D1545980

SECULARISM IN
ANTEBELLUM AMERICA

SECULARISM

* · IN ANTEBELLUM AMERICA · *

— WITH —

REFERENCE TO GHOSTS, PROTESTANT SUBCULTURES,
MACHINES, AND THEIR METAPHORS;

FEATURING DISCUSSIONS OF

MASS MEDIA, *MOBY-DICK*, SPIRITUALITY,
PHRENOLOGY, ANTHROPOLOGY, SING SING STATE PENITENTIARY,
AND *SEX* WITH THE NEW MOTIVE POWER

— · —

John Lardas Modern

THE UNIVERSITY OF CHICAGO PRESS

CHICAGO AND LONDON

PUBLICATION OF THIS BOOK
HAS BEEN AIDED BY A GRANT FROM
THE BEVINGTON FUND.

———

JOHN LARDAS MODERN is assistant professor of religious
studies at Franklin and Marshall College and the author of *The Bop
Apocalypse: The Religious Visions of Kerouac, Ginsberg, and Burroughs*
(2001).

The University of Chicago Press, Chicago 60637
The University of Chicago Press, Ltd., London
© 2011 by The University of Chicago
All rights reserved. Published 2011.
Printed in the United States of America

20 19 18 17 16 15 14 13 12 11   1 2 3 4 5

ISBN-13: 978-0-226-53323-0 (cloth)
ISBN-10: 0-226-53323-9 (cloth)

An earlier version of chapter 1 appeared as "Evangelical Secularism
and the Measure of Leviathan" in *Church History*, vol. 77, No. 4 (2008):
pp. 801-876. Copyright © 2008 American Society of Church History.
Reprinted with the permission of Cambridge University Press. An
earlier version of chapter 4 appeared as "Ghosts of Sing Sing, or the
Metaphysics of Secularism" in *Journal of the American Academy of
Religion* 75:3 (September 2007): 615-50. Reprinted by permission of
Oxford University Press.

Library of Congress Cataloging-in-Publication Data

Modern, John Lardas.
Secularism in antebellum America : with reference to ghosts, Protestant subcultures, machines, and their
metaphors : featuring discussions of mass media, Moby-Dick, spirituality, phrenology, anthropology,
Sing Sing State Penitentiary and sex with the new motive power / John Lardas Modern.
p. cm. — (Religion and postmodernism)
Includes index.
ISBN-13: 978-0-226-53323-0 (cloth : alk. paper)
ISBN-10: 0-226-53323-9 (cloth : alk. paper)   1. Secularism—United States—History—
19th century.   2. Protestantism—United States—History—19th century.   3. United States—Religion—
History—19th century.   I. Title.   II. Series: Religion and postmodernism.
BL2760.M58 2011
211'.6097309034—dc23
2011023613

♾ This paper meets the requirements of ANSI/NISO Z39.48-1992
(Permanence of Paper).

For Libby, Leo, and Max

Air, in its common condition, is a thin transparent fluid, so subtile that it cannot be handled, and when at rest it cannot be felt. That it is a body, however, is quite obvious, because we feel its impression or force when agitated as wind, or when we wave our hand quickly through it. In the quick motion of the hand, we feel that it is partially opposed by something; and in inhaling breath into the lungs, we feel that we are drawing something through the mouth—that something is air...This ocean of air penetrates into all unoccupied places...hardly any thing, indeed, that we see in nature or art, is free from air.

Chambers's Information for the People: A Popular Encyclopædia (1851)

CONTENTS

ILLUSTRATIONS

ACKNOWLEDGMENTS

The book before you is difficult to skim—no less for its content than for the life behind it. Which is to say that my effort owes much, if not everything, to those individuals, communities, and institutions that have given me the most precious of writerly resources: time, strength, cash, and patience.

Many readers made the process of writing a rewarding one. Alan Thomas at the University of Chicago Press has offered crucial support and keen intelligence from the very beginning. Tom Carlson has been a valued conversation partner throughout, not to mention an inspirational grammarian. John Corrigan and Tracy Fessenden offered, first and foremost, recognition of the ideas and arguments contained herein. Their generous and amazingly detailed readings have helped me clarify my own. Simon Coleman, William Connolly, Charles Hirschkind, Leigh Schmidt and Ann Taves gave critical feedback on the conference circuit. Richard Allen cleaned up the rough edges in the last stages of manuscript production.

I am also indebted to a small coterie of readers who forged through a thicket of draft (and detritus) at one point or another and saw things that I did not: Annette Aronowicz, Courtney Bender, Chip Callahan, Finbarr Curtis, Stephen Cooper, Lisle Dalton, Mark Elmore, Gabriel Levy, Kathryn Lofton, Tomas Matza, David McMahan, Kerry Mitchell, and William Robert.

The book before you has, by design, a ridiculous number of footnotes. I would like to thank James Gulick and Rob Haley for digging deep in order to obtain materials that seemed not to appear on any digital map. Jeanne Dreskin, Johanna Gosse, Michael Kassler-Taub, and Frank Pittenger helped compile a formidable archive from which I will continue to draw. Numerous individuals gently (and sometimes virtually) guided me through the folders and boxes—at the Rhode Island Historical Society, the Rare Books and Special Collections at the University of Rochester, the Darlington Memorial Library at the University of Pittsburgh, the Friends Historical Library at Swarthmore College, Special Collections at Millersville University, the Rare Book and Manuscript Library at the University of Pennsylvania, and the photography collection at Mystic Seaport Museum.

A surprising amount of capital undergirds this project. With the support of the Humanities Center at Haverford College I traveled to the Pitt Rivers Museum Archive. There I encountered E. B. Tylor and first considered the question of what constituted anthropological knowledge. Tamara Goeglein and the Provost's Office at Franklin & Marshall College funded my excursion to Rhode Island (on a research tip from David Morgan). With the support of the Charles and Barbara Kahn Endowment at Franklin & Marshall College, my sabbatical year was guaranteed to be a productive one.

I would also like to thank the National Endowment for the Humanities for funding my research fellowship at the Winterthur Museum and Country Estate. Greg Landrey, Rosemary Krill, Jeanne Solensky, Emily Guthrie and the rest of the Winterthur staff allowed me to complete this project in a timely fashion. And as with any mode of enlightened governance I am required by law to inform you that any views, findings, conclusions, or recommendations expressed in this book do not necessarily reflect those of the National Endowment for the Humanities.

I benefited immensely from those institutions that hosted iterations of the argument herein: Rutgers University (Camden), Hartwick College, and the Tri-College American Studies Colloquium. It was at the latter talk in 2004 that Peter Schmidt encouraged me to organize my thoughts about the excesses of rationality in antebellum America. At a small but lively conference on Religion, Aesthetics, and Global Media at the University of California, Davis I gained a greater appreciation for strange circulations. I also want to thank audiences (anonymous and otherwise) at the University of Chicago Divinity School and Florida State University.

Before any formal words appeared, my students at Franklin & Marshall College and Haverford College heard most everything in this book. Their reactions and feedback have been invaluable. As I began to write Dan Chambers built quite a fine room in which to concentrate amidst varied acoustics. Around this time I participated in the Young Scholars of American Religion Program, the seeds of an intellectual community from which I still draw sustenance. Under the banner of Buca di

Beppo I had the privilege of meeting Judith Weisenfeld, Tracy Leavelle, Christopher White, Henry Goldschmidt, and Sylvester Johnson among others.

As the book has taken shape in the past year or so, many other environments have left their mark. On this note, I would like to thank the good people at *The Immanent Frame*—Jonathan VanAntwerpen, Chuck Gelman, and Nathan Schneider—for asking the right questions. I also owe much to the Social Science Research Council and discussions revolving around the working group on Spirituality, Politics, and Public Engagement (led fearlessly by Omar McRoberts and Courtney Bender and funded by the Ford Foundation). There I have encountered the best minds of my generation holding forth on the time of the now.

A number of friends and colleagues have added texture that is both epistemic and social: Max Adams, Christina Beltran, Book Club and the Brotherhood, Matthew Budman, Kevin Carroll and all the folks at Solid Side Vinyl, John Carter, Tony Chemero, My Aunt Debbie, Dennis Deslippe, Mary DiLullo, Joel Eigen, Ken Firestone, Brian Frailey and Dogstar Books, Lee Franklin, Hank Glassman, Lisa Jane Graham, Nicole Heller, David Hargis, Jessica Todd Harper, Matthew Hoffman, Alison Kibler, Ken Koltun-Fromm, Scott Lerner, Teb Locke, Maria Mitchell, Mommalicious, Nick Montemarano, Marci Nelligan, Eliza Reilly, Amelia Rauser, Joanna Rosenberg, Bethel Saler, Sarah Schwarz, David Sedley, Bill Seeley, Michael Sells, Toni Shanahan, Gus Stadler, Ann Steiner, Mr. Suit, Guillaume de Syon, Peter Williams, Kerry Sherin Wright, Scott Wright, and Chris Zafiriou.

I continue to register my debt of gratitude to the religious studies department at the University of California, Santa Barbara, not least of all for allowing me to write (and to file) a rather unwieldy dissertation in 2003. That document—a history of *Moby-Dick* as it was received, engaged, and written over in the twentieth century—was an exercise in unreason that prepared me to write the book at hand. For as I investigated the network of Melvillean interpreters I discovered that I, too, was one—ever always a penultimate reader. In Santa Barbara I learned much about the art of interlocution from Catherine Albanese, Giles Gunn, Richard Hecht, Roger Friedland, and Philip Hammond. And I am grateful to my friends (many already named) who helped me begin thinking about ghosts under the shadows cast by the Santa Ynez Mountains—John Baumann, Anna Bigelow, Drew Bourn, Darryl Caterine, Suzanne Crawford O'Brien, Beth Currans, Florie Downey, Caleb Elfenbein, Dan Michon, Matt Miller, Ellen Posman, Tom Price, Jeff Ruff, Elijah Siegler, and Wendy Wiseman.

Throughout this process—from inchoate musing to overdetermined footnotes—my family has been a source of love and joy. Diane Lardas has, for decades now, fostered in me a determined curiosity. John and Susan Kleine, the Elwyn clan, and the Littles have provided a life outside of the mind for which I am grateful. Libby, Leo, and Max—the Moderns to whom this book is dedicated—I thank you for having made the doors of the wonder world swing open.

PROLOGUE

Published in London in October 1851 and a month later in New York City, *Moby-Dick; or, the Whale* is written in a variety of dialects and genres—from Shakespearian prosody, Swiftian wit, and the argot of whaling to frontier adventure and the reasonable parables of natural science. The story is set within the mid-nineteenth-century whaling industry and concerns a number of things, including the possession of Captain Ahab by forces unseen, his pursuit of the white whale, and the related quest by the young sailor Ishmael to gain interpretive leverage on these forces, the pursuit, and the whale. Central to the style, substance, and narrative arc of the novel is the looming presence of Moby Dick, a sperm whale who is feared to be both ubiquitous and immortal. For the majority of the book the white whale is a highly charged idea, an excuse it would seem for the author to relate the finer points of how brute nature is conquered, manufactured, and put up for sale. The whale assumes a biological character, in and of itself, only at the very end of Ishmael's "tale" when the air aboard the *Pequod* has become so saturated with the idea of Moby Dick that a typhoon envelops the "noble craft," forcing it off course and toward its final confrontation with the whale.

Moby-Dick is also a ghost story.

For the white whale possesses a strange materiality, a presence whose authority operates from a distance, affects the individual personality, and provokes responses in the form of human activities, technics, and institutions. Yet the creature of the sea inhabits the same reality as each of the characters—from Ahab and his "phantom" oarsmen to Starbuck and Aunt Charity to the "savage" harpooners, Queequeg, Daggoo, and Tashtego. They are as susceptible to the whale as the whale is to them. There is mutual acknowledgment, direct contact, dependency, blood. These seemingly polar identities of the whale, amidst a rather intricate and elegant play of language, have not only collapsed but have shown themselves to be mutually constitutive. In this sense Moby Dick is at once worldly and divine, creature and creator. Moreover, "the idea of the great whale himself" is "overwhelming." It is a dangerous force that confounds the notion of language as precise in its markings. It confounds any mode of perception that neatly divides up the world into matter and spirit, message and media. And it calls into question the distinction between the silence of the solitary subject and being subject to incantations.

As a historian of nineteenth-century American religion, I am indebted to *Moby-Dick*. I have become obsessed with how this novel addresses the material resonance of social symbols, its mind-bending scrutiny of distant happenings reverberating under the skin. In its language of steam and electricity *Moby-Dick* seems to suggest that a state of enchantment is not the exception that proves the rule of an Enlightened, civilized evolution of human being but rather that enchantment itself is the rule.[1]

---

1. To insist upon an enchanted subject is not simply to reverse a traditional boundary of Enlightenment critique but to acknowledge that the boundary itself possesses its own historicity and makes its own spectral demands. For rather than view enchantment as the exception that proves the rule of a calculating and calculable subject, enchantment becomes the working assumption, a state of nature that calls into question more static versions of human nature. To make enchantment a working assumption is to think, historically, about the implications of Jacques Derrida's case for the necessity of hauntology in any critical project. "To haunt does not mean to be present," writes Derrida. Moreover, it is "necessary to introduce haunting into the very construction of a concept. Of every concept, beginning with the concepts of being and time. That is what we would be calling here a hauntology. Ontology opposes it only in a movement of exorcism. Ontology is a conjuration" (Jacques Derrida, *Specters of Marx: The State of the Debt, the Work of Mourning, and the New International*, trans. Peggy Kamuf [New York: Routledge, 1994], 161). This move wrests disenchantment from the narrative yoke of modernity, questioning the very premise of instrumental calculation as opposed to legitimating it. In other words, one must recognize the distinction between enchantment and disenchantment as integral to the modern secular imaginary and not as some natural difference between two modes of consciousness. Here, I am sympathetic with Max Weber's inquiry into a particular kind of rationalization that emerges within the constraints of modernity. The spread of such reason through routinization and institutionalization, as Weber himself implies, did not necessarily make disenchantment an affective norm. On the contrary, the excess of instrumental reason gave rise to rather impressive and righteous irrationalities. On disenchantment as an ideal, see Max Weber, "Science as a Vocation," in *From Max Weber: Essays in Sociology*, ed. H. H. Gerth and C. Wright Mills (New York: Oxford University Press, 1958), 139. On the excess of reason leading to all manner of intractable hallucinations, see Theodor W. Adorno and Max Horkheimer, *Dialectic of Enlightenment*, trans. John Cumming (New York: Continuum, 1993) and Zygmunt Bauman, "Uniqueness and Normality of the Holocaust," in *Modernity and the Holocaust* (Ithaca: Cornell University Press, 1989), 83–114.

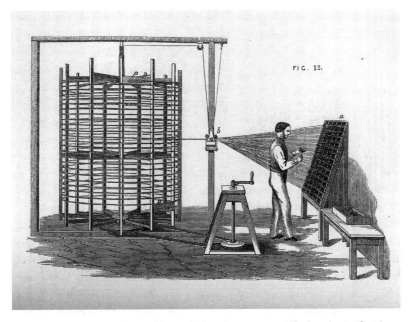

FIGURE I · Warping Mill turned by a winch and rope. From Alfred Barlow's *The History and Principles of Weaving by Hand and Power* (London: Sampson Low, Marston, Searle & Rivington, 1878), 70.

In addressing the tangled relationship between subjectivity and environmental pressures, *Moby-Dick* narrativized, in an ethnographic key, human responses to the "subtle agencies" pervading everyday life. Whereas early ethnographers addressed primitive societies in order to justify the superior position of their own, Melville was interested in the atmospheric conditions that permitted his own society to justify itself in the present. Instead of legitimating the assumptions of sovereign individuality and Manifest Destiny that undergirded the systematic extermination of Native Americans and the continued enslavement of African Americans, Melville chose to explore the cannibalistic "spirit" of America that allowed for such assumptions to be made in the first place. By extending the focus from primitive history to the American present, *Moby-Dick* suggested that America was enchanted by the spirit of vanquishment, what he would later call "the metaphysics of Indian-hating." This spirit was manifest in the brutalities of slavery and in the insular subjectivities assumed by whites in their exploitation of both humans and the natural environment. It was evidenced in the systematic extermination of those groups who stood in the way of America's imperialistic ambitions. In coming to reside in the aptly named *Pequod*, a "cannibal of a craft," this spirit of subjugation had come home to roost.[2]

1. Loomings

"Call me Ishmael," he implores early on, casting his lot with whatever is set apart from an American order conceived in terms of providence, empire, illumination. This imperative sounds a rupture between words and their meaning, between a name and the identity it discloses. *Call me Ishmael.* There is an admission, here at the beginning of a chapter entitled "Loomings," that signs are ever lacking, promising more than they can deliver. Words, for the person who has asked you to call him Ishmael, can not be trusted to encompass one's sense of self. Nor, for that matter, can words be trusted to represent certain knowledge of a relatively stable world. A murk permeates Ishmael's language of recall—"some years ago . . . never mind how long . . . little or no money . . . nothing particular . . . hazy about the eyes." A damp drizzle had become the substance of his soul. Something was admittedly opaque, both inside and out, a state of indistinction that had become *almost* unbearable. It was as if Ishmael was already at sea.

"Looming" is an adjective, a seaman's term for appearing on the horizon through mist or darkness (OED). Loomings, the plural noun, are those things that appear indistinct, distorted, magnified on account of atmospheric conditions. That which looms is threatening because it calls into question one's point of orientation, that is, one's foundational assumptions of order, clarity, and legibility. Loomings are anathema to immediate comprehension. They undermine one's capacity to distinguish, for nautical purposes, the horizon from one's immediate circumstances. Loomings are also those things that becloud commonsense visions of self and society, those things that run against the grain of a quickly conjured systematicity. They are, for lack of a better phrase, neither subjective nor objective. They are beyond the scope of precise linguistic covering. And finally, loomings refer to a network of threads, loom being that which holds the warp threads in taut alignment for the purpose of interweaving the weft threads that feed into it.

By the time Ishmael introduced himself, the port city of New York had

---

2. Herman Melville, *The Confidence-Man: His Masquerade* (London: Longman, Brown, Green, Longmans, & Roberts, 1857), 201.

TEN CYLINDER ROTARY TYPE-REVOLVING PRESS

FIGURE 2 · Ten Cylinder Rotary-Type Revolving Press, circa 1856. Robert Hoe's *A Short History of the Printing Press and of Improvements in Printing Machinery from the Time of Gutenberg up to the Present Day* (New York: Robert Hoe, 1902), 35.

become the primary node through which language circulated in and beyond the United States. Between 1842 and 1853 the American publishing
industry expanded ten times faster than the population. Much of this activity was either located within the "insular city of the Manhattoes" or else
depended upon its market for print materials and especially readership.[3]

The unprecedented expansion and extension of an American media
sphere in the first half of the nineteenth century owed much to sheer
innovation—from technologies of production to those of distribution
through strategies of reception. The technics were matters of massive production, rapid response, and sensitivity to the demands of "public opinion."
Publishers, for example, claimed to be sharpening the interpretive skills of
each individual they reached, particularly the "objective natures" of those
within urban centers like New York. Reading closely—with voluntary
attention—would prevent one from being overwhelmed by the daily barrage
of words: on street signs, handbills, banners, wagons, and even people (in
the form of sandwich boards); in the crime and court reports of the penny
presses as well as their steady flow of gossip, advertising copy, and information about national and world events.[4] Objectivity was a self-conscious
and necessary virtue in such a distracting environment.[5] It was instrumental in securing reasoned contemplation. And it habituated the concept of
"news" by promising a certitude to be found in one's readerly engagement
with it. The "human interest story," for example, was first and foremost
about seeing things as they really, truly were. Consequently, even the most
"trifling moment"—even one's own—became significant when located in
"time and in space" and seen in terms of "causes" and "consequences."[6]

---

3. Steam printing presses and papermaking machines did not simply facilitate the extension
of commercial activity into remote regions of the country and the psyche, but ushered in a
situation of unprecedented linguistic density. As the transportation and distribution systems
became more reliable (the Erie and Champlain canals were completed in the 1820s, prepaid
postage instituted in 1847), local booksellers became a permanent fixture in a burgeoning
information economy. While the upper classes made up most of the market for books, newspapers, and other publications, a high literacy rate motivated publishers to make their wares
ever more affordable. Semiotic density was due both to technological innovation and also to
emerging market conditions, felt most intensely within urban spaces. Ronald J. Zboray, *A
Fictive People: Antebellum Economic Development and the American Reading Public* (New York:
Oxford University Press, 1993), 3-4, 55, 69, 94. See also Dan Shiller, *Objectivity and the News:
The Public and the Rise of Commercial Journalism* (Philadelphia: University of Pennsylvania
Press, 1981), 13, 17.
4. David M. Henkin, *City Reading: Written Words and Public Spaces in Antebellum New York*
(New York: Columbia University Press, 1998).
5. "Beware of Your Own Subjectivity," *New-York Evangelist* 20 (October 4, 1849): 157.
6. So argued the *New York Herald* in March 1837. Cited in Michael Schudson, *Discovering the
News: A Social History of American Newspapers* (New York: Basic Books, 1978), 27-28.

Despite such encomiums to objectivity, Ishmael remains hard-pressed to state directly who he is or to explain why, exactly, he has felt compelled to go to sea as a common sailor.[7] Before revealing that "chief among [my] motives was the overwhelming idea of the great whale himself," Ishmael runs through a series of explanations that connote a similar degree of excess. His goal is to "see a little into the springs and motives which being cunningly presented to me under various disguises, induced me to set about performing the part I did."

In dissecting his own decision, he admits the possibility of having been cajoled "into the delusion that it was a choice resulting from my own unbiased freewill and discriminating judgment." Perhaps his decision may be attributed to "the invisible police officer of the Fates, who has . . . constant surveillance of me, and secretly dogs me, and influences me in some unaccountable way—he can better answer than anyone else." The answer, however, is not to be found in the official utterance of the gods. It appears on a handbill, an ephemeral piece of paper. In the sign-saturated environs of the city, "the grand programme of Providence" was no longer a transcendent affair. Instead, it was immanent, utterly devoid of mythical or holy hue, revealed to Ishmael in a series of headlines that staged past history and future biography as part of the same theatrical production:

"Grand Contested Election for the Presidency of the United States.

"WHALING VOYAGE BY ONE ISHMAEL.

"BLOODY BATTLE IN AFFGHANISTAN."

Having been put down for a "shabby part of a whaling voyage" by "those stage managers, the Fates," Ishmael seems to be following a script not of his own choosing. He is literally surrounded by words that have noth-

---

7. The intensification of self-instruction could be seen as contradiction by such figures as Thomas Carlyle who, in a book owned by Melville, expressed horror over the religio-political role publishers were assuming. Melville borrowed a copy of Carlyle's *Heroes, Hero-Worship and the Heroic in History* from Evert Duychinck in the summer of 1850. Merton M. Sealts Jr, *Melville's Reading: Revised and Enlarged Edition* (Columbia: University of South Carolina Press, 1988), 163. "Writing brings printing," wrote Carlyle, "every-day extempore Printing, as we see at the present. Whoever can speak, speaking now to the whole nation, becomes a power, a branch of government. . . . Those poor bits of ragpaper with black ink on them;—from the Daily Newspaper to the sacred Hebrew Book, what have they not done, what are they not doing. . . . All this, of the importance of . . . how the Press is to such a degree superseding the Pulpit, the Senate, the Senatus Academicus and much else, has been admitted for a good while; and recognized often enough, in late times, with a sort of sentimental triumph and wonderment" (*On Heroes, Hero-Worship and the Heroic in History* [London: Chapman and Hall, 1840], 152–53).

ing, essentially, to do with him—here the 1844 election of James Polk, the first president to win without a majority, and the First Anglo-Afghan War (1839-42). Nevertheless, these words are affective, intimate, prescriptive. These words are auratic, hinting at unseen forces that were shaping and directing them. Having already recognized the failure of a name to deliver on its promises of legibility and meaning, Ishmael now must consider how words also exceeded themselves (and their promises) upon delivery. By the end of the opening chapter, words themselves become ciphers of power, part of empirical reality and not simply pointing to it. A chain of signification that originates from nowhere in particular, weaving itself over the skin and underneath.

2. A Modern Book

Shortly before the publication of *Moby-Dick*, Herman Melville was both reticent to summarize its content and pessimistic about its reception. "What's the use of elaborating what, in its very essence, is so short-lived as a modern book? Though I wrote the Gospels in this century, I should die in the gutter." Perhaps Melville's sour mood reflected his sense that *Moby-Dick* was so prophetically embedded in its historical moment as to offer little in the way of imaginative escape. "Infinite socialities are within me," he declared soon after publication, refusing to answer the question of ultimate reference, the question of what exactly his book was about. God *or* the process by which infinite socialities made their way in? The lack of precision was inevitable. For it was "not so much paucity as superabundance of material that seems to incapacitate modern authors."[8] As Melville implied, his "modern book" was ephemeral *because* it was about everything. A manic attempt to encompass a reality that was intimate yet exceeded the bounds of conceptual formulation.

For *Moby-Dick*, among other things, was Melville's response to a world whose capacious replication was at once secretive and a matter of human design. As Melville suggested in a letter to Nathaniel Hawthorne in April 1851, shortly before the publication of *Moby-Dick*, if God could not explain his own secrets, how could humans ever be up to the task of explaining their

---

8. Herman Melville, *Correspondence*, vol. 14 of *The Writings of Herman Melville*, ed. Lynne Horth (Evanston: Northwestern University Press and the Newberry Library, 1993), 192, 212; A Virginian Spending July in Vermont [Herman Melville], "Hawthorne and His Mosses," *The Literary World* (August 17 and 24, 1850): 303f.

own? And what price would they pay in pursuit of self-disclosure? "We incline to think that God cannot explain His own secrets," wrote Melville,

> and that He would like a little more information upon certain points Himself. We mortals astonish Him as much as He us. But it is this *Being* of the matter; there lies the knot with which we choke ourselves. As soon as you say *Me, a God, a Nature,* so soon you jump off from your stool and hang from the beam. Yes, that word is the hangman. Take God out of the dictionary, and you would have Him in the street.

Humans, in other words, in their desire to clarify complexity and contain surplus by way of naming, had become as complex, if not more so, than the God who had created them. Instead of the inscrutability of God, Melville seemed more concerned with the inscrutability of social existence. Opacity, creatureliness, submission—each was a theological effect that resided in the most seemingly mundane activities. The bewildering conditions created by humans had, moreover, generated a dangerous insistence upon categories and categorical difference. But it was precisely this insight that was life-affirming—an insight into the seductions of language and the capacity of words to fix neat distinctions that compelled Melville to ask, "what's the reason, Mr. Hawthorne, that in the last stages of metaphysics a fellow always falls to *swearing* so?"[9] Melville's warning about saying "Me, a God, a Nature" is transgressive. For he suggests his unwillingness to subscribe to any interpretive enterprise that left unquestioned the plurality of its own ground or object of inquiry. For to posit some universal and static quality to existence was to end one's own.

Melville's letter is amazingly suggestive in how it frames *Moby-Dick* as a work situated between theology and anthropology.[10] Antebellum life, in my rendering of Melville's rendering, has everything to do with this streetwalking God who is at once unsettling and determinative. It is a God who haunts the human subject yet erases that moment of haunting as it is hap-

9. Melville, *Correspondence*, 186–87. On the "invention of an acategorical thought," see Michel Foucault, "Theatrum Philosophicum," in *Language, Counter-memory, Practice: Selected Essays and Interviews by Michel Foucault,* ed. Donald F. Bouchard (Ithaca: Cornell University Press, 1977), 186–87.

10. According to Melville, the problem in need of interpretation was not the will of God but the God-like agency by which the collective was made to cohere. See Jenny Franchot, "Melville's Traveling God," in *The Cambridge Companion to Herman Melville,* ed. Robert S. Levine (New York: Cambridge University Press, 1998), 157–85, and Susan L. Mizruchi, *The Science of Sacrifice: American Literature and Modern Social Theory* (Princeton: Princeton University Press, 1998), 99.

pening. It is a God who incorporates such fleeting moments into the project of defining the sentience of human nature as disenchanted, thereby
perpetuating its own enchantments and stability. For in a book that Melville offhandedly referred to as the "gospels of the nineteenth century,"
God is who disappears into the crowd, into the processes of sociality, after
its name has been taken out of the dictionary. Yet in its generous portrayal
of the sensorium on land and at sea, Melville empathized with myriad
practices of unknowing (as opposed to depicting his characters as falsely
knowing). Or to put this another way, Melville's subject matter, among
other things, was the dense and complex practices in which individuals
learn to know what not to know—the bare human struggles to keep the
excessively haphazard and stubbornly uncertain at bay. And like others
who practiced this dark science of genealogy, Melville did not revel in this
excess but attempted to see the shadows it cast.[11]

Melville's story is both a prophetic and paradigmatic scene of modernity—its emergence, its parameters, and its limits. In *Moby-Dick*, Leviathan
once again becomes linked to the idea of social organization. In this respect, *Moby-Dick* may be seen as a rewriting of Thomas Hobbes's *Leviathan
or The Matter, Forme, and Power of a Commonwealth Ecclesiastical and Civil*
(1651). For Hobbes, the social order becomes a problem that is explained
not by theological intervention but by a theory of social control. The title
of Hobbes's treatise comes from the book of Job, a sea-monster who "is
king over all the children of pride." Hobbes's mortal god was just that—a
human apparatus that functioned to distill the detailed will of a Protestant
God for the purposes of organizing existence after the Fall. Civil society
was dependent upon each and every individual being possessed by his or
her "Corporeall Spirit," that is, the spirit of one's essential reason.[12] For

11. On genealogy, see Friedrich Nietzsche, *A Genealogy of Morals*, vol. 10 of *The Works of Friedrich Nietzsche*, ed. Alexander Tille (New York: The Macmillan Company, 1897), and Michel Foucault, "Nietzsche, Genealogy, History," in *Language, Counter-memory, Practice*, 139–64. See also Melville's contemporary, Frederick Douglass, who wrote of the way that history imprinted itself upon the body in order to ridicule the supposedly neutral conclusions of racialist science. Douglass was painfully aware of how the theories of Josiah C. Nott and Samuel Morton had perpetuated a feedback loop between representation and political reality. "Thus," he wrote, "the very crimes of slavery become slavery's best defence." In turning the assumptions of Nott and Morton against them, Douglass wrote that "fashion is not confined to dress; but extends to philosophy as well." "A man is worked upon by what he works on. He may carve out his circumstances, but his circumstances will carve him out as well" ("The Claims of the Negro Ethnologically Considered" [1854], in *The Life and Writings of Frederick Douglass*, ed. Philip S. Foner [New York: International Publishers, 1950], 2:295, 298, 304–5).
12. See Paul C. Johnson on how "spirit possession" functioned as a colonialist trope against which notions of self-possession, the good society, and proper civic comportment were con-

it was precisely such singular possession, in awe of a terrifying monster, that guaranteed rational agency and the smooth workings of the State.

As Michel Foucault has argued, new modes of statecraft developed between the appearances of *Leviathan* and *Moby-Dick*. Across Europe and America there appeared new modes of governance that utilized statistics, probability, and the leverage of the "population" in order to generate the normal range of individual behavior.[13] As linear, top-down impositions of authority gave way to situations in which one's horizon of possibility, as opposed to one's physical frame, was acted upon, the arts of government became increasingly concerned not with men per se but with

> men in their relations, their links, their imbrication with those other things which are wealth, resources, means of subsistence, the territory with its specific qualities, climate, irrigation, fertility, etc.; men in their relation to that other kind of things, customs, habits, ways of acting and thinking, etc.; lastly, men in their relation to that other kind of things, accidents and misfortunes such as famine, epidemics, death, etc. The fact that government concerns things understood in this way, this imbrication of men and things, is I believe readily confirmed by the metaphor which is inevitably invoked in these treatises on government, namely that of the ship. What does it mean to govern a ship? It means clearly to take charge of the sailors, but also of the boat and its cargo; to take care of a ship means also to reckon with winds, rocks, and storms; and it consists in that activity of establishing a relation between the sailors who are to be taken care of and the ship which is to be taken care of, and the cargo which is to be brought safely to port, and all those eventualities like winds, rocks, storms, and so on; this is what characterizes the government of a ship. . . . Government, that is to say, has a finality of its own, and in this respect again I believe it can be clearly distinguished from sovereignty.[14]

In Foucault's rendering, the State became more affecting than effective, manifest not in external force but in the technics one adopted in order to cultivate the self. Hence the imbrication of the freedom of men and their

structed in the works of Hobbes, Locke, and Kant. "An Atlantic Genealogy of Spirit Possession," *Comparative Studies in History and Society* 53 (2011): 393–425.

13. See, for example, A. B. Johnson, "Advantages and Disadvantages of Private Corporations," *Hunt's Merchants' Magazine* 22 (December 1850): 626–32.

14. Michel Foucault, "Governmentality," in *The Foucault Effect: Studies in Governmentality*, ed. Graham Burchell, Colin Gordon, and Peter Miller (Chicago: University of Chicago Press, 1991), 93–94.

WHALES.   579

are obliged to leave the northern seas and get clear of the ice by August.

The flesh of this animal is a dainty to some nations; and the savages of Greenland, as well as those near the South Pole, are fond of it to distraction. They eat the flesh and drink the oil, which to them is an exquisite delicacy. The finding a dead whale is an adventure considered among the fortunate circumstances of their lives. They make their abode beside it, and seldom remove till they have left nothing but the bones.

FIGURE 3 · Sperm Whale from *Parley's Panorama; or, Curiosities of Nature and Art, History and Biography*, ed. S. G. Goodrich (House & Brown, 1851), 579.

submission to things. Consequently, Foucault insisted that "power must be analysed as something which circulates, or rather as something which only functions in the form of a chain. It is never localized here or there, never in anybody's hands, never appropriated as a commodity or a piece of wealth. Power is employed and exercised in a netlike organization. And not only do individuals [such as the crew of the *Pequod*] circulate between its threads; they are always in the position of simultaneously undergoing and exercising this power."[15]

15. Michel Foucault, "Two Lectures," in *Power/Knowledge: Selected Interviews & Other Writings, 1972–77*, ed. Colin Gordon (New York: Pantheon Books, 1981), 98.

Moby-Dick captures something about this shift in the way individuals begin to feel the circulation of ideas and fluidity of institutional logics.[16] Rather than a singular, unified, and sovereign structure that demands reasonable submission for the benefit of all involved, Melville's leviathan was that which unified by way of generating agencies from within, provoking theorizations of interior states and sensibilities in all who encountered even the rumor of the whale, linking free wills together in shared "sympathies and symbolizings." And lest we forget, the white whale catalyzed the smooth operations aboard the *Pequod* (by way of catalyzing all manner of reasoned introspection) even as it posed a mortal threat to the security of all on board.

Moby Dick, in contrast to Hobbes's naturalized State, did not impose but rather brought "into play relations between individuals."[17] It convinced those who encountered it that self-possession was not only natural but worth defending, no matter what the cost. And because it had no discernible qualities other than its opaque complexity, the possessive force of Moby Dick was indirect. Leviathan, in Melville's rendering, functions as "empty cipher," generating schemes by way of the presence ascribed to it—"subtle deceits, not actually inherent . . . but only laid on from without." Whereas Hobbes's Leviathan defined the terms of human association, the "accumulated associations" of Moby Dick achieve the same end through spectral means.

Hobbes's account of an enlightened accumulation of social agencies is challenged, on its face, by the radical sense of original sin that so preoccupied Melville while writing his own treatise of the economy of human behavior and emotions. In *Moby-Dick*, there is a kind of theological attention paid to those imaginative and ominous acts that went into naturalizing the State, what Hobbes insisted was "but an artificial man." Throughout the novel, Moby Dick is more often felt than seen, an intangible medium of existence rather than a fixed and stable message. "For some time past, though at intervals, the unaccompanied, secluded White Whale had haunted those uncivilized seas most frequented by the Sperm Whale fisherman. But not all of them knew of his existence; only a few of them, comparatively, had knowingly seen him." As a "fabulous rumor," the

16. See for example "The Philosophy of Advertising," *Hunt's Merchants' Magazine* 23 (November 1850): 580–83.

17. Michel Foucault, "The Subject and Power," in *Michel Foucault: Beyond Structuralism and Hermeneutics*, 2d ed., ed. Hubert L. Dreyfus and Paul Rabinow (Chicago: University of Chicago Press, 1983), 217.

white whale has been invested with naturalistic descriptions and "the real living experience of living men," that "did in the end incorporate themselves all manner of morbid hints, and half-formed foetal suggestions of supernatural agencies." The enchanting quality of the white whale is often aligned with "the message-carrying air" whose anonymity and invisibility catalyzes both personal responses and institutions. It knows you but does not acknowledge you. It imparts meaning upon the "whole visible world; which while pauselessly active in uncounted modes, still eternally holds its peace, and ignores you, though you dig foundations for cathedrals."

In the whale's "wake of creamy foam, all spangled with golden gleamings," the reader begins to glimpse the generative power of an American discourse: social mores, epistemic rituals, and habits of imagination that bind the crew of the *Pequod* together in common cause. For like the white whale, discourse does not exist as a matter of measurement. It does not act directly and immediately upon individuals. It is rather an airy substance that presses upon one's actions. It is an amorphous constellation of ideas and moral vectors that cannot be named in the certain terms of empirical analysis. Discourse has neither center nor contour. It is "strange, frightening, and perhaps maleficent."[18] And like the white whale, the searing reality of discourse demands an attention to its spectral presence, the material trace of its metaphysics.[19] So I begin here, at the outset, with the recognition of discourse as monstrous.

18. Michel Foucault, "The Order of Discourse," in *Language and Politics*, ed. Michael J. Shapiro (New York: New York University Press, 1984), 108.

19. In *Moby-Dick*, the atmosphere is dramatized as an agent in its own right—immaterial, formless, and invisible yet possessing motive force. For "the wind that made great bellies of their sails, and rushed the vessel on by arms as irresistible; this seemed the symbol of that unseen agency which so enslaved them to the race." Yet the atmosphere is less than omnipotent. Independence is dependent upon how one goes about interpreting and coming to terms with it. "Who aint a slave?," exclaims Ishmael. "Tell me that." Ishmael here suggests that one's sense of sovereignty is ever premised upon an admission of submission. "Well, then, however the old sea-captains may order me about—however they may thump and punch me about, I have the satisfaction of knowing that it is all right; that everybody else is in one way or other served in much the same way—either in a physical or metaphysical point of view." There was, perhaps, honesty as well as expiation to be found in jettisoning the markers of sovereign individualism. Elizabeth B. Clark notes, as millions of African Americans remained enslaved in the south, the image of the suffering slave could express degrees of guilt, anxiety over social forces, or perhaps a questioning of some basic assumptions of white male privilege. On the trope of the suffering slave, see Elizabeth B. Clark, "'The Sacred Rights of the Weak': Pain, Sympathy, and the Culture of Individual Rights in Antebellum America," *Journal of American History* 82, no. 2 (Sept. 1985): 463–93.

3. Haunted Modernity

Life is, and has been for a very long time, a haunting process in which one's actions are acted upon by others from a distance—people, to be sure, but also and perhaps more importantly, concepts, representations, and words. Modernity, then, is haunted not because of an aberration in consciousness or a return of the repressed but in the contemporary necessity of coming to terms with and providing terms for ghosts.[20]

In grappling with the metaphysical issues raised in Hobbes's *Leviathan*, *Moby-Dick* frames modernity as haunted, a necessary precondition for gaining an appreciation of it in terms other than its own. As such, *Moby-Dick* was part of a distinctive mode of cultural analysis that emerged on both sides of the Atlantic, a style of anthropological inquiry that was saturated with the language of ghostly possession. By the mid-nineteenth century, the link between modernity and excess had become almost commonplace—excess projections, excess repression, excess credulity, excess rationality, excess bureaucracy, excessive political rationality, and so on and so forth. Years earlier, for example, Alexis de Tocqueville had written that in America "everything is in motion" around you, but "the hand which gives the impulse to the social machine can nowhere be discovered."[21] Among Melville's contemporaries, the anonymous powers of spirit informed the Gothic works of Edgar Allen Poe and Melville's close friend, Nathaniel Hawthorne.

Two years before the publication of *Moby-Dick*, Congregationalist minister Horace Bushnell made a theological case for the aura of language itself. According to Bushnell, God was immanent in the fixtures of nature

20. Essential works that have focused on the haunted character of modernity include Avery F. Gordon, *Ghostly Matters: Haunting and the Sociological Imagination* (Minneapolis: University of Minnesota Press, 1997); Michael T. Taussig, *The Devil and Commodity Fetishism in South America* (Chapel Hill: University of North Carolina Press, 1980); Michael Taussig, "Maleficium: State Fetishism," in *The Nervous System* (New York: Routledge, 1992), 111–40; and Terry Castle, *The Female Thermometer: Eighteenth-Century Culture and the Invention of the Uncanny* (New York: Oxford University Press, 1995). In taking issue with definitions of enchantment as a modality of unreflexive reasoning—a false (Marx), repressive (Freud), or regressive (Adorno) consciousness—Jane Bennett makes the case for the ethics of enchantment in *The Enchantment of Modern Life: Attachments, Crossings, and Ethics* (Princeton: Princeton University Press, 2001). Enchantment, in Bennett's estimation, becomes a relentless commitment to self-reflexive consciousness, a relentlessness that reaches the point of questioning whether there is an ontological ground to be reflexive about.

21. Alexis de Tocqueville, *American Institutions and Their Influence* (New York: A. S. Barnes & Co., 1851), 67.

as much as in the words uttered about the nature of things, in the explanations that were espoused, and the worlds that were created in light of those explanations. According to Bushnell, the whole of human activity registered itself in terms of "spiritual hieroglyphs," marks to be deciphered by humans in the service of worshipping their creator. In making his case for an "atmosphere of meaning," Bushnell argued that the "outer world, which envelops our being, is itself language, the power of all language," written by the "universal Author." This was nothing less than the "publicity" of God as amplified by human activity. Social life, according to Bushnell, was affective. If performed according to the script of "Christian nurture," conversations and their tone, the "expression of the eye, the face, the look, the gait, the motion," business practices, even railroads and telegraphs,— all could precipitate a "sweet sense of estrangement." As Bushnell once wrote, "the walk, the solitary chamber even, are haunted unawares by a feeling which must be called social."[22]

Decades earlier Alexander Bryan Johnson's *A Treatise on Language: or, The Relation which Words Bear to Things* (1828 and 1836) had called for recognition of the fact that language had come to assume a life of its own. Johnson posited the existence of a para-linguistic reality, a medium that was itself a product of *an economy of* verbal interaction. Johnson was a local banker in upstate New York who had taken a keen interest in the value of currency. From Johnson's desk in Utica, signs circulated in increasingly massive and dense orbits even as their referents faded into the abstractions of the "credit system." Johnson's was an insight into a phantom economy, a complex and stable rationality divorced from the material world.[23] This mood carried over into his study of language and its hazards. "We usually say that words are signs of things," wrote Johnson. "Practically," however, "we make things the signs of words." For Johnson, this was a crisis of empiricism and representation, or more precisely a failure to represent

22. Horace Bushnell, "Preliminary Dissertation on Language," in *God in Christ: Three Discourses* (Hartford: Brown and Parsons, 1849), 30; Horace Bushnell, *Spirit in Man: Sermons and Selections*, ed. Mary Bushnell Cheney (New York: Charles Scribner's Sons, 1910) 442, 111; Horace Bushnell, *Christ in Theology: Being the Answer of the Author, Before the Hartford Central Association of Ministers, October, 1849, for the Doctrines of the Book Entitled "God in Christ"* (Hartford: Brown and Parsons, 1851), 46; Horace Bushnell, "Revelation" (1839), cited in *Horace Bushnell: Selected Writings on Language, Literature, and American Culture*, ed. David Lester Smith (Chico, Calif.: Scholars Press, 1984), 29; Horace Bushnell, "Unconscious Influence," in *Sermons for the New Life*, 2d ed. (New York: Charles Scribner, 1858), 188–92; Mary Bushnell Cheney, ed., *The Life and Letters of Horace Bushnell* (New York: Charles Scribner's Sons, 1903), 88.
23. For a contemporary account, see Caitland Zaloom, "The Derivative World," *The Hedgehog Review: Critical Reflections on Contemporary Culture* 12 (Summer 2010): 20–27.

the empirical. It was a failure to interpret "language with reference to its meaning in something other than words." Although not inclined to reduce the "something other" of language to divine immanence (Bushnell criticized Johnson for "ignoring language as a vehicle of the spirit"), Johnson argued that signs had begun to shape their signifiers in significant ways.[24] A feedback loop had been created. For although language may have originated as the creation of humans, it was now creating them. An unseen force molded beliefs and behaviors in its image—"some unverbal subjective something in man's consciousness" or some "objective unverbal thing that our senses reveal." Like Bushnell, Johnson was sensitive to the conjuring effects of language. Once humans began to interpret "any given word or set of words by other words," Johnson feared that they would "pursue a round without end." His response was to exorcise, through reason, the "demon who delights in our infirmities."[25]

In moving away from the God-soaked grammars of theology, Karl Marx made a memorable case for the anonymous spirit of capitalism. The experiential acceptance of modernity's economic order, he argued, was akin to participating in a spiritualist séance, the conjuring force of capitalism being "far more wonderful than 'table-turning' ever was."[26] What mattered for Marx was the excessive materiality of circulation. Commodities, not concepts, had assumed an agency of their own, independent of the individual who used them. The ideology of capitalism—this strange way of doing business—Marx treated as a savage system, a society unaware of what it was really doing. The Anglo-European models of social interaction and the moral good were unhinged, forms of fetishism and often scenes of brutality. There was something both deceitful and ravenous about the metaphysics of capitalism. Those who subscribed to it without question were no better than the animists they viewed with contempt on the colo-

24. Alexander Bryan Johnson, *A Treatise on Language, edited with a Critical Essay on his Philosophy of Language* (Berkeley and Los Angeles: University of California Press, 1947), 40, 161. Charles L. Todd and Robert Sonkin, *Alexander Bryan Johnson: Philosophical Banker* (Syracuse: Syracuse University Press, 1977), 105; Bushnell, "Preliminary Dissertation," 44.

25. Todd and Sonkin, *Alexander Bryan Johnson*, 156–58, 166; Johnson, *A Treatise on Language*, 36, 42. According to Johnson, demystification was long overdue. "Science" had "long lost the favor of practical men, and is almost abandoned, with alchymy [sic] and catholicons, to the dreams of enthusiasm." Given his dismissal of magic, Catholicism, and those Protestants taken up by revivalism, Johnson found a receptive audience in those freethinkers who saw him as dismantling the sovereignty of a Christian God. He was, however, a committed Presbyterian, serving as president of the Union Tract Society as well as the Oneida Evangelical Society.

26. Karl Marx, *Capital: A Critique of Political Economy*, ed. Friedrich Engels, trans. Samuel Moore and Edward Aveling (New York: International Publishers, 1992), 1:76.

nial peripheries. They, too, were haunted by what they, themselves, had put into circulation—the commodity and its directives. Yet they were unable to recognize their own labor, their own imprint. And herein lies the mystical heart of capitalism—the material imprint of the human, the mark of its own agency, it erased. According to Marx, the rich, poor, and laboring classes alike had become as deluded as those attending a parlor séance. Like spiritualists, Marx's contemporaries were ignorant of the hardest of truths. They did not know themselves because they could not admit that it was they who were the enchanters.

4. Madness

Shortly before composing *Moby-Dick*, Melville encountered George Adler, a German émigré and professor at the City University of New York. Melville met Adler as he was traveling from New York to London to sell the publishing rights to his novel *White Jacket*. Adler, noted Melville in his journal, was "full of the German metaphysics" and "the author of a formidable lexicon, (German & English); in compiling which he almost ruined his health. He was almost crazy, he tells me, for a time." Indeed, Adler would soon became a semi-permanent resident of Bloomsdale Asylum in upper Manhattan. But here, in the middle of the Atlantic Ocean, Adler idealized knowledge as a means of control. Disenchantment was the most profound lesson he had taken from his readings of British and German Romanticism:

> Walked the deck with the German, Mr. Adler, till a late hour, talking of "Fixed Fate. Free-will, foreknowledge absolute" &c. His philosophy is *Colredegian*: he accepts the Scriptures as divine, & yet leaves himself free to inquire into Nature. He does not take it, that the Bible is absolutely infallible, & that anything opposed to it in Science must be wrong. He believes that there are things out of God and independant [*sic*] of him,—things that would have existed were there no God:—such as that two & two make four; for it is not that God so decrees mathematically, but that in the very nature of things, the fact is thus.[27]

27. Herman Melville, *Journals*, ed. Howard C. Horsford and Lynn Horth (Evanston: Northwestern University Press, 1989), 4–5; G. J. Adler, *A Dictionary of the German and English Languages* (New York: D. Appleton, 1848). For a short biographical sketch, see Lyman R. Bradley, "George J. Adler, 1821–1868," *The German Quarterly* 7 (November 1934): 152–56.

Adler, according to Melville, waxed poetically about a notion of divine order that was neither transcendent nor active but wholly immanent and inert. According to Adler, Christian divinity was not so much animate as subsidiary and complementary to an overarching scheme of order in which things pulsated at their own pace. Universal laws of "Nature" "would have existed were there no God." Adler's was a heady and practical reading of European romanticism, his way of acknowledging issues of aesthetics—terror, the ludicrous, and the sublime—so as to diffuse their disruptive potential.[28] The world was infinitely complex but so too was the mind's eye in its capacity for calculation.

As a member of the American Ethnological Society, Adler infused his work in philology with a certain confidence about the universal and seamless qualities of language. Adler and other proponents of "the scientific character and value of linguistic researches" argued that language, as opposed to God or even biology, was that which bound the human race together.[29] For philologically inclined ethnologists like Adler, "the study of human language" could serve to complement the sacrament of "physical science," which had "penetrated the heavens" and "traced out and systematized the laws of the imponderable agencies on which depends the motions and the changes of the visible universe." Philology, in other words, could at once extend the inquiries of science into territories once reserved for theologians and provide access to a universal code that was not strictly empirical.[30]

Adler assumed that truth was evident in the marks of human communication and self-evident to those who gazed intently enough upon it. Yet for Adler, efforts to peel back the layers of surface existence were not necessarily comforting. For after his encounter with Melville Adler became increasingly distraught about a looming "conspiracy" involving colleagues, students, and hired hoodlums who were "determined to vex me out of existence." As Adler lamented, "I have been made the object of a systematic and invidious persecution" and was leading "a life of a discouraging uncertainty." He had been *"seized of my personality and of my substantial*

---

28. See, for example, Adler's translation of Jean Paul Richter's "On the Ludicrous," in *The Literary World* 220 (April 19, 1851): 309-10 and 223 (May 10, 1851): 370-71.
29. "The Unity of Language and of Mankind," *North American Review* 152 (July 1851): 164, 179.
30. Ibid., 167-68. "Human language may be considered not so much the offspring, or the organ of communication, as the embodiment, the proper manifestation of the human soul. It reveals to us all we know of other human souls, and probably all, or nearly all, that each of us knows of his own."

being, by which I make myself an accountable, a moral and a religious agent." Consequently, Adler "was confined to my bed most of the time" because "it was painful and disgusting for me to be awake." The only comfort Adler found was reading "'Hegel's Logic' for two or three hours a day." In 1853 Adler was, in his words, *"converted into an insane man by the oath of two physicians"* and committed to Bloomsdale Asylum. Adler soon began sending letters from the asylum that detailed perceived grievances. Such missives did not precipitate any official response. But strangely, they did intensify the secretive and "nefarious business of subjugation." For rather than being ignored, his tormentors continued to act in public without being detected. As Adler lamented, his letters had been "answered by spectral demonstrations (not unlike those of ghost-rappers)."[31]

———

The integrated narrative of *Secularism in Antebellum America* revolves around Melville's scene of writing as he composed *Moby-Dick*. In keeping with Melville's critical perspective, mine is a particular history of ghosts as they became tangible in the lives of antebellum Americans who, in one way or another, found themselves subject to modernity's effects. My goal, in attending the haunted terrains of America circa 1851, is not to exorcise them as regrettable sites of consciousness. My goal instead is to appreciate haunting as a "social phenomenon of great import," integral to what it means to be modern, what it means, perhaps, to speak of a "modern book" and, by extension, to be alive within a secular age whose freedoms carry with them their own coercions and their own madness.[32]

31. G. J. Adler, *Letters of a Lunatic, or A Brief Exposition of My University Life, During the Years 1853-54* (New York: Author, 1854), 18, 17, 30-31, 14, 24, 28, 22.
32. Gordon, *Ghostly Matters*, 7.

The Metaphysics

OF SECULARISM

"But if we disintegrate verbal units, that is vaporize the containers, then the explosion could not take place in effect would never have existed—"

"Perhaps—I am a chemist not a prophet—It is considered axiomatic that the nova formula can not be broken, that the process is irreversible once set in motion—All energy and appropriations is now being channeled into escape plans—If you are interested I am empowered to make an offer of evacuation—on a time level of course."

"And in return?"

"You will simply send back a report that there is no evidence of nova activity on planet earth."

WILLIAM S. BURROUGHS, *Nova Express* (1964)

1. On Declarations of Independence and Nova Effects

How does it feel to live within a secular age? Or as the philosopher Charles Taylor asked: what is at stake when faith, "even for the staunchest believer, is one human possibility among others"? What are the effects, religiously speaking, of living in a world that naturally divides itself into a series of choices to be made, sold, and tried on for size? The answers to such questions exceed even Taylor's own magisterial effort to offer a phenomenology of secular modernity in the Anglo-European West. Taylor identifies the nineteenth century as a moment when a particular feeling of independence was forged and when declarations of religious freedom made their way across Europe and North America. The nineteenth century, suggests Taylor, did not efface religion. It changed it. For it was during this time that piety and belief became subject to a "nova effect, the steadily widening gamut of new positions" vis-à-vis the religious, "some believing, some unbelieving, some hard to classify." The nova effect, in other words, generated an unprecedented potentiality of responses to and habituations of something conceived of as the religious. For whether the religious was engaged with reverence, hostility, or indifference, the range of choices that emerged, not to mention the ability to choose, were remarkable and representative achievements.[1]

---

1. Charles Taylor, *A Secular Age* (Cambridge, Mass.: Harvard University Press, 2007), 3, 423. Taylor points to such achievements as the difference that secularization makes in Anglo-European history. Secularization, for Taylor, involves not the decline of religion but has to do with developments that made religion something in the world that could be chosen or not, something that could be known, categorized, consumed, and/or feared. As with any secularization thesis, regardless of particulars, Taylor's is invested in marking the *sine qua non* of modernity—a difference without which modernity would not be. As Vincent Pecora has noted in his critical survey, secularization has come to assume multiple meanings and to serve multiple agendas within the academic, political, and legal realms. In its most simplistic iteration, secularization is an advertisement for the propriety of its own desire, sociologists announcing the retreat of religion into private life, conservatives bemoaning the diminishment of its categories and institutions, or perhaps foreign policy-makers calling for the eradication of religion that was not true, at the level of hearts and minds. In a more sophisticated guise, secularization signifies a transformation of the religious within the West—its rationalization and/or its form assuming worldly content. Since the publication of Max Weber's *The Protestant Ethic and the Spirit of Capitalism* (1904), substantial readings of the place and function of religion within modernity have marked a shift or rupture in practices revolving around the concept of religion. Vincent P. Pecora, *Secularization and Cultural Criticism: Religion, Nation, and Modernity* (Chicago: University of Chicago Press, 2006).

Talal Asad has done much to show how the relationship between the religious and the secular became both a metaphysical and practical matter within various arenas of European Christianity. Rather than posit a thing called religion that recedes or becomes re-entrenched or undergoes a revision to its essential nature, Asad insists upon attending to the practices and ideas that contribute to new concepts of religion. In his focus on the co-articulation of religion and secularity, Asad interjects the question of discourse into a previous debate between Karl Löwith and Hans Blumenberg over the meaning and prospects of secularization. Asad, *Formations of the Secular: Christianity, Islam, Modernity* (Stanford, Calif.: Stanford University Press, 2003), 191.

Shortly after World War II Löwith argued the secular age was an excession of the religious, "a mistaken Christianity that confound[ed] the fundamental distinction between redemptive events and profane happenings." Modernity was an illegitimate heir to religion because in turning Judeo-Christian eschatology into secular theodicy it could excuse all manner of colonial violence and injustice in the present as the inevitable working out of progress. Blumenberg, rather than view modernity as a regressive rendering of theological sensibilities, conceptual structures, and institutions, argued that secularization was marked by an "innocent confidence" revolving around a bad fit between contemporary questions and preestablished epistemic needs. "What mainly occurred in the process that is interpreted as secularization," wrote Blumenberg, "should be described not as the transposition of authentically theological contents but rather as the reoccupation of answer positions that had become vacant and whose corresponding questions could not be eliminated." New attitudes toward progress, for example, were a formal reoccupation of Christian expectation rather

Taylor does not grapple much with the historicity of the nova effect, that is, the *effects* upon *it*, the contingent threads that make up its weave and tensile strength. Yet his query—what does it feel like to live within a secular age?—is a profound question of aesthetic matters and their history. It is profound because it points to the fact that any viable description of the nineteenth century must account for how one's identity becomes bound up with one's relationship to the religious. Such a description must explain those processes—emotional, epistemological, ethical—in which religion becomes naturalized as an option rather than an obligation. Such a description must also address a situation in which individuals feel the authority of their choices or, at the very least, arrive at a place in which some choice can and must be made. The nova effect, in other words, does not exist in essence. It is rather a mood or sensibility in and through which choices are made and made to feel decisive.

What Taylor calls the "nova effect" has long been a working assumption among Americans in general and scholars of antebellum America in particular. Indeed, the mid-nineteenth century has a storied place in the American imagination of religion and its freedoms. This story has many elements, some more persistent than others.

In the fractious decades leading up to the Civil War, it is said, economic structures and political sensibilities were coming together that would help secure, however fragilely, a more just future in which religion, itself, would become liberated.[2] In the decades that followed, violence, racism, and intolerance may not have ceased. But there was momentum, a tangible expansion of religious freedoms that would soon create a viable diversity.[3] Evangelicalism expanded at an accelerated pace.[4] Together, denomina-

---

than a strange extension—born of "novel experiences." I am interested in what constitutes the novelty of these experiences and their significance. Karl Löwith, *Meaning in History: The Theological Implications of the Philosophy of History* (Chicago: University of Chicago Press, 1949), 203, 30; Hans Blumenberg, *The Legitimacy of the Modern Age* (Cambridge, Mass.: MIT Press, 1983), 63, 65, 31.

2. G. P. Putnam, ed., *The World's Progress: A Dictionary of Dates with Tabular Views of General History* (New York: G. P. Putnam, 1851), 146–55.

3. Barbara Welter, *Dimity Convictions: The American Woman in the Nineteenth Century* (Athens: Ohio University Press, 1976), and Albert J. Raboteau, *Slave Religion: The Invisible Institution in the Antebellum South* (New York: Oxford University Press, 1978). For an implicit and subtle critique of trends within the first wave of social history, see R. Laurence Moore, *Religious Outsiders and the Making of Americans* (New York: Oxford University Press, 1986). See also Walter Benn Michaels, *Our America: Nativism, Modernism, and Pluralism* (Durham: Duke University Press, 1997).

4. Nathan O. Hatch, *The Democratization of Christianity* (New Haven: Yale University Press, 1989).

tional fault lines and recombinations generated a plurality of individual-isms. The influx of immigrants fueled both the creativity and institutional-ization of non-Protestant faiths.[5] Spiritualism and other aspirant religions attracted crowds and individuals who considered themselves progressive reformers.[6] Intentional communities were not uncommon. The promise of science and scientific technics such as phrenology was evidence of a vibrant pluralism in thought and deed. And finally, self-consciously sec-ular pursuits—the market, in particular—were quickly gaining ground as many Americans were learning to live with neither God nor creed.[7] Such events, it has been said, unsettled traditional hierarchies of religious authority, not to mention those of gender, race, and class, conditioning possibilities for the emancipations that were to follow. Fragmentation, pluralism, creativity—such analytics have since become part and parcel to the historical treatments of this period.[8] The age of the "first person singular."[9] A hallowed moment when a large segment of the population, finally, had become (or would soon become) liberated enough to believe what they wanted to believe.[10]

5. Jay P. Dolan, "The Immigrants and their Gods: A New Perspective in American Religious History," *Church History* 57, no. 1 (1988): 61–72. For an explicit conflation of political diver-sity and personal freedom, see Diana Eck, *A New Religious America: How a "Christian Coun-try" Has Become the World's Most Religiously Diverse Nation* (New York: HarperOne, 2001).

6. Ann Braude, *Radical Spirits: Spiritualism and Women's Rights in Nineteenth-Century America* (Boston: Beacon Press, 1989); Leigh Eric Schmidt, *Heaven's Bride: The Unprintable Life of Ida C. Craddock, American Mystic, Scholar, Sexologist, Martyr, and Madwoman* (New York: Basic Books, 2010).

7. James Turner, *Without God, Without Creed: The Origins of Unbelief in America* (Baltimore, Md.: Johns Hopkins University Press, 1985).

8. On the persistence/promotion of scholarship that universalizes religion and celebrates its liberation as a particularly American phenomenon, see Kevin M. Schultz and Paul Harvey, "Everywhere and Nowhere: Recent Trends in American Religious History and Historiogra-phy," *Journal of the American Academy of Religion* 78 (March 2010): 129–62.

9. Ralph Waldo Emerson, *Journals of Ralph Waldo Emerson, 1824–1832*, ed. Edward Waldo Emerson and Waldo Emerson Forbes (Boston: Houghton Mifflin Company, 1909), 164.

10. Histories of American religiosity, even when they complicate simplistic narratives of democratic triumph by focusing on limitations or incompleteness of the project, often leave unquestioned the status of the subject whose piety depends on either/or conceptions of agency, intentionality, and deliberation. In assuming the former, the works cited above leave unthought the historical contingencies that have made religion synonymous with belief and religious practice a consistent reflection of conscious assent. In assuming the latter, they are blinded to what Daniel Walker Howe identifies as the middle ground in which beliefs *are* practices, democratization can be repressive, and discipline is a kind of choice ("The Evangelical Movement and Political Culture in the North during the Second Party System," *Journal of American History* 77, no. 4 [March 1991]: 1220). For works that have not slighted the fact that the subjects of American religion are always, simultaneously, subject to power relations, see Robert A. Orsi, *Thank You, St. Jude: Women's Devotion to the Patron Saint of Hope-*

The invocation of close ties between agency and the freedom to believe is not incorrect. Indeed, it reflects much of what antebellum Protestants were saying at the time. "True religion," as it was referred to across the Protestant spectrum at mid-century, was grounded deep within the self. Belief in turn was conceived of as a choice rather than obligation, the cause of practice rather than the effect. Moreover, belief was an epistemic virtue, a choice made self-evident given that religion was not merely a "sentiment" but something that "one must be able also to put . . . out of him, as a theory, that he may contemplate it, study it, fit it to himself and himself to it."[11] In becoming the object of increasingly systematic attention, religion was bound up with seeing the world clearly, with knowing the self knowing it without mediation. Piety not only corresponded to divine script but was also the means of revealing essential principles of the human — reason, coherency, and legibility — to the human in the name of human progress. Such progress served as both incentive and epistemological horizon. In other words, the story of the nova effect, circa 1851, has had a strange way of reproducing what it takes for granted — that religion, at its best, is the exercise of one's freedom in private that is also beneficial to the public sphere.[12] At its worst, religion is untrue — a perversion of consciousness and/or a scheme of social control.[13]

Stories of the nova effect, expressed either by contemporary scholars or antebellum Americans, are not untrue. There have indeed been remarkable improvements, expansion of choices, extensions of freedom. Yet there

---

less Causes (New Haven: Yale University Press, 1996); Ann Taves, Fits, Trances, and Visions: Experiencing Religion and Explaining Experience from Wesley to James (Princeton: Princeton University Press, 1999); Susan Friend Harding, The Book of Jerry Falwell: Fundamentalist Language and Politics (Princeton: Princeton University Press, 2000); Leigh Eric Schmidt, Hearing Things: Religion, Illusion, and the American Enlightenment (Cambridge, Mass.: Harvard University Press, 2000); John Corrigan, Business of the Heart: Religion and Emotion in the Nineteenth Century (Berkeley and Los Angeles: University of California Press, 2002); Tracy Fessenden, Culture and Redemption: Religion, the Secular, and American Literature (Princeton: Princeton University Press, 2007); Richard J. Callahan Jr, Work and Faith in the Kentucky Coal Fields: Subject to Dust (Bloomington: Indiana University Press, 2009); Courtney Bender, The New Metaphysicals: Spirituality and the American Religious Imagination (Chicago: University of Chicago Press, 2010); Kathryn Lofton, O: The Gospel of an Icon (Berkeley and Los Angeles: University of California Press, 2011).

11. Henry W. Bellows, "Spiritual Discernment," in Re-Statements of Christian Doctrine (Boston: American Unitarian Association, 1867), 32.

12. On military conquest as a way to exercise one's religious freedom while extending "freedom from superstition" to the colonial subject, see "Prescott's Conquest of Peru," The North American Review 65 (October 1847): 372.

13. On the "ghostly domination" of the Roman Catholic Church, see Rev. Nicholas Murray, The Decline of Popery and its Causes (New York: Harper & Brothers, 1851), 9.

are other stories to tell when examining the dense measures of antebellum experience, other truths to consider that unsettle the congealed mythos of religious freedom and pluralistic evolution.[14] For despite the fact that a range of Protestants conceived of their religion as integral to securing their independence, the conception itself was not solely of their own making. On the contrary, the conviction that one was religious or not in the antebellum period was a haunted and haunting affair.

Secularism in Antebellum America tells another kind of story about the feelings, epistemic moves, and habits of being that made the nova effect a living possibility. For what defines the secular imaginary at mid-century, I argue, was not the liberatory profusion of either/or propositions involving the will to believe or not. I neither assume the capacity for utilitarian calculation nor project it upon the wills of others. I argue instead that the secular imaginary occurred at the levels of emotion and mood, underneath the skin. Consequently, this study does not take religion for granted as a natural site of knowledge or practice. Declarations of independence should be read with a degree of critical distance.[15] Religious freedoms are rarely, if ever, unprecedented.[16] For as I will show in the chapters that follow, the "true religion" known and practiced by a significant number of antebellum Americans was anything but natural. On the contrary, it was really made up—by individuals, to be sure, but also by forces only tangentially related to them and never quite in their control. To focus on the disciplinary air of the secular age is necessarily to focus on something that may seem anathema to either antebellum Americans or contemporary historians who imagine selves as having certain inherent traits. These selves have the capacity to access, immediately, their own thoughts, and they are set apart from organized forces and systemic structures, a removal that guarantees both the political and epistemological premises of the agentive self. But agency is not an either/or prospect. It is circuitous. It happens, but always in and through "instruments, techniques, procedures, levels of

---

14. Stories that have informed and inflected my own include Ann Douglas, *The Feminization of American Culture* (New York: Alfred A. Knopf, 1977), Ronald Takaki, *Iron Cages: Race and Culture in 19th-Century America* (New York: Knopf, 1979), and Christopher Newfield, *The Emerson Effect: Individualism and Submission in America* (Chicago: University of Chicago Press, 1996).

15. On the ironic demeanor of the historian, see Catherine L. Albanese, "Narrating an Almost Nation: Contact, Combination, and Metaphysics in American Religious History," *Criterion* 38 (Winter 1999): 2-15, 44.

16. Winnifred Fallers Sullivan, *The Impossibility of Religious Freedom* (Princeton: Princeton University Press, 2005).

application, targets," and concepts.[17] And it is this thought that I would like to bring to bear upon antebellum religious history.

To put a finer point on it, *Secularism in Antebellum America* contends that human agency was and remains an open question. And it is precisely this openness that is the historiographic first principle of this book, a mode of storytelling that appreciates the impossibility of complete self-disclosure.[18] For those living within a secular imaginary, decisions about religion were often one's own, yet the range of available choices had been patterned and shaped by circumstance. Institutions making their invisible demands. Media generating models of particular choices. Machines enabling you to interact with your decisions and those of others. A choice being made before it presents itself as such. Unseen somethings haunting the day.[19]

2. The Truth of Religion in Antebellum America

I have chosen the name secularism to refer to that which conditioned not only particular understandings of the religious but also the environment in which these understandings became matters of common sense. Rather than signal a decreasing influence of the religious, secularism names a conceptual environment—emergent since at least the Protestant Reformation and early Enlightenment—that has made "religion" a recognizable and vital thing in the world.[20] To make inquiries into secularism is

17. On discipline as a modality of power that involves, simultaneously, its exercise, resistance, and inscription, see Michel Foucault, *Discipline & Punish: The Birth of the Prison* (New York: Vintage Books. 1995), 215.
18. A negative anthropology underlies my commitment to the normativity of enchantment and is manifest in how I approach historical subjects as well as in the form and content of the story that unfolds. To figure enchantment as a state of unknowing is not to reduce it to false consciousness. On the contrary, it is to frame enchantment and the unknowing that it portends as a kind of knowledge, or more precisely, as a space of knowledge creation. On the "work-like or poetic character of the human creature," see Thomas A. Carlson, *The Indiscrete Image: Infinitude and Creation of the Human* (Chicago: University of Chicago Press, 2008). Carlson writes of a creativity premised upon indiscretion, that is, the undefinability of human being. "What is distinctive about man," writes Carlson, "as a poetic work, or as a creature who creates even himself, is his lack of limit or definition, his lack of distinction, or more precisely, his lack, as a work, of distinctive resemblance to any definite model or archetype: his being, in short, the open and ongoing work of an 'indiscrete image'" (32–33).
19. Don DeLillo, *Underworld* (New York: Scribner, 1997).
20. In what follows I do my best to refuse narratives that chronicle the disappearance or retreat of religion into private realms. I also question those arguments that document the appearance of cultural forms and attitudes that came to usurp the authority of religion in the

to ask how certain concepts of religion (and the social formations that revolve around them) became consonant with the way things were—in essence—as portrayed by a secular political order. Such inquiry requires a sensitivity to how individuals imagined and assumed their place within society vis-à-vis these concepts and social formations. It also directs attention to the styles of reasoning that determine the truth of religion and/ or its falsity, that enable a person to know the world and objects within it along a religious-secular continuum.[21]

To begin to make inquiries into secularism, one must appreciate not only the construction of the religious/secular binary (and the concepts of reason, ethics, and the political that undergird it) but also the viral quality of secularism. There is, of course, something uncanny in the recognition of secularism as a disciplinary structure that is, first and foremost, invested in its own evolutionary progression. In that regard, secularism is monstrous, a presence of its own and not simply an effect of classification or a means of conferring legitimacy. For in its ability to convince a wide range of individuals of their conviction, secularism was, in the American grain, "something like an imperial discourse."[22] Although never

---

secular age. That story has been told, perhaps, too many times—"secular" forms and attitudes as vehicles of piety and/or transpositions of religious sentiment. Representative studies include John Lardas, *The Bop Apocalypse: The Religious Vision of Kerouac, Ginsberg, and Burroughs* (Urbana: University of Illinois Press, 2001). Although such studies have been valuable in prising open the category of the religious, reimagining what is religious about history, and even reflecting upon the desire to know about "religion," they have not, by and large, challenged the categorical dominance of the "secular." Within a work like *The Bop Apocalypse* the essential division between the religious and the secular remains essentially intact. For when ostensibly secular/worldly/mundane activities are shown to possess a religious cast, there is an implicit sense of corruption, of religion infiltrating the secular. Formally, such instances possess the air of a crime scene, of violation, transgression. Such instances also call attention the degree to which the difference between the religious and the secular has been secured in everyday as well as academic life. This amazing trick of history—so thoroughly achieved that the difference between the religious and the secular has become a matter of common sense—has had a double effect. First, it has had a pronounced influence on how religious actors and institutions define themselves as religious. Secondly, this achievement has allowed such actors and institutions to occlude from public consideration their own complex identity and conditions of possibility.

21. Over the past decade a number of works have shown how secularism is bound up with those forces that have defined (and continue to define) religion and its relationship to truth, institutions, and subjectivity. See William E. Connolly, *Why I am Not a Secularist* (Minneapolis: University of Minnesota Press, 1999); Asad, *Formations of the Secular*; Saba Mahmood, *Politics of Piety: The Islamic Revival and the Feminist Subject* (Princeton: Princeton University Press, 2005); and Gil Anidjar, "Secularism," *Critical Inquiry* 33, no. 1 (Autumn 2006): 52–77.

22. Foucault, "Nietzsche, Genealogy, History," 148–49. Secularism, then, is not simply a fantastic translation of material conditions, "a mere epiphenomenon of its morphological base."

articulated as such, secularism conjured a natural presence. The categories and sensibilities that it generated were aggressively self-evident for those who adopted them, setting the terms that all arguments about religion would have to adopt in order to become intelligible. But the concept of true religion was not natural. Nor was its definition as an interior and, more often than not, highly rationalized belief.

Secularism, in other words, cannot be approached as an ideological ruse. It neither deceived nor promulgated inaccurate representations of reality. On the contrary, secularism has been part and parcel to the very constitution of the real. For in supplying both the ground and ingredients of the freedoms enacted in the name of true religion, secularism did not distort reality as much as it provided a particular kind of justification for it. *Secularism in Antebellum America* is about the ways, means, and effects of this provision in 1851 or thereabouts. It surveys scenes of secularism at mid-century, which is to say, it dwells upon the aesthetics of religious conviction and practice in the lives of antebellum Americans.[23] Rather than offer a sweeping account of antebellum religious history, I explore the historicity of antebellum Protestantism, or more precisely, the processes by which particular ways of being religious took hold within a range of

---

On the contrary, secularism is an effervescent phenomenon—"a *sui generis* synthesis of individual consciousnesses." Such a synthesis, writes Durkheim, "is a whole world of feelings, ideas, and images that follow their own laws once they are born. They mutually attract one another, repel one another, fuse together, subdivide, and proliferate" (*The Elementary Forms of Religious Life* [1912], trans. Karen E. Fields [New York: The Free Press, 1995], 426). Within the immanent frame of secularism, not everybody shares the same ideas or attitudes but a majority share the same grammars of fear, desire, and expectation.

23. My encounter with historical subjects has been informed by works that address the emotional and perceptual frequencies of ideas, including William James, *Essays in Radical Empiricism*, ed. Ralph Barton Perry (New York: Longmans, Green, and Co., 1912); Emile Durkheim, *The Elementary Forms of Religious Life*; and Walter Benjamin, "The Work of Art in the Age of Mechanical Reproduction," in *Illuminations*, ed. Hannah Arendt (New York: Schocken Books, 1968), 217–51, and "One-Way Street," in *Selected Writings*, vol. 1: *1913–1926*, ed. Marcus Bullock and Michael W. Jennings (Cambridge, Mass.: Harvard University Press, 1996), 444–88. Such works explore the matter of mood, that is, the "space between the content of thought and the institutionalization of the world" (Donald M. Lowe, *History of Bourgeois Perception* [Chicago: University of Chicago Press, 1982], 1). See also Michael Taussig, *Mimesis and Alterity: A Particular History of the Senses* (New York: Routledge, 1993), and Alain Corbin, "A History and Anthropology of the Senses," in *Time, Desire, and Horror: Towards a History of the Senses*, ed. Alain Corbin, trans. Jean Birrell (Cambridge: Polity Press, 1995), 181–95. Corbin writes that the "history of sensibility" implies "discovering the configuration of what is experienced and what cannot be experienced within a culture at a given moment" (182). On the burgeoning field of the study of emotion and the study of religion, see John Corrigan, ed., *The Oxford Handbook of Religion and Emotion* (New York: Oxford University Press, 2008). See also Jason C. Bivins, *Religion of Fear: The Politics of Horror in Contemporary Evangelicalism* (New York: Oxford University Press, 2008).

Protestant subcultures at mid-century. How, in other words, did a range of Protestants—from the committed to the experimental to the erstwhile—arrive at and make the choices they did?

In taking the metaphysics of secularism as its subject, this book addresses an economy of social forces in terms that are anathema to a strictly empirical account of society and life within it.[24] Although I am interested in the first principles of secularism, I do not ascribe a stable or consistent ontology to them. Nor do I portray secularism as a singular entity. I assume, as a matter of analytical faith, that whatever we are talking about when we talk about secularism exceeds our capacity to name it. It is my contention that to address the immanent frames of secularism one must possess a certain degree of humility when naming the phenomena in question. Consequently, this story is experimental, an attempt to measure the surplus of secularism, to be attuned to the resonance of its component parts. It is a story that is at odds with the stories its subjects tell about themselves and their capacities.[25] It is a story that does not adopt a model of society that operates according to communicative reason and transparent relations between those who inhabit it. It is a story that remains suspicious of a model of subjects who possess direct access to themselves, whose consciousness is a responsibility undertaken rather than a process pieced together from "discursive traditions whose logic and power far exceeds the consciousness of the subjects they enable."[26]

Metaphysics, suggested Foucault, meant dealing with the "materiality of incorporeal things—phantasms, idols, and simulacra." Consequently, I address the metaphysics of secularism in terms of its spectral power, a process of "transcendent mediation" in which concepts of true religion take

24. The term *meta ta physika* is of Greek origin ("after the things of nature"). In the most general sense, metaphysics refers to the first principles of things: being, substance, essence, time, space, cause, identity, etc. For a fuller account of the etymological history and philosophical applications of this term, see Roger Hancock, "History of Metaphysics," in *The Encyclopedia of Philosophy*, ed. Paul Edwards (New York: Macmillan Publishing Co. and The Free Press, 1967), 5:289–300. Within the American intellectual climate of the late eighteenth and early nineteenth centuries, "metaphysical" was often code for superstition, occultism, and Catholicism.

25. On resonance as a subversion of individual reason and the democratic collective, see "On the Occult Sciences," *The Living Age* 5 (June 21, 1845): 575. On the savage capacities to hear and use resonance to communicate across great distances, see "Natural Music Telegraph," *Scientific American* 4 (October 7, 1848): 18. "The savage ear is more instinctive to sound than that of the civilized European, yet civilized in this respect far outshines barbaric instinct, for while certain understood sounds may be communicated to a great distance on the Banns of the Niger the whole movements of an army may be regulated by a bugle on the banks of the Thames."

26. Asad, *Formations*, 1–8; Mahmood, *Politics*, 32.

hold at the level of affect and practice.[27] Among evangelicals, for example, true religion revolved around the concepts of voluntary attention and systematicity. For Unitarians and other liberal Protestants, true religion was identified in terms of self-culture, spiritual discernment, and spirituality. For those who did not (or no longer) identified themselves denominationally, concepts such as sympathy, spiritual intercourse, culture, and kindness became general markers for the truth of the human condition. Such concepts, I argue, were compatible in so much as they articulated a situation in which there was a truth to religion to be discerned and, moreover, that the individual was ultimately responsible for the cultivation of this truth for the salvific benefit of self and others.[28]

Throughout this book I pay close attention to how concepts of true religion served to conflate, in distinctive ways, moral agency with the directives of political security in the lives of individuals. Each chapter illuminates specific pathways through which particular concepts of true religion carried with them a normative sociality to which individuals aligned themselves. For it was by way of conceptual mediation that description became prescription and sense transformed into a common fund of meaning. Concepts such as voluntary attention or spirituality exceeded the marks that constituted their literal meaning. They were also styles of representing the self to the self and others. They were used to focus one's thoughts and to carry oneself throughout the day. They generated structures of consciousness through which the world was felt, experienced, and acted upon.[29] They were, for all intents and purposes, capillary, repeating

27. Michel Foucault, "Theatrum Philosophicum," in *Language, Counter-memory, Practice: Selected Essays and Interviews by Michel Foucault*, ed. Donald F. Bouchard (Ithaca: Cornell University Press, 1977), 170, 169; Asad, *Formations*, 5.

28. Again, I am sensitive to how Protestant theological traditions were continuous with behaviors and institutions of so-called secular life in antebellum America. But rather than offer general claims about the relationship between religion and modernity, I am committed to investigating consequential moments in which 'religion' and its truth became sites of immense attention, mediation, and circulation. Secularism, then, has much to do with informational density and the intensification of attention directed at concepts of religion. Indeed, I am tempted to claim that whatever we are talking about when we are talking about secularism revolves around the power and capaciousness of semiotic machines, which is to say that I am tempted to argue that secularization might be considered to be the difference that semiotic technologies make in allowing individuals to inhabit and practice concepts of religion.

29. My inquiry into secularism asks how the conceptual constellation of religion becomes generative of what Durkheim called effervescence. As Durkheim observed, "categories are social things" that constitute "a system of active forces—not a nominal being, and not a creation of the mind" (*Elementary Forms*, 441). What, then, is the significance of effervescence moving out from "individuals pressing close to one another" to the moral force that concepts themselves generate, from the repeated actions of bodies to the categories that organize those bodies?

themselves across different sites, making their way into and underneath the skin.[30]

In antebellum America secularism moved across a number of sites — evangelicalism, liberal Protestantism, burgeoning fields of mental science, spiritualism, ethnographic inquiry, moral reform, etc. Consequently, chapters are scenic rather than synthetic. Weaving in and out of Melville's scene of writing, I conduct inquiries into the local effects of secularism rather than universal causes. Chapters explore the habituations of religion in the precincts of evangelicalism, within the liberal orbits of Unitarianism, phrenology, and Protestant mental science, among spiritualists as well as others who found themselves at the limits of (or beyond) explicitly Protestant markings. Each chapter accounts for the denominational and/or institutional affiliations of individuals. But I am not interested in measuring whether one mode of affiliation was dominant or more influential than an other.[31] I do, however, contend that the concept of true religion possessed its own political charge. Despite differences of articulation within there was a viral set of first principles about the truth of religion. To be sure, these principles have morphed and congealed. But they also repeat, as narrative and affect.

The first chapter, "Evangelical Secularism and the Measure of Leviathan," explores the circulation of true religion within the evangelical media sphere. Much of its focus is on the missionary and publishing enterprise of the American Tract Society (ATS), a transdenominational enterprise that used print technology, demography, statistics, and all manner of "systematic organization" to convert what it called the "population" or the "masses." I am interested in the significance of "true religion" as it became central to the stories evangelicals told themselves in order to be themselves. This chapter moves from a critical assessment of contemporary scholarly accounts of evangelicalism to one of the first histories of evangelicalism — Robert Baird's *Religion in the United States* (1843). Moving from narrative frames to corporeal registers, I then explore how the con-

30. On conceptual constellations assuming ethical force in the lives of individuals, see Asad, *Formations*, 25-26, 78. See, also William Burroughs and Brion Gysin, *The Third Mind* (New York: Viking Press, 1978).

31. I recognize from the outset that my interest in charting the resonance between different articulations of Anglo-American Protestant piety runs counter to a generation of scholarship that has done much to demonstrate the import of various fault lines within Protestantism and/or has emphasized the significance of those groups and religious sensibilities that were external to Protestantism. I am not so much questioning these findings as their premises. For when religious pluralism is defined in institutional terms — denominational and/or affiliative — particular kinds of consolidations tend not to be noticed.

cept of "true religion" plays out in the encounter between the workforce of ATS and its public, between the logic of the institution and the individual reader. This chapter foregrounds the role that mass media played in the experience of true religion and, perhaps more significantly, in the viscerality of circulating words.[32]

The second chapter traces the emergence of spirituality as a marker of liberal Protestant piety. It dwells upon the shift in ontological status of "spirituality" as it moved from signifying a quality of God (and marking his immunity from material conditions) to a practice of human immunization. I am particularly interested in how spirituality emerged as an epistemic virtue—a means of accessing unfettered knowledge about the nature of the human, the nature of divinity, and the nature of nature itself. This knowledge was pursued by way of theorizing affect, of harnessing the surplus of one's interior life. This pursuit, in turn, itself depended upon the promises of immediacy in an increasingly mediated world. This chapter is roughly chronological. It begins with the theological abstractions of William Ellery Channing and Boston Unitarianism. It then moves through the transdenominational pedagogies of mental and moral science to phrenological applications of spirituality. Spirituality was a fundamental human faculty, located at the crown of one's head and "discovered" in 1842 by Orson Fowler. Spirituality could be cultivated alongside "Veneration," "Hope," and other religious sentiments. This chapter concludes with a discussion of the conceptual life of spirituality within a burgeoning spiritualist subculture, a means of training oneself to imagine one's piety as all-encompassing, ever-connected, yet wholly unencumbered.

The third chapter tells a story about Lewis Henry Morgan, a Rochester lawyer and founding figure in the institution of American anthropology. The geographical and psychic scenes of Morgan's career intersected with evangelical revivalism and séance spiritualism, as well as with the advance of technological networks in the form of telegraph wires and railway lines. Morgan was a lukewarm Presbyterian whose ambivalence toward the corporate character of religion was manifest in his inquiries into the lifeways of the Iroquois. He self-consciously distanced himself from the formalities of religion, choosing instead the language of spirit and spirituality to describe his own scientific pursuits, the native populations that he studied in detail, and the evolution of human history. In wavering between sym-

---

32. For an account of the resonating effect of media practices among contemporary evangelicals, see William E. Connolly, "The Evangelical-Capitalist Resonance Machine," *Political Theory* 33, no. 6 (December 2005): 869–86.

pathetic longing for Native Americans and objective distance, Morgan was crucial in the development of the culture concept, a key term of anthropological comprehension. Moreover, in such wavering one can see how a style of liberal piety becomes embedded in disciplinary and institutional settings that are ostensibly secular. For within his own drama of spirituality, Morgan performed many of the roles in the elaborately staged drama of secularization (the much talked-about process through which the secular is said to have shown itself as natural and inevitable, that is, non-ideological). Morgan's desire to translate the language of religion into self-consciously secular forms pitted independent rationality against received faith, consigned primitive survivals to the dustbin of history, and envisioned the industrialization of the frontier.

The fourth chapter, "The Touch of Secularism," addresses how "true religion" became a hinge for organizing the population of the women's wing of Sing Sing State Penitentiary. As in previous chapters, I am interested in the compatibility of different formations of mid-century Protestantism. And I dwell again on this compatibility at the level of biopolitics. Here I focus explicitly on two figures, Eliza Farnham, "free-thinker," memoirist, and matron of the women's wing, and John Edmonds, aspiring politician and president of the New York Prison Association. Both would embrace séance spiritualism in the 1850s. Before their spiritualist turn, however, Farnham and Edmonds instituted a phrenological agenda of criminal reform in the mid-1840s to the dismay of the Methodist chaplaincy. On the one hand, their reforms anticipated their future correspondences with the spirit-world. On the other, even as they replaced an evangelical program of instruction with a phrenological one, they retained and extended the metaphysics of secularism in a new key.

In conclusion, I pose the question of agency within the immanent frame of the secular age. I focus, specifically, on the sensuous engagement with machines as depicted in the lives of Captain Ahab and John Murray Spear. Both Ahab and Spear, I argue, were representative of a new kind of agency born of deterministic schemes. In the spring of 1854, Spear "copulated" with the "new motive power," a device of "metal, magnets, and copper plates" that the spirit of Benjamin Franklin had instructed him to build. As one witness later described the scene, Spear "desired to submit himself to an operation" and "was encased . . . in an apparatus . . . composed of a combination of metallic plates, strips, and bands . . . and including, at proper locations, some of the precious metals, jewels, and other minerals alleged to enter prominently into the constitution of the human body." Upon being encased, Spear entered into a trance state for over an hour and entered into relations with the machine. One witness, "described 'a stream of light, a sort of *umbilicum*, emanating (from [Spear]) to and enveloping the mechanism.'" Spear was found in a "condition of extreme exhaustion. The witness concluded that 'virtue,' of *some* sort, 'had gone out of him,' by this novel mode of transfer."[33]

Together, these chapters attend to the powers of public Protestantism circa 1851—its ingredients, its processes, and its effects. There are substantial and subtle works that explore the often violent impact of this circulating ethic upon those who were not born into its scheme of economic and political blessings.[34] This study, however, is primarily interested in those who were. Rather than portray this period as one of unprecedented religious freedom and experimentation, I dwell instead upon the inscriptions made by a relatively privileged subculture upon themselves and others. Consequently, I seek to glimpse the force relations that were involved in and established by conceiving of and inhabiting religion in a particular way. For what is most remarkable about this period, I contend, was not the so-called flowering of religious pluralism and competitive strife but a resonance between different statements about religion—issued simultaneously by conservative evangelicals, liberal, experimental, and erstwhile Protestants.[35]

What idioms, I ask, were made available to these Americans for living, religiously? What styles of reasoning allowed these individuals to recognize their beliefs, whatever their content, to be true? What imaginings of social life enabled them to assume that their practices conformed to how the world was and/or should be in essence? And finally, what were the consequential effects of these choices, beliefs, and practices—upon them-

---

33. John Murray Spear, *The Educator: Being Suggestions, Theoretical and Practical, Designed to Promote Man-Culture and Integral Reform with a View to the Ultimate Establishment of a Divine Social State on Earth*, ed. A. E. Newton (Boston: Office of Practical Spiritualists, 1857), 245.

34. See, for example, Saidiya V. Hartman, *Scenes of Subjection: Terror, Slavery, and Self-Making in Nineteenth-Century America* (New York: Oxford University Press, 1997) and Susan M. Ryan, *The Grammar of Good Intentions: Race and the Antebellum Culture of Benevolence* (Ithaca: Cornell University Press, 2003).

35. The effects of secularism take hold against the backdrop of what it is not—not religion in general, but bad religion as racially coded as an incapacity for self-governance. Those who were deficient in religion, who had wholly misconstrued its truth, who possessed an excess of religion, who possessed diseased bodies yet did not own their own labor. It goes without saying that the inhabitations of religion that I explore in this book were dependent upon all manner of power relations—exclusionary practices in both conception and deed. See, for example, Matthew Estes injunction that "masters" be "required to attend to the religious conditions of their Slaves" (*A Defence of Negro Slavery as its Exists in the United States* [Montgomery: Press of the Alabama Journal, 1846], 259).

selves, but also upon others who ostensibly chose, believed, and practiced the truth of their religion in everyday life?

3. Styles and Subcultures of American Protestantism

What is most remarkable about verbal and corporeal expressions of true religiosity issuing from the precincts of mid-century Protestantism is how two realms were simultaneously imagined: (1) the sphere of the religious in which piety became idealized as a mode of immediate cognition, intentionality, and self-mastery, and (2) the sphere of the secular in which cognitive control was not only promoted as natural (and therefore neutral) but also protected from the illegitimate claims of others.

Among evangelicals, for example, particularly those concerned with the most efficient means of producing piety, "true religion" became a matter of "systematic organization" of the self. The key to worldly success was the same as that for salvation, namely, "proper government" and "mastery over" oneself. Self-possession, then, was also a political act, a "great public blessing" in which the individual "carries a pleasant atmosphere with him wherever he goes" for the purpose of inviting others to possess themselves as well.[36] Among mid-century evangelicals there was a desire to recover the ideal symbiosis between saint and citizen.[37] Atheism, licentiousness, and irreligion, by contrast, were illegitimate forms of civic engagement because they were matters of being possessed, "contrary to the nature of religion." In other words, they did not correspond to the truth, that is, the potential of the human. Therefore, those possessed by them had "no right, by any law in the United States . . . to come forward and propagate opinions and proselytize."[38]

True religion, among Unitarians, was the exercise of one's capacity for "spiritual discernment."[39] A "deliberateness and independence of judg-

36. David Magie, *The Spring-Time Of Life; Or, Advice To Youth* (New York: American Tract Society, 1855), 211, 225–26.
37. Michael Walzer, *The Revolution of the Saints: A Study in the Origins of Radical Politics* (Cambridge, Mass.: Harvard University Press, 1965), 208–12.
38. Robert Baird, *Religion in the United States of America, or an Account of the Origin, Progress, Relations to the State, and Present Condition of the Evangelical Churches in the United States with Notices of the Unevangelical Denominations* (Glasgow: Blackie and Son, 1844), 252.
39. Bellows, "Spiritual Discernment," 19–34. See also James Walker, "Spiritual Discernment" (1854–58), in *Reason, Faith, and Duty: Sermons by James Walker* (Boston: Roberts Brothers, 1877), 202–21.

ment" would, ideally, free the individual from "casual rumor and loose conversation." On the one hand, such cognition was focused on divinity. "Unitarianism is the system most favorable to piety, because it holds forth and preserves inviolate the spirituality of God." To know this immaterial dimension of God was, on the other hand, to discern something essential about the self. "Spiritual freedom" was the result, a state which "liberat[ed] the intellect, conscience, and will, so that they may act with strength and unfold themselves forever. The essence of spiritual freedom is power." It was *this* power—the disclosure of an interior life that was once hidden—that was prerequisite for civic engagement. Such power was an antidote to the "ignorant masses" who had not yet discerned who they were in essence. For it was only after individuals had become liberated in a religious (rather than a political) sense that they should even enter the arena of 'secular' politics.[40]

For séance spiritualists, piety revolved around an enhanced understanding of one's links with the spirit-world.[41] As "determined *foes* of Ignorance, Error, Injustice and tyrannical Institutions," spiritualists held that such understanding was necessary to initiate democratic participation with all humans, past and present. "We, therefore, declare it to be 'our highest duty,' to become enlightened concerning ourselves," wrote trance-medium Andrew Jackson Davis. For spiritualists, America was to become a "REPUBLIC of SPIRIT embosomed and gestating in the dominant political organism." It was to be based on reason, "new classification of States; some new centres of governmental administration."[42] This republic was truly religious. It was "innate." And it "spontaneous[ly]" produced "the elements of our spiritual being." It was anathema to the teaching of "heathen divines" and the "relic[s] of barbarism" being peddled by Catholicism.[43]

40. William Ellery Channing, "Self-Culture," in *The Works of William E. Channing, D.D.* (Boston: American Unitarian Association, 1889), 24; "Unitarian Christianity," in *Works* (1889), 388; "Spiritual Freedom," in *Works* (1889), 174. See also Thomas C. Upham, *Principles of the Interior or Hidden Life; Designed Particularly for the Consideration of Those Who are Seeking Assurance of Faith and Perfect Love* (Boston: D. S. King, 1843).

41. On the theory of correspondence underlying spiritualist metaphysics, see Catherine L. Albanese, *A Republic of Mind and Spirit: A Cultural History of American Metaphysical Religion* (New Haven: Yale University Press, 2007), 13–15, 214–16, 253.

42. Andrew Jackson Davis, "The Principles of Nature. Declaration of Independence," *The Spirit Messenger* (May 31, 1851): 337–40; Andrew Jackson Davis, *Beyond the Valley; A Sequel to "The Magic Staff:" An Autobiography of Andrew Jackson Davis* (Boston: Colby & Rich, 1885), 64. On the republican politics of spiritualism, see Brett E. Carroll, *Spiritualism in Antebellum America* (Bloomington: Indiana University Press, 1997).

43. J[oel] Tiffany, *Lectures on Spiritualism* (Cleveland: J. Tiffany, 1851), 249, 344.

Politics, then, was modeled on the "political economy" of the spirit-world and dependent upon the earthly embrace of social circulation. Spiritualists saw in the spirit-world a code of governance that guaranteed freedom on earth. Moral autonomy did not threaten nor was it impeded by circulation. On the contrary, independence was premised upon one's interconnect-edness. Such freedom for spiritualists promoted an "infinite" variety of character based upon a singular model of the human.[44]

There is a peculiar symmetry marking each of these statements. Across the range of Protestant subcultures both the religious and the secular could lay claim to how the world was in essence. Both heaven and earth became the inheritance of a rational human species, a hard-won triumph against the forces of savagery and barbarism.[45]

Alexis de Tocqueville noted the irony of how Americans set piety apart from the political even as their piety assumed a rather aggressive politi-cal agenda and yielded all number of political effects. Religion, observed Tocqueville, "never intervenes directly in the government of American society [and] should therefore be considered as the first of their politi-cal institutions." So although legal rhetoric may have called for a clear demarcation of church and state, religion was that which suffused pri-vate faith with public reason. "Thus while the law allows the American people to do everything; there are things which religion prevents them from imagining and forbids them to become."[46] Consequently, the power of compatible statements about the truth of religion was to secure a sharp

44. Robert Hare, *Experimental Investigations of the Spirit Manifestations, Demonstrating the Existence of Spirits and Their Communion with Mortals* (New York: Partridge and Brittan, 1855), 88–89, 113.

45. Nowhere is this kind of desire more apparent than in scientific efforts to locate, define, and eradicate "bad" religion from the public arena. As embryonic works of comparative religion and anthropology, taxonomies of the world's religions placed the very notion of the "religious" at a distance in order to better secure its place. See, for example, George Smith, *The Patriarchal Age: or, the History and Religion of Mankind* (New York: Lane & Scott, 1851) and E.G.S., "American Ethnology," *The American Whig Review* 9 (April 1849): 392–93. In the antebellum grain, "bad" religion could be exhibited by irrational "savages" and Christian "enthusiasts" alike. In either case the excesses of religion were to be contained. Under the relentless gaze of philologists, ethnographers, missionaries, and anti-revivalists, the world's religions were transformed into so many specimens and evidentiary bodies that could be dis-sected, prioritized, and alphabetized. See, for example, Richard Hughes Seager, *The World's Parliament of Religions: The East/West Encounter, Chicago, 1893* (Bloomington: Indiana Univer-sity Press, 1995) and Tomoko Masuzawa, *The Invention of World's Religions or, How European Universalism Was Preserved in the Language of Pluralism* (Chicago: University of Chicago Press, 2005).

46. Alexis de Tocqueville, *Democracy in America*, ed. J. P. Mayer, trans. George Lawrence (Garden City: Anchor Books, 1969), 292.

distinction between private and public in theory while erasing the boundary between piety and politics in practice. For with varying degrees of intensity and inflection, the Protestant focus on the self assumed the existence of a bounded, perhaps even immunized, interiority. Yet this space of freedom was conceived of as actively guaranteeing the potential for others to achieve that very same freedom. For as the individual came to know himself knowing the world, he would catalyze conditions for others to know themselves knowing that very same world.[47]

What gives cause for concern is the creation of a public space whose legitimacy is founded upon an order that is both universal and rational, a space that insists upon its natural neutrality, a space that claims to guarantee open political debate even as it forecloses discussion about its legitimacy, its neutrality, and its openness within the arena it has created. Tracy Fessenden has recently referred to this paradoxical space in terms of what she calls the development of "nonspecific Protestantism" in American history. "In the United States," writes Fessenden, "whose founding documents aimed to unite a presumptively (if diversely) Christian population under the mantle of religious tolerance, the rule of noninterference between religion and government, far from consigning all religions equally to the silent margins of the political, instead created the conditions for the dominance of an increasingly nonspecific Protestantism over nearly all aspects of American life, a dominance as pervasive as it is invisible for *exceeding the domains we conventionally figure as religious.*"[48] This version of Protestantism was nonspecific because it belonged to no single group or movement in particular. It went without saying because it came without saying, resonating across various differences in creed, civic engagement,

47. Noting the publication of the thirteenth edition of *Democracy in America*, the *New-York Evangelist* lauded this discussion of consent as confirmation of religion's political truth ("Religion and Civil Order," *New-York Evangelist* 22 [November 1851]: 180). More recently, William E. Connolly has taken up this passage to argue that in America "the separation of church and state allows monotheism to install its effects in the hearts of the people and the presumptions of their institutions below the threshold of political debate" (Connolly, *The Ethos of Pluralization* [Minneapolis: University of Minnesota Press, 1995], 170). These effects of monotheism not only include patriotic righteousness but also involve how political engagement itself is normalized as public and progressive, an activity among sovereign, disenchanted individuals, made in the image of God.

48. Fessenden, *Culture and Redemption*, 61. "The secularization of American Protestantism," argues Fessenden, was "inseparable from its expansion" (59). As will be addressed in the first chapter, this "effect of Protestant consensus" is still very much a reality "for American religious historiography" (17)—a matter of looking at religion as a way of orienting oneself to the world, of making meaning, of overcoming or, at the very least, living within human limitations *rather* than thinking about the ways in which the world orients humans, makes them meaningful to themselves and others, and defines for them what is possible and what is not.

racial and sexual politics. This nonspecific Protestantism interacted with institutions of commerce, consumerism, and journalistic objectivity even as it structured the ways of church governance and the means of missionary outreach. Having fueled the energies of disestablishment in the Revolutionary period, it had now come to channel them into more experiential and/or more reasonable forms of piety. And finally, this nonspecific Protestantism articulated a politics in the service of naturalizing democracy, moral autonomy, and, most notoriously, freedom *from* religion and the freedom *to* practice it.[49]

Consequently, the most significant development, religiously speaking, in antebellum America was how religion exceeded itself, or at the very least, its dictionary definitions. Transcending both doctrinal and denominational differences, a somewhat hazy metaphysics assumed hegemonic status both within Protestant practice and across a number of other sites— in the formal innovations as well as the content of mass media, in encomiums to objectivity and in therapeutic approaches to selfhood, in the advent of human sciences such as anthropology, as well as in the moral reforms enacted by an ostensibly secular state that remained neutral on questions of religion. This is not to claim that these ostensibly secular formations were mere extensions of Protestantism but rather to argue that in this moment of emergence, during this eruptive play of forces, both the religiosity of Protestantism and the secularity of the democratic nation-state conformed to an unmarked and unacknowledged metaphysical scheme that made possible and governed them both.[50] (Again, the first principles of this metaphysics revolved around a common faculty of human reason whose judgment was secured in the separation of social life into private and public realms.) For under the sign of this nonspecific Protestantism there occurred a mutual imbrication between the religious and the secular. To be clear, I am not making the familiar case for the collaboration of the religious and the secular. Instead, I wish to attend to the strange processes

---

49. Such freedoms were integral to processes in which racial hierarchies become inevitable and determinative. For as notions of freedom were forged in relation to concepts of religion, whiteness took hold as both natural and empty of any specific content. Of course, this taking-hold did not happen apart from what white Protestant subjects were attempting to immunize themselves from—Catholics, immigrants, African Americans, and other insufficient forms of humanity. For example, "freedom of religion" could become a rallying cry for those who supported the military campaign in Mexico as well as those who opposed it. "Progress of Democracy, vs. Old Fogy Retrograder," *The Democratic Review* 30 (April 1852): 302; "Calhoun's Speech Against the Conquest of Mexico," *The American Review* 1 (March 1848): 230.

50. Michel Foucault, *The Archaeology of Knowledge and the Discourse on Language*, trans. A. M. Sheridan Smith (New York: Pantheon Books, 1972), 72.

by which the religious and the secular were made compatible. In other words, the difference between the religious and the secular was ever less than stark, their similarity the result of a long-distance triangulation with the metaphysics of secularism.

There was a process of normalization at work here, a process in which legitimate ways of knowing the world and living within it were established. Simultaneously, illegitimate ways were excluded as unacceptable—failures on the part of individuals and, perhaps, entire communities, to assume their full humanity. Consequently, I approach statements about religion and the practices that revolved around them in light of their exclusionary processes. Such statements and practices contributed to hierarchies of race and gender. And such exclusions were, of course, directed against bodies that failed to adequately perform their prescriptions and served to disqualify such bodies from entrée into a state of so-called freedom. Such exclusions, however, were also inscribed upon the bodies who performed the prescriptions of Protestant normativity with little or any questioning.

4. The Epistemics and Politics of Secularism

Rather than view antebellum religious history as predominated by this or that religious sensibility—be it an evangelical experientialism, liberal intellection, or metaphysical speculation—or even as a consolidation of the mainstream-denominational form, I approach antebellum religious history in terms of an unacknowledged and often invisible consensus that occurred at the level of first principles. To be clear, secularism cannot be reduced to the content of any one statement about Protestant religiosity. It can be approached only indirectly—in terms of the resonance between statements and their cumulative effect; as that which made a host of statements about true religion possible; as the epistemic criteria used to verify the truth or falsity of piety; as that which made piety feel right to the self and appear convincing to others. So although secularism did not exist in essence, it has everything to do with how this metaphysics manifested itself, affectively, by way of epistemic pursuit and political concern. Secularism, in other words, achieved an effective unity in the diversity of its public articulation.[51]

51. Foucault, *Archaeology of Knowledge*, 72, 118. To focus on the metaphysics of secularism is to see differences between varieties of Protestantism as non-oppositional, as matters of conceptual utterance. Differences, in other words, had as much to do with the conditions through which knowledge was acquired and the emotional weight such acquisition carried

The metaphysics of secularism registers its effects during interplay between epistemology and politics, between an empirically sensitive style of reasoning and the desire to organize the component parts of society into a working population. In antebellum America the metaphysics of secularism resided within the affective compatibility between Scottish Common Sense reasoning and republican principles of governance. For it was this compatibility that both habituated and secured versions of true religion emanating from the precincts of Anglo-Protestantism.

In the nineteenth century Scottish Common Sense was integral to developments within Protestantism—from its "vast subterranean influence" upon professional theology to its inflections of evangelical conversion narratives and modes of scriptural attention, and from its impact upon practices of "spiritual discernment" among liberals to the metaphysics of phrenology as well as the various designs and justifications for spirit-seeing.[52] Common Sense assumed that every human was endowed with the capacity for radical reflexivity and epistemic independence, that is, to become immediately aware of the process of awareness as the basis of objective knowledge. "The power of reflection upon the operations of their own minds," wrote Thomas Reid, a popular source of the Scottish Enlightenment in America, "is greatly improved by exercise; and until a man has got the habit of attending to the operations of his own mind, he can never have clear and distinct notions of them, nor form any steady judgment concerning them. His opinions must be borrowed from others, his notions confused and indistinct." To pay attention to one's own mental operations was not simply to reveal the self to the self. On the contrary, such attention would also allow the individual "to think with precision and accuracy on every subject, especially on those subjects that are more abstract." Or as Henry Ward Beecher, an evangelical preacher who dabbled in phrenology and possessed liberal sympathies, declared: "Men are like open books, if looked at properly."[53]

---

as they did with any explicit doctrinal rift. Consequently, what transpires is not an analysis of Protestant counter-publics but compatible formations within the imperial discourse of secularism.

52. Sydney Ahlstrom, "The Scottish Philosophy and American Theology," *Church History* 24 (September 1955): 267–68. Ahlstrom writes that Scottish Common Sense Realism inflected not simply the Princeton Presbyterians and the polemics of Charles Hodge but also nourished the moderate Calvinism of David Tappan, the Unitarian flowering at Harvard, and the "New Haven Theology."

53. Thomas Reid, *The Works of Thomas Reid with an Account of His Life and Writings by Dugald Stewart* (New York: J & J. Harper, 1822), 1:375; Henry Ward Beecher, "The Study of Human Nature," in *Lectures on Preaching* (London: T. Nelson and Sons, 1872), 113.

In both the seminary and the village, the manipulation of Common Sense was pervasive at mid-century, its promises of immediacy and transparency appealing to the lonely (and attentive) evangelical, to the Unitarian seeker and the phrenological examiner, to the would-be spirit-seer and the ethnographer as well as to those whose sensibilities were explicitly hybrid. As a decidedly non-Humean strain of the Scottish Enlightenment made its way across the Atlantic, Common Sense reasoning meant to approach the world as ultimately legible and to assume the burden of translation, that is, of making the unknowable known and the invisible verifiable. It also implied the need to take the measure of one's emotions so as to better grasp how they were themselves an integral part of cognition. Feelings, then, were privileged in order to put them in their proper place. For with the dissemination of Scottish philosophy to middle-class audiences, emotion became a "mental process subject to scientific investigation and analysis."[54]

Evangelicals embraced the tenets of Common Sense in order to confirm the viability of self-examination that was integral to processes of conversion. Unitarians embraced Scottish philosophers in order to confirm their Enlightened understanding of God and to appeal to the reasonableness of revelation. Spiritualists, too, appealed to a mode of extrasensory perception, what Davis would later call "*sixth* sense," as the means to verify the empirical truth of the spirit-world. In each instance the abiding mystery of the Calvinist Godhead was displaced by the comforting possibility of an *a priori* knowledge of the universe confirmed through natural vision and expression. Indeed, among evangelicals and liberals alike, "reason" promised to reveal "fixed laws" of the human. This anthropology, in turn, would confirm the capacity for individuals to read their situations in light of God's script, and God's in light of their own. Across the range of Protestant subcultures, there existed imagined spaces of noninterference, spaces of conversion, self-knowledge, wisdom, and spirit-seeing.[55]

54. Corrigan, *Business of the Heart*, 295.
55. See, for example, S. Stanhope Smith, *The Lectures, Collected and Improved, which have been Delivered for a Series of Years in the College of New Jersey; on the Subjects of Moral and Political Philosophy* (Trenton: D. Fenton, 1812); A. A. Livermore, *Reason and Revelation* (Boston: American Unitarian Association, 1838), 1; William Ellery Channing, "Self-Culture," 15, 27; "Christian Worship" (1836), in *Works* (1889), 410; Andrew Jackson Davis, *The Principles of Nature, her divine revelations, and a voice to mankind*, ed., with an introduction and biographical sketch of the author, by William Fishbough (New York: S. S. Lyon and Wm. Fishbough, 1847), 101; Andrew Jackson Davis, *The Philosophy of Spiritual Intercourse* (revised, restereotyped, and enlarged) (Boston: Colby & Rich, 1880), 350–53.

In its promise to reveal the correspondence between physical and meta-physical laws, Common Sense was much more than an epistemic stance. For many interpreters, Common Sense guaranteed a touch of the real, guaranteeing a direct encounter between the senses and the object world as the basis for mechanics, calculation, and computation. Such calculability was the primrose path to disenchantment, a means of demystifying "spectral illusions."[56] Common Sense did more than secure a bounded and unmediated interiority. It also guaranteed the political conditions of transparency, a social environment in which subjects were not only agentive but whose agency could be trusted and perhaps even predicted. Common Sense, then, was manifest not simply in a reasonable attitude toward piety but, more importantly, in the individual's conception of piety as a matter of political efficacy.

To this end, Common Sense was the key to conjuring the politics of the American Revolution or, more precisely, to perpetuating the political horizon of republicanism. Independence combined with communal grounding. An ongoing project of introducing "every American" to the "science of government."[57] "Some form of government" was necessary, at least "until all men are so far under the control of their higher faculties that none will trespass upon the rites of others." In the meantime, the solution to the "governmental problem" was republicanism. It was just and antimonarchial. It was the only form of governance that guaranteed "self-government." Still retaining its revolutionary hue, republicanism ceased to be a formal doctrine at mid-century. It became, rather, a pervasive and protean sentiment inculcated by "republican mothers," the school system, political parties, and clergymen.[58] In republican imaginaries social life became a process of maximizing epistemic independence while engaging in the same project as those around you. The "possibility of a permanent and well-ordered republic, on so extensive a scale . . . depends on the INTELLIGENCE and VIRTUE of the people"

56. "Superstitions," in *Chambers's Information for the People: A Popular Encyclopedia* (Philadelphia: J. and J. L. Gihon, 1851), 2:333. See also William Grier, *The Modern Mechanic: A Scientific Guide and Calculator* (Boston: Bradley, Dayton, & Co., 1861), 8.

57. Andrew W. Young, *Introduction to the Science of Government* (Buffalo: Geo. H. Derby and Co., 1851), frontmatter.

58. "Republicanism the True Form of Government—Its Destined Influence, and Improvement, No. 1," *American Phrenological Journal* 8 (1846): 270-71; "Republicanism . . . No. 2," 339. See also Linda K. Kerber, "The Republican Mother: Women and the Enlightenment: An American Perspective," *American Quarterly* 28 (Summer 1976): 187-206; Jean Baker, "From Belief into Culture: Republicanism in the Antebellum North," *American Quarterly* 37 (Autumn 1985): 532-50.

and capacity for the "Almighty ruler of nations" to create the conditions of cultivation.[59]

The diffusion of secularism in antebellum America was in part a product of a metaphysics that enveloped practices of reason across a range of Protestant (from conservative to liberal) and post-Protestant (freethinking and self-consciously scientific) subcultures. Both evangelicals and Unitarians envisioned their own piety as a distillation of republican virtue. For American phrenologists, republican virtue was a biological ideal. Spiritualists, too, sought to reform the social order through an appeal to the equality and republican virtue that they believed governed the order of the spirit-world. And finally, Lewis Henry Morgan was a vocal advocate of republican politics, as were penitentiary reformers who hewed closely to Benjamin Rush's admonition to create a society of "republican machines." Indeed, for the majority of Americans interested in optimizing the epistemic conditions for the population as a whole, republicanism was both the justification and blueprint.[60] For in order for everyone's reason to flourish, society must be a place that fostered immediate access to knowledge rather than mediate its acquisition. It must be a place in which knowledge circulated freely, unencumbered by illegitimate pressures. It must be a place which individuals were transparent to themselves, given how transparency between them had already been guaranteed.

And it was here, in this symmetry between an approach to knowledge as politically efficacious and a politics that secured what it meant to be a knowing human subject, that secularism may be glimpsed. Back and forth between feeling that one's ideas were good for the world and feeling like one knew what one knew because the world had confirmed it. And it was this loop between politics and epistemics—how to become and usher in what one already knew—that inflected how a range of Protestant subcultures felt themselves to be truly religious.[61]

59. W. C. Taylor with C. S. Henry, *A Manual of Modern History*, 5th ed. (New York: D. Appleton and Company, 1851), 784–85.

60. Mary Poovey, *A History of the Modern Fact: Problems of Knowledge in the Sciences of Wealth and Society* (Chicago: University of Chicago Press, 1998), 182f. Poovey argues that strains of Scottish Common Sense were integral to emerging modes of liberal governmentality. For example, Francis Hutcheson's contribution to this emerging art of state maintenance in the eighteenth century was to link the operation of human passions with mathematical reasoning. By wedding mathematical language with descriptions of moral apprehension, Hutcheson "proved" that humans could be trusted to govern themselves by themselves and for themselves.

61. In addition to self-consciously Protestant circles, the cultivation of epistemic virtue in the service of republican cohesion was esteemed in both lyceum lectures and educational curricula. See, for example, William Hosmer, *The Young Man's Book, or Self-Education* (Cincinnati:

5. Technologies of Secularism

The promise of systematicity was the most tangible effect of the inter-play between Common Sense and republicanism. The "human faculties," wrote Francis Hutcheson, "form a machine, most accurately subservient to the necessities, convenience, and happiness of a rational system."[62] In antebellum America, the promise of systematic treatment of the human, by the human, and for the human was most associated with technology (*technologia*, from the Greek meaning systematic treatment). Technological advances made in the first half of the nineteenth century included mecha-nization of factory floors, the spread of rail lines and telegraph wires, the extension of trade and postal routes, the increased capacity to produce and disseminate information. Such phenomena were, of course, products of the village Enlightenment and the market revolution. Tradesmen and inventors steeped in the vernacular know-how of Common Sense were as integral to these advances as the political elites and businessmen who sup-plied an overlay of laissez-faire republicanism to such enterprises.[63]

The metaphysics of secularism assumed a tangible presence in the world with advances in machines and mechanized circulation. The "power and value of steam," for example, lay in its ability to catalyze the kind of self that both Common Sense and republicanism depended upon.[64] The "rapid circulation of men and ideas" promised to decentralize authority and to create the perfect conditions for Common Sense discernment. To make in-

---

Henry W. Derby, 1855). To this end, the nexus between Common Sense and republicanism was present among social reformers, freethinkers, 'secular' publishers, elites, and the work-ing class. This nexus informed the human and natural sciences and helped legitimate emerg-ing forms of economic exchange, speculation, production, and consumption.

62. Francis Hutcheson, *An Essay on the Nature and Conduct of the Passions and Affections with Illustrations on the Moral Sense* (1742). Cited in Daniel Walker Howe, *Making the American Self: Jonathan Edwards to Abraham Lincoln* (Cambridge, Mass.: Harvard University Press, 1997), 64.

63. David Jaffe, "The Village Enlightenment in New England, 1760-1820," *The William and Mary Quarterly* 47, no. 3 (July 1990): 327-46.

64. Indeed, nascent theories of secularization were often embedded in discussions of tech-nological innovation. Jacob Bigelow, for example, employed steam power as a metaphor of new kind of power relations affecting the social sphere. "In modern times," wrote Bigelow, "the application of philosophy to the arts may be said to have made the world what it is at the present today. It has not only affected the physical, but has changed the moral and politi-cal condition of society" (*Elements of Technology* [Boston: Hilliard, Gray, Little, and Wilkins, 1829], 3-4). On the need for Christianity to harness "the mechanical tendencies of the pres-ent age [that] have drawn men into new relations, and placed them in densely-congregated masses, where peculiar temptations more readily beset them," see "What is Machinery Do-ing for Us?" *The Living Age* 12 (January 30, 1847): 202.

formation universally accessible guaranteed a transparent political sphere, leaving no space for power to congeal. Any resistance, then, would be futile.[65]

In the "future extension of industry," wrote geologist and meteorologist Arnold Guyot in 1849, "we may, perhaps, foresee" in America "a true social world, transcending in grandeur and unity the most impressive spectacles of human greatness." The Swiss émigré, enamored with reading the surfaces of the earth, wrote of an expanding field of forces that would silently instruct and invisibly refine social life within "the modern world." According to Guyot, political matters were becoming atmospheric. "Rome accomplished her task by brute force [but] America is doing hers by persuasion. Drawing to her the free will of the sons of all the races, she binds them by one faith, and is thus preparing a true brotherhood of man." New modes of media, material exchange, and social connectivity were emergent. And according to Guyot, they promised to decentralize authority, emancipate the populace from external obstacles, and promote, at the level of conviction, self-guided choice and action. "Reciprocal influence" had become "joined to the community." This was "the distinctive feature of modern society" and "exalt[ed] the powers of man to a degree hitherto unknown."[66]

Such epistemic and political liberation was premised upon the technological intensification of connectivity and circulation, processes that Guyot described in the etymological (*religare*, meaning to "bind fast") and vernacular ("faith") terms of religion. Networks of rail lines and telegraph wires, according to Guyot, were not simply material evidence of American empire but also precipitated liberatory modalities of being and thinking, new political horizons, and, most importantly, a consummation of true

---

65. "The Progress of Man," *American Phrenological Journal* 13 (April 1851): 83; "The Power and Value of Steam," *American Phrenological Journal* 11 (1849): 196. Imperial ambitions often accompanied the funding of mechanical initiatives and ventures that would render horses "obsolete" just as "Indians" had been. Railways became the exoskeleton and telegraph wires the nervous system of an aggressive political body. "Annexation," *Democratic Review* 17 (July 1845): 9. As *The New York Herald* reasoned, "Steam and electricity, with the natural impulses of a free people, have made, and are making, this country the greatest, the most original, the most wonderful the sun ever shone upon. . . . Those who do not mix with this movement—those who do not go on with this movement—will be crushed into more impalpable powder than ever was attributed to the car of Juggernaut. Down on your knees and pray" (citations in Takaki, *Iron Cages*, 149, and Kenneth Silverman, *Lightening Man: The Accursed Life of Samuel F. B. Morse* [Cambridge: Da Capo Press, 2004], 243).
66. Arnold Guyot, *The Earth and Man: Lectures on Comparative Physical Geography, in its relation to the History of Mankind* (1849), trans. C. C. Felton (Boston: Gould and Lincoln, 1855), 325-26, 314.

religion. According to Guyot, the future was a matter of machines. "Perpetual movement, a fever of locomotion, rages from one end of the continent to the other. The American uses things without allowing himself to be taken captive by them. We behold everywhere the free will of man overmastering nature."[67]

Guyot and myriad others within the institutional orbits of Protestantism were at the forefront of advancing technologies and technics integral to the development of network society. Not only did networks promise to order and organize the social world, they also promised to harness that world so as to actualize the individuals within it. Systematic treatment. Managing one's expectations. Machine layered upon machine in order to produce an unprecedented precision and efficiency of being.[68]

By the mid-nineteenth century the history of evangelicalism had become all but equivalent to the story of technological triumph. "The power of steam has achieved wonders, which have ceased to be regarded as wonders from their common and every-day occurrence." Such was "the progress and developments of this progressive age," opined the *New-York Evangelist* in 1852.[69] As was consistent with their history of mission, evangelicals embraced any development that would further the reach of the gospel and endorsed the proposition that the "power and preeminence" of nations "will depend upon new discoveries and applications of science. Battles will soon be fought by engineers instead of generals, and by mech-

67. Ibid., 322-24, 299-300. See also Arnold Guyot, "'The People of the Future,'" *The Home Missionary* 24 (November 1851): 153-55.
68. Eli Bowen, *The United States Post-Office Guide* (New York: D. Appleton and Co., 1851), 1-7; Albert Bigelow, "The Post Office System as an Element of Modern Civilization," *Yale Literary Magazine* 16 (1851): 333-35. The concept of organizational control, of course, was not new. See, for example, the numerous administrative networks established by the government in the early years of the nineteenth century—the federal court system, the national banking system, the stage coach system, and the distributing apparatus for public lands. Richard R. John, *Spreading the News: The American Postal System from Franklin to Morse* (Cambridge, Mass.: Harvard University Press, 1995, 300 n. 2). My discussion of networks has been informed by James R. Beniger, *The Control Revolution: Technological and Economic Origins of the Information Society* (Cambridge, Mass.: Harvard University Press, 1986) as well as Mark C. Taylor's discussion of the philosophical challenges posed by advancing schemes of circulation and distribution in *The Moment of Complexity: Emerging Network Culture* (Chicago: University of Chicago Press, 2001). For more technical discussions of networks, see Alexander R. Galloway and Eugene Thacker, *The Exploit: A Theory of Networks* (Minneapolis: University of Minnesota Press, 2007). For an appraisal of networks and their metaphors in the nineteenth century, see Laura Otis, *Networking: Communicating with Bodies and Machines in the Nineteenth Century* (Ann Arbor: University of Michigan Press, 2001).
69. "Railroads," *New-York Evangelist* 23 (Oct. 1852): 178.

anisms in place of men."[70] For evangelical missionaries during this period, statistics were fast becoming the measure of success—calculating with a degree of certainty the most efficient means of securing the attention and subsequently the eternal life of the population. Indeed, the power of trans-denominational media enterprises like the American Tract Society (ATS) lay in their ability to conserve their energies, to make sure their effects were feeding back into their causes.

For evangelical missionaries the logic of feedback control was integral to generating the Kingdom of God on earth. As strategies for managing business blurred into those of managing the souls of the population, ATS implemented a media network that connected printing presses with path-ways of distribution with technics of dissemination with the cultivation of voluntary attention and habits of reading. Both the colporteurs who distributed tracts and those to whom they distributed them were encour-aged to imagine themselves as agents of evangelical truth and participants within an exceptional and emancipatory narrative. In addition to distrib-uting tracts door-to door, colporteurs were also charged with gathering in-formation and feeding it back to the national headquarters of ATS, which in turn used such data to streamline future publishing and distribution efforts. Given its emergent picture of social life as a complex interplay of forces, ATS sought to engineer God's kingdom on earth by approaching the abstract notion of the population as a series of linked individuals and their own missionary efforts in terms of "universal circulation."[71]

Evangelicals were not the only Protestant subculture that became enam-ored with the potential of networks. By the mid-1840s, the firm of Fowlers and Wells had turned phrenology into a "true religion," a public spectacle, and a thriving publishing enterprise. The brothers Orson and Lorenzo Fowler, alongside the businessman Samuel Wells and his wife Charlotte Fowler, endorsed the idea that phrenology was "destined to form a new era in Christianity."[72] Their stated goal was to "Phrenologize Our Nation," phrenology being "the crowning essence of true religion." According to

70. Thomas Ewbank, A Descriptive and Historical Account of Hydraulic and Other Machines for raising Water, Ancient and Modern; with Observations on Various Subjects Connected with the Mechanic Arts: Including the Progressive Development of the Steam Engine (New York: Bangs, Platt, and Co., 1851), vi.

71. Robert Baird, The Christian Retrospect and Register; A Summary of the Scientific, Moral, and Religious Progress of the First Half of the XIXth Century (New York: Dodd, 1851), 188.

72. "Boston Phrenological Society," American Phrenological Journal 2, no. 5 (February 1, 1840): 235.

phrenology, the human psyche was itself organized like a network—a series of interlinked faculties whose ideal state was utter equilibrium. Under the auspices of Fowlers and Wells, phrenology became an advertising phenomenon that addressed the psychic economy of the individual.[73]

The "religion" of phrenology was an amalgam of evangelical sensibility and concerted appeal to liberal sympathies, the latter being yet another site that strategically embraced the ideal of networks.[74] According to Unitarian leaders, for example, the redemption of America would be made possible "by modern improvements, by increased commerce and traveling, by the post-office, by the steam-boat, and especially by the press,—by newspapers, periodicals, tracts, and other publications. Through these means, men of one mind, through a whole country, easily understand one another, and easily act together." Such collective action would, ideally and perhaps ironically, revolve around practices of "spiritual discernment" and "spirituality," the preferred and privatized terms for piety among mid-century liberals (and deemed a full-fledged faculty by Orson Fowler in 1842). On the one hand, the "circulations of industry" would strengthen the "chain of sympathies," binding Americans in a common Christian cause.[75] On the other hand, this cause was envisioned as the consummation of the essential particularity of each individual. Spirituality, then, was premised upon the assumption that individuals were inherently connected to each other but yet instinctively capable of differentiating themselves from one another.

This ambiguous concept of spirituality played a dramatic role in the

---

73. By the 1850s the signs of phrenology were proliferating, as Fowlers & Wells became the largest mail-order business in New York City. "The American Phrenological Journal for 1849," *American Phrenological Journal* 11 (1849): 10; "Progression a Law of Nature: Its Application to Human Improvement, Collective and Individual," *American Phrenological Journal* 8 (August 1846): 240; Allan S. Horlick, "Phrenology and the Social Education of Young Men," *History of Education Quarterly* 11 (Spring 1971): 25.

74. As the *American Phrenological Journal* instructed, readers were to missionize their neighbors by measuring their heads—this direct approach being the "best mode of convincing unbelievers of its truth" ("Rules for Finding Organs," *American Phrenological Journal* 11 [1849]: 116). On the appeal to liberal sympathies, see the republication of Channing's sermon, "The Arrogance of Wealth—by Dr. Channing," in *American Phrenological Journal* 5:139-41. Fowlers & Wells explicitly targeted Unitarians. See for example the "phrenological conversion" of a contemporary doubting Thomas—the anti-phrenologist S. Dean, a "Unitarian clergyman of acknowledged talents, and considerable critical acumen" (*American Phrenological Journal* 4, no. 7 [July 1842]: 176-78).

75. William Ellery Channing, "Remarks on Associations," in *Works* (1889), 139; William Ellery Channing, "The Union," *Christian Examiner* 6 (1829): 159-60; see also William Henry Channing, *The Life of William Ellery Channing, D.D.* (Boston: American Unitarian Association, 1899), 283.

development of anthropological comprehensibility and in the reforms instituted at Sing Sing State Penitentiary. Within the burgeoning institution of anthropology, the culture concept served as a way to approach the ambient links of network sociality as legible, liberating, and potentially salvific. Among Protestant prison reformers, the metaphor of automation became central to how they approached the rehabilitation of the criminal body in relation to other criminal bodies. Both culture and the penitentiary were systematic treatments of the social, fluid in their design and intended effect.

Networks also played a vital role within spiritualist circles—networks of rope held by participants in a séance circle, "a vast nervous network of spiritual communication" between heaven and earth, networks of transportation, and networks of subtle energies.[76] Railroads, for example, became biological, "the friction of the car-wheels and axels" generating a therapeutic field of energy. For spiritualists, railroads were positively sacred. As Andrew Jackson Davis argued, to be in the proximity of a railway car and to feel its vibrations was to inhabit a space of theological inquiry where "eternal truths" could be examined.[77]

Moreover, spiritualists claimed that technological advances and the evolution of "commercial instrumentalities" were driven by spirit-power. Spirits "made and managed" such things as railroads and steamboats in order to bring to light the transmission of human spirit across space and time. As has been well documented, spiritualists embraced network technologies as apocalyptic, that is, as revealing something essential about the world and as enabling humans to correspond with that essence. Spiritualists used telegraphic, electrical, and financial metaphors in order to explain the automaticity of the spirit-world. "The great bank of heaven," wrote the medium Robert Hare, "of which our Heavenly Father is president and director, and in which his beloved children, the whole human family, are shareholders." "Money, he continued, "seems in most instances necessary to the effectual exercise of that fellow-feeling in the cultivation of which human virtue pre-eminently consists."[78] What was envisioned here was a feedback loop, a perpetual engine of human progress that was dependent

76. William Henry Channing, "The Judgment of Christendom," *The Spirit of the Age* 1 (October 27, 1849): 264.
77. "Health Promoted by Railroads," *American Phrenological Journal* 11 (1849): 97–98; Andrew Jackson Davis, *Magic Staff: An Autobiography of Andrew Jackson Davis* (Boston: Bela Marsh, 1867), 442.
78. Andrew Jackson Davis, *The Philosophy of Spiritual Intercourse* (New York: Fowlers and Wells, 1851), 31, 49; Hare, *Experimental Investigations*, 113, 88, 89, 136.

upon the accumulation and circulation of material capital, which was promoted by spirits who in turn answered to a God who made available the capital and the means of accumulation and circulation.

On one level, the discursive alignment of Protestant subcultures revolved around a shared metaphysics steeped in the directives of Common Sense and republicanism. On another level, the power of a nonspecific Protestantism owed much to the specifics of Protestant engagement with networks. For it was through the imagination of machines and in the reliance upon their metaphors that the metaphysics of secularism took hold. Yet even as the metaphysics of secularism saturated the public sphere, the power of secularism cannot be reduced to matters of media exposure. For to appreciate the power of secularism at mid-century, one must also attend to the responses elicited by emerging networks.

6. Phenomenologies of Secularism

The metaphysics of secularism was secured in the process of response— the agentive encounter between individuals and the manifestations of systematicity, feedback, and automation. Bound up with iron, steam, and electricity, such encounters also involved the language of networks taking effect on a corporeal register. So whereas the Protestant deployment of network technologies amplified their epistemological claims *about* the truth of religion, it was the experiential encounter with networks, and the explanation of this encounter, that served to intensify the security *of* this truth.[79] The emerging network society at mid-century was a looping process, an application of secularism's metaphysics, which in turn seeded the ground for future and more extensive applications. But this process was not without friction, for it was the diffusion, circulation, and density of secularism's metaphysics that could also confound expectations of an inviolable interiority, of freedom, of choice.

79. As the experience of systematicity became more common—its materiality, circulations, and automated capacities—technology registered itself at the level of language, providing terms, metaphors, and inflections with which to think, live, and dream. So although technology may not possess an agency of its own, its determinative force may be glimpsed in how it was imagined and represented as, in fact, having an agency of its own. See, for example, Charles Caldwell, "Thoughts on the Moral and Other Indirect Influences of Rail-Roads," *The New-England Magazine* 2, no. 4 (April 1832): 288–300; Charles Fraser, "The Moral Influence of Steam," *Hunt's Merchant Magazine* 14 (June 1846): 499–515; Samuel Beman, "The Power and Influence of Commerce," *Hunt's Merchant Magazine* 23 (December 1850): 632–40; "The Influence of Railroads," *Scientific American* 7 (November 22, 1851): 76.

The harnessing of steam, for example, led not only to revolutions in industry but also to innovations such as the Fourdrinier paper machine and the Napier steam press, dramatically increasing printing productivity. As networks of print and later electronic information became ever more viable, local markets crossed paths and became more densely woven.[80] A national economic infrastructure was further secured by the "American system" of manufacturing. The novelty of this system and its reliance upon principles of interchangeability (and machines that made parts for other machines) was celebrated at the Crystal Palace Exhibition in 1851 (London) and 1853 (New York). The circulation of individuals themselves and the expansion of the northeastern rail network also contributed density to the weave of the social. By the time the first health insurance company was incorporated in 1847, machines and their metaphors had come to possess an affective intensity. With the spread of the telegraph, for example, information "anticipates every step he takes, and works against him in every place. It makes the whole land to know him, for it flashes his likeness in every direction, and thus creates the man in a thousand different localities. . . . It spreads over the land a network of intelligence."[81] The materiality of networks, in other words, had come to make demands upon the senses, seeping in and haunting the imagination.

By mid-century, the referentiality of networks was quickly moving from the language of thread and silks[82] to the language of biology and blood flow[83] to the concepts of political economy[84] and social interdependence.[85] And so even as the interlocking and mechanized systems registered their effects, so too did their metaphors. Consequently, the emergence of network society was not just about machines and institutional

80. Charles Sellers, *The Market Revolution: Jacksonian America, 1815–1846* (New York: Oxford University Press, 1991). See also David A. Hounshell, *From the American System to Mass Production, 1800–1932* (Baltimore: Johns Hopkins University Press, 1984).

81. "The Influence of Great Men," *New Englander and Yale Review* 11 (May 1853): 256.

82. "Captain Hall's Voyage to the Eastern Seas," *The North American Review* 26 (April 1828): 529; "The Prado of Madrid," *The Living Age* 6, no. 63 (July 26, 1845): 190.

83. "Miscellanies of Literature," *The United States Democratic Review* 9 (September 1841): 299; J. R. Buchanan, "The Anatomy of the Brain," *Buchanan's Journal of Man* 1 (August 1849): 291; "Recent Revelations of the Microscope," *The Living Age* 9 (May 2, 1846): 232.

84. "Political Economy," *The North American Review* 47 (July 1838): 79; "What Constitutes Real Freedom of Trade?" *The American Whig Review* 12 (October 1850): 356; "What Impression Do We and Should We Make Abroad?" *Putnam's Monthly Magazine* 2, no. 10 (October 1853): 349.

85. "Mr. Van Buren's Title to Re-election," *The United States Democratic Review* 7 (April-May 1840): 293; O. A. Brownson, "The Present State of Society," *The United States Democratic Review* 54 (July 1843): 34.

applications of them. More significantly, the advance of network technologies made possible concrete ways of imagining the self within a vast
scheme of relationality. This was the revelatory quality of networks, not
changing or determining human nature but generating new kinds of sociality, new experiences of permeability, new ways of knowing the self and
the world, and new metaphors and expressive grammars for imagining a
society in which individuals experienced, with unprecedented intensity,
the relations within that society.[86] As the *New-York Evangelist* opined in
1850, "When we come to examine the constitution of society, we shall find
ourselves surrounded by an atmosphere of influences in which every element is in constant vigorous action and re-action."[87]

For someone like Congregationalist minister Edward Hitchcock, the
moral force of networks was apocalyptic—the revelation of deep relationality. In 1851 Hitchcock turned his attention from the study of chemistry and the prevention of nervous disorders to more general processes
in which "different things [act] upon one another." He proposed a "telegraphic system of the universe" in which "our words, our actions, and
even our thoughts, make an indelible impression on the universe." His
vision of a closed network of material and spiritual forces was premised,
self-consciously, upon science—principles of chemistry, biology, mechanics, optics, and electricity. This vision was also premised upon a "peculiar"
substance, the "odic force," discovered by Baron Reichenbach, that "exists
in all bodies, and throughout the universe . . . analogous to magnetism,
electricity, light, and heat, yet distinct from them all." Hitchcock saw the
presence of this "odic force" as guaranteeing universal connectivity, perfect transparency, and universal access to history. The presence of this
force also exposed the complicity of the self in all manner of economies,
social, biological, as well as cosmic.[88]

With the spread of rail lines and telegraph wires as well as the extension of mass-mediated forms into every day life, Americans in the northeast confronted a social environment that increasingly announced itself as
interconnected. And as Hitchcock's example attests, there was something
strange about experience within a public sphere rooted in republican sen-

86. Edwin T. Layton Jr, "Technology as Knowledge," *Technology and Culture* 15 (1974):
31–41.
87. "Streams of Influence," *New-York Evangelist* 21 (May 2, 1850): 69.
88. Edward Hitchcock, *The Religion of Geology and its Connected Sciences* (Boston: Philips,
Sampson, and Company, 1851), 41–11, 424, 440. See also Edward Hitchcock, *Dyspepsy Fore-
stalled and Resisted: or Lectures on Diet, Regimen, and Employment* (Amherst: J. S. and C. Adams,
1831).

timent and Common Sense epistemics, not to mention his desire to orient himself to something that did not exist in essence yet was everywhere around him.[89] Hitchcock was not alone in suggesting that experiences of social density were often in tension with the explanatory schemes of Common Sense and republicanism that had conditioned their possibility. Conceptual resources could fail, at least initially, to convincingly account for the kind of experiences ushered in by networks.

For as these principles of Common Sense and republicanism began to circulate in and among people who had already adopted them, they were rendered both suspect and ripe for redirection. For example, the advance of network technologies served to exacerbate and reframe the anxiety over tyranny at the heart of republican politics. Across the Protestant spectrum, the centralized power of metaphorical monarchies was no longer conceived of as an exterior matter. On the contrary, it had diffused into the social environment of which one was already a part. Liberal Protestants, for example, were concerned with how the individual could avoid being "turned into a mere tool, copy, echo of the public will and the public voice." According to Unitarian minister James Walker, the task of "act[ing] from his own spirit" had been made ever more difficult by the "whole machinery of party and popular agitation," including "pamphlets, periodical publications, newspapers, meetings, speeches, agencies." Mechanized enchantment had become a threat, given the increasing capacity of media to act upon "whole communities at once . . . as if you heard the clatter of the machinery by which their hands are lifted up."[90]

So even as networks were thought to expand the possibilities of human freedom, there were accompanying fears over the programmatic aspects of life, the source of which could be enigmatic—"some force coming from nowhere and costing nothing, yet increasing according to the

89. Bruce Robbins, ed., *The Phantom Public Sphere* (Minneapolis: University of Minnesota Press, 1993).

90. James Walker, "Public Opinion," in *Reason, Faith, and Duty: Sermons Preached Chiefly in College Chapel* (Boston: Roberts Brothers, 1877), 239, 228–29, 222. This anxiety, pervasive within liberal precincts of antebellum Protestantism, was perhaps related to what Tocqueville called the "overpowering strength" of "present democratic institutions of the United States." Tocqueville, who had consulted with Channing on his first visit to the United States, had warned of a "submissive silence" that could accompany mass democracy. Such concern was shared by Channing, Bellows, and other Unitarian leaders who not only warned parishioners about the tyranny of the majority but also about the tyranny that resulted when the majority itself became enchanted—a "delusion" that "takes on the laws of an epidemic" as "in the witchcraft times." Alexis De Tocqueville, *American Institutions and Their Influence*, notes by John C. Spencer (New York: A. S. Barnes & Co., 1851), 261, 264; Walker, "Public Opinion," 232.

cube of velocity."[91] Such fear and uncertainty, laden with conspiracy (or paranoia depending on your degree of empathy), was premised on experiential insights into the self-regulating potential of machines, their obfuscating effects, and the capacity for networks to disabuse individuals of their capacity to regulate themselves.[92] Anxious questions abound. What happened when principles of efficiency, mechanization, and interchangeability became values? Did railroads and telegraphs operate according to the "law of social contagion"? To what extent had private opinion become increasingly susceptible to control from a distance?[93]

Across the range of Protestant subcultures, answers to such questions often involved degrees of xenophobia and revolved around the seductive qualities of distributive networks. The "spirit of popery," for example, threatened to corrupt from the inside out.[94] More generally, there were heightened concerns over "moral epidemics" and the unseen contagion of crowded spaces.[95] The perception of such threats, as Jenny Franchot has suggested, "figured crucially in the construction of antebellum Protestant subjectivity." The fact that such threats multiplied, diffused, and recombined at mid-century—extending to Masonic cabals and various

91. "New Motive Power and the Spiritual Rappings," *Scientific American* 7 (September 20, 1851): 3.

92. See, for example, the relationship between public safety and steam engine regulators. "Rail-road News," *Scientific American* 7 (November 8, 1851): 57.

93. Horace Bushnell, *Barbarism The First Danger: A Discourse for Home Missions* (New York: American Home Missionary Society, 1847), 27; Horace Bushnell, *Views of Christian Nurture* (Hartford: Edwin Hunt, 1848), 83, 110; Peter G. Washington, "Post Office Department," *United States Postal Guide and Official Advertiser* 2 (1851): 98.

94. Such concerns, of course, were bound up in a defensive masculinity. Anti-Catholicism, for example, was often expressed as a defense of women from predatory priests. Clerical authority, in turn, represented a threat to masculine freedom in general and a republican public sphere in particular. Popery was a "slightly modified paganism" in which religion became utterly impersonal, that is, an "unqualified and slavish submission" to the "will of superiors" (*The Spirit of Popery: An Exposure of Its Origins, Character, and Results* [New York: American Tract Society, 1840], 129, 327). Catholicism was anathema to civilized progress because it was "inimical to nationhood" and possessed no single country of origin. Susan M. Griffin, *Anti-Catholicism and Nineteenth-Century Fiction* (Cambridge: Cambridge University Press, 2004), 4.

95. John F. Watson, "Bible Thoughts," 447. Watson Family Papers, Box 1A. Joseph Downs Collection and Winterthur Archives, Winterthur Museum and Library, Winterthur, Del. Watson's concern was noted as he read "Moral Epidemics," *Chamber's Edinburgh Journal* 428 (April 11, 1840): 89–90. "There *is* a remarkable analogy between diseases of the body and diseases of the mind, and it is shown in nothing more strikingly than in the tendency of some morbid mental conditions to spread, like common bodily ailments, and take possession of great bodies of people. Some of the most puzzling things in the history of superstition may be explained upon this principle."

enthusiasms—signaled their atmospheric quality, their ability to seep without leaving a mark. The thematics of captivity that Franchot has identified as shadowing America's "official version of itself as the land of liberty" was in transition at mid-century.[96] Its drama had moved inward.[97]

This shift to a thematics of seduction was, perhaps, most fully encapsulated by the trope of "female influence." On the one hand, women were most prone to seduction—subject to the evils of fashion or the leering mesmerist but also, more affirmatively, to the workings of the Holy Spirit. On the other hand, women were the most seductive, religiously speaking. Under the canopy of mid-century Protestantism, women possessed the highest capacity for influencing others. Such influence was due to the natural qualities of women, for better or for worse. Women could be considered benevolent force through which social values were transmitted across generations. They were also deceptive and dangerous, a potential force of corruption, wielding their charms toward deceptive ends.[98]

"Female influence" was invoked in order to conjure a sense of neural contagion, a sense of original sin divorced from its theological referent. "The art of lying," so "closely allied to that of advertising, was invented in

96. Jenny Franchot, *Roads to Rome: The Antebellum Protestant Encounter with Catholicism* (Berkeley and Los Angeles: University of California Press, 1994), 99, 87.

97. This shift within Protestant subcultures from a thematics of captivity to that of seduction coincided with rising fears over confidence-men who did not coerce but gained the trust of their victims, manipulating them, as it were, from the inside. This shift also occurred as fears over slave rebellions began to outpace those of Indian conspiracies. Although this was a product of both a governmental policy of Indian removal and intensifying debates over slavery, it is important to note how the identity of the captor moved from an exterior and 'sovereign' community (Native American) to a diffuse and, in some sense, internal network of enslaved bodies. Karen Haltunnen, *Confidence Men and Painted Women: A Study of Middle-class Culture in America, 1830–70* (New Haven: Yale University Press, 1982). On the capacity of statistics to spur fear and uncertainty, stoking the fires of racist paranoia, see "Reflections on the Census of 1840," *Southern Literary Messenger* 9 (1843): 340-52. See also the paranoid (as opposed to conspiratorial) rhetoric of nativism that would emerge in the 1850s in which "foreign influence" was multitiered and in effect nonessential. J. Wayne Laurens, *The Crisis: or the Enemies of America Unmasked* (Philadelphia: G. D. Miller, 1855).

98. Mrs. Gore, "Evil Influence of Fashion," *Brother Jonathan* 2, no. 8 (June 18, 1842): 221; Jonathan French Stearns, *Female Influence and the True Christian Mode of its Exercise* (Newburyport: John G. Tilton, 1837); "Woman—Her Phrenology, Sphere, Perfection, and Influence," *American Phrenological Journal* 11 (1849): 177-82,, 250-51. See also Barbara Welter, "The Cult of True Womanhood: 1820-1860," *American Quarterly* 18 (Summer 1966): 151-74; Douglas, *Feminization of American Culture*, 45-46, 69, 73. Douglas notes that middle-class women in antebellum America, alongside Protestant clergy, adopted the rhetoric of influence in order to redefine themselves as forces of social uplift. Douglas charts what she sees as a loss of ethical nerve as both groups eschewed more direct strategies of political suasion in favor of the psychology of moral influence.

Paradise . . . but its scientific application to trade was reserved for a more advanced stage of civilization." Technics, precision, and expertise. The philosophy of advertising, of selling the consumer to the product, was at once neurological and militaristic. "The human brain is of a most impressionable substance. As the continuing dropping of water, to adopt a time-honored simile, wears away the solid rocks, so the continued repetition of an assertion, false or true, produces an ever deepening imprint on the sensorium of mortals . . . Those whose life is mainly sensuous, and who have not made human nature itself a subject of study, are utterly without shield or ward against an engine of war that pours forth its missiles with a certainty of aim. There is no resisting . . . an advertisement."[99]

In antebellum America, the most pervasive advertisements were those for the self. Attention to the technics and politics of inviolable selfhood was integral to conceptions of religious freedom (and subsequent invocations of the nova effect). Yet such attention was often accompanied by unease over eroding boundaries—between private and public, interior and exterior, one's physical frame and the body politic.[100] The extension of networks across land and psyches generated opportunities to experience firsthand the dense and sometimes dangerous weaves of sociality in which one was embedded.[101] With the small sensations of deep complicity with others and the world around, the essential sovereignty of self was thrown into doubt. Consequently, negotiations over the status of boundaries and the telos of causation were urgent matters at mid-century. Such negotiations, I contend, became an issue because the particulars of experience within network society often exceeded the explanatory franchises of Common Sense and republicanism brought to bear upon them. These moments of unease, however, were more often fleeting than substantial. For rather than precipitate a radical revision of first principles (or even negation), such disturbances often served to renew the authority of secularism.

99. "The Philosophy of Advertising," *The American Whig Review* 16 (August 1852): 121-22.

100. See also the argument that female influence was being overemphasized at the expense of understanding "male influence" and the influence of society in general in Hugo Reid, *Woman, Her Education and Influence with a General Introduction by Mrs. C. M. Kirkland* (New York: Fowlers & Wells, 1852), 41-45. This and other statements speak to how the expectation of transparent relations with the world and the desire to make oneself transparent to the self was ever in tension with the dramatic increase in media and the circulation of signs, an intensification in which signs begin to reinforce one another by way of reflection and synchronous vibration.

101. Networks themselves were often identified as forces akin to nature, storms that laid bare the permeable boundaries of the self. "Curiosities of Railway Traveling," *Harper's New Monthly Magazine* 2 (January 1851): 194-95; Robert MacFarlane, "The Printing Press," *American Phrenological Journal* 12 (May 1851): 109-12.

7. The Evacuation of Dread

Sociality, in the age of networks, generated all manner of strange dissolutions. As "mental action" was "thrown into the locomotives," difficulties arose in naming the source of its power when there was no center to speak of.[102] For as the pace of modernization accelerated, so too did the awareness of energies coursing through society and the individual psyche. Many Americans suspected "secret causes and agencies" of registering their effects invisibly, indirectly, and from a distance. And despite their acknowledged materiality, accounts from the antebellum period speak of somethings that are bodiless and just out of reach.[103] Everyday life, particularly for those who most seemingly benefited from the advance of networks, was increasingly experienced in terms of spectrality, haunting, and contagion. It is the historicity of this experiential unease within Protestant subcultures that is of analytical concern, particularly in light of a mid-century environment strewn with messages of disenchantment, transparency, and calculability.[104] The key to understanding these perceptions is the fact that specters became a matter of intense public scrutiny.

In 1848 Maggie and Kate Fox garnered widespread publicity with their claims of strange knockings in the basement of their Hydesville home, about thirty miles east of Rochester. In the wake of the "Rochester knockings" a preexisting publicity surrounding the "reality of ghosts" gathered

102. John Murray Spear, "Of the Electric Motor" (June 2, 1860), Box 1, Folder 48, 17. Sheldon Papers, Darlington Memorial Library. University of Pittsburgh.

103. John Barton Derby remarked in 1835 that there was "a kind of sleight o'hand and mystery about" the effects of politics in the abstract. The citizen rarely, if ever, "feels its *direct* action," he mused. "And it is only by some irregularity in the system, that he becomes conscious of subjection to higher powers than his own paternal state government" (*Political Reminiscences* [Boston: Homer & Palmer, 1835], 171).

104. On instances of political paranoia, see "The Mystery of Iniquity: A Passage of the Secret History of American Politics," *The American Review* 1 (May 1, 1845): 441-53. See also the collected tracts, "New Threats to Internal Security (1825-1860)," in *The Fear of Conspiracy: Images of Un-American Subversion from the Revolution to the Present*, ed. David Brion Davis (Ithaca: Cornell University Press, 1971), 66-101. For literary assessments, see Henry D. Thoreau, "The Commercial Spirit of Modern Times Considered in its Influence on the Political, Moral, and Literary Character of a Nation," in *Early Essays and Miscellanies*, ed. Joseph J. Molden Hauer and Edwin Moser (Princeton: Princeton University Press, 1975), 115-18. See Walt Whitman's description of the "magnetic" attraction of daguerreotypes in the "phantom concourse" of Plumbe's Gallery in 1846 ("Visit to Plumbe's Gallery," *The Gathering of the Forces*, ed. Cleveland Rogers and John Black [New York: G. P. Putnam's Sons, 1920], 2:116). See also Margaret Fuller's 1843 discussion of the "daemoniacal" as "indissolubly linked with the existence of matter" (*Memoirs of Margaret Fuller Ossoli* [Boston: Phillips, Sampson and Company, 1852], 225).

momentum.[105] Lyceum circuits were booked with mediums, mesmerists, trance healers, and other occult practitioners. Romantic Hermeticism assumed a scientific sheen and became, in the words of historian Catherine L. Albanese, a "tool in a new technology of spirit." Many Americans during this period were exposed to articles, maps, and demonstrations of haunted political terrains in which the material possessed spiritual attributes, and vice versa. And indicative of the entangled horizons of ghosts, machines, and their metaphors, early communiqués from the spirit world often sounded like grinding gears and steam.[106]

Spiritualists, in general, were quick to incorporate the metaphors of media and mechanical regulation into their worldview, as evidenced by notions of "spiritual telegraphy" and the "new motive power."[107] John Murray Spear's comment on the mechanism of "Universal Activity" was typical: "between the Grand Central Mind and all inferior minds there subsists a connection, a telegraphic communication, by means of what may be termed an Electric chain, composed of a greater or lesser number of intermediate links." Invoking the metaphor of the network, Spear declared that "independence does not exist; self-generation is a fallacy. INFLUX is the grand truth."[108]

By the mid-1850s, séance spiritualism—the liberal extension of liberal Protestantism—had woven various explanatory threads of ontic mediation and spiritual intercourse into a loose institutional canopy. Indeed, spiritualism had generated an entire theology around gestures within liberal Protestantism toward the utter connectivity of earthly existence and its

105. Walter Cooper Dendy, *The Philosophy of Mystery* (New York: Harper & Brothers, 1845), 12. The conceptual space of spiritualism became increasingly viable with the publication of the mystical writings of Swedenborg, the outburst of spirit communication among Shakers in the late 1830s, and the healing sessions held by trance physician Andrew Jackson Davis (the "Seer of Poughkeepsie") in the 1840s.

106. Albanese, *Republic of Mind and Spirit*, 199; Horace Greeley, "Spirit and Matter," in *The Rose of Sharon: A Religious Souvenir for MDCCCLII*, ed. C. M. Sawyer (Boston: A. Tompkins and B. B. Mussey & Co., 1852), 130–39; Eliab W. Capron and Henry D. Barron, *Singular Revelations: Explanation and History of the Mysterious Communion with Spirits, Comprehending the Rise and Progress of the Mysterious Noises in Western New-York, Generally Received as Spiritual Communication* (Auburn: Finn & Rockwell, 1850), 58.

107. For a provocative reading of the occult desires and effects of telegraphy, see Jeremy Stolow, "Salvation by Electricity," in *Religion: Beyond a Concept*, ed. Hent de Vries (New York: Fordham University Press, 2008), 668–86. See also Jeffrey Sconce, *Haunted Media: Electronic Presence from Telegraphy to Television* (Durham: Duke University Press, 2000). Sconce argues "that many of our contemporary narratives concerning the 'powers' of telecommunications have, if not their origin, then their first significant cultural synthesis in the doctrines of Spiritualism" (25).

108. Spear, *The Educator*, 517, 328–32.

relationship with the spirit-world. And perhaps most significant in terms of the metaphysics of secularism, "occult and invisible operators" not only allowed the dead to speak to the living but would precipitate *"emancipation from all Fear and Superstition."*[109]

The perpetual circulations of the spirit-world transformed mediation from a potentially disturbing experience into one that empowered.[110] Spirits themselves confirmed that such mediation was in fact a distillation of republican politics. The result, counterintuitively, was an ontology of pure independence. Basing their "affirmations . . . upon the demonstration . . . of fact, science, and natural law," spiritualists welcomed the directives of strangers, departed loved ones, and a revolving line-up of "worthies" that included George Washington, Thomas Jefferson, Benjamin Franklin, William Ellery Channing, Isaac Newton, Lord Byron, and Martha Washington. Within this "republican" government, "ministering angels" used neither rhetoric nor "coercion" but openly "impressed" moral order "upon" those who were "constitutionally unable to resist the sentiment which, like a magic spell, operates upon their sense of right, and overrules any rebellious passion." "When spirit laws are understood," declared Franklin in 1851, "every one will rejoice to be governed by them."[111]

The popularity of spiritualism owed much to how séances made sense of the experience of mediation. To attend a séance was to interact with the abstraction of the public—people and forces that had nothing essentially to do with you.[112] As representative citizens, mediums often posited spirit-power as incalculable and then proceeded to calculate it—an archetypal performance of their agency.[113] "Intelligent beings," for example, were

109. Emma Hardinge, *Modern American Spiritualism: A Twenty Years' Record* (New York: Author, 1870), 10-12; Andrew Jackson Davis, *The Present Age and Inner Life: A Sequel to Spiritual Intercourse* (New York: Partridge and Brittan, 1853), 71.

110. George Clayton Jr, *Angelology: Remarks and Reflections Touching the Agency and Ministration of Holy Angels* (New York: Henry Kernot, 1851).

111. Hardinge, *Modern American Spiritualism*, 11; Hare, *Experimental Investigations*, 138, 89, 113; Isaac Post, *Voices from the Spirit World, Being Communications from Many Spirits, by the Hand of Isaac Post, Medium* (Rochester: Charles H. McDonell, 1852), xi.

112. As the medium Eliza Brown confessed, she was in possession of 923 "communications which have been given through me." The majority, she noted, were "from spirits who were *strangers* to me, and many of them are addressed to persons whom I have never met." Many spirits, wrote Davis "were strangers to me, in the sense that I had never seen them before; and yet they were friends to the doctrines of this philosophy" (Davis, *Present Age*, 140, 78). On the public sphere as an "environment of strangerhood," see Michael Warner, *Publics and Counterpublics* (New York: Zone Books, 2002), 74-75.

113. Davis, for example, offered a taxonomy of spirit inscription: from the vibratory medium "whose body, not mind, is under the partial control of invisible powers" to the pulsatory medium who receives sensual impressions and no longer needs an alphabet to the neurological

"beyond our vision," yet their "influence" could be measured in "sounds, impressions and various other means."[114] In their preoccupation with discerning the laws of spirit, spiritualists ritualized the ethics of legibility. Within the darkened parlor or public hall, they imagined themselves as part of a vast public sphere. On the one hand, spiritualists openly addressed epistemological and political dilemmas of opacity and mediation, respectively. On the other hand, it was their manner of explaining these dilemmas that, more often than not, diffused their unsettling charge. Encounters with ghosts were often comforting, mundane affairs, as notable as having tea with friends or making cheese at home.[115]

Ghosts were domesticated within spiritualist venues, their mediating presence used to rearticulate the ground of agency in its epistemic and political registers. Like evangelicals, spiritualists located piety in the act of voluntary attention—not to the Bible but to spirit messages to be decoded. Underlying spiritualist piety was the desire to read the signs of spirit-inscription in order to make legible the process by which the spirit world registered its effects. Many surfaces, including bedroom walls, body parts, handkerchiefs, and pantaloons, were marked with "hieroglyphic representations." On March 15, 1850, for example, in Stratford, Connecticut, a turnip fell to the ground. On it was a message that revealed something about the ethical desires underlying spirit communiqués. The marks upon the turnip were "entirely arbitrary" in relation to any language that had previously existed. The "singular characters" were, instead, "signs of the times." The message, written in a language from the future and deciphered by Davis: *You may expect a variety of things from our society.*[116]

By the early 1850s spiritualism had become a vernacular resource for a large swath of Americans. It provided terms to those seeking to come to terms with the "atmospheric" effects of modernization. Spiritualism, although never challenging denominational Protestantism in terms of sheer numbers or institutional heft, nonetheless provided a language that addressed the materiality of spirit. This book, then, is not a history of spiritu-

---

medium whose "mind, though influenced to some extent by the spirit present, is nevertheless left to reflect, meditate, and invite thoughts through its accustomed methods" (Davis, *Present Age*, 130, 140, 145). See also Taves, *Fits, Trances, and Visions*, 178.

114. Capron and Barron, *Singular Revelations*, 35.

115. "Diary of Maria M. Fifield," Sunday, July 18th, 1858. Doc. 389, Joseph Downs Collection and Winterthur Archives, Winterthur Museum and Library, Winterthur, Del.

116. Davis, *Philosophy of Spiritual Intercourse*, 47, 55–56.

They are, therefore, entirely arbitrary,—having no affinity, in either their grammatical structure or interior signification, with any ancient or oriental language that ever existed among men. They are rather "signs of the times" which mankind may confidently expect to realize when external or terrestial conditions are favorable to their development.

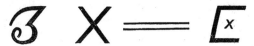

When I first saw these figures I recognized them as being, to a certain extent, analogous to some characters* which I read upon a SCROLL which was presented to my mind on the seventh of March, 1843. The interpretation of the above, according to my interior impressions, is literally as follows : " *You may expect a variety of things from our society.*" Here is an answer to the inquiry, respecting the *object* of spiritual visitings to present such trifling manifestations. The spirits

FIGURE 4 · "When spirits make or write characters, for the purpose of arresting public attention, they do not employ those instrumentalities which we use but adopt altogether different agencies." From Andrew Jackson Davis's *Philosophy of Spiritual Intercourse; Being an Explanation of Modern Mysteries* (New York: Fowlers and Wells, 1851), 55.

alism or metaphysical religiosity. Rather, it dwells upon phenomenological registers of haunting. Consequently, I seriously consider the testimony of spiritualists and the use of occult metaphors, in general, because I am interested in experience within the secular age, or more precisely, the intimate encounters with its discursive effects.

Haunting, in its various guises at mid-century, is the most revealing locus for analyzing the metaphysics of secularism—in terms of physical impact as well as material persistence.[117] Consequently, this book dwells

117. I draw inspiration here from Alex Owen's magisterial account of occultism in fin-de-siècle Britain, *The Place of Enchantment: British Occultism and the Culture of the Modern* (Chicago: University of Chicago Press, 2004). Owen delineates two forms of enchantment and shows how enchantment gets taken up as an extension but also a critique of modern projects of calculation. On occultism as both critique and extension of the social imaginary of late-nineteenth-century colonialism, see Gauri Viswanthan, "The Ordinary Business of Occultism," *Critical Inquiry* 27, no. 1 (Autumn 2000): 1–20.

upon those processes by which individuals came to understand and live with spirit laws. For these processes in which specters became (anxious) objects of knowledge, I contend, speak to the dynamism of secularism and the security of its metaphysics. What is perhaps even more unsettling, however, is that such processes served to foreclose possibilities for recognizing what was spectral about modernity. For as the experiences of structures without seams and strategies without subjects achieved a degree of coherence, such experiences were only *potentially* unnerving. Rather than challenge, they often served to legitimate the core principles upon which Protestant pieties were founded. As Francis Wayland suggested at mid-century, such foreclosure was inevitable. "I am built railroad fashion," wrote Wayland, the author of a popular textbook in Common Sense philosophy and republican virtue. "I can go forwards, and, if necessary, back; but I can't go sideways."[118] The experience of haunting, in other words, rather than introduce discontinuity into one's being, often fueled the repetition of sovereignty, uninterrupted and in control.[119] For what is most remarkable about mid-century Protestantism is how anxieties over invisible, indirect, and regulatory powers served to unsettle *and* secure the metaphysics of secularism.

Rather than disturb at the level of first principles, the recognition of "unconscious influence" and other strange agencies aswirl in social life led, more often than not, to a hardening of the epistemic and political ground that had been momentarily disturbed. And it is this process—an evacuation of dread and a suturing of various ruptures—that serves as a leitmotif of the chapters that follow: the receipt of spiritualist communiqués, the reformation of the criminal body at Sing Sing State Penitentiary, the ethnographic agenda of Lewis Henry Morgan to discern the mysterious interrelationality of social life, the will to internalize phrenological blueprints as maps of one's own agency, the Unitarian insistence that sal-

118. Francis Wayland and H. L. Wayland, *A Memoir of the Life and Labors of Francis Wayland* (New York: Sheldon and Company, 1868), 2:150.
119. The experience of contradiction followed by a tentative reconciliation, anxiety followed by assuagement—this, perhaps, is a central trope of a modernity in which crises are experienced, sold, and, now, cross-marketed in terms of their overcoming. To be clear, this conceptual space of haunting was not a matter of false consciousness but one of discursive practice. Russ Castronovo has suggested something akin to this in *Necro Citizenship: Death, Eroticism, and the Public Sphere in the Nineteenth-Century United States* (Durham: Duke University Press, 2001). Castronovo argues that an occult public sphere idealized passivity as a democratic sensibility, depoliticization as a political virtue, and spiritualized pressing material concerns.

vation depended upon one's relations with *and* immunization from society, and finally, in evangelical efforts to address the particularity of souls from a distance, to mediate them through the abstraction of the population, a moment exemplified when a multi-tiered national media institution entered into, by way of the colporteur, the ramshackle quarters of the unconverted.

8. Phantasmaphysics

In antebellum America the metaphysics of secularism assumed a ponderous and formidable materiality. Its claims to that which was most natural, that which was certainly true, and that which was excessively real were relentless. In forging numerous and circuitous paths in the lives of individuals, secularism spurred the imagination of identity, mediated actions, and animated institutional logics vis-à-vis the question of religion. Among antebellum Protestants, new words and new practices sprang up whose imperative was to consolidate a continuity (as opposed to equivalence) between piety and citizenship. Some versions of religion became all but equivalent to the aspirations of a progressive, Enlightened nation-state. Citizenship became utterly consistent with particular versions of piety and moral transformation. The compatibility between the range of Protestant practices and secular modernity speaks to the power of an atmosphere saturated with metaphysical commitments of a particular type, an affective environment in which the truly religious and the truly secular were inscribed, seamlessly and simultaneously, with the mark of the real. So rather than a history of religion per se, this book is a genealogical investigation into those formations—social, conceptual, and technical—that enabled a broad Protestant majority, circa 1851, to convince themselves that they were religious. For revolving around the truth of these convictions at mid-century was an atmosphere in which you could feel as if you were living within a secular age.[120]

120. As a storyteller, my desire to render the diffusions of secularism is premised in part on my ability to perform its promise of systematicity. My use of systematicity, then, as a formal device, is both necessary and strategic. For before gaining any leverage upon a frame that is immanent, one must first submit to the fierce wishfulness of systematicity—not as a matter of choice but as a matter akin to breathing in the air. It is my sense that critical inquiry has little, if anything, to do with prescriptive statements about an outside, a space beyond the effects of secularism and the intricacies of their making. To hedge one's bets in favor of

The atmosphere of secularism, despite its human hue, had nothing essentially to do with those people who lived in and through it.[121] It was anonymous but not quite impersonal. This conceptual space, then, is best approached as a discursive formation—a mix of human agency, the agency of concepts, and the affective appeal of particular technics of self-governance. Secularism, in antebellum America, was neither totalizing nor utterly determinative. It did, however, possess a kind of agency, defined, barely, as the threshold reflexivity of feedback operations. In each of the chapters that follow, I attempt to glimpse the dynamism of secularism by showing how its metaphysics assumed an almost biological presence—what Foucault calls the "incorporeal materialism" of discourse—in the practices of evangelicalism, Unitarianism, phrenology, spiritualism, anthropology, and prison reform.[122]

This book is comprised of a series of ghost stories. These stories dwell upon Anglo-Americans, circa 1851, and how their recognition of forces that were neither visible nor strictly corporeal served to consolidate the metaphysics of secularism. To be sure, the encounter with spectral entities varied according to the desires and fears animating them. Yet within each of these ghost stories one can witness how tensions within Common Sense epistemics and the political imaginary of republicanism were resolved. These ghost stories, in other words, explore how particular moments were aggressively not recognized for the excesses they portended

---

transcendence is no substitute for critique. Acknowledgment of immanence is necessary, I contend, for gaining any leverage upon the limitations and exclusions of secularism. Consequently, this book is an attempt to write across a secular imaginary, turning its words, expectations, and templates against themselves. I have learned much from those figures who address the possibilities and limitations of immanent critique—Herman Melville, of course, but also Walter Benjamin, Ralph Ellison, Laurie Anderson, William S. Burroughs, Don DeLillo. And like those figures I harbor a perhaps naïve and possibly hubristic hope that the effect of words on the page will somehow be enough, an affective sign that something like resistance is possible in the readerly commitment to the work itself. See "Détournement as Negation and Prelude," in The Situationist International Anthology, ed. and trans. Ken Knabb (Berkeley: Bureau of Public Secrets, 1995), 55–56 ("Le détournement comme négation et comme prélude" originally appeared in Internationale Situationniste no. 3 [Paris, December 1959]). See also John Lardas, "Smells Like Moby-Dick," SPEAK Magazine (Spring 2000): 82–89.

121. On the phenomenology of the "inapparent," see Tyler Roberts, "Exposure and Explanation: On the New Protectionism in the Study of Religion," Journal of the American Academy of Religion 72, no. 1 (2004): 161. See also Jenny Franchot's insistence that scholars of religion "need to move among theoretical discourses on the invisible—whether theological, psychoanalytic, anthropological, or rhetorical" ("Religion and American Literary Studies," American Literature 67 [December 1995]: 836).

122. Foucault, Archaeology of Knowledge, 231; "Theatrum Philosophicum," 169.

or else addressed in terms that occluded their excessive nature. For it was in these non-recognitions and occlusions that secularism emerged as a space of conceptual viability, generating and securing substantial kinds of knowledge about the truth of religion as a matter of choice and conscious assent.[123]

123. Foucault writes that "in every society the production of discourse is at once controlled, selected, organized and redistributed by a certain number of procedures whose role is to ward off its powers and dangers, to gain mastery over its chance events, to evade its ponderous, formidable materiality" ("The Order of Discourse," in *Language and Politics*, ed. Michael J. Shapiro [New York: New York University Press, 1984], 109).

CHAPTER 1

EVANGELICAL SECULARISM AND THE
MEASURE OF LEVIATHAN

Steam has of course been noticed ever since the heating of water and boiling of victuals were practiced. The daily occurrence implied by the expression 'the pot boils over' was as common in antediluvian as in modern times. . . . From allusions in the most ancient writings, we may gather that the phenomena exhibited by steam were closely observed of old. Thus Job in describing Leviathan alludes to the puffs or volumes that issue from under the covers of boiling vessels.

THOMAS EWBANK, *A Descriptive and Historical Account of Hydraulic and Other Machines for Raising Water, Ancient and Modern: with Observations on Various Subjects connected with the Mechanic Arts: including the Progressive Development of the Steam Engine,* 12th ed. (1851)

1. America's God

Statistics point to a "surge" in evangelical publications as well as in the practices of evangelical piety in the first half of the nineteenth century.[1] In order to explain these parallel trends, however, mere measurement falls short in adequately addressing the strange power evangelical media institutions assumed during this period. In 1825, for example, the American Tract Society announced its agenda of "systematic organization," a directive that applied equally, *and simultaneously*, to words on the page, to readers on the ground, and to the airy abstractions of the nation-state:

1. Mark A. Noll, *America's God: From Jonathan Edwards to Abraham Lincoln* (New York: Oxford University Press, 2002), 162-70.

49

So long as public opinion maintains its existing supremacy, who does not feel the immense importance of moulding it by a moral and religious influence, and of securing and augmenting our civil and political liberties by the most unconfined diffusion of the lights of science and religion throughout a community whose political existence depends on the intelligence, and, more especially, on the integrity of the people.[2]

In this chapter, I will approach the "immense" project of "moulding" public opinion by focusing on the combinatory effects of specific evangelical media practices. These practices included the representation of the population as an object of redemption and religious inquiry; the promotion of a subject-centered epistemology as prerequisite for being included in such a large-scale project of redemption; the differentiation of "true religion" from imperfect or corrupt forms of political behavior; the deployment of mass media to shape the meanings of democratic progress and social transparency; and finally, the sensuous cultivation of rational reading habits in light of these meanings.

Each of these media practices was double-edged, targeting *"the local situation and habits of the people."*[3] And each revolved around the desire for systematicity—not in the sense of direct control but in "securing and systematizing the exertions of others." For example, both major evangelical media organizations, the American Tract Society and the American Bible Society, subscribed to a "practical system" of "doing good which is level to every capacity, and adapted to every condition." The conditions that "demand[ed] the employment of a system combining catholicity, itinerancy, directness, and permanence" were matters of demographic calculability. These conditions included "the vastness of our territory and the sparseness of the population; the enormous increase of foreign emigration; the inadequacy of ministerial instruction and other means of grace; the meager supply of religious reading; the prevalence of vicious books; the neglect of Christian duty in visiting the abodes of the destitute; [and] the existence of error in numberless forms." Such issues, however, could only be addressed "on a vast scale" by addressing individuals "at the fireside, through the eye and the ear."[4]

---

2. *Address of the Executive Committee of the American Tract Society to the Christian Public* (New York: D. Fanshaw, 1825), 12.

3. *An Abstract of the American Bible Society, Containing an Account of its Principles and Operations* (New York: Daniel Fanshaw, 1830), 38.

4. *A Brief Analysis of the System of the American Bible Society, Containing a Full Account of its Principles and Operations* (New York: Daniel Fanshaw, 1830), 29; *Address of the Executive Com-*

In coordinating the production of information about "true religion" with information they had previously gathered about intimate, domestic details, evangelicals made their calculations in terms of "the masses [who] have their rights, as well as individuals."[5] To be sure, the statistically driven efforts of evangelical media did not seek to eradicate the idiosyncrasies of everyday life (sin was, after all, originary). On the contrary, they sought to account for the private realm in such a way as to bring it into the orbit of a community that was in the process of being imagined. Such efforts were effective inasmuch as they made the imagination of the social the primary function of each and every individual.[6] Evangelical publishers, in this scheme, were "a mighty throbbing heart gushing [their] thrilling thought-currents through all the swelling arteries of the world's life."[7] Individual readers, in turn, were conduits of this "life blood" pouring into them "with accelerated force."[8]

Despite evangelical claims to the contrary, "systematic organization" did not yield hard data. It was, however, tangible—in the same way a child's imagination of God's omniscience or the adult's imagination of his or her complicity in an invisible network of social vectors has affective and lasting results. Or as the children's tract *The History of Jonah* (1833) suggests, its own power of instruction was not coercive but ever a looming prospect. For to invite the reader to imagine how God knows "all things that all the people in the world, are now thinking, feeling, saying, and doing" was to "promote . . . active piety" and "call into exercise the reflecting and reasoning powers."[9]

According to contemporary testimony, the "moral power of the [evangelical] press" consisted of something more than the formal properties of Latin letters lying flat. Rather, the power consisted of the active residue of signification that accompanied these letters: from the desire that suffused

---

mittee, 5. See also *Brief Analysis of the System of the American Bible Society*, 126–27; *Twenty-Fifth Annual Report of the American Tract Society* (New York: American Tract Society, 1850), 62.

5. [R. S. Cook], *Home Evangelization: A View of the Wants and Prospects of Our Country, Based on the Facts and Relations of Colportage* (New York: American Tract Society, 1849), 111.

6. See Michel Foucault, "The Subject and Power," in *Michel Foucault: Beyond Structuralism and Hermeneutics*, 2d ed., ed. Hubert L. Dreyfus and Paul Rabinow (Chicago: University of Chicago Press, 1983), 208–26. See also Michel Foucault, *Security, Territory, Population: Lectures at the Collège de France, 1977–1978*, ed. Michel Senellart, trans. Graham Bell (New York: Palgrave, 2007), 12.

7. Cited in David Paul Nord, "Religious Reading and Readers in Antebellum America," *Journal of the Early Republic* 15, no. 2 (Summer 1995): 247.

8. *Address of the Executive Committee*, 12.

9. T. H. Gallaudet, *The History of Jonah, for Children and Youth* (New York: American Tract Society, 1833), 10, 4.

FIGURE 5 · Jonah with whale from *The History of Jonah, for Children and Youth* (New York: American Tract Society, 1833).

their composition to the gears and steam that produced them to the intricate strategies that marked their dissemination, delivery, and reception. Descriptions of "the machinery of this system" were pervaded by the language of indeterminacy, incandescence, and automation.[10] As Henry Ward Beecher noted, the experiential form of the first convention of the American Bible Society anticipated its function. It was a "sublime spectacle," he wrote. Each attendee had "had his own mind prepared by an agency which he had scarcely recognized, and of whose ubiquitous influence he had no knowledge." In "bringing the Gospel into contact with those who absent themselves from the sanctuary," tract societies would "be the means of incalculable good." The "power of the press" was "resistless." Its "*mechanical arrangements* for multiplying" and the "magnitude" of its operation guaranteed its "indefinite expansion."[11] Even critics could not help but be impressed by the organizational effects of evangelical media. As Unitarian

10. *The Bible Agent's Manual* (New York: American Bible Society, 1856), 3. The American Tract Society is now based in Garland, Texas. Its motto: "Always Telling Someone."
11. Beecher cited in Robert Baird, *The Christian Retrospect and Register; A Summary of the Scientific, Moral, and Religious Progress of the First Half of the XIXth Century* (New York: Dodd, 1851), 237; *Instructions of the Executive Committee of the American Tract Society to Colporteurs and*

William Ellery Channing wrote, "an electric communication [was] established" between the members of voluntary societies that enabled them to accomplish "wonders." But Channing also expressed concern over the "minute ramifications of these societies, penetrating everywhere," noting that "one of the most remarkable circumstances or features of our age is the energy with which the principle of combination or the action by joint forces, by associated numbers, is manifesting itself. . . . This principle of association is worthy the attention of the philosopher, who simply aims to understand society, and its most powerful springs."[12]

In light of such testimony, this chapter will address, rather than quantify, the cumulative effect of evangelical media practices. As I will demonstrate, the "systematic organization" of media in the form of information as well as the bodies and imaginations that encountered such information was, indeed, "immense." Evangelical media practices, I argue, made possible particular conceptions of the self, the social, and the means to understand them both; manufactured somewhat narrow definitions of "true" religion and interpretive propriety; shaped characters who could readily adopt these conceptions, assume these means, and adapt themselves, in practice, to these definitions. Simply stated, the power of evangelical media must be approached in terms of the conceptual spaces they helped initiate and foreclose in antebellum America.

From this perspective, evangelical media practices structured both the meaning of "true religion" and the subsequent expectations of mundane life. Neither religious nor secular, the significance of evangelical media lies in the power they assumed in defining a particular symmetry among piety, epistemology, and politics. Like the Scottish Sunday School teacher in *Catherine Warden; or, the Pious Scholar*, evangelical media institutions "aim[ed] to make [students] understand what they committed to memory, not only as subjects of belief, but as incitements to action—subjects that directed them in their conduct towards God, towards their fellow-men,

---

Agents (New York: American Tract Society, 1848), 99–100; Nord, "Religious Reading," 247; [R. S. Cook], *Home Evangelization*, 65–66.

12. William Ellery Channing, "Remarks on Associations," in *The Works of William Ellery Channing* (Boston: American Unitarian Association, 1889), 139–40. For another critical account of the excesses of voluntary associations, see *An Appeal to the Christian Public, on the Evil and Impolicy of the Church Engaging in Merchandise; and Setting Forth the Wrong Done to Booksellers and the Extravagance, Inutility, and Evil-working, of Charity Publication Societies* (Philadelphia: King & Baird, 1849). For a critique of the efforts of the ATS to "modernize" and to alter traditional texts by Jonathan Edwards, Richard Baxter, and others, see *Proceedings of the Synod of New York and New Jersey* (New York: Roe Lockwood and Son, 1845).

and in the manner in which they ought to attend to the eternal salvation of their own souls."[13] Within the strange loops professed here—the back and forth between memory and action, reading and belief, piety and social ethics—evangelicalism was baptized in the spirit, rather than in the name, of secularism.

In conceptualizing the essence of religion and promoting this essence in terms of private reason and social ethics, evangelical media practices both contributed to and were informed by the discursive formation of secularism in antebellum America. Rather than being the antithesis to religiosity, evangelical secularism was constituted by those feelings, expectations, and practices that animated definitional categories about religion and was manifest in the deployment of those definitions at the level of the population. To frame evangelical media practices in terms of secularism—a "conceptual environment that presupposes certain ways of defining how religion, ethics, the nation, and politics relate to each other"—shifts the analytical emphasis from the meaning-making activities of evangelicals to the question of how evangelicals (and others) were made meaningful to themselves.[14]

R. S. Cook, secretary of the American Tract Society, spoke to this process in 1849 when he described his encounter with the printing presses at the society's headquarters in New York City. "Twelve of these oracular machines pursue their endless task, without weariness or suffering; preaching more of Flavel's sermons in a week than he preached in a lifetime—dreaming Bunyan's Dream over a thousand times a day—reiterating Baxter's 'Call' until it would seem that the very atmosphere was vocal with, 'Turn ye, turn ye; for why will ye die?'"[15] For Cook the biological presence of either Flavel or Baxter was no longer necessary for their words to be meaningful, that is, effective.

At mid-century, evangelical secularism was quite literally amorphous, haunting words, animating ethical sensibilities, motivating and coordinating practices without announcing itself as such. Consequently, evangelical secularism must be approached indirectly. A metaphysical solvent rather than a substantive ideology, evangelical secularism was a highly charged atmosphere in which epistemology continuously dissolved into politics,

13. William Dunn, *Catherine Warden; or, the Pious Scholar* (New York: The American Tract Society, ca. 1841), 4.

14. Jon E. Wilson, "Subjects and Agents in the History of Imperialism and Resistance," in *Powers of the Secular Modern: Talal Asad and His Interlocutors,* ed. David Scott and Charles Hirschkind (Stanford: Stanford University Press, 2006), 180.

15. Cook, *Home Evangelization,* 65–67.

politics into epistemology. Because evangelical secularism cannot be re-duced to any one thing and, for that matter, did not even exist at the level of empirical reality, this chapter will move across a number of interrelated sites, no single one of which captures the phenomenon in question: evan-gelical reviews of "infidel" fiction, evangelical histories of evangelicalism, evangelical representations of true and false religion, the logic, practices, and statistical presentations of evangelical media institutions, and finally, evangelical instructions on how to read, what to read, and why. Together, resonating, these sites added up to more of a medium than a message, more than the sum of individual actions, and more than the words on any page.

2. Reading Melville and the Question of Mediation

Given his firsthand encounter with both the missionary cause and evan-gelical media, Herman Melville's fiction may be as good a place as any to begin exploring what he once referred to as "evangelical pagan piety."[16] Melville's first novel, *Typee: A Peep at Polynesian Life during a Four Months' Residence in the Valley of the Marquesas* (1846), was about the specter of can-nibalism. It was also condemned by evangelical, and in Melville's words, "senseless" reviewers who "go straight from their cradles to their graves & never dream of the queer things going on at the antipodes."[17]

Typee is told in the first person. Tommo, the narrator, is a young sailor who abandons his whaling ship and ends up chronicling the customs, laws, and habits of the Marquesan islanders. Tommo pays particular at-tention to the "Typee," which "in the Marquesan dialect signifies a lover of human flesh." The question of whether the Typee are *really* cannibals is integral to both the substance and arc of his narrative. At the beginning of the novel, for example, Tommo recounts his conversation with the "na-tives of Nukuheva" and writes that it was "quite amusing" to "see what earnestness they disclaimed all cannibal propensities on their own part, while they denounced their enemies—the Typees—as inveterate gorman-dizers of human flesh; but this is a peculiarity to which I shall hereafter have occasion to allude." And allude he does to this disclaimer, compar-ing the "system" of Typeean ritual to the practices of Protestant mission-

16. Herman Melville, *Moby-Dick; or, the Whale,* ed. Hershel Parker and Harrison Hayford (New York: W. W. Norton, 2002), 83.

17. Herman Melville, *Correspondence,* vol. 14 of *The Writings of Herman Melville,* ed. Lynne Horth (Evanston: Northwestern University Press and the Newberry Library, 1993), 65–66.

aries. Throughout his narrative, Tommo juxtaposes the humanity of the Typee with the "death-dealing machines" of "white civilized man" and the abuses committed in "the business of mission." Having "evangelized into beasts of burden" everyone in their path, the "cruelty" of missionaries was "remorseless." According to Tommo, the "atmosphere" of the Typee was "cool [and] delightful." The "tainted atmosphere of a feverish civilization" had become self-consuming. This process of turning life against itself, like cannibalism, was also unspeakable. "How feeble is all language to describe the horrors."[18]

Melville's "voluptuous" prose struck a chord among American evangelical leaders, for whom speech meant much. They responded quickly, attacking Melville for his "slurs and flings against missionaries" as well as his "utter disregard of truth."[19] A common refrain among evangelicals was Melville's "flagrant" infidelity. Although never defined with any theological rigor, such infidelity was assumed to be anathema to piety and, more significantly, detrimental to the cultivation of civilized sensibility. For example, in William Oland Bourne's "Typee: The Traducers of Missions," there is more at stake than Melville's "pertinacity of misrepresentation." For as Bourne insisted, his rather lengthy review in *Christian Parlor Magazine* was not an "analysis of [*Typee*'s] contents, its literary execution, or its claims to fidelity." Bourne, instead, took issue with the threat that *Typee*'s circulation posed. Despite the fact that *Typee* was a "work coming from the press of one of the first houses in this country, and published simultaneously by the same house in London," it was nonetheless "an apotheosis of barbarism! A panegyric of cannibal delights. An apostrophe to the spirit of savage felicity!" If left unaddressed in public, Bourne suggested, *Typee* threatened to infiltrate sensibilities, to mediate the masses "like the ominous characters of blood" traced by primitive tribes. Attempting to invert Melville's inversion of cannibal and Christian, Bourne likened *Typee* to an "omnipotent and talismanic 'TABU'" object, one borne of deceit and obfuscation. *Typee* was a violation of the kind of circulation guaranteed

18. Herman Melville, *Typee: A Peep at Polynesian Life during a Four Months' Residence in the Valley of the Marquesas* (New York: Signet Classics, 1964), 38, 224, 42, 144–145, 222. For an excellent discussion of the trope of cannibalism in *Typee*, see Geoffrey Sanborn, *The Sign of the Cannibal: Melville and the Making of a Postcolonial Reader* (Durham, N.C.: Duke University Press, 1998), 75–118. For a defense of missionary activity in the Marquesas, see Harlan Page, *Memoir of Thomas H. Patoo, A Native of the Marquesas Islands* (New York: American Tract Society, ca. 1840).

19. H. C., *New-York Evangelist* (9 April 1846): 60.

by democratic exchange. In its animistic allure, the very language of *Typee* could corrupt the capacity of individual readers to make judgments by and for themselves.[20]

Bourne, it should be noted, did not fit neatly within evangelical categories of self-identification. On the one hand, Bourne was a self-styled reformer and "free-thinker." He called for the "brilliant establishment of Christianity in the hearts of people" of "insulated tribes" and believed that "the presentation of a written and printed language" was essential to the task. Bourne also promoted the "Liberty that angels use" and argued for the abolition of slavery based on what he viewed as the republican-inflected teachings of Jesus. On the other hand, Bourne was a member of the National Institute for the Promotion of Science. He was also a poet of some renown and the author of works that owed much to the liberal currents of Transcendentalism and "free-thinking" sensibilities.[21]

What bound together Bourne's allegiances was his commitment to language as a source of metaphysical truth and his interest in shaping the context in which language was practiced, that is, produced, disseminated, and received.[22] Words, in their evangelical, scientific, and Romantic registers, could embody the immediacy of truth, whether that truth referred to the divine and/or human condition. In Bourne's idealistic rendering, language was not necessarily a process of mediation but could function as a natural expression of metaphysical order. It could be relied on to provide certain knowledge of God, world, and self. Bourne inhabited a space in which ideological currents of evangelicalism and Romanticism intersected. His commitment to a particular kind of social space and to the linguistic practices within it undergirded Bourne's apostrophic condemnation of *Typee*'s publicity.

Bourne's commitment also explains his choice to riff on Melville's more voluptuous phrasings and narrative threads, re-presenting them as an egregious example of what did not count for either divine or human truth. Stringing a random selection of Melville's words together with his own, Bourne distilled what he believed to be the essence of *Typee*'s literary

---

20. [Wm. Oland Bourne], "Typee: The Traducers of Missions," *Christian Parlor Magazine* 3 (July 1846): 74.

21. Ibid.; William Oland Bourne, "The Divine Mission," in *Poems of Hope and Action* (New York: George P. Putnam, 1850), 99. See also "The Doom of the Children," *Southern Literary Messenger* 10 (April 1844): 201–6.

22. William Oland Bourne, "Sonnets to Franklin's Printing Press," *Southern Literary Messenger* 10 (October 1844): 583–84.

"abandon." Assuming the voice of Tommo as he succumbs to the "beaute-
ous nymph Fayaway," Bourne writes:

> Come, oh Celestial Spirit of Primitive Bliss! and waft me on thy golden
> pinions to the lovely abodes of the Typeans! . . . Come, oh yearning soul of
> the angelic Fayaway! let me henceforth be the chosen partner of thy tabued
> pleasures! let me bask beneath the mild ray of thine azure eye, and repose
> on the swelling oval of thy graceful form! . . . With thee let me sport on
> the mirror-surface of thy sacred waters, and ramble beneath the refreshing
> shades of the cocoa and the palm![23]

In his deliberately outrageous impersonation, Bourne plays on the double
meaning of infidelity, depicting Tommo's penetration as a modality of sin
and pleasure and not of truth. Tommo rambles beneath. Tommo is in-
toxicated by the beauty of natural form. He loses himself to nature but
gains no knowledge of its secrets. Tommo's desire, it seems, was pleasur-
able. But it was also a perversion of Bourne's evangelical, scientific, and
Romantic sensibilities, each depending on a wholly unified subject and a
conception of Nature that corresponded to this unification.[24]

The infidelity that Bourne ascribed to *Typee* evoked disunity, bodily and
psychic penetration, the excessive emotionality of the feminine, and all
that threatened to infringe on the rugged and autonomous reason of the
solitary reader. By contrast, Bourne's re-presentation of *Typee* relied on
the assumption that his imagined audience would be able to discern truth
when it was presented to them. All publicity was good publicity, given
that individual readers could potentially exercise their common reason.
All publicity was good publicity when there existed ontological distinctions between private and public, individuals and the concepts they use.
Deliberate promotion, in other words, rather than prohibition was the
most effective response to Melville's infidelity. To secure *Typee*'s presence
in public as an object of collective discrimination would ensure that its
"tabu" powers were kept in check.

The decision by Bourne (and his editors) to publicize a fictional and

23. Bourne, "Typee," 75.
24. Bourne's assumption that language could be used to secure the unification of self was
poignantly on display in 1865, when he established the "Left-hand Writing" award for Union
soldiers who had lost their right arms in battle. As editor of *The Soldier's Friend*, Bourne issued
prize money to disabled veterans who displayed the "best specimen[s] of left-hand penman-
ship." Such monetary incentive, it was presumed, would allow soldiers to achieve spiritual
integrity despite their physical loss.

carefully constructed "extract" from *Typee* was indicative of their faith in a public sphere properly constituted as republican. For as *Christian Parlor Magazine* insisted, "the American Christian Citizen" possessed "reverence for the laws of his country, and a scrupulous submission to them. . . . Liberty in its just definition, the liberty for which our fathers struggled, is not freedom from law, but freedom according to law, and on this point it is to be feared we need instruction and warning. The theory of republicanism is eminently beautiful."[25] Republicanism, in other words, was *not* a theory but a systematic reflection of moral law. It was that which regulated reasoned exchange and democratic dialogue. It was, for all intents and purposes, a mediating principle that guaranteed epistemological immediacy (a most significant dimension of what I am calling secularism). Consequently, Bourne could be confident that his "extract" of *Typee* would be received and understood according to certain tendencies, particular structures of feeling that would render obvious Melville's infidelity. "To give circulation to such statements as our author makes may seem unwise," wrote Bourne, "but as extracts from it of the nature we condemn are obtaining a channel through the public journals, we have determined to do our part in the work of making him known to the public."[26]

According to Bourne, circulation and unimpeded flow of literature — particularly, but not exclusively, evangelical literature — would secure the conditions of republican governance.[27] This version of circulation, however, was of a particular type — words moving through space in a sustained and orderly fashion, empowering individuals rather than compromising (that is, mediating) their individuality. "The Press," argued Bourne, now driven by the "expansive force of steam," had "opened the resources of science to millions of thinking, active, aspiring minds, and poured abroad over the world floods of light which are heaving and swelling in their fullness, as each new inquirer delves to the nether rock, points his glass into the blue depths, or touches the unconscious matter with the galvanic probe to learn its mysteries."[28] Like an engine's conversion of steam into

25. "The American Christian Citizen," *Christian Parlor Magazine* 2 (November 1845): 195.

26. Bourne, "Typee," 75.

27. William Oland Bourne, "British Oppression," *Southern Literary Messenger* 9 (August 1843): 506-7. A republic was commonly held to be "a form of government in which the people, or at the very least a large portion of them, are acknowledgedly the source of power, and have the direct appointment of the officers of the legislature and executive" (cited in "Principles of Civil Government," in *Chambers's Information for the People: A Popular Encyclopædia*, 15th ed. [Philadelphia: J. & J. L. Gihon, 1851], 1:329).

28. Wm. Oland Bourne, "Science and Priestcraft," *Christian Parlor Book Devoted to Science, Literature, and Religion* 9 (July 1852): 80.

a "perpetual circular movement," mass media would transform the world. It embodied the spirit of objectivity. It would enact a permanent separation of truth from fiction by "converting" individuals who would then convert mystery into reliable knowledge, circulating that knowledge and making it available to the entire populace.[29] Print technology, in the right hands, would initiate a mastery of nature at the level of public opinion. A massive penetration of Nature's mirrored surfaces would in turn offer a sustained defense of metaphysical truth from the obfuscating (and less weighty) claims of infidel novelists.[30]

At stake in Bourne's "review" of *Typee* was the impurity of its language, understood as a confusion and corruption of the human enterprise. For Bourne, harnessing the technological means of circulation would purify the process of signification. It would reveal the complementary claims of evangelicalism and natural science, showing them to be bound up in the same scheme of universal order. Print technology, in other words, would enable individuals to identify this order, to live their lives in harmony with this order, and to align their thoughts and actions with how the world was in essence.[31] If the "Press" were allowed to perform its mission, it would secure the physical conditions of a social space in which all words (not to mention beliefs and actions) could be collectively judged according to the degree to which they corresponded to the metaphysical order of that space.

Again, Bourne's faith in print technologies was premised on the wholly ironic concept of non-mediating mediation. His faith was equal parts "sola scriptura," Common Sense visions of ordinary language, and Romantic poetics, the latter captured most strikingly in Ralph Waldo Emerson's ambiguous notion of the poet as creating the truth of the world by submitting

29. "The Steam-Engine," in *Chambers's Information for the People*, 15th ed., 2:85.
30. Bourne's insistence on the promise of techno-science was not limited to rhetoric. In 1857, Bourne received a U.S. patent for a machine that deployed a current of air to separate gold from the quartz matrix in which it was found. Later, in 1860, Bourne would receive a U.S. patent for his "improved bed for ore-separators." This invention resembled his "Improved Gold Separator" in producing "an intermittent or continuous current of air or water upward from beneath the bed for the purpose of effecting a concentration or separation of the heavier from the lighter materials." Like Bourne's vision of the power of the press to enact a natural separation of truth from fiction, both of these machines would rapidly and effectively deposit the heavier and more valuable substances "while the lighter pass off over the waste edge of the machine" ("Improved Gold Separator," *Scientific American* 2, no. 8 [18 February 1860]: 113). See also Bourne's "Specifications of Letters Patent No. 30,290" (9 October 1860).
31. On the imagery of kinesis and motion within the genre of American Romanticism, see Catherine L. Albanese, *Corresponding Motion: Transcendental Religion and the New America* (Philadelphia: Temple University Press, 1977).

to its unmodifiable metaphysics.[32] At root in each was a vision of autonomy or autonomous meaning achieved through linguistic incorporation,
of consciousness merging with the natural or spiritual "facts" that words
signified. Bourne assumed that because words were organic containers of
truth, the perpetual circulation of them could make universal knowledge
universally accessible to all who chose to recognize its universality.[33] In
making this wager on the "interplay of reality with itself," Bourne sought
to play the "game" of "not interfering, allowing free movement, letting
things follow their course; *laisser faire, passer et aller*—basically and fundamentally . . . acting so that reality develops, goes its way, and follows its
own course according to the laws, principles, and mechanisms of reality
itself."[34] And it was precisely this kind of unmediated state of things—the
natural "option of circulation"—that Bourne understood as metaphysical
truth and, by extension, the fundament of social order as well as the natural state of human consciousness.

———

In keeping with his flirtations with "free-thinking" and his home missionary efforts, Bourne's faith was in non-mediating mediation. Following the
legal disestablishment of religion, evangelical reformers like Bourne established a "Benevolent Empire" of voluntary associations that approached,
"systematically," issues of life, death, and the various impediments to

32. On the shift from a republican to a corporate form of liberalism within the work of Emerson, see Christopher Newfield's *The Emerson Effect: Individualism and Submission in America*
(Chicago: University of Chicago Press, 1996).
33. In a review of *Typee* and Melville's second novel, *Omoo*, Horace Greeley wrote of Melville
being "positively diseased in moral tone, and will be fairly condemned as dangerous reading for those of immature intellects and unsettled principles." Greeley, editor of the *New
York Tribune*, avid reader of Marx and Engels, a Fourierist, and a political radical, was no
evangelical. But adopting the language of infection Greeley's concerns resonated with those
espoused by Bourne as well as others in the evangelical press. Novels written by the likes
of Melville were considered dangerous, not because of their worldliness, but because they
resulted in an "ill-regulated and over-excited imagination." They were not consistent with a
properly constituted public because they were not consistent with themselves. "Unsanctified
literature," linked with criminality, unreason, and alcoholism, threatened the "mind" of the
individual and the "morals" of the *"population of the land."* Greeley's 1847 review is cited in
Hershel Parker, *Herman Melville: A Biography*, vol. 1, *1819–1851* (Baltimore: Johns Hopkins
University Press, 1996), 531. See also Annie Apswood, "Confessions of a Novel Reader," *The
Christian Parlor Book* 6 (October 1849): 181–85; "The Irreligious Element of General Literature," *Christian Parlor Book* 6 (September 1849): 154–55; M. M. Backus, "Novel Writers and
Publishers," *Christian Parlor Magazine* 1 (May 1844): 19–23.
34. Foucault, *Security, Territory, Population*, 48.

salvation—rampant materialism, alcoholism, dueling, swearing, and the profanation of the Sabbath.[35] The majority of associations that emerged in the first half of the nineteenth century were heavily invested in print media as a missionary organ, an embrace of publicity consummated in periodicals like the *New-York Evangelist* and *Christian Parlor Magazine* and, most significantly, in such print-centered organizations as the American Bible Society (1816) and the American Tract Society (1825). In contrast to earlier publishing collectives, the ABS and ATS were highly coordinated affairs and national in scope.[36]

Financed by wealthy businessmen, administered by agents at the local level, and coordinated at the national level, these organizations sought to maximize soteriological profits within a "moral economy." In their drive toward efficiency, the ATS and ABS were interdenominational. They did not involve themselves in sectarian debate (all of their publications required approval by each member of a modestly diverse publishing committee), and they were loathe to address hot-button cultural issues like abolitionism. Instead, they concentrated on the bare bones of evangelical piety—that destitute souls were in need of conversion, that salvation would come in the form of recognizing one's destitution and accepting Christ's death as a pardon, and, finally, that such conversion signified one's acceptance into an immortal community. Although the moment of conversion could happen in a variety of contexts, reading—and the kind of epistemic empowerment instantiated by reading—was a privileged vehicle for maintaining the emotional assurance of redemption.

"Universal circulation" was common rhetoric of evangelical publishers as well as an explicit agenda. "Systematic" production and distribution was pursued in the service of aligning the saving grace of God and a secular space of social interaction. Ever preoccupied with production numbers and circulation statistics, evangelical publishers suggested that the so-called secular world (media, technology, and the marketplace in which publicity was achieved) would bring about its own transformation, religiously

35. See, for example, Steven Mintz, *Moralists & Modernizers: America's Pre-Civil War Reformers* (Baltimore: Johns Hopkins University Press, 1995) and Robert H. Abzug, *Cosmos Crumbling: American Reform and the Religious Imagination* (New York: Oxford University Press, 1994).
36. The distribution of Bibles, tracts, Almanacs, and classic texts of Puritan devotion was not unprecedented in antebellum America. The ATS, ABS, and the American Sunday-School Union (1824) modeled themselves on previous publishing cooperatives such as the New England Tract Society (1814), the Massachusetts Society for Promoting Christian Knowledge (1803), and the colonial project of the Society for Propagating the Gospel among the Indians and Others in North-America (1787).

speaking. In 1851, for example, the ATS reported that the *"power of the press"* had precipitated the "aggressive movement by which the masses" have been "reached and supplied" with "6,567,795 copies of standard religious works." These works (as well as promotional literature about the efficient and effective dissemination of them) were designed for continuous circulation (unlike, say, the fleeting circulation of newspapers). The circulating presence of Bibles and tracts would secure "the authority of the divine Legislator." Such circulation would also serve to overcome political disorder and make manifest the uniformity of consciousness. "We do believe that if good men beheld each other's goodness through a nearer medium, and one less obscured, they would be more under the direction of a reciprocated confidence."[37]

The "Benevolent Empire," then, was not simply a matter of brick, mortar, or even the warm bodies of reformers or church attendees. On the contrary, it was an empire of semiotic technology and informational density. Such "reciprocated confidence" was more ethereal, perhaps, than bodies, but nonetheless tangible. "What elements of power are here entrusted to us!" proclaimed Presbyterian Robert Baird in 1851, the "us" referring to evangelical media organizations in general. "These arts of printing that multiply the Word of God literally with every minute; these accumulations of capital still active, still accumulating; these means of communication over sea and land, through the broad earth—who does not hear the voice of God in all these?"[38]

Baird, the author of *Religion in the United States* (1843), one of the first and most comprehensive histories of evangelicalism, was simply repeating a common theme—the celebration of mass media accompanied by an anxious denial of the affective role evangelicals played in mediating the messages they produced and distributed.[39] The ABS, for example, claimed

37. *Twenty-Fifth Annual Report*, 66–67; Cook, *Home Evangelization*, 8.
38. Baird, *Christian Retrospect and Register*, 188.
39. Media practices of evangelicals sought to generate habits: "the state[s] of feeling and action formed by the repetition of the same train of thought and the same course of conduct" (T. S. Clarke, "The Power of Habit," *Christian Parlor Magazine* 1 [July 1844]: 86). David Paul Nord has devoted much attention to the strategies of persuasion pursued by evangelical publishers; see his *Faith in Reading: Religious Publishing and the Birth of Mass Media in America* (New York: Oxford University Press, 2004). In this book and in a series of substantial articles, Nord has done much to illuminate the motivation and technics of tract and Bible societies in antebellum America. Nord's incisive approach to the history of evangelical media, however, often avoids genealogical excavation of the categories evangelicals used to understand themselves and others. See also Paul C. Gutjahr, *An American Bible: A History of the Good Book in the United States, 1777–1880* (Stanford: Stanford Univer-

that "its sole object [was] to promote the circulation of the Holy Scriptures without note or comment," as if their notes or comments or strategies of distribution did not affect the community they were promoting.[40] Similarly, in their inaugural address, the executive committee of the ATS described their enterprise as the most "practical system" of addressing the "extended population" precisely because it cultivated what was most natural and common within individuals—their capacity to "weigh" and "deposit" information directly into consciousness.[41]

Although the evangelical press may not have been among those included in Tommo's critique of "the business of mission," the effects of evangelical publishing were as intense, microscopic, and impervious to description. This despite the fact that by the close of 1853, the ATS dutifully reported that 116,435,000 tracts were in circulation, a total of 982,619,267 individual pages (leaving aside tracts published in foreign languages, broadsheets, or Almanacs!).[42] Numbers, however, do not do justice to the power of evangelical representation. R. S. Cook, for example, in his attempt to describe the effects of the ATS, struggled to articulate (and justify) its new and seemingly apophatic form of power. It "does not plant churches or supply pastors; it does not send forth men as public heralds of the Gospel; it does not administer ordinances; it does not advocate or defend the peculiarities of any particular sect." On the contrary, he wrote, "it paves the way for permanent religious institutions. . . . It spreads the leaven of truth among the masses that most need its power. Though restricted in the scope of its agencies, it is unrestricted in the range of its adaptation. It can go everywhere [even] if it cannot do every thing; and all its tendencies are purely evangelical and saving."[43] For Cook, the power of the evangelical press was precisely its non-mediating power of mediation. It allowed you to become yourself. It was akin to the Holy Spirit. And it was Cook, here,

---

sity Press, 1999) and Candy Gunther Brown, *The Word in the World: Evangelical Writing, Publishing, and Reading in America, 1789–1880* (Chapel Hill: University of North Carolina Press, 2004).

40. *Abstract of the American Bible Society*, 26, 29. The position of the ABS was theologically consistent with American copyright law in which was established a republican notion that the proprietary value of text was disseminated at publication (*Wheaton v. Peters*). Meredith L. McGill, *American Literature and the Culture of Reprinting, 1834–1853* (Philadelphia: University of Pennsylvania Press, 2003), 48, 63–64.

41. *Address of the Executive Committee*, 5.

42. *Twenty-Ninth Annual Report of the American Tract Society* (New York: American Tract Society, 1854), 22.

43. Cook, *Home Evangelization*, 74–75.

who was both a subject of secularism and an agent who theorized it into existence.

The "system" of evangelical media was, indeed, remarkable in making "personal religion a personal concern [for] all the millions it reaches."[44] In representing the essence of "true religion" as it was manifest in history as well as within consciousness and social life, evangelical media promoted (with the peculiar force that accompanies words that announce themselves as metonyms of God's will) particular styles of being an ordinary human and particular strategies for representing this ordinariness to the self. Or to borrow a description from Tommo, mining the wicked ironies of his prose, the power of evangelical media to define the relationship between sacred importance and secular minutiae was akin to primitive ritual. "So strange and complex in its arrangements is this remarkable system," he writes, that "I am wholly at a loss where to look for the authority which regulates this potent institution." "Situated as I was in the Typee valley, I perceived every hour the effects of this all-controlling power, without in the least comprehending it. Those effects were, indeed, widespread and universal, pervading the most important as well as the minutest transactions of life. The savage, in short, lives in the continual observance of its dictates, which guide and control every action of his being."[45]

3. Systematicity and the Metaphysics of Evangelical Secularism

My re-presentation of Tommo's description of the "remarkable" systematicity of the Typee valley calls attention to the metaphysics of evangelical secularism, a discursive power that affected the manner in which antebellum Americans such as Bourne assumed a range of subject positions. Bourne's hybrid identity, for example—evangelical, reformer, freethinker, Romantic poet, engineer—becomes less hybrid when one accounts for his sustained commitment to a metaphysical order, an exterior space of regularity to which each of his various practices sought correspondence.[46] For

44. *Twenty-Fifth Annual Report*, 63.
45. Melville, *Typee*, 247, 250.
46. Michel Foucault, *The Archaeology of Knowledge and the Discourse on Language*, trans. A. M. Sheridan Smith (New York: Pantheon, 1972), 55. Timothy Mitchell, utilizing Martin Heidegger's concept of enframing, refers to such commitments as the most common of performances within Anglo-European modernity. "The Stage of Modernity," in *Questions of Modernity*, ed. Timothy Mitchell (Minneapolis: University of Minnesota Press, 2000), 26.

Bourne, as for evangelical publishers in general, there was no essential distinction between component parts of reality. Everything operated within, and according to, a universal pattern. In reflecting the very principles of existence, this notion of order made each component part of physical nature appear to work in terms of an overarching network of meaning. This order encompassed life *as it was in essence*. It brought a searing realness of consistency to bear *on* the present and affirmed utter continuity *between* the past and the future. And finally, this "remarkable" systematicity fixed the relationship between the religious and the secular in such a way that the "most important" and "minutest transactions of life" became ontologically indistinct.

For a range of conservative Protestants, systematicity was bound up in a style of reasoning in which the various possibilities of truth or falsehood had already been determined. On the one hand, systematicity had everything to do with the way evangelicals approached expressly religious issues—God and providential history, piety as well as the Bible. First and foremost, systematicity was the essence of "true religion." It was the grammar of piety and resulted in "the voluntary consecration of one's entire self, body, soul, and spirit, 'a living sacrifice, holy and acceptable unto the lord.'" Systematicity was also the nexus between human ethics and divinity. "System in beneficence tends to make free-will offerings the fruit of a more *cheerful* spirit, and renders beneficence a *delight*, as it is a duty." On the other hand, systematicity had everything to do with how evangelicals approached worldly experience, preempting any ruptures such experience may have portended. As the principle of life itself, systematicity conferred "*consistency and efficiency* to the character of Christians, by bringing *their life into harmony with their doctrines and professions*."[47] Evangelicals also relied on the concept of systematicity to distinguish "true religion" from all that was infidel—bad religion, to be sure, but also suspect politics and corrupt epistemologies. Atheism, irreligion, and licentiousness were by definition asystematic, inconsistent with either "organic laws of the State" or "any laws whatsoever." That which was "contrary to the nature of religion" was also contrary to nature and "subversive" of "virtue, morality, and good manners."[48]

In what follows, I will chart the metaphysics of systematicity as it as-

47. Edward A. Lawrence, *The Mission of the Church; or, Systematic Beneficence* (New York: American Tract Society, 1850), 141–42, 145.
48. Robert Baird, *Religion in the United States of America, or an Account of the Origin, Progress, Relations to the State, and Present Condition of the Evangelical Churches in the United States with Notices of the Unevangelical Denominations* (Glasgow: Blackie and Son, 1844), 273.

sumed physical form in the reading lives of white evangelicals in the northern United States. I am particularly interested in how the notion of systematicity was deployed by evangelicals in the mid-nineteenth century—in media representations and their circulations. This media sphere possessed a technological hue, a distinct valuation of "systematic treatment." "Systematic organization," for example, was a well-worn phrase among evangelical leaders who embraced technics and technologies for missionary purposes. It signified not only mechanical forces now at their disposal but also the kind of world these forces would help usher in. Or as William Oland Bourne wrote in the *Christian Parlor Book* a few years after he had reviewed *Typee*, steam engines were "now moulding the world to the might of their genius." Although "ingenious devices" had historically been "used to operate upon [the population's] ignorance, their fears, and their credulity," they would now serve the purposes of evangelicalism by severing the chains of epistemological and political despotism.

Bourne's story of evangelical triumph was also a story of disenchantment and increasing political security. Technological innovation—or more precisely, the circulation of knowledge about specific innovations pertaining to the "elastic force of vapors"—promised to liberate humanity from priestcraft and superstition. It would do so not by argument but by detailing the mechanisms of their skilled manipulation of the populace. Citing early theorists of feedback technologies—Archimedes and Hero of Alexandria (whose treatise had just been translated into English)—Bourne then celebrated the "splendid labor agent of Watt" and "the fiery steed of Stephenson" as having brought to public attention the inner workings of "priestly workshops" and "superstitions palmed upon the people." According to Bourne, self-regulating technologies, once "stripped of their coverings," would reveal the essential order of the universe, "enlighten man, and lead him onward to his God."[49]

For Bourne, such exposure was but the latest development in the Protestant Reformation, a moment in which the "wonderful and ennobling revelations" of "Science" would transform human life into a systematic proposition, akin to "the locomotive of Stephenson." Bourne, here, was cribbing from Thomas Ewbank's treatise on hydraulics and "air machines," the twelfth edition having been published in 1851.[50] Ewbank,

---

49. Bourne, "Science and Priestcraft," 80, 80-81, 84. See *The Pneumatics of Hero of Alexandria, from the Original Greek*, trans. and ed., Bennet Woodcroft (London: Taylor Walton and Maberly, 1851).

50. Ibid., 83; Thomas Ewbank, *A Descriptive and Historical Account of Hydraulic and Other Machines for raising Water, Ancient and Modern; with Observations on Various Subjects Connected*

the U.S. commissioner of patents (1849–52), had traced the history of human manipulation of natural elements—water, fire, and air. In an effort to reveal the "impostures of the heathen priestcraft," Ewbank had celebrated the "diffusion" of practical knowledge by way of technology. Such diffusion, he argued, would expose those "who applied some of the finest principles of science to the purposes of delusion." Ewbank's agenda was to communicate to "the GREAT MASS of our species," providing them with "DESCRIPTIONS OF USEFUL MACHINES" in order to produce "more useful member[s] of society." Knowledge of air machines would expose the "effectual frauds" of the "governors of the heathen" and all manner of "state tricks."[51] In Bourne's reading of Ewbank, evangelicalism became the privileged vehicle for applying scientific principles to the population in order to secure the humanity of those within it.

Bourne's insistence on evangelicalism's continuity with technological innovation was neither insignificant nor unique.[52] In 1851, for example, John Maltby argued that "Christianity" was not simply amenable to "secular progress" but that it was an essential component of it. Maltby was a Congregationalist minister and member of the American Board of Commissioners for Foreign Missions. Earlier in his career he had called for a home missionary "system" that would "bring the most remote parts of our nation into cordial cooperation, awaken mutual interest in the same grand and harmonious design, produce a feeling of brotherhood, and thus bind us all together by a new chord of union."[53] By 1851, the "grand and harmonious design" had become a first principle. The "nineteenth century," wrote Maltby, was distinguished by the "engrossing" idea of "Progress," not only "in *one* thing" but "in *every* thing;—Progress in Literature,—Progress in Science,—Progress in the application of Science to the arts of life." As opposed to earlier epochs with other ideals—Poetry, Philosophy,

with the Mechanic Arts: Including the Progressive Development of the Steam Engine, 12th ed. (New York: Bangs, Platt, and Co., 1851), 387.

51. Ewbank, *A Descriptive and Historical Account*, 2–4, 382. Ewbank would make visible the workings of power, guiding the reader into "the secret recesses in their temples!—places where their chemical processes were matured, their automaton figures and other mechanical apparatus conceived and fabricated, and where experiments were made before the miracles were consummated in public" (viii).

52. See, for example, "Railroads," *New-York Evangelist* 23 (October 1852): 178.

53. Maltby's "Connection between Domestic Missions and the Political Prospects of our Country" (1825) is quoted in Michael H. Harris, "'Spiritual Cakes upon the Waters': The Church as a Disseminator of the Printed Word on the Ohio Valley Frontier to 1850," in *Getting the Books Out: Papers of the Chicago Conference on the Book in 19th-Century America*, ed. Michael R. Hackenberg (Washington, D.C.: Center for the Book, Library of Congress, 1987), 110.

National Glory, for example—the age of Progress did not lead "off in a single line of pursuit" but hurried "men upon different lines of endeavor." It also had no foreseeable end, "resulting in improvements indefinitely various,—inventions startling as miracles,—and wealth like the golden veins of an exhaustless mine."[54]

Whether or not this "idea" of the "age" would precipitate an advance in "human welfare," however, depended on "the presence or absence of Christianity in the counsels that shall guide this Progress." Maltby lashed out against those who "flatter" themselves, who tell themselves that they "know how to refuse the evil and choose the good," and who are "fool-hardy" and "rash" in believing that Progress has nothing to do with "re-vealed religion." Such individuals were like children playing with "surgical instruments." They had failed to embrace the rule of life itself. "They will physic away their health, cut their fingers, and may be, their throats besides!"

A crass humanism, in other words, was not a viable option in an age of Progress. It is here that two versions of the secular emerge, the first being the adjective that refers to the "permanent good of the world" and the second being the chaotic world of "human passions."[55] This latter version of secularity functioned as a straw man for Maltby. This was secularity as a condition of obfuscation. It was anathema to "secular progress" and was akin to infidelity—irrational, senseless, and blind to the object(ive) lesson "on the pages of history." If such secularity is allowed to triumph, warns

54. Rev. J. Maltby, "Secular Progress and Christianity," *Christian Parlor Book* 7 (January 1851): 278–79. All citations are from this article unless otherwise noted. According to Karl Löwith's theory of secularization, imperialism, colonialism, and nationalism are so many sublimations of religion—inappropriate and chauvinistic reformulations of Christianity that are perversions of it. As Löwith laments, "the "striving for gain and the striving for power are in themselves insatiable, the more so as they become satisfied and connected with the eschatological hope in a final fulfillment" (*Meaning in History: The Theological Implications of the Philosophy of History* [Chicago: University of Chicago Press, 1949], 202).

55. Within evangelical discourse, the notion of the "secular" was deployed with ambivalence. On the one hand, the secular world was a haven of infidelity and "terrible moral convulsions." In its inaugural address, for example, the executive committee of the American Tract Society condemned what it called "modern liberality" associated with "Voltaire and his infidel associates." This view of the world "discovers no difference between the precious and the vile, and which consists in a virtual indifference to all religious opinions" (*Address of the Executive Committee*, 77–78). The secular connoted relativism, obfuscation, anarchy—all that exceeds or, worse, threatened to exceed the promise of order. "Secular pursuits," then, were not simply worldly but undisciplined, un-American, an affront to order itself. But on the other hand, secularity also connoted progressive overcoming, the mark of epistemic clarity and political transparency *in potentia*. See Cook, *Home Evangelization*, 117. See also *Profane Swearing* (New York: American Tract Society, 1825).

Maltby, progress will cease. Americans will be "thrown fatally from the track," their fossilized fate to be examined by a future generation "as the Mastodon relics of other ages have been."

Religion, in this version of secularization, was integral to the progress of "human welfare" yet also dependent on it. Christianity had initiated "the voyage we are [now] making." It was the only "counsel" that could effectively steer the ship of state from the "soundings of the lee-shore" and secure the permanence of present conditions. Yet these conditions— philosophical, scientific, political, economic, medical, and technological progress—were precisely those which had enabled Christianity to assume control over the present. Anyone who denied this historical fact was "guilty of high treason against the race." Maltby, then, was not simply advocating the adoption of Christian principles throughout every sphere of social life but calling attention to the principles that made piety and "human welfare" effectively the same. Such principles were primordial. They were outside the flux of time yet extant in the stirrings of the age. And if recognized and embraced for what they were—systematic principles of metaphysical order—they would guarantee the prosperity of the age, a time in which Christianity and secular progress would perpetually reinforce one another.[56]

"True religion," according to evangelicals, not only corresponded to divine script but was also the means of revealing essential principles of the human—reason, coherency, and legibility—to the human in the name of human progress. Because evangelical piety was consistent with principles of universal reason and the principal vehicle for universal morality, "true religion" was that which best reflected the metaphysics that *already* governed secular existence. This agenda—of reproducing religious life by calling attention to its "secular" credentials and aspirations—was not contradictory. On the contrary, this maneuver was incredibly successful and perfectly consistent with how evangelicals understood themselves to be— truly religious rather than simply religious or merely Christian.[57]

Gil Anidjar's argument about the relationship between Protestant Christianity and the metaphysics of colonialism is not unrelated to such mid-century collusions between evangelicalism and systematicity.[58] For in their embrace of a particular version of modernization, evangelicals

---

56. See also W. P. Strickland, *History of the American Bible Society, From its Organization to the Present Time* (New York: Harper & Brothers, 1849), xxvi–xxvii.
57. Gil Anidjar, "Secularism," *Critical Inquiry* 33, no. 1 (Autumn 2006): 60.
58. Ibid., 59.

sought to govern themselves "by the deliberate choice of goals and rational selection of means." In breeding "a judicious concern for the actual workings of society," evangelicals like Maltby and Bourne represented a "different way of thinking power" and "a different way of thinking the relations between the Kingdom of Heaven and the Kingdom of Earth." Confronted by the anxious prospect of somehow losing reality, evangelicals made reality, itself, in addition to God, an object of their belief. In doing so, evangelicals "reincarnated" themselves as secular and elaborated a "peculiar discourse" about themselves. This discourse was, of course, composed of signs referring to the substance of evangelicalism — creeds, practices, history, etc. But in addition to being a group of intertwined representations, this "peculiar discourse" was also composed of practices that systematically formed the objects to which these signs referred.[59]

4. Every Hour the Effects of Common Sense

Historian Mark Noll, more than any other scholar of his generation, has called attention to the peculiar stories evangelicals told themselves about themselves at mid-century. In *America's God*, Noll charts the making of what he calls the "evangelical synthesis"— the integration of Scottish Common Sense philosophy and republicanism that, by mid-century, had become "an ethical framework, a moral compass, and a vocabulary of suasion for much of the nation's public life." Noll argues that antebellum evangelicals were so adept at promoting this "synthesis" that they forged what he calls "America's God." This ethereal object of worship was not simply the province of self-proclaimed evangelicals but, more importantly, served as an ideological horizon for the majority of Americans. "Theologians," Noll surmises, "translated the historic Christian message into the dominant cultural languages of politics and intellectual life so successfully that these languages were themselves converted and then enlisted for the decidedly religious purposes of evangelism, church formation, moral reform, and theological construction." By integrating the grammars of piety, politics, and epistemology, evangelicals both reflected and spurred an emergent na-

---

59. Daniel Walker Howe, "The Evangelical Movement and Political Culture in the North during the Second Party System," *Journal of American History* 77, no. 4 (March 1991): 1216; Terrence Martin, *The Instructed Vision: Scottish Common Sense Philosophy and the Origins of American Fiction* (Bloomington: Indiana University Press, 1961), 5; Foucault, *Security, Territory, Population*, 286; Foucault, *Archaeology of Knowledge*, 49; Anidjar, "Secularism," 59-61.

tional imaginary. "The key moves in the creation of evangelical America," writes Noll, "were also the key moves that created secular America."[60]

According to Noll, evangelicals absorbed Common Sense reasoning as a method of "examining one's own consciousness as object, treating the deliverances of consciousness as data, gathering these data inductively into broader conclusions (even 'laws'), about the nature of human existence itself."[61] Such data, according to evangelical readings of Dugald Stewart, Francis Hutcheson, and Thomas Reid, were reliable, anterior to, and independent of subjective experience.[62] For evangelicals interested in making faith an epistemological proposition, Common Sense offered a philosophical defense of the immediacy of consciousness and the essential continuity between thinking subject, object world, and divinity. "Such is the manner of true faith; it realizes the fact, that heaven is really engaged *about us, with us, and in us*. . . . There is a virtue, and there is a power in this faith, not from the logic by which it may be sustained and defended, but" because "reason belongs to it, because it derives its light from the Divine Logos, the source of knowledge and wisdom. . . . True Christian faith is, therefore, incapable of denial"[63] (italics mine). This style of reasoning was a matter of governance, of cultivating the capacity to observe consciousness and to act determinatively on that knowledge. Faith, and the reason that "belongs to it," were potentially in each of us, waiting to be organized.

Subsequently, the promise of Common Sense reasoning was also, by definition, a public matter. The sense of a latent political order within Common Sense resonated with the ideals of republicanism, a mode of polity whose "ideological flexibility" enabled evangelicals—as well as a great number of Americans regardless of their orientation to the truth of religion—to fold "public life into the drama of redemption." In its broad appeal, the republican will to virtue came to signify not only "disinterested service to the common good" and the prerequisite for public morality but also "a life guided by God's will and cultivated in personal and domestic devotion." In becoming a "public spirit," virtue would precipitate both po-

---

60. Noll, *America's God*, 9, 443. Indeed, the most compelling thing about Noll's work is how he demonstrates, inadvertently perhaps, the power of a discourse whose formations include both religion and politics. See also Noll's *The Civil War as Theological Crisis* (Chapel Hill: University of North Carolina Press, 2006).

61. Ibid., 94.

62. On the Common Sense dimensions of American theology in general, see Sydney E. Ahlstrom, "The Scottish Philosophy and American Theology," *Church History* 24, no. 3 (September 1955): 261.

63. George Moore, *Man and His Motives* (New York: Harper & Brothers, 1848), 211. See especially the English Baptist physician's chapter on "Self-Management."

litical security and private morality, citizenship and salvation. According to Noll, "the ebb and flow of meanings" between "the spheres of secular and religious discourse" was a fundamental source of American modernity. "Coruscating evangelical energy"—in catalyzing particular approaches to interiority, objectivity, moral agency, social ethics, and the market—was instrumental in the formation of an antebellum public sphere.[64]

Noll's version of this public sphere was a space that Americans entered into voluntarily, a space in which evangelicalism "communicated above all a system of inner motivation" and "promot[ed] resentment against traditional, aristocratic political authority."[65] Within this space, Americans could exercise their rational autonomy, deliberate, and decide what was true, good, and beautiful in a fashion approaching the democratic ideal.[66] Noll, for his part, is writing against the "social control" thesis as an explanation for how evangelicals became so dominant at mid-century—in religion, in politics, in general cultural significance.[67] According to Noll, viewing the evangelical surge at mid-century in terms of evangelicals' desire to regulate themselves and the world around them does not do justice to the complexity of that desire or to its effects. Building on scholarship that grants "religious actors" the proper degree of "self-awareness" and "agency," Noll's version of evangelical dominance is a story of "intuitively persuasive reason" taking hold, autonomy being cultivated, and political liberties expanding.[68]

Noll accepts at face value the stories mid-century evangelicals told themselves in order to be themselves, defining human agency according to formal properties of belief and degrees of interiority. Noll's story of individuals achieving both epistemic and political leverage is one that originates and plays out on the level of conscious choice, conscious action, indeed, on the level of consciousness alone. The play of ideas happens independently from the bodies and contexts these ideas inhabit, that is,

---

64. Noll, *America's God*, 91, 90, 56, 439, 175.
65. Ibid., 188.
66. This assumption is shared by a great number of evangelical historians, including Nathan O. Hatch in *The Democratization of Christianity* (New Haven: Yale University Press, 1989). For a classic statement, see Sidney E. Mead, "From Coercion to Persuasion: Another Look at the Rise of Religious Liberty and the Emergence of Denominationalism," *Church History* 24, no. 4 (Dec. 1956): 317-37.
67. Noll is responding, in part, to Paul E. Johnson's *A Shopkeeper's Millennium: Society and Revivals in Rochester, New York, 1815-1837* (New York: Hill & Wang, 1978).
68. Noll, *America's God*, 189. Addressing Jürgen Habermas's discussion of the "bourgeois public sphere," Noll writes that this model "fits the American situation well" but not perfectly given the overarching emphasis on the rights of the individual (188-89).

from the conditions that mediate those ideas.[69] Noll's argument, then, is a reception history of evangelical ideals with no critical discussion of reception; a chronicle of the desire for epistemological and political immediacy with no sustained attention to how this desire was mediated; and finally, a rendition of the antebellum public sphere that leaves unquestioned the historical conditions of its possibility.[70] To be fair, this is not part of Noll's agenda. But in leaving out those issues that would, perhaps, call into question the boundary between the religious and the secular that underlies his argument about the migration of meanings, Noll forestalls an exploration of the circumstances that have enabled the story he is telling to become so persuasive.

Tracy Fessenden has recently explored what she calls "the Protestant-secular continuum," the invisible consensus of American Protestantism that has enabled histories like Noll's to be written, and more ominously, to be accurate.[71] Not only do such histories assume a secularized understanding of piety as the meaning-making actions of a lone individual, but they also align this piety with definitive versions of human nature and potential. As we shall soon see in the historical narrative of Robert Baird, representations of evangelicalism as integral to a democratic social space have long served to mediate, seamlessly and all but invisibly, attempts to measure the historical importance of evangelicalism. As Michael Warner has suggested in a different context, the appealing ideal of the public sphere as an unmediated and deregulated space is not of recent vintage but rather gained momentum throughout the nineteenth century. This concept of the public sphere, in addition to being an enabling fiction, leaves little if any room to acknowledge the regulatory dimensions of mediation.[72]

Noll's failure to account for issues of mediation—that is, how evangelicalism took hold at the level of intuitive reason—is odd given that the me-

69. Dugald Stewart, *Elements of the Philosophy of the Human Mind* (Boston: James Munroe and Company, 1855), 3.

70. As John Corrigan notes in his review of *America's God*, Noll pays little attention to practices beyond those of intellection (*The Journal of American History* 91, no. 2 [September 2004]: 595-96).

71. Tracy Fessenden, *Culture and Redemption: Religion, the Secular, and American Literature* (Princeton: Princeton University Press, 2007), 9.

72. Michael Warner, *Publics and Counterpublics* (New York: Zone, 2002), 67-74. See also Warner, *The Letters of the Republic: Publication and the Public Sphere in Eighteenth-Century America* (Cambridge, Mass.: Harvard University Press, 1990). As Charles Hirschkind has written, building on Warner's insight, "this conception of a public builds in a structural blindness to the material conditions of the discourses it produces and circulates" (*The Ethical Soundscape: Cassette Sermons and Islamic Counterpublics* [New York: Columbia University Press, 2006], 106).

dia practices of evangelicals played such a massive role in promoting the synthesis of theistic Common Sense and Christian republicanism. For according to evangelicals at the time, it was in and through media that these styles of reasoning and political imagination would be made real. The ATS, for example, became a primary vehicle for disseminating the tenets of Scottish Common Sense to the American public. Leading purveyors of Common Sense such as Archibald Alexander (who helped establish Princeton Theological Seminary, a major hub of Common Sense throughout the nineteenth century) lent their support to the ATS, their editorial oversight, and even their hand-picked contributions to the publishing docket.[73] Robert Baird, a formidable agent of evangelical publicity at mid-century, claimed that the triumph of evangelicalism as a republican power was premised on the "liberty of the Press" and "the systematic periodical distribution of tracts." Here was a celebration of the commons and a refusal to consider any possible exclusions. All of reality was included. Because it was being "driven by steam," the "great power" of the press to "circulate" would make God's Word a tangible entity. It would be made real, verifiable, effective—a miracle Baird himself had witnessed as an agent for the American Bible Society and American Sunday-School Union.[74]

In drawing attention to the evangelical penchant for the systematic organization of mass media, mine is not a subtle reclamation of the social control thesis. The "industrialization of evangelicalism in America"[75] resulted in the control of neither society nor self. On the contrary, the media practices of evangelicals generated sensual criteria for evaluating the true, the good, and the beautiful—for others, to be sure, but, more importantly, for themselves. America's God, from this perspective, was not simply a theological product—a mere representation of the divine passed between elites—but also a political effect of secularism. For in addition to infusing politics and reason with a divine imprimatur, America's God also served to authorize certain norms about the human in relation to "true religion," regardless of whether that human had chosen to be redeemed. Noll, to his credit, is ambivalent about the incorporation of piety by the directives of modern science and the evangelical preoccupation with issues better left to those pursuing political security rather than eternal salvation. I, too, am troubled by the process in which "the notion of government" became

73. Archibald Alexander, *Practical Truths* (New York: American Tract Society, 1852), 387.

74. Baird, *Christian Retrospect and Register*, 57, 62, 165; *Religion in the United States*, 376–77.

75. David Paul Nord, "The Evangelical Origins of Mass Media in America, 1815–1835," *Journalism Monographs* 88 (Association for Education in Journalism and Mass Communication, College of Journalism, University of South Carolina, 1984): 4.

the "controlling paradigm to explain what was good or evil about the functioning of the universe."[76] I am more troubled, however, by the viral effects of that paradigm and how "the spheres of secular and religious discourse" were actively constructed by evangelicals, why the conditions of ebbing and flowing became a primary focus of evangelical practice, and, finally, how the concepts of "true religion" and "secular progress" were aligned in such a way as to become *practically* equivalent.

The remainder of this chapter explores the "evangelical surge" in terms of its capillary effects on the lives of the populace. It charts a process by which the metaphysics of evangelical secularism assumed a degree of physicality. This process was bound up with how evangelicals wielded new technologies and oriented themselves vis-à-vis technology, that is, the "systematic treatment" of the human, by the human, and for the human. The corporealization of evangelical secularism may be glimpsed in the historical treatments of evangelicalism (both now and then); in the way evangelicals delimited the concept of "true religion" and legitimated the "business of mission"; through the technological pathways in which the message of evangelicalism arrived and circulated among strangers; and finally, in the way evangelicals sought to regulate the aesthetics of literary reception by framing reading as a biological practice. By taking seriously the mechanics of coruscation and the logic of intuitive persuasion, one may begin to appreciate the strange contours of secularism and its reverberations in everyday life. Consequently, mine is an attempt to reassess the role media representations and practices played in the making of an evangelical public sphere. These representations and practices, I argue, were an instantiation of secularism to the extent that they naturalized hierarchical patterns implicit in the equation of saved souls and "best subjects" of civil society.[77]

5. A Conversion Narrative of Evangelical Secularism

I began this chapter with reference to Noll's magisterial treatment of evangelicalism not simply to point out its limitations but to evoke a persistent desire among Protestant subcultures to represent themselves vis-à-vis the American population. *"The Christian History of Society has never yet been written,"* wrote reformer Thomas Grimke in 1833. "When the pen of some future Luke shall record its eventful scenes, that Christian History will

---

76. Noll, *America's God*, 443.
77. "The Science of Sciences," *New-York Evangelist* 19 (15 June 1848): 97.

be founded, not so much on the annals of Churches, as on those of social institutions, whose spirit is regenerating the nations, whose influence is pervading, with life-instilling energy, all the classes, and the very depths and recesses of society."[78] Protestant reformers like Grimke were becoming self-conscious, even anxious, about their own history and the ways in which this particular history related to the evolution of American society. For in addition to becoming rather adept in the technological aspects of representation, Protestant leaders aspired to make their story public, to get the word out in an increasingly saturated media environment, and to make those words part of the story they were telling. For Grimke, the "energy" of Christianity, its power and para-institutional scope, the way it flowed in and through an entire population, had become an issue in need of historical and celebratory explanation.

One of the first and most comprehensive histories to proffer such an explanation was Robert Baird's *Religion in the United States of America* (1843). It is a remarkable text, suffused with a desire to write the history of its own present. Baird graduated from Princeton Theological Seminary in 1822 and remained active in local affairs as both a tutor and occasional minister. When Princeton's first printing press went into operation in 1824, a "blaze of philanthropic zeal [broke] out" and a number of organizations were formed. "The Bible cause, the Colonization scheme, the Sunday Schools, the cause of popular education—the Tract cause—the Missionary cause, were all espoused by organized association and received the aid of the new press." As superintendent of the Nassau Bible Society, Baird helped coordinate the statewide effort of Bible distribution by inserting circulars into "almost every newspaper in the commonwealth." He also advised local agents in collecting information on "several important topics not immediately connected with their Biblical operations"— age, literacy rates, educational status, and disabilities. Baird "was one of the most efficient agents employed in this enterprise," whose work led to the allocation of state funds to support public schools.[79] Soon after, Baird became an agent for the American Bible Society, traveling around New Jersey and distributing Bibles to those destitute in body, mind, and spirit. He performed similar work for the American Sunday-School Union and

---

78. Thomas S. Grimke, *The Temperance Reformation* (1833), quoted in Charles I. Foster, *An Errand of Mercy: The Evangelical United Front, 1790–1837* (Chapel Hill: University of North Carolina Press, 1960), 123.

79. John Frelinghuysen Hageman, *History of Princeton and its Institutions* (Philadelphia: J. B. Lippincott, 1878), 1:238–39; Henry M. Baird, *The Life of the Rev. Robert Baird, D.D.* (New York: Anson D. F. Randolph, 1866), 44–45.

became involved in the transatlantic Evangelical Alliance. As secretary of that organization, Baird performed missions in southern Europe and wrote numerous works to promote its cause and to position evangelicalism as a global phenomenon.

Baird composed *Religion in the United States* while living in Geneva, Switzerland. First published in Glasgow, Baird's work was directed at both European and American audiences. It was representative of the evangelical desire to organize religious identity as something that could be narrated, historically and progressively. Baird's explanation of evangelical power, in other words, possessed an air of inevitability.[80] According to Baird, evangelical piety was taking hold among the populace not simply because it provided the most direct access to divinity but also because it complemented the pursuits of liberty, virtue, and knowledge. In framing the progress of evangelicalism as both an epistemological and political matter, Baird's history defined religion as an *essentially* interior phenomenon that was *essentially* related to the evolution of civil society. In its detailed account of what evangelicals viewed as the inspired movement from "religionism" to "true religion," secularism emerged as the effective subtext of *Religion in the United States*.[81]

Baird's treatise on the political aspects of "true religion" may be read in part as a response to the "fanciful conjecture" of Alexis de Tocqueville.[82] Baird took particular issue with Tocqueville's suggestion that religion was a "ready-made opinion," adopted by Americans "without examination" and therefore not subject to rigorous philosophical debate. Baird also rejected Tocqueville's suggestion that democracy could be compromised by "complicated rules" of "public opinion." Such rules, wrote Tocqueville, "are both minute and uniform" and constituted a disciplinary "network"

---

80. For other historically minded, missionizing, yet less comprehensive accounts of evangelicalism as "agreeable to the doctrines of Christianity," see Charles Buck, *A Theological Dictionary: Containing Definitions of all Religious Terms* (Philadelphia: W. W. Woodward, 1825), 170; John Hayward, *The Book of Religions; Comprising the Views, Creeds, Sentiments, or Opinions, of all the Principal Religious Sects in the World Particularly of All Christian Denominations in Europe and America* (Boston: Albert Colby and Company, 1842); J. W. Barber, *History of the Most Important and Interesting Religious Events, Which have Transpired from the Commencement of the Christian Era to the Present Time* (Boston: L. P. Crown and Co., 1848); James Porter, *A Compendium of Methodism Embracing the History and Present Conditions of its Various Branches in All Countries; with a Defence of its Doctrinal, Governmental, and Prudential Peculiarities* (Boston: Charles H. Peirce and Co., 1851).
81. "Religion and Religionism," *New-York Evangelist* 21 (29 August 1850): 138.
82. Baird, *Religion in the United States*, 54.

that does "not break men's will, but softens, bends, and guides it."[83] In Baird's estimate, Tocqueville did not appreciate the subtlety of republican governance—the way in which it promoted the free exchange of individual opinions, thus guaranteeing that public opinion would be an organic representation of the whole.[84] It was obvious to Baird what was happening in America: a full-scale reformation in which "true religion" would finally and fully triumph precisely because the people, as a whole, were allowed to exercise their freedom to practice it.

Such wide-scale freedom was made possible by Scottish Common Sense philosophy, what Baird referred to as the "handmaid" of evangelical piety. According to Baird, Common Sense was not equivalent to piety but offered a convincing explanation of the mechanics of piety to those who practiced it. Consequently, evangelicals proficient in the writings of "[Thomas] Reid," "Dugald Stewart," and other Scots (with the notable absence of David Hume) could rest assured that their faith operated in accordance with "the faculties and powers of the human mind, and of the principles which govern its operations." In this reading of Common Sense, piety was a wholly voluntary process consisting of the investigation of "facts, or the relations of phenomena, respecting the operations of mind itself, and the intercourse which it carries on with the things of the external world."[85] Or as the Rev. Albert Barnes wrote, "Christian piety" was the "index of intellectual advancement" and integral to the advance of "modern science." Because piety called "forth the active powers of the mind," it produced "true independence of thinking and investigation."[86] As Baird and leaders like Barnes attested, faith was first and foremost a matter of securing knowledge in the immediacy of the moment.

Within Baird's sweeping narrative there existed a deep interdependency between "principles that guide the operations of the human mind" and "the laws of our moral constitution."[87] Common Sense, in other words, was not simply consistent with evangelical piety but was, by extension, an

83. Alexis de Tocqueville, *Democracy in America*, ed. J. P. Mayer (New York: Anchor, 1969), 692.

84. Baird accused Tocqueville of lacking in Common Sense—having no evidence for his slander and no capacity for deduction "according to the principles of the Baconian philosophy" (*Religion in the United States*, 54–55).

85. Baird, *Religion in the United States*, 438–39; John Abercrombie, *Inquiries Concerning the Intellectual Powers and the Investigations of Truth* (New York: J. & J. Harper, 1832), 33.

86. Albert Barnes, "Influence of Religion upon the Intellect," *Christian Parlor Book* 6 (August 1849): 111–13.

87. Baird, *Religion in the United States*, 439, 463.

effective and just means of governance. Or as Thomas Reid, one of Baird's acknowledged sources, wrote, it was not "impossible that reasonable men should agree in things that are self-evident." It was, therefore, "desirable" that the "decisions of common sense . . . be brought into a code, in which all reasonable men should acquiesce."[88] The uniformity of consciousness, in other words, guaranteed the potential demystification of social relations (not to mention just leadership and civil obedience). For Baird, "sympathetic feelings" were the natural extension of such uniformity. Such feelings, in turn, fueled this process of demystification by generating a network of individuals in which political power circulated unimpeded. Because "God has decided, that the social and sympathetic feelings of our nature ought to be enlisted in the cause of religion," reasoned Baird, "it would be strange, indeed," if "that powerful principle which binds man to his fellow" were "never employed by the Holy Spirit in bringing those who act in masses, on every other subject, to act, at least sometimes together in coming to the 'obedience of truth.'" In Baird's rendering, such truth was contained within the bonds of co-existing individuals rather than being externally imposed on them. Consequently, individuals became metonymic extensions of the same "truth," interchangeable because they were all equally subject to it.[89]

Baird affirmed, at every turn, the progress of evangelicalism in America, aided by his "statistical view" of what was to be done if "religion [was] to keep progress with the increase of the population."[90] In Baird's depiction of the "religious economy of the United States," the particularity of the individual was emphasized even as it receded into the background. According to Baird, "the energy of action possessed by the voluntary principle" was the *sine qua non* of both personal piety and political progress. This "energy" saved souls, to be sure, but also maximized "liberty" for the

88. Thomas Reid, *Essays on the Intellectual Powers of Man*, ed. James Walker (Cambridge: John Bartlett, 1851), 353.

89. Baird, *Religion in the United States*, 471–72. Baird here was drawing on the notion of sympathy as expressed in Adam Smith's *The Theory of Moral Sentiments* (1759), an idea (and a text) that was widely circulated in antebellum America. See, for example, the lengthy review of the 1817 edition published by Wells & Lilly in *The North American Review* 8 (March 1819): 371–96.

90. Ibid., 289–90. Relying on census data, Baird calculated the rate of increase of the population and made projections for the coming decades in the service of refining the missionary strategies of evangelicals. See also chapter 12, "A Brief Geographical Notice of the United States" (63–69), as well as Baird's anxiety over the U.S. population—particularly its "comparative thinness" and "floating . . . character"—as "a great obstacle to the progress of religion" (73, 76).

population as a whole. Within Baird's narrative, the voluntary principle was not simply an article of faith but "extend[ed] itself in every direction with an all-powerful influence." In its "vast versatility," suggested Baird, "the voluntary plan in America" animated both "true religion" and political liberation, enabling the causes of one to feed off the effects of the other. The "wide application of the voluntary principle" made possible something systematic: a natural (yet noninstitutional) union between the fundamentals of piety and the organizing principle of the population. So while "true religion" was a voluntary affair, a matter of achieving, independently, immediate knowledge of Christ, such private acts existed for the sake of the "voluntary system." Americans, in exerting themselves to "the utmost," would become living ciphers—not of God but of their true selves, giving structure to the human spirit by continuously organizing its presence.[91]

Religion in the United States paralleled emergent histories of civil society—works of political economy that, despite their somewhat different emphases regarding the logic of populations, nonetheless assumed that a logic did, in fact, exist.[92] *Religion in the United States*, like Henry Carey's *Harmony of Interests* (1851), to name but one contemporary work of political economy, aggressively recognized the population as a living system, something that would tend toward stability if only managed properly.[93] Assumed in both of these narratives was a present conflict between the individual and the collective will. Both narratives also implied the necessary existence of a third entity in and through which this tension could dissolve.[94] Whereas Carey explicitly labeled this entity the "American Sys-

91. Ibid., 59, 395, 286, 288, 410, 292, 396, 71-72, 77. "The American people, taken as a whole," wrote Baird, were "mainly characterized by" something they all shared, "a disposition to depend upon their own exertions to the utmost" (43). This will toward self-exertion was the necessary precondition for the security of the State as well as the primary effect of that security. For other examples of Baird's language of automaticity, see 311, 326, 352, 388.
92. Works of antebellum political economy sought to demarcate a civic space set apart from the workings of state government and owed much to yet another figure in the Scottish Enlightenment, Adam Ferguson and his *Essay on the History of Civil Society* (1767). See, for example, Francis Leiber, *On Civil Liberty and Self-Government* (Philadelphia: Lippincott, Grambo, and Co., 1853). And finally, it should be noted that the working title of Baird's history was *The Religious Economy of the United States* (Baird, *The Life of Rev. Robert Baird*, 203-4).
93. Henry Carey, *Harmony of Interests, Agricultural, Manufacturing, and Commercial* (Philadelphia: J. S. Skinner, 1851). According to Carey, the State was a mediating force, a system that provided direct access for those who lived within it—to each other, to the market, to the land, to truth itself.
94. Whereas Baird posited voluntarism as that which mediated the collective will *and* guaranteed the autonomy of the individual, in *Harmony of Interests* a fluid, almost viral rationality

tem," Baird danced grammatically around its edges, alluding to its divine pedigree and approaching this forceful presence most often in terms of the "voluntary principle." In both works, however, a formless and continuous power enabled both the population and the individual within it to organize themselves in relation to one another *and* independently from one another. So in both renderings of the modernization process, private and public were ideally distinct but *potentially* conflated. Individuals were each part of the same system into which they were born. Consequently, liberty or salvation depended on recognizing and perfecting one's integration within a totality that was, itself, subject to perfection.

Baird's language regarding this totality was often ambiguous given that it was for him both sacred and profane, a worldly matter as well as sanctified. Baird's portrayal of civil society and the "Holy Spirit" in terms that resembled one another was consistent with his desire to integrate them. It was also consistent with the myriad ways in which Baird positioned voluntarism as the means to secure the public presence of order and the presence of divinity within the individual. As the direct object of voluntary action, civil society was *all but* equivalent to the "existence, the personality, the offices, and the saving operation of the Holy Spirit."[95] But then again, not exactly. For at no juncture did Baird explicitly equate the Holy Spirit with the order precipitated by the voluntary actions of humans. Both, however, were immanent reverberations of an ultimate source. And it was precisely the presence of this source between the lines of Baird's text that allowed him to use the logics of civil society and the Holy Spirit all but interchangeably. Baird's progressive narrative, then, left the lingering impression that both divine reason and political rationality corresponded to something, quite literally, in between. Although embodied in the "systematic effort" and "manner" of evangelicals, it was unknown to all but God. It remained unutterable within the public sphere that it alone was responsible for creating and maintaining. "How beautiful is this spirit!" Baird exclaimed in a letter to the *New-York Evangelist*. "It seeks to do good

---

assumed this dual function. Carey employed statistics to confirm various interrelations that already existed within the population and suggested how they could be more effectively promoted in the name of "perfect self-government." Society would become a "harmony of interests," an economy that revolved around ideological and material loops of production, exchange, and consumption—the "establishment of *real* free-trade." Pure circulation as a state of affairs was, according to Carey, the best way to secure the presence of the State, the latter being the tangible and manageable dimension of human rationality that transcended any single individual (*Harmony of Interests*, 229, 208).

95. This line appears in the American edition of *Religion in the United States* (New York: Harper & Brothers, 1844), 321.

without attracting to its possessor the regards of the public. It is unknown to all but God himself. And yet how liberal!"[96]

Coursing between the lines of Baird's narrative of divine reason and political rationality was an implicit insistence on a rule of order from which both followed. This subtext of order allowed Baird, on the one hand, to posit a categorical boundary between the religious and the secular and, on the other hand, to delimit this boundary in such a way that it would be effectively and efficiently overcome.[97] Such overcoming was guaranteed by the fact that evangelicalism possessed a worldly telos and the world a religious one. Such were the stories that evangelicals told themselves at mid-century. *A tentative separation. Mediation. Systemization. The inevitable revelation of utter continuity between God, civil society, and self.* Such was the dream of transparency and perfect order—"a place for everything, and everything in its place; a time for everything, and everything in its time."[98]

Religion in the United States was written in the spirit, rather than in the name, of secularism, a medium through which the "gigantic" synthesis of personal piety and civic order would unfold.[99] Baird's account of evangelical progress, then, was not simply an account. It was also a conversion narrative, one in which the population, conceived as a singular and dynamic entity, was as convertible as the individual. On the one hand, *Religion in the United States* chronicled the conversion of the American people into an ordered and intrinsically stable system. On the other, it sought to make a particular "State" exist in reality, encouraging individuals to think of themselves as part of a voluntary assembly.[100] Indeed, the subtitle of Baird's work—*An Account of the Origin, Progress, Relations to the State, and Present Condition of the Evangelical Churches in the United States with Notices of the Unevangelical Denominations*—celebrated the fact that evangelicalism

96. Cited in "Benevolence upon Principle," *New-York Evangelist* 16 (16 January 1845): 10.

97. Baird, *Religion in the United States*, 298–300, 414-15, ix. As Fessenden argues, this maneuver allowed Baird to figure America as a de facto Protestant nation, "subtly align[ing] religious identity with political identity" (*Culture and Redemption*, 62–63).

98. "System," *New-York Evangelist* 23 (5 August 1852): 128. In Baird's words, the difference between the "temporal well-being of the Human race" and the "enlargement of the kingdom of the Messiah" was a difference in register and not in essence (*Christian Retrospect and Register*, iv).

99. Baird, *Religion in the United States*, 221.

100. "Men are so constituted," wrote Baird, as to become "'co-workers for God' in promoting his glory, and the true welfare of their fellow-men." Like these individuated "co-workers," different denominations "resembled" the "various corps of an army, which, though arranged in various divisions, and each division having an organization perfect in itself, yet form but one great host, and are under the command of one chief" (*Religion in the United States*, 411, 499).

and the "State" were progressively folding into one another. The symbolic boundaries between the religious and the secular spheres were inherently collapsible precisely because Baird was up to something much more significant than simply calling for the rationalization of piety or even the sanctification of social order already extant. He was also hinting at a macrocosmic law to which all things, eventually, would correspond, a future to which the present inevitably referred.

Consequently, the "State" to which evangelical churches were progressively relating was not viewed as institutional. It did not impose order, externally, on the populace. On the contrary, Baird conceived of the "State" as in no way resembling an "it." Rather, the "State" was an energy that operated within human history, a non-mediating medium that would allow individuals to act voluntarily, on their own terms, as a people.[101] As a control variable for both "religion" and the organization of the population, this energy made the evolution of evangelicalism and social order part of the same horizon of possibility. Moreover, this energy secured the meaning of evangelicalism as emancipation from the fetters of artificial, and therefore unreasonable, authority. Although Baird approached this energy in and through the language of voluntarism, it remained essentially unnamed within his account. Like Tommo, Baird was at a loss to name it. This regulatory energy, however, was nothing less than the spirit—not "Holy" per se, but that of secularism.

6. Interlude: The Incorporation of Infidelity

In Baird's hands, secularism was not simply the unnamed subtext of true religion. It was also that which defined ideas and actions that were outside the terrain of this truth. Near the end of *Religion and the United States*, for example, in a section titled "Efforts of the American Churches for the Conversion of the World," Baird defended government policies of Indian

---

101. Like Cook, Baird's submission to secularism helped theorize secularism into existence. Baird's portrayal of the population as both potentially autonomous and sovereign with respect to institutions was not surprising given the degree to which evangelicals distrusted histories that revolved around the institutional development of Christianity. Such histories threatened to portray Protestantism in a Catholic light, that is, focusing on "the medium through which we become Christians" at the expense of charting the circulating presence of the "Holy Spirit" ("The Work of Dr. Schaff on Protestantism," *New-York Evangelist* 16 [11 September 1845]: 146). On the irony of Protestant faith becoming a mediating formation whose presence goes largely unacknowledged, see Max Weber, *The Protestant Ethic and the Spirit of Capitalism* (New York: Charles Scribner's Sons, 1958).

removal. He also celebrated the efforts of the American Board of Commissioners for Foreign Missions (ABCFM) in terms that extended his previous argument about religious and political progress. "Their object," wrote Baird, was to "plant the institutions of the gospel where they do not exist" such that they "acquire a self-supporting, self-propagating energy." The training of a "native ministry" was tantamount to making the "great system of missionary operations" more efficient, the primary goal being that the native population learn to regulate itself. Here, the spirit of secularism assumed a colonial hue. As Baird proclaimed (quoting the ABCFM's *Thirty-Second Annual Report*), "in most of our missions we are opposed by three formidable obstacles, namely distance, expense, and climate. England was opposed by the same obstacles in her conquest of India. And how did she overcome them? By employing native troops; and it is chiefly by means of them she now holds the great populous country in subjection. We too must have native troops in our spiritual warfare. Why not have an army of them? Why not have as numerous a body of native evangelists as can be directed and employed?" Missionary activity, in other words, was a matter of geopolitical security, of promoting "true religion" in the service of making native populations assume political responsibility for themselves. It was also the means of bringing the global population into the evangelical fold. "Is not Providence," asked Baird, "affording us the means of stamping our own peculiarities of mind and character upon the less earnest and active nations which we have left so far behind us in social development?"[102]

Baird's treatment of foreign missions is revealing inasmuch as it calls attention to the force relations generated by evangelical narratives of "true religion."[103] Within this consequential conceptual space, "true religion" became the antithesis not to the "secular" world in general but to "false religion" in particular—animists, fetishists, polytheists, Catholics, "errorists," and all those whose practices did not conform to the public sphere as constituted by evangelicals. For in addition to conditioning the relationality between true religion and the redemption of the population,

102. Baird, *Religion in the United States*, 692–93, 697, 695. See also *Report of the American Board of Commissioners for Foreign Missions Presented at the Thirty-Second Annual Meeting* (Boston: Crocker & Brewster, 1841), 46; Baird, *Christian Retrospect and Register*, 165. On "mission apologetics" and the "language of spiritual expansionism," see William R. Hutchison, *Errand to the World: American Protestant Thought and Foreign Missions* (Chicago: University of Chicago Press, 1987), 46–61.
103. On the concept of a "religio-political force field," see David Chidester, *Patterns of Power: Religion and Politics in American Culture* (Englewood Cliffs, N.J.: Prentice Hall, 1988).

evangelical narratives conditioned the meaning of their antitheses—infidelity and insecurity.

In antebellum America, the "religions" of others became an object of intense scrutiny among various home missionary movements and a distinctive narrative thread of evangelical publications. The ATS, for example, devoted a significant part of its budget not only to reaching the "heathen governments" of "foreign and pagan lands" but also to publicizing their success. The criteria for measuring religions and the judgments that ensued were the epistemological immediacy of Common Sense and the political transparency promised by republicanism. Infidelity, as any number of articles and tracts attested, was caused by "man's want of knowledge" and a population's "lack of information" about itself as much as it was by innate depravity. Infidelity, in other words, was a matter of reasoning and social organization as much as theology. It evoked, first and foremost, a state of being excessively mediated. Evangelicals, then, were not necessarily free from sin, but they were certainly not infidels, given that they knew how to know as individuals within a group setting.[104]

The tract *Visit to the Chinese Coast*, for example, reads: "The inhabitants [of China] are very numerous. . . . They have many curious laws and customs, and in some respects are a very wise people." Continually noting the magnitude of the Chinese population—*"three hundred millions"*—the tract grudgingly acknowledges their achievements—constituted by their "curious" traditions and, one imagines, by the sheer fact that there are so many of them. But neither the wisdom nor the numbers amount to much good. Theirs was an unsystematic knowledge, a collective wisdom that bore no relation to the way things were in essence. Subsequently, the tract accuses them of infidelity, impugns their intellect, and points out their silliness, excitability, and senselessness. This was no way to run a country.[105] The "poor Chinese," we learn, have been utterly distracted when presented with missionary translations of the Bible. "Many dif-

104. *Twenty-Sixth Annual Report of the American Tract Society* (New York: American Tract Society, 1851), 112–53; David Nelson, *The Cause and Cure of Infidelity* (New York: American Tract Society, 1841), 13. The evangelical critique of monarchy and superstition went hand in hand, exemplified in two accounts that appeared on opposite pages of the ATS's *American Messenger* (January 1858): 2–3. In "East India Company and Missions," recent turmoil in India is attributed to "divine judgments upon the English government." In "A Cannibal King Converted," the king of the "Feejee Islands," Thakambau, is reported to have given up his crown and "confess[ed] the sins of his former life."

105. Charles Gutzlaff, *Visit to the Chinese Coast* (New York: American Tract Society, ca. 1840), 4.

ficulties attended the circulation, for the Chinese are very conceited." Not only did they "think that all the rest of the world are savages," the Chinese were obsessed with their "idols" and with building "monuments of Satan's power" rather than tending to the business of political security and managing their "overcrowded population." Their wisdom, in other words, was circumstantial, superficial, and a mediated product of desperate and crowded living conditions. They were incapable of practicing "true religion" because they were incapable of appreciating the metaphysical order behind the surface of things. As one missionary admitted, "I had often the mortification to learn, that my auditors had all the while been intimately surveying my clothes, while they scarcely heeded my exhortations."[106]

Contrary to the so-called wisdom of the East, the case for the "tremendously true" doctrines of Christianity was self-evident. "Let them display, in its *professed eye-witnesses*, similar *proofs of veracity*," went a popular argument from the eighteenth century reproduced as tract 123 by the American Tract Society. Mocking the "impostures of Mahomet," "Heathen Deities," and "Deists," it declared in no uncertain terms: "LET THEM SUBMIT TO THE IRRESISTIBLE CERTAINTY OF THE CHRISTIAN RELIGION." The "truth" of evangelicalism was a function of its relationship to imposture and the "fact" that it could and would be verified by the population: "1. That the fact be such as men's *outward senses* can judge of; 2. That it be performed *publicly*, in the presence of witnesses; 3. That there be *public monuments and actions* kept up in memory of it; 4. That such monuments and actions shall be established, and commence, *at the time of the fact*."[107]

"True religion" in this scheme was wholly secular; false religion a perversion of the epistemological and political order of things. Unlike true religion, false religions deviated from an understanding of the real as a reasonable, coherent, and legible enterprise.[108] They were that which stood outside the progressive interplay of evangelicalism and the unfolding of modernity. Consequently, evangelicals were wholly on the inside with God, securing secular "prosperity" on earth in order to secure his divine standing. The inaugural address of the ATS confirmed:

---

106. Ibid., 11, 7, 9. On the "unparalleled" density of the population of China's eastern seaboard, see "Population of China," *American Messenger* (April 1858): 15.

107. *Leslie's Method with the Deists; and Truth of Christianity Demonstrated* (New York: American Tract Society, 1836), 20, 1–2.

108. Anidjar, "Secularism," 58–60.

The state of our country is one of unparalleled prosperity . . . our population is becoming "as the sand which is by the sea in multitude." . . . The light of science and the arts is diffusing its influence through every part of our growing Republic. Our plans of internal improvement and public utility are raising our dignity and glory in the view of future ages; and our happy religion, born of God, descended from Heaven, and dwelling in undisturbed security in the Western World, has already exerted its efficient power in forming here, a people for his praise.[109]

Evangelicals, in this scenario, were merely responsible for maintaining this elegant system of feedback. Security was always at risk from the outside precisely because it had been virtually achieved within.

Although foreign missions such as the ABCFM tended to the salvation of individual souls, their target was the native society itself. To effect the moral conditions of a society, it was thought, would naturally lead to the transformation of individual character. Assuming the population to be the primary object of their project, missionary power, like that of English colonizers, came to depend on "the systematic redefinition and transformation of the terrain on which the life of the colonized was lived."[110] Integral to this management of the atmosphere, the space between moral conditions and moral character, was the printing press and the circulation of Bibles, testaments, and tracts in a host of native tongues. At work here was an assumption about the universalism of truly religious language as well as a confidence that the words themselves would signify truth despite the restless sensoria of the heathen crowd.

7. Secularism and the Business of Mission

At mid-century the power of evangelical secularism was not simply a subtext of narratives *about* "true religion" or even infidelity. The metaphysics of secularism was also gaining physical traction in and through evangelicals' conception of America as an organizable social space, their strategies of organization, and the problems generated in the process of systemization.[111] "The propagation of the gospel in other lands," wrote Baird, "forms a natural sequel to what has been said of their endeavors to

---

109. *Address of the Executive Committee*, 14–15.
110. David Scott, "Colonial Governmentality," *Social Text* 43 (Autumn 1995): 205.
111. Asad, *Formations of the Secular*, 190–91. See also Leonard Bacon, "Responsibility in the Management of Societies," *New Englander and Yale Review* 5 (January 1847): 28.

plant and to sustain the institutions of the gospel on their own soil."[112] Or as the American Home Missionary Society declared in 1849,

> we wish every minister in the land, would make himself familiar with the *geography* of our country. Let him study its map; observe the length of its territories, its great slopes and basins, its systems of rivers and plains, the distribution of its products, the extent of its coasts. Let him consider the political history of our country; how the states have come in, one after another, how the centre of representative population has been moving westward, and has now passed the Alleghanies [*sic*], and is going on with accelerated speed. Let him take the established ratio of increase of population—three per cent., compound, per annum—as deduced from sixty years past, and let him work out, by a short arithmetical process, the numbers for the next half-century. Let him compute the relative rates of foreign immigration and natural increase, and infer what share *strangers* are to have in forming institutions for *our* children. Let him weigh well the adaptedness, condition and power of the various organizations for benefiting our people, and learn how the money and labor can be most efficiently applied. Let him ascertain what Home Missions have already achieved; and on what fields and in what proportion their action is still most desirable.[113]

Evangelical media institutions positioned themselves at the frontline of an epic battle—waged in "foreign and pagan lands" but more importantly on their own soil. In pursuit of a "systematic personal Christian effort for the salvation of men," organizations such as the ATS and ABS were interested not so much in the direct confrontation with the intimate details of sin but rather in the distant management of the American population performed with military precision. According to R. S. Cook, a secretary for the ATS, the pace of American expansion and western immigration threatened to "baffle[] all the calculations of political economists and all the enterprises of Christian benevolence." Neither numerical assessment nor traditional missionary outreach could keep pace. With the advent of steam power, "the barriers of civilization were all thrown down, and the restraints [on] public opinion, neighborhood influence, and gospel truth were cast off." Although the "difficulties" of "evangelization" had become "overwhelming," the evangelical press was up to the challenge, considering itself "one of the mightiest weapons for the maintenance and defense of

---

112. Baird, *Religion in the United States*, 665.
113. "How Shall They Secure This?" *The Home Missionary* 21 (April 1849): 266.

truth."[114] The ATS instructed its agents: "It is not enough to plant a fort on the borders of the enemies' country, dangerous only to those who assail it, or come within the range of its guns; but it is also required that the church-militant should be *in the field*, extending its conquests to every hamlet and every heart." Once the *"aggressive principle"*[115] had been effectively deployed, an "army of Bibles" and tracts would secure order just as standing armies had done in the past. With the "dangers of ignorance and vice" threatening to overwhelm the "home field," the problem of the "masses" came to the fore.[116]

In seeking to make "personal religion a personal concern [for] all the millions it reaches," the ATS approached the population as a network of discrete nodes. Within this "system," the individual became an element internal to the trends, problems, and prospects of the population.[117] Tract distributors, in addition to delivering this centrally produced message about personal religion to distant locales, distributed surveys and gathered statistical data in order to "adapt[] to the multiplied wants of the people."[118] These traveling agents of the ATS, proclaimed Archibald Alexander, had become "more efficient and no less necessary" than the police.[119] Alexander's comment is striking in how it trumpeted evangelical reform societies as a new form of power looming on the nineteenth-century horizon, a point hinted at by the historian Nathan O. Hatch when he describes evangelical media's "democratic urge to multiply."[120]

---

114. Or as the New York Auxiliary of the Protestant Episcopal Society for the Promotion of Evangelical Knowledge contended, "the press, in the hands of a truly faithful ministry, and of an intelligent pious laity, is one of the mightiest weapons for the maintenance and defense of truth" ("Christian Toleration," *New-York Evangelist* 20 [19 April 1849]: 58). *Instructions of the Executive Committee* (1848), 99-100; Cook, *Home Evangelization*, 7, 11, 6.

115. Cook, *Home Evangelization*, 53; see also Archibald Alexander's discussion, "Christianity in its Nature Aggressive," in which he equates Christ's injunction to be "doers of the word" with an admirable intolerance. "Christianity is so intolerant," he reasoned, "that it will bear no other religion; it seeks to overthrow every other system" (*Practical Truths*, 33).

116. "A Standing Army of Bibles," *New-York Evangelist* 22 (11 September 1851): 149; Cook, *Home Evangelization*, 7, 11, 8.

117. *Twenty-Fifth Annual Report*, 63. For the persistent focus on the population, see the tables of population statistics that appeared in many of the *Christian Family Almanacs* (published by the ATS) at mid-century as well as articles such as "Area and Population," *New-York Evangelist* 20 (22 February 1849): 32.

118. Cook, *Home Evangelization*, 63-64. See also the unedited and handwritten reports of tract society agents in Providence, R.I., in which there is a persistent attention to demographic changes: "American Tract Society Records, 1832-35," Rhode Island Historical Society. My thanks to David Morgan for directing me to this archive.

119. Alexander, *Practical Truths*, 54.

120. Hatch, *The Democratization of Christianity*, 142.

The institutional logic of evangelical media was undergoing a profound shift in the first half of the nineteenth century. Both the ATS and ABS were on the cutting edge of articulating rationales for corporate organization and deploying strategies of bureaucratic management.[121] The "home field" had long been a site of missionizing impulses, from the Puritan stronghold in Massachusetts Bay through the first and second Great Awakenings. Although the ideological edge of the Protestant faith being pushed had remained somewhat consistent—freedom of conscience over and against the worldly claims of government and ecclesiastical institutions—the cultivation of piety, by mid-century, had become a matter of systematic treatment.[122] In their "systematizing mania," antebellum evangelicals sought to create, maintain, and manage the conditions of circulation—of words, people, and ultimately spirit.[123] Although the messages produced by evangelical missionaries were not radically different from their predecessors, the ways and means of mediation were undergoing an unprecedented transformation. The difference that new media technologies and semiotic strategies made in recasting the production, distribution, and reception of evangelical words was substantial in making secularism a metaphysical solvent.

Like previous reformers, evangelical media organizations were wary of civil interference even as they insisted that religion should be a political force. But the logic by which evangelicals arrived at such a conclusion as well as the techniques adopted to pursue this logic had shifted. The arguments of an earlier generation of post-Puritans—those like Congregationalist Ezra Stiles, for whom the practice of "true religion" would perfect "our system of dominion and civil polity"—were still being made.[124] But not exclusively. For now the relationship between forms of civil polity and the Kingdom of God was subject to reversal. According to the logic of the evangelical press, for example, "universal circulation" would eventu-

121. Peter Dobkin Hall, "Religion and the Organizational Revolution in the United States," in *Sacred Companies: Organizational Aspects of Religion and Religious Aspects of Organizations*, ed. N. J. Demerath III, Peter Dobkin Hall, Terry Schmitt, and Rhys H. Williams (New York: Oxford University Press, 1998), 101.

122. Noll refers to this shift as an "epidemic of organization" (*America's God*, 198).

123. Ronald J. Zboray, *A Fictive People: Antebellum Economic Development and the American Reading Public* (New York: Oxford University Press, 1993), 136–37; Foucault, *Security, Territory, Population*, 29. I use the word "spirit" here to refer to the "disposition of the mind of intellect" as well as "the principle of animal life, common to men and animals" (*A Dictionary of the Holy Bible, for General Use in the Study of the Scriptures* [New York: American Tract Society, 1859], 436).

124. Cited in Noll, *America's God*, 64.

ally usher in God's Kingdom on earth. Or as the ATS predicted: "a spiritual telegraph, stretching from one abode to another, will constitute the net-work by which the great family of man may be bound together in a common brotherhood, along whose wires the electricity of love, kindled at the cross, may flash around a regenerate world."[125]

The logic of religion perfecting and perpetuating the state, although still very much part of evangelical identity at mid-century, had mutated. So, too, had the institutional practices of governmental reason that evangelicals adopted in "press[ing] home the claims of God, and unfold[ing] the riches of Christ, in ten times ten thousand abodes." Whereas an earlier generation had relied on local outreach and the face-to-face contact of itinerancy, tract and Bible societies were decidedly more bureaucratic in orientation and virtual in their effects. But this mutation was not simply a matter of scale or even of the technologies of print involved. The procedural logic of statecraft was undergoing a massive transformation in the early nineteenth century that had everything to do with the urge to multiply the "spiritual good of the masses."[126]

Evangelical media organizations readily integrated these new approaches to political knowledge, declaring that their "system [was] not needless, even in the land of the Puritans." In their efforts to produce the most efficient means of enveloping "our whole country" with the language of "true religion," the ATS and ABS adopted strategies of corporate man-

---

125. Cook, *Home Evangelization*, 31–32; *Twenty-Sixth Annual Report*, 66–67.

126. *Twenty-Fifth Annual Report*, 63; *Twenty-Sixth Annual Report*, 70. In the aftermath of the American revolution, government officials had moved away from viewing the individual in his or her unique particularity and citizenship as the general (and artificial) state with which such particularity corresponded. Rather, they began to consider the individual to be a citizen, *in potentia*, and particularity as simply a variation on the essential nature of the human. The individual, in other words, was no longer the primary object of governmental reason. The individual was instead a statistic, an endlessly reproducible effect of how one approached the population. For someone like Thomas Jefferson, governmental reason was a matter of surveying the territory of the United States as a container of raw data—abstract "inhabitants"—which could be calculated in such a way as to identify trends, problems, and possible reconfigurations. Michel de Certeau, "Believing and Making Other People Believe," in *The Practice of Everyday Life* (Berkeley and Los Angeles: University of California Press, 1988), 177–89; Theodore M. Porter, *The Rise of Statistical Thinking, 1820–1900* (Princeton: Princeton University Press, 1986); and Ian Hacking, "Biopower and the Avalanche of Numbers," *Humanities in Society* 5, nos. 3/4 (Summer/Fall 1982): 279–94. On colonialism and calculability, see David Kazanjian, *The Colonizing Trick: National Culture and Imperial Citizenship in Early America* (Minneapolis: University of Minnesota Press, 2003), 110–11; Patricia Cline Cohen, *A Calculating People: The Spread of Numeracy in Early America* (Chicago: University of Chicago Press, 1982), 112–14; and "Population—Poor Laws—Life-Assurance," in *Chambers's Information for the People*, 15th ed., 2:289–305.

agement.[127] To control the means of production, each organization consolidated its printing and binding operations in a central location. Each employed the "judicious and systematic division of labor," cost-accounting techniques, differential pricing, and elastic modes of production.[128] Each organization also coordinated local distribution routes. "General agents" for the American Tract Society, for example, were "expected to ascertain the condition and plan for the cultivation of all parts of their field; to secure the services of valuable colporteurs; to confer personally with candidates; to encourage those in the field; to communicate intelligence for the public journals, and to perform much other labor for the promotion of the general interests of the cause committed to his hands." In setting up channels of transport, securing depositories, and coordinating the efforts of Auxiliary Societies, general agents sought "efficiency" within the system.[129] The goal of evangelical publishers was to facilitate "constant intercourse" within a network: to disseminate tracts and Bibles "with cheapness, security, and expedition to the most distant places."[130]

Although not designed for economic profit, evangelical publishers nonetheless internalized the logic of the market.[131] By re-envisioning the market's goal of pure circulation in terms of spirit rather than money, they understood themselves as participants in a moral economy. By adopting the practices of economic calculability, "Christian publishing houses" sought to maximize the production of souls rather than capital. And in anticipation of the consumer economy, evangelical publishers were in the business of catalyzing desire. Rather than simply meet and fulfill the existing needs of the "ductile masses," their directive of redemption entailed having production drive demand, to "form the appetite and create the ne-

127. *Twenty-Fifth Annual Report*, 87, 25–26. On the rise of corporate practices of management and internal communication in the nineteenth century, see JoAnn Yates, *Control Through Communication: The Rise of System in American Management* (Baltimore: Johns Hopkins University Press, 1989).

128. *Abstract of the American Bible Society*, 27, 29; Cook, *Home Evangelization*, 5, 100–102. See also *Brief Analysis of the System of the American Bible Society*, 34–36, 81–83.

129. *Twenty-Fifth Annual Report*, 56. Similarly, the ABS was "conducted by Managers, under whose inspection, and by whose control, all its business is transacted." Such managers had "no other interest in the institution than a desire for the advancement of its glorious object" (*Abstract of the American Bible Society*, 25–26).

130. *Fourth Annual Report of the American Bible Society* (1820). Cited in *The Christian Herald* 7, no. 7 (5 August 1820): 218; as well as in Nord, *Faith in Reading*, 71.

131. The ATS, for example, made decisions according to the logic of the market even as it designated the market as "secular." The market was secular, not in essence, but on account of the economic motive behind contemporary practices of it. The logic itself was sound. The incentives were not. Economic reasoning, in other words, was not profane when practiced in the service of moral calculations.

AMOUNT PRINTED AND CIRCULATED.

There have been *printed* during the year, according to the Depositary's statement annexed, 1,040,500 volumes, 7,931,500 publications, 285,914,500 pages; and *circulated* 886,692 volumes, 7,837,692 publications, 269,984,615 pages. The total amount circulated since the formation of the Society, is 6,567,795 volumes, 119,826,867 publications, 2,777,087,404 pages; including 121,725 volumes (8,115 sets) of the Evangelical Family Library, 94,026 volumes (2,089 sets) of the Christian Library, 30,993 volumes (775 sets) of the Youth's Library, and 85,848 volumes (12,264 sets) of the Youth's Scripture Biography.

DEPOSITARY'S STATEMENT OF PUBLICATIONS PRINTED AND CIRCULATED, 1851.

PUBLICATIONS OF THE SOCIETY.	Printed during the past year.		Circulated the past year.		Printed since the formation of the Society.		Circulated since the formation of the Society.		Remaining in the Depository and Sheetroom, April 1, 1851.	
	COPIES.	PAGES.	COPIES.	PAGES.	COPIES.	PAGES.	COPIES.	PAGES.	COPIES.	PAGES.
TRACTS.—English Duodecimo	4,921,000	38,612,000	4,794,971	32,176,352	97,274,250	851,787,000	91,535,060	806,670,541	5,730,190	45,116,459
Foreign Languages do.	634,000	5,040,000	714,457	4,441,492	6,579,500	59,068,000	5,723,783	49,017,576	355,717	64,677,754
Children's Tracts, English and Foreign Languages	506,000	10,164,000	779,961	14,713,922	7,949,000	149,334,000	6,663,577	138,777,139	1,285,423	10,556,861
Broadsheets, Handbills, and Cards	504,000	504,000	350,871	350,871	5,560,116	5,560,116	5,049,451	5,049,451	510,665	510,665
Family Christian Almanac	310,000	16,120,000	310,000	16,120,000	2,796,493	132,400,590	2,796,493	132,400,590		
Tract Magazine and Monthly Distributer					1,443,000	24,757,952	1,443,000	24,757,952		
New Series 18mo	16,000	512,000	740	27,492	68,000	2,584,000	47,708	1,681,017	20,292	902,983
Total Tracts	6,891,000	70,952,000	6,951,000	67,830,129	121,670,359	1,225,491,658	113,259,072	1,158,354,566	8,411,287	67,137,092
VOLUMES.—12mo bound Tracts, Eng., Ger., and Fr.			4,542	2,178,100	137,274	54,807,820	114,884	50,791,340	22,300	4,016,480
Duodecimo volumes	111,000	48,978,000	84,873	48,343,169	617,461	299,009,556	456,945	234,331,802	160,516	64,677,754
Octavo volumes	1,000	425,000	71	45,866	6,500	3,978,000	5,363	2,447,558	1,137	1,530,442
Miscellaneous duodecimo volumes			1,743	258,954	104,484	21,559,552	99,527	20,966,632	4,957	592,920
Volumes 18mo, including 121,725 vols. Family Library; 94,026 vols. Christian Library; 30,993 vols. Youth's Library, and 85,848 vols. Scripture Biography, circulated,	676,000	120,457,000	590,752	114,251,370	5,569,443	1,198,198,034	4,958,273	1,135,681,761	611,170	63,516,273
Volumes 32mo	64,000	13,154,000	47,569	8,683,880	376,850	72,711,877	262,817	46,457,794	114,033	26,254,083
Pocket Manuals, 128 to 479 pages each	124,000	18,464,000	88,537	13,574,572	501,945	82,783,442	301,910	68,074,346	110,035	14,709,096
Volumes in Foreign Languages	64,500	13,484,500	69,605	14,818,265	366,000	75,565,500	274,604	59,336,794	91,396	16,228,706
do. in Indian do.					3,472	644,811	3,472	644,811		
Total Volumes	1,040,500	214,962,500	886,692	202,154,486	7,683,429	1,809,258,592	6,567,795	1,618,732,838	1,115,634	190,525,794
Total Publications	7,931,500	285,914,500	7,837,692	269,984,615	129,353,788	3,034,750,250	119,826,867	2,777,087,404	9,526,921	257,662,846

FIGURE 6 · Publications Printed and Circulated, 1851. *Twenty-Sixth Annual Report of the American Tract Society* (New York: American Tract Society, 1851).

cessity for tenfold greater issues." Otherwise, "self-interest would shape the supply to the demand," and the market itself would assume power over the evangelical hand guiding it. If this were allowed to happen, "the mightiest agent God has given to the world for moulding public opinion and sanctifying the public taste, would be moulded by it."[132]

Tracts, themselves, were considered an effective way to represent and manage the individual opinions that made up the public. The ATS solicited new tracts from readers of tracts—with prize money and the promise that, if chosen, their tract would "be fitted in the highest possible degree to meet the moral wants of this great community." A tract in this scenario was nondisposable, catalytic, a self-sustaining presence that would align individual opinions with the same script. Tracts fed off of themselves in a protective manner, continually charging and recharged by their own propensity for circulation among the populace. "One book prepares the way for another," precipitating the "reflex influence" of missionary action and forging new channels of providential influence. The "power" of tracts,

132. *Thirtieth Annual Report of the American Tract Society* (New York: American Tract Society, 1855), 37; *Twenty-Sixth Annual Report*, 66; *Proceedings of a Public Deliberative Meeting of the Board and Friends of the American Tract Society* (New York: American Tract Society, 1842), 61; Cook, *Home Evangelization*, 107.

although taking hold during the "mystic flash" of solitary study, was "cumulative." Tracts were electric, like the charge of a battery. They did not simply "bind where circumstances part" but, more importantly, generated and sustained a "wide field" in which Society agents could potentially intervene.[133]

8. Colportage: So Strange and Complex in its Arrangements

In order to ensure the salvation of each and every member of the population, evangelical media organizations sought to "penetrate[] the remote and sparsely settled districts of the country."[134] This agenda was, of course, made possible by the multitiered structure of tract and Bible societies, but the burden of "hunt[ing] up the scattered families unblest yet even with the influence of a newspaper" was shouldered by itinerant book peddlers. The ABS had utilized, from its inception, field agents to "secure a greater share of patronage than can be procured in any other way." In 1841, the ATS followed suit. Building on its network of local distributors, the ATS instituted the colportage system in order to keep pace with the "rapid *increase* of our population." Colporteurs, like ABS agents, were salaried members of the ATS, carefully recruited and chosen "to combine with the press . . . the *prayerful, personal agency of individual Christians.*" Colporteurs were also subject to elaborate instruction manuals and trade publications such as the *American Messenger,* devoted to their continuing training in the field. By 1851, the ATS was employing over five hundred colporteurs and even owned steamboats for missions along the Mississippi River. In the span of ten years, colporteurs had charted more than two million missions and visited over eleven million individuals (approximately half of the population).[135]

As instruments of "public relations," colporteurs were to avoid "religious controversy" in their office and "should be silent on topics of po-

---

133. "Circular—New Tracts," *The American Tract Magazine* 7 (November 1832): 133-34; *Twenty-Sixth Annual Report,* 66-67; *Bible Agent's Manual,* 2; Nord, "Religious Reading," 247; *Twenty-Fifth Annual Report,* 10; Nord, "Religious Reading," 247; *Colporteur Reports to the American Tract Society, 1841-1846* (Newark, N.J.: The Historical Records Survey, 1940), 52.

134. Cook, *Home Evangelization,* 108; *Twenty-Fifth Annual Report,* 63; *Twenty-Sixth Annual Report,* 66.

135. Cook, *Home Evangelization,* 76-78, 108-9; *Abstract of the American Bible Society,* 37; *Twenty-Sixth Annual Report,* 48; *Instructions of the Executive Committee of the American Tract Society to Colporteurs and Agents* (New York: American Tract Society, 1859), 10. The French term *colporteur* derives from the pack a book peddler carried *(porter)* around his neck *(col)*: Nord, *Faith in Reading,* 97-98; *Twenty-Fifth Annual Report,* 100.

litical agitation." Their charge consisted merely of "advanc[ing] the reign of Christ in our world; interfering with none of those points in which the spiritual, devoted followers of Christ are unhappily sundered from each other."[136] The goal of each colporteur was to become an anonymous presence in the lives of those who "did not believe in religion." Each person they encountered was to become a node in the expanding network of evangelical power. Colporteurs were to divest themselves of personal opinions so as not to "offend local prejudices" and were instructed to treat each individual they encountered in the same depersonalized manner.[137] Colporteurs, like the "true religion" they served, were idealized as neither controversial nor political. In their wholly acceptable anonymity, colporteurs operated according to universal principles of truth.

Conceived as an objective cipher, colporteurs were an integral part of a "system" of "mechanical execution" envisioned, largely, as nonmediating.[138] Colporteurs, nonetheless, practiced a hands-on approach, as evidenced by their detailed reports. Besides their supply of books and tracts, the most important item the colporteur carried with him was his field journal. "The colporteur was expected" to "visit *every abode*; and his reports, based on personal observation furnish perhaps, the most available materials for a moral census of the country."[139] This "moral census" reported on the presence or absence of religious literature in the household as well as on personal reading habits. It included information about denominational affiliation or lack thereof, health, geography, "mode of settlement," ethnic backgrounds, the "intellectual and moral condition" of those encountered, and "the prevalence of error, and the means of corruption among the masses."[140] The goal of this census was to gain interpretive leverage on the moral condition of the "whole population"—Baptists, Methodists, Presbyterians, Dutch Reformed, Quakers, Catholics, Mormons, Universalists, infidels, and freethinkers, that is, "to gather authentic facts, which should in the aggregate present a fair and accurate view of *the country as it is*."[141]

136. *Instructions of the Executive Committee* (1848), 70–71.
137. *Twenty-Fifth Annual Report*, 91; *Instructions of the Executive Committee* (1848), 71–72.
138. *Twenty-Sixth Annual Report*, 34.
139. *Colporteur Reports*, 65; Cook, *Home Evangelization*, 12.
140. *Colporteur Reports*, 77, 83–84, 63, 67, 46, 50, 53; Cook, *Home Evangelization*, 10, 35, 37. See also the colporteur reports from rural districts in *Twenty-Third Annual Report of the American Tract Society* (New York: American Tract Society, 1848), 71–76.
141. *Colporteur Reports*, 63; *Twentieth Annual Report of the American Tract Society* (New York: American Tract Society, 1845), 73; Nord, *Faith in Reading*, 103. See also *Instructions of the Executive Committee* (1848), 21.

Rather than perform the same presentation for each family, colporteurs were encouraged to incorporate *"special adaptations of the Society's labors to the wants of his field,* by the presentation of which he may increase both his efficiency and acceptableness." By "adapt[ing] his remarks to the condition of those he addresses," a colporteur was better able to elicit information from "the people," regardless of religious affiliation or lack thereof.[142] By adjusting, on a case-by-case basis, to the information they had gathered, colporteurs and Bible Society agents would "put in motion that system of operation which is best fitted to the *local situation, habits, and moral condition of the people.*"[143] As R. S. Cook wrote in his instructions to ATS agents, "the *variety of the Society's publications,* and their adaptation to the multiplied wants of the people, is greater than is often apprehended."[144]

The objective of colporteurs was not simply to disseminate tracts but also to survey the effects of tracts on their audience, to measure these effects in terms of demographics, and to feed back this information to the local branch society and ultimately to the national organization. The national organization could then adjust its strategies of dissemination and modify their instruction to agents in the field.[145] By gathering statistical data and relaying it back to the relevant branch society, colporteurs were at the cutting edge of developing an archive that could then be used at the national level. "It is almost entirely through the discoveries made by [Branch] Societies, in their various districts, and their subsequent activity in the work of distribution, that the beneficent object of this Institution can be thoroughly effectuated, and the precious boon dispensed where it is most pressingly required."[146]

Decisions about production and strategy were reflexive, dependent on the "moral and religious statistics" colporteurs were collecting about "the people." Once the population had become a matter of "immediate inspection," field agents could respond swiftly to demographic shifts. "The *adaptation of colportage* to every class and condition of our varied population" had the effect of making the population appear as a naturally given entity. The use of information — compiling data, processing information, chart-

---

142. *Instructions of the Executive Committee* (1848), 91; see also the dialogues crafted by Archibald Alexander in which a colporteur interacts with a "cottager," a "farmer," an "aged man," and a "Roman-Catholic" (*Practical Truths,* 247–353).
143. *Abstract of the American Bible Society,* 38.
144. Cook, *Home Evangelization,* 63–64, 109. See also "Narratives Illustrating the Usefulness of Religious Tracts" as appended to *The Address of the Executive Committee.*
145. Colporteur reports would sometimes question existing instructions and ask for further guidance in light of experience in the field (*Colporteur Reports,* 108).
146. *Abstract of the American Bible Society,* 42.

ing aggregate patterns, and acting on those perceived patterns—secured the validity of that information not in essence but as semiotic leverage for advancing their cause at the level of the population. "Timbre is scarce in Nebraska," reported one colporteur. "Families settle along river branches and rills. For several years, therefore, the laborer in this field will have to use such a system as I adopted. The state of morals in many of the towns along the river is deplorable; some infidel publications are already in circulation. Labor now, while the people are in this forming state, seems especially promising of good."[147]

The colportage system played an integral role in targeting the potential to be properly socialized, promoting individuals' imagination of themselves as part of a divine network of which they were already a part. "These instrumentalities," reported the ATS, "constitute one of the most powerful levers for the elevation of the human race." Colporteurs, in other words, were instrumental in targeting the population as a series of individuals. "I Visited every family," reported one colporteur, "& as a general rule conversed on the subject of personal religion." From the perspective of the colporteur, individuals were but metonyms of an essential order on the cusp of being actualized. Just as steam was converted to power according to the laws of thermodynamics, colporteurs sought to organize individuals they encountered into a working social system. "One has said that 'the colporteur enterprise is in morals what steam is in mechanics.' Whether it turns large wheels or small ones, there is precision, energy and expansion."[148]

As "laborers in the cause of truth and right worship," colporteurs embodied the institutional logic of the ATS, the success of which depended less on the absolute coordination and control of its own activities and more on its capacity to make the air dense with the concept of "true religion."[149] In report after report, colporteurs described their own success in terms of a convincing articulation of "true religion" via their tracts rather than the lasting salvation of those they encountered, the latter being the sole purview of God's judgment. These encounters are even more remark-

147. *Colporteur Reports*, 16; *Abstract of the American Bible Society*, 23; Cook, *Home Evangelization*, 83; "Pioneer Colportage," *American Messenger* (April 1858): 15.
148. *Instructions of the Executive Committee* (1859), 10; *Colporteur Reports*, 16; J. M. Sturtevant, "The American Colporteur System," *The American Biblical Repository* 55, no. 23 (July 1844): 230.
149. American Tract Society Report [Rhode Island Historical Society], October 1832, 24. On the formal structures of organization reflecting the spirit of their institutional environments rather than the letter of their mission statements, see John W. Meyer and Brian Rowan, "Institutionalized Organizations: Formal Structure as Myth and Ceremony," in *The New Institutionalism in Organizational Analysis*, ed. Walter D. Powell and Paul J. DiMaggio (Chicago: University of Chicago Press, 1991), 41–62.

able in demonstrating how opposition to the colporteur was expressed through recourse to a concept of religion that had everything to do with interior deliberation, the immediacy of knowledge, and the fact that a religion was either true or not depending on the quality of that deliberation or knowledge. As the bulk of the reports attest, the notion of a religion that is true, that one possesses it or not, that one should be interested in it or not, infused the colporteur encounter.

Saturated with the ethos of republican self-rule and the epistemic assumptions of Common Sense, the terrain of the colporteur encounter was often contested but rarely overcome. "In one district a woman refused taking a tract [because] it was a free country [and] every one had a right to enjoy their own opinion" about religion. Similarly, an irritated Universalist "said that religion was a good thing . . . but did not want any body to come tell him about his state." Another man "did not believe the tracts were true," having previously read an error-ridden tract "about a young lady who lived in the town where he formerly resided." After the agent explained to him that this tract "was not published by the American Tract Society," the man's skepticism subsided. A similar disposition toward religion was shared by a Catholic who rejected a colporteur's assertion that her doctrines "were contrary to common reason and [her] own sense." She countered with the "truth" of her religion conceived of as an interior and transformative assent to how things were in essence. Another man told a colporteur that he had already read the tract being offered "and there was nothing in it." But "he then began to read the tract to me," wrote the colporteur, "remarking on it as he went along. He inquired why the exact date was not put down? He said it was a fact they could not prove. . . . I soon found that he wished to dispute with me and as he said he was going to convert me to his religion I very soon found that he was a Roman Catholic and he began to reason with me to convince me that *that* was the only true religion." After some back and forth on ecclesiastical history, the colporteur stated that he did not consider any "denomination of religion as sufficient without a change of heart." The man agreed "and with this remark and an urgent request to call again I left him. Was there no influence exerted on that man's mind? The judgment day will show."[150]

150. Jonathan Cross, *Five Years in the Alleghanies* (New York: American Tract Society, 1863), 37–38; American Tract Society Reports [Rhode Island Historical Society], February 1834, 20; May 1833, 5; June 1833; February 1833, 9–11. David Morgan cites this final example in noting the "limits of studying production" and warning scholars not to "be swept away by [ATS] propaganda." Morgan's timely inquiry into the reception of tracts suggests a range of responses—from complicity and acquiescence to what he calls "resistance," "rejection,"

Even if the colportage system failed to get the entire population on the same page, individual reports speak of success in soliciting, even from detractors, eerily standard categories of religious normalcy and deviancy. To the degree that it was successful on this count, colporteurs cultivated a particular version of piety, affecting how individuals came to know themselves and how they would act in accordance with that knowledge. A colporteur presentation, then, was instrumental, a moment when the line between description and prescription blurred and the individual was provided with the terms of his or her individuality. Most important, such instrumentality was not lost on those encountered and surveyed by the colporteur.

To be observed by an agent of a national organization was to note the signifying aura of the rather ordinary-looking gentleman at your door. As one colporteur reported, he had "endeavored as much as circumstances would permit to leave a favourable impression on the minds of the people of the principles on which the work was prosecuted — explaining briefly the organization of the Society, its object, &c." Another ATS agent reported his conversation with a woman who was initially "reluctant." "I conversed with her some length of time endeavoring to convince her that these messengers of salvation have undoubtedly been instrumental in converting thousands of . . . souls. As I was about leaving her she asked me the title of the Tract. After telling her of the contents of it she rec'd it without hesitation and promised to read it with attention." To hear about the benevolent exploits of the ATS or the ABS was to sense an immense power directly in front of you, particularly for those who had yet to be fully integrated into a burgeoning economy of information. "As we would expect," wrote one colporteur, individuals often took "a deep interest in the work of the Society." To sense, however fleetingly, the "moral census" being compiled was to inhabit the psychological space of a statistic. "Tell

---

and "abrupt opposition" ("Studying Religion and Popular Culture: Prospects, Presuppositions, Procedures," in *Between Sacred and Profane: Researching Religion and Popular Culture*, ed. Gordon Lynch [London: I. B. Tauris, 2007], 30–33). To be sure, colporteur encounters did not simply reproduce the institutional agenda of saving souls or even the modest goal of successfully depositing tracts into households. But this is often the irony of institutions whose success depends more on generating semiotic fields than in successfully fulfilling the promise of their propaganda. The ATS, then, reproduced the categories by which true religion was understood. On institutions "as both supraorganizational patterns of activity through which humans conduct their material life" and "symbolic systems through which they categorize that activity and infuse it with meaning," see Roger Friedland and Robert R. Alford, "Bringing Society Back In: Symbols, Practices, and Institutional Contradictions," in *The New Institutionalism in Organizational Analysis*, eds. Powell and DiMaggio, 233–63.

them," instructed the national office, "that you come to offer at cost the publications of a benevolent society supported by thirteen different denominations of Christians and *then* explain to them the character of your volumes" (emphasis mine).[151]

To entertain the company of a visiting colporteur was to recognize yourself, implicitly, as an object of calculation. On the one hand, such recognition catalyzed an awareness of the moral calculus employed by the colporteur as he compiled your data, normalizing a series of binary relations integral to secularism (true religion versus false, religious affiliation versus unchurched, salvation versus "spiritual destitution," literacy versus illiteracy, temperance versus corruption). Such awareness served to intensify the authority of the colporteur's missionary premise precisely because it suggested that you were a subject who could, in fact, calculate the morality of your person and those around you. On the other hand, such recognition involved a fleeting yet powerful feeling of being a social atom that was normal precisely because you were subject to social laws.[152] For to receive a tract, book, or Bible from a colporteur was to receive a tangible sign, however small, of a vast organizing logic that was neither visible nor easily recognized. There was joy in such recognition, based not on intimacy but rather on an intimate knowledge of a network that could not, by definition, assume a singular identity. "As I called at one house this lady said on coming to the door 'how happy I am to see my tract distributor.'" The colporteur was taken aback by the intensity of the emotional display. "This lady," he took care to note, "was an entire stranger to me."[153]

At its most successful, the colporteur encounter assured the individual that he or she was significant in the universal scheme of things, that you were not alone even when you were, that even your most intimate failings possessed a social explanation (and not simply a theological one). Even encounters that colporteurs deemed to be failures could be considered successful on this count, catalyzing paranoid visions of an encroaching market or state apparatus. Although most of the people visited by colporteurs "knew" the ATS as a "giving institution," some, for example, insisted that "book-huckstering was a money making affair" and accused colporteurs of "roguery" after hearing "enough already about the Tract Society." "We have frequently had to defend" ourselves "against the charge of *dishonesty*

---

151. *Colporteur Reports*, 110, 28, 108. American Tract Society Report [Rhode Island Historical Society], September 1832, 14.

152. On the psychological power of statistics, see Ian Hacking, *The Taming of Chance* (Cambridge: Cambridge University Press, 1990).

153. American Tract Society Report [Rhode Island Historical Society], January 1833, 2.

and *of speculating* in *selling* Sacred scriptures!" wrote a trio of colporteurs in New Jersey. "A Gentleman in one instance expressed the belief that the *public money* of New Jersey was in some way appropriated, in part, to pay for these religious books—He could not tell *how* it was done—but said that he was under that impression!"[154]

The New Jersey gentleman's suspicions were perhaps unfounded, but they were not surprising given that the Society advertised—in annual reports, in speeches and sermons, in promotional tracts—its own organizational acumen. Annual reports of the ATS detailed their own business practices as a form of missionary outreach. Production numbers, distribution charts, and testimonials to the organization were "strict records of the power of religion and the grace of God."[155] In a tract published by the ATS, the Rev. Edward A. Lawrence argued that the model of "systematic beneficence" adopted by associations such as the ATS was essential to the vitality of evangelicalism. "Let them study the character and operations and claims of the various humane and benevolent associations, as exhibited in their lucid and condensed reports and other publications."[156] Other tracts took a more personal approach, relating stories of colporteurs' perseverance and success as a mark of the society's perseverance and success.[157]

Like a colporteur visitation, such meta-commentaries generated a phenomenological key by furnishing "the best illustrations of the efficiency for good, under God, of this enterprise." The presentation of "data" invited individuals to read the meaning of their own sociality and to organize their lives in accordance with the political imagination being promoted by evangelical media. Words about the distribution of words and their circulation among "the people" became tangible referents of the "public"—something that was immaterial and whose reality was purely mathematical. Meta-commentaries served the mission of media organizations by presenting knowledge about the public to the individual—the

154. *Colporteur Reports*, 78, 111, 67, 40.

155. *Twenty-Fifth Annual Report*, 41. Such reports, however, were careful to differentiate evangelical publishing from mere marketing. Tracts were not commodities. On the contrary, they were distributed in "the most inoffensive and unobtrusive way; with no magisterial authority; no claims of superior wisdom or goodness; and no alarm to human pride or forwardness" (*Address of the Executive Committee*, 6).

156. Edward A. Lawrence, *The Mission of the Church; or, Systematic Beneficence* (New York: American Tract Society, ca. 1850), 9. For a critique of such self-promotion leading to complacency among the populace, see "Systematic Benevolence," *New Englander and Yale Review* 9 (February 1851): 18.

157. *Anecdotes, Illustrating the Beneficial Effects of Religious Tracts* (New York: American Tract Society, 1832); "The Colporteur," published in the ATS's *The Child's Paper* 3 (December 1854): 45.

82   TWENTY-SEVENTH ANNUAL REPORT.   [1852.

SUMMARY VIEW OF COLPORTAGE IN THE SEVERAL STATES.

STATES.	Colporteurs.	Time of service. (M. D.)	Volumes sold.	Vols. granted.	Public or prayer meetings.	Families destitute of all religious books.	Families Rom. Catholics or fatal errorists.	Families habitually neglecting evan. preach'g.	Families conversed or pray'd with.	Whole number families visited.	Families destitute of the Bible.	Families supplied with Bibles or Testaments.
New England---	20	108 1	17,708	4,468	731	2,215	-----	3,227	14,998	21,733	515	----
Vermont------	4	18 27	2,121	582	83	359	231	879	1,389	3,021	54	93
Rhode Island ---	2	18	1,758	325	124	67	79	256	1,357	1,537	----	----
Connecticut ----	4	9 24	2,549	154	14	30	71	156	727	2,186	9	8
New York------	52	349 7	43,090	14,013	1,534	15,605	20,852	27,950	48,342	93,784	14,366	1,856
New Jersey ----	5	40 10	7,338	1,745	126	534	1,278	2,388	6,284	13,006	166	104
Pennsylvania---	63	337 8	74,514	13,168	1,032	2,195	5,080	6,405	23,550	63,376	2,344	1,352
Delaware ------	3	5 13	592	173	7	190	44	201	404	686	84	----
Maryland ------	8	73	5,145	2,614	240	765	770	1,015	3,985	12,135	----	----
D. of Columbia--	1	3 7	297	192	51	30	86	21	303	510	6	5
Virginia ------	53	282 4	34,470	12,337	1,642	2,462	492	2,502	16,769	28,072	1,080	548
North Carolina--	5	26 16	4,303	1,680	127	2,217	79	594	2,838	4,329	624	478
South Carolina--	4	6 25	595	114	50	10	3	9	140	378	----	----
Georgia -------	12	62 25	9,611	3,107	240	1,218	18	599	3,777	8,728	353	251
Alabama-------	9	70 15	12,175	3,202	431	538	102	471	3,494	6,996	529	307
Florida --------	2	13 17	1,874	813	35	110	9	37	174	776	55	41
Mississippi -----	6	40 24	10,943	2,393	174	588	15	196	2,647	3,801	413	352
Louisiana ------	8	75	9,816	2,339	69	1,547	3,302	3,637	4,638	12,164	1,727	985
Texas ---------	8	52 11	5,668	1,101	233	508	270	374	924	4,304	326	248
Arkansas------	1	4 29	949	163	73	65	4	125	353	496	38	13
Tennessee-----	22	122 23	19,757	4,790	536	2,907	309	1,381	7,788	14,264	1,116	404
Kentucky ------	15	76 3	10,411	3,095	149	2,084	753	1,698	2,803	10,878	816	427
Ohio ----------	56	384 2	61,783	19,786	949	4,725	4,060	6,422	28,934	63,634	2,090	1,808
Michigan ------	14	88 18	11,829	3,529	413	1,475	725	3,621	11,733	16,791	405	241
Indiana -------	17	114 16	14,286	5,034	614	3,303	1,173	3,344	9,313	24,361	1,504	652
Illinois -------	31	186 17	25,829	7,459	843	3,102	2,360	5,370	17,478	30,370	1,562	630
Missouri ------	22	139 26	21,167	5,848	850	2,483	1,394	2,277	6,831	18,122	1,496	995
Iowa ---------	6	38 7	3,564	1,044	190	238	416	732	2,704	5,635	189	147
Wisconsin-----	12	75 8	9,463	4,009	448	3,545	2,160	5,091	9,892	16,868	1,552	420
Canada -------	7	60 25	8,871	2,369	375	1,123	1,318	360	4,706	11,340	1,273	742
Mexico -------	1	11 23	1,545	1,261	7	2,214	1,809	2,724	1,245	4,286	1,977	420
Total----	473	2,897 11	434,021	122,907	12,390	58,452	49,262	84,062	240,520	498,567	36,751	12,793

FIGURE 7 · Summary View of Colportage 1852. *Twenty-Seventh Annual Report of the American Tract Society* (New York: American Tract Society, 1852).

reading habits of the population, its contours, its common elements. The functionality of these presentations depended on their visibility, their verification of a particular model of the public sphere directed at individuals on the verge of accepting its terms.[158]

Colporteurs may not have been able to determine, with absolute certainty, whether "any cases of conversion" could "be traced to some of the vol[ume]s."[159] Their very presence, however, not to mention the presence

158. *Twenty-Fifth Annual Report*, 64. Publicity was also an integral part of God's final judgment; see *The Sailor's Friend* (New York: American Tract Society, ca. 1825), 8.
159. *Colporteur Reports*, 64.

of the materials they carried with them, inspired the individuals they encountered to recognize themselves in a particular way and their place in the world from a particular vantage point. Such moments were tremendously complex. They were haunted by a systematicity that included the publishing agenda of the national organization, the distribution of tracts through the network of colportage, colporteurs gathering data and measuring the effects of reading, the auxiliary societies then measuring the results of these measurements, national officials receiving and translating this knowledge into further matters of decidability surrounding what tracts would be produced and when, where to distribute them, how to measure their effects, what to tell colporteurs and why. And so on and so forth.

"We leave the naked statistics to speak for themselves."[160]

9. Technologies of Voluntary Attention

In addition to their complex system of distribution and self-promotion, evangelical publishers were equally concerned with interior matters. Tracts, for example, were highly personalized affairs. Each tract was conceived and produced with an eye toward its target audience—community leaders, poor families, children, the physically or spiritually afflicted, drunkards, deists, or freethinkers.[161] Each tract was meant to be read in one's spare time and relied on the drama of direct address—"Sailor!" called out one tract, "this is the only haven of safety for your immortal soul."[162] Some tracts were even written as letters addressed directly to the reader.[163] As Harriet Beecher Stowe wrote in the *New-York Evangelist*, reform organizations were only useful to the extent that they cultivated the "interior or hidden life" as the locus of piety. For Stowe, versed as she was in the affective power of the written word, the "whole state of the times seems to call for an effort to bring back the Christian mind to a deeper internal scrutiny and life."[164]

Such nostalgia was premised on the fact that the solitary act of read-

160. Cook, *Home Evangelization*, 92.

161. See, for example, *Twenty-Sixth Annual Report*, 15–22, and *Twenty-Seventh Annual Report of the American Tract Society* (New York: American Tract Society, 1852), 18–22.

162. *The Sailor's Friend*, 5. See also Charles P. McIlvaine, *Importance of Consideration* (New York: American Tract Society, ca. 1835) and *The Talking Bible* (Philadelphia: American Sunday-School Union, 1851).

163. *Friendly Conversation* (New York: American Tract Society, ca. 1840).

164. Harriet Beecher Stowe, "The Interior or Hidden Life," *New-York Evangelist* 16 (April 1845): 61.

ing had been the lifeblood of evangelicalism since Luther's claim of "sola scriptura." Words, according to the tradition of Protestant hermeneutics (particularly as that tradition was cut with Scottish Common Sense), were not animate in and of themselves. They were anchored in but separate from the world of objects. They possessed no material force of their own but directly pointed to real reality, be it the natural world, intentionality, or God.[165] Because language was technically inert, words could be evaluated as more or less encompassing of the metaphysical veracity to which they referred. The consequences of language, then, were potentially predictable. Evangelical publishers, for example, sought to harness the representative potential of words in order to produce the clarifying effects of "truth." Because language, at base, was the means of "specific and individual description," evangelicals within the media were confident that "we are enabled to determine and fix the meanings of words in particular use; so as to give clear and intelligible definitions. . . . If this were not true we should have no physical science, and the labors of Newton, Davy, and Cuvier would turn out an utter failure."[166]

Drawing on this model of textual piety in an age of mass media, evangelical reformers derived comfort from the fact that words could provide direct access to, and personal clarification of, metaphysical order. By preaching the "Gospel to the eye," evangelical publishers imagined themselves as providing a more intimate, more immediate, and more reliable encounter with "Evangelical Truth" than could be provided by other methods.[167] In claiming to address "the mind through *the eye*" as the "living ministry" addressed the mind "through *the ear*," the ATS made a not-so-subtle case for the superiority of the written word over speech.[168] Tracts were not only more indelible versions of God's word—Latin letters lying flat that could be scrutinized by the reasoning guaranteed by Common Sense—but could be passed around, cut up and rearranged, discussed with visual certainty, and instantly recalled, unlike last Sunday's sermon.[169] Although generally

165. Charles Hodge, *Collection of Tracts in Biblical Literature* (Princeton, N.J.: Princeton Press, 1825), 58; Gardiner Spring, *A Dissertation on the Rule of Faith, Delivered at Cincinnati, Ohio, at the Annual Meeting of the American Bible Society* (New York: Leavitt, Trow, and Co., 1844), 78.

166. "Dr. Bushnell's View of Language Considered," *New-York Evangelist* 20 (15 November 1849): 182.

167. Cook, *Home Evangelization*, 50.

168. See David Morgan's "The Aura of Print," in *The Lure of Images: A History of Religion and Visual Media in America* (New York: Routledge, 2007), 7–36.

169. Nord, "Religious Reading," 262. This was in keeping with how Scottish Common Sense affirmed a decisive gap between subject and object yet denied that the distractions of con-

in favor of revivalist means of missionary outreach, evangelical publishers, not surprisingly, privileged reading as a process in which the individual could achieve "mastery over" thought and, by extension, eternal salvation.[170] Such mastery is exemplified in the confession of a "profane drunkard" and self-proclaimed "wickedest man" in the county who, on his way home from a bar, began reading a tract "with the word *Eternity* in large letters at the head of it." Being "worse for liquor" at the time, "my attention got fixed on the word *Eternity*, and I became alarmed at my state as a sinner. By the time I got home I was nearly sober. I read it and reread the tract until I had it committed to memory." Six months later the man was sober and had built a church on his property.[171]

Given their faith in language as an objective cipher of metaphysical truth, evangelical publishers promoted a particular kind of literacy as securing both "the happiness of life and the immortal interests of the soul."[172] In addition to being the most reliable vehicle for ascertaining the laws of physical existence, the act of reading promised "the discovery of the real nature of God" and knowledge of his "infinite glory."[173] In the name of aiding readers in ascertaining "Evangelical Truth" in non-biblical works, the ATS issued instructions on how to achieve self-mastery in the process of reading. The goal was to counteract the submission of "one's self to the control of fancy" and to resist becoming "the plaything of every literary harlequin who chooses to amuse and delight us." This masterful subject could then possess the real meaning of words as opposed to living "in an imaginary world." To grasp this meaning one had to read with empirical sensitivity and to approach words with technical precision. For this meaning had substance and could be objectively seen. "'We should read with *diligence*," with "*attention*," with "*practice*" and "*prayer*." "We should read with reflection—think of what we read—ponder it—compare it—weigh it—make our observations—form our own conclusions."[174]

According to evangelical treatments of the subject, the act of reading

sciousness played any role in constituting the world of perception. On this point, see Ahlstrom, "The Scottish Philosophy," 268.

170. "Training of the Mind," *New-York Evangelist* 22 (27 March 1851): 53.

171. Cross, *Five Years in the Alleghanies*, 111–12.

172. Cook, *Home Evangelization*, 52. Numerous articles on reading habits appeared in the ATS periodical, *American Messenger*.

173. *The New Birth* (New York: American Tract Society, ca. 1830), 5–6.

174. "Habits of Reading," *American Messenger* (August 1843): 33; and "The Manner of Reading," *American Messenger* (October 1845): 43. See Nord's transcription of both in *Faith in Reading*, 161–63.

was a privileged ritual of cultural production.[175] Reading was also the privileged vehicle for authorizing the peculiar discourse of evangelical secularism. On the one hand, reading would provide the most viable means of internal scrutiny demanded by "true religion." In this moment of deep examination, secular obfuscation ceased to exist precisely because the reader's "understanding is illuminated with the knowledge of *himself*." This rite of self-culture would break the "charms" of the "world" and "worldly men."[176] On the other hand, reading was a particular form of submission to the orderly essence shared by self and world, a "cultivation and development" of "mental powers" that cannot be forgone "without criminality." To "undertake seriously and systematically, a process of self-education" via reading was a "moral obligation" that would serve the "good of the country." The Bible, for example, in addition to being the readerly occasion for spiritual agency, was also a code of political security based on the continued execution of that agency. "We have a higher reason for pressing the Bible into politics," declared the *New-York Evangelist*. "*The well-being of the state imperiously demands it*. . . . All depends upon a *conformity of affection and action* to the teachings of this book. The good of the country, therefore, is promoted just as its *sentiments*—its laws and institutions come into sympathy with this legislation of heaven" (my emphasis).[177]

For evangelicals, reading promised to align the condition of the soul with the conditions of civic order. As "great instrument[s] of moral renovation," tracts precipitated and perpetuated the loop between epistemology and social conscience, "self-government" and the "rule of others." Helen Cross Knight's *The Rocket*, for example, celebrates reading and technology, or more precisely, reading as a technology of evangelical secularism. *The Rocket*, like other tract narratives, addresses issues of piety as they arise in settings that were not explicitly religious. And like many tract writers, Knight makes clear distinctions between right and wrong, piety and sin, but generates

---

175. "Books for the Fire," *New-York Evangelist* 20 (November 1849): 188. A book was judged, religiously, on the basis of its potential to contribute to the intense practice of "self-government" and, more importantly, whether it promoted both personal morality and political stability. "Bad" books, by contrast, threatened to emasculate the evangelical public sphere. "No man can do his friend or child a more real service," instructed the ATS, "than to snatch out of his hand the book that relaxes and effeminates him, lest he destroy his solids and make his fibre flaccid" ("Bad Books," *American Messenger* [March 1858]: 10).

176. *The Closet Companion; or, A Help to Self-Examination* (New York: American Tract Society, ca. 1830), 1–2; *The New Birth*, 9.

177. J. Alleine, *Pause and Think, Am I a Christian?* (New York: American Tract Society, 1831), 4; "Self-culture," *Christian Parlor Magazine* 1 (October 1844), 187; "The Supremacy of the Bible," *New-York Evangelist* 23 (19 August 1852): 133.

little tension between the truth of religious faith and the inherent order of the world.[178] Tracts such as *The Rocket* inspired readers to think about the world and interpret its signs. They informed readers as to why they should feel particular ways within the particularity of the social. "Words produce actions," intoned the keynote speaker at the 1856 convention of the American Baptist Publication Society. "The public mind, and consequently public and private transactions, are pre-eminently the product of the *Press*. From books men derive *thoughts*. These thoughts become *motives*; and those motives *action*. . . . The printed page, then, is a thing of power."[179]

The Rocket tells the story of George Stephenson (1781–1848) and his son, Robert (1803–59), civil engineers and railroad pioneers. The reader is first introduced to George, a young, illiterate boy whose first job was to tend the pumping engine at a coal factory in Newcastle, England. George "loves his engine" and keeps "it in prime order." In his "mastery" of machinery, George wanted to know more about technology. He "wished he knew the history of engines, and how they were thought out at first. Somebody told him about Watt, the father of steam-power, and that there were books which would satisfy his curiosity. Books! What good would books do poor George? He cannot read."[180]

As a plotting device, George's illiteracy was the first obstacle that, once overcome, would lead to both his salvation and "secular progress." By his late teens, George had learned to read "by the light of his engine-fire." George's reading "was to open the gates into great fields of knowledge. Read he must." George soon became well known (and more justly compensated) as an "engine doctor." Watt's steam engine had been "a curious success in its way," setting George on his path and "other minds thinking." A few years later, George introduced his son, Bobby, to "the curious and cunning power of machinery." Inspired by his father, Bobby stored "his mind with principles, facts, and illustrations" to discuss at home. Soon the son became as knowledgeable as the father when it came to matters of Scottish Philosophy. "The Edinburgh Encyclopedia was at his command as was James Ferguson's *Astronomy Explained*."[181]

---

178. [Helen Cross Knight], *The Rocket* (New York: American Tract Society, 1860). Knight wrote many works geared toward the doctrinal instruction of children. See, for example, *Reuben Kent at School, or, Influence as it Should Be* (Philadelphia: American Sunday-School Union, 1844) and her memoir of London Tract Society founder Hannah More—*A New Memoir of Hannah More; or, Life in Hall and Cottage* (New York: M. W. Dodd, 1853).
179. Cited in Nord, "Religious Reading," 247.
180. Knight, *The Rocket*, 13.
181. Ibid., 15, 24, 31, 26–28.

The remainder of *The Rocket* charts the Stephensons' engineering feats and celebrates their role in extinguishing the technophobia of the "ignorant and unthinking" masses. Their prized engine, the Rocket, was the Stephensons' contribution to the political stability of the entire globe. It was a "blessing for the world," taking its "place as one of the grand moving powers of the world." It is only in the last few pages that a recognizable religious tone is struck when Knight suddenly locates the development of the railway within the prophecies of Isaiah: "Men make good tools and instruments for themselves. They forget they are perfecting them for God also, who is using them, and who will use them to make known the precious gospel of his Son."[182] In its depiction of the political and divine orders engineered by the Stephensons, *The Rocket* stands out for its attention to technologies of automation.[183]

What is most interesting about *The Rocket*, then, is the way it invites the reader to imagine a world and its contents as calculable. It narrativizes the evangelical imperative, expressed elsewhere as the need "to act rationally, with a just reference to probable results, and these cannot be ascertained except by the exercise of our talent for calculation. Some calculations are very hard to be made, and the hardest are often the most important. Such especially is the case with those which relate to the eternal interests of the soul."[184] As Knight makes clear, the Stephensons were heroic examples. Their "singleness of purpose," Knight informs her reader, will "bring you safe to his sweet presence in heaven at last." They were smart, energetic, calculating. "*Neglect nothing,*" was their motto. To "neglect nothing" was to transform the mind into a kind of engine in which "calculations more or less intricate must be constantly made." This imperative was neither religious nor secular but something else entirely.[185] It was the cultivation of a particular code of epistemic virtue, what might be called secular objectivity.[186] Such virtue, furthermore, replicated the institutional logic of evan-

182. Ibid., 41, 99–100, 107. Such time-saving technologies should also allow for a more rigorous observance of the Sabbath (108): "Every railroad corporation is bound to be a Sabbath-keeping corporation. It *makes time enough* to do its work" (111).

183. *The Rocket* also stands out for its progressive narrative of benevolent capitalism. Like the prized engine of the story's title, "trade is one of the great progressive elements of the world. It goes ahead. It will have the right of way. It will have the right way, the best, safest, cheapest way of doing its business. Yet it is not selfish, its object is the comfort and well-being of men" (58).

184. "Heavenly Arithmetic," *New-York Evangelist* 19 (1848): 33.

185. Knight, *The Rocket*, 119–20, 114; see also *What is a Star?* (New York: American Tract Society, 1848).

186. See, for example, A. Keith, *The Evidence of Prophecy* (New York: American Tract Society, ca. 1825) as well as *The Seaman's Spy-Glass; or God's Ways and Works Discovered at Sea* (New

gelical media. "It is an important thing to think," wrote one ATS agent in the field. "The Christian should be a thinking, considering, reflecting person . . . thinking accurately, . . . thinking connectedly," and "banishing from his mind every subject which was not worthy of continuous and systematic thought." The agent then retorted, "But what has this to do with a tract report, say you?" His answer: "thinking awakens *feeling* and if we *felt* more we should strive to do more for *feeling* produces action. . . . If Christians *felt* more, they would act with greater efficiency—We should then see many of the members of our churches who ought to be Tract Distributors but who are not" become part of, and not simply the objects of, the ATS (my emphasis).[187]

The Rocket was part of a vast evangelical literature revolving around the sensuous subject of readerly attention.[188] The code of epistemic virtue that tracts were in the business of promoting, however, did little to recognize such emotive force. According to the Presbyterian minister J. H. M'Ilvaine (a "life member" of the ATS), "voluntary attention" immunized readers from "all the influences that may be at work upon us . . . so numerous and so powerful, that they constitute a disturbing element in the truthfulness of our judgments and conclusions." M'Ilvaine insisted that human consciousness, in its natural state, was resistant to forces of mediation coursing through culture.[189] If working properly, nothing could prevent it from discerning "those general laws and principles by which the facts connected with any subject are bound together."[190]

York: American Tract Society, ca. 1825), in which piety is equated with the navigational talents of a ship's captain. See also the genealogy of epistemic virtues in Lorraine Daston and Peter Galison, *Objectivity* (New York: Zone, 2007).

187. American Tract Society Report [Rhode Island Historical Society], March 1833, 12–15. The agent adds that once tracts were distributed to heathen "living in ignorance" and "abominable idolatry," that is, "get[ting] Tahiti to read," then "we may be disposed to think more highly of them."

188. See, for example, T. Carlton Henry, *Letters to an Anxious Inquirer, Designed to Relieve the Difficulties of a Friend under Serious Impressions* (Philadelphia, Key & Biddle, 1833), 177–94; John Angell James, *The Anxious Inquirer After Salvation* (New York: American Tract Society, 1838), 1–11; *Novel-Reading* (New York: American Tract Society, 1840).

189. J. H. M'Ilvaine, *A Discourse upon the Power of Voluntary Attention* (Rochester, N.Y.: D. M. Dewey, 1849), 21. "Voluntary attention" would also enable the individual to bid at an auction with assurance because that individual would make "allowance for the effect which the excitement of competition, and the arts of the salesman have upon judgment" (22).

190. Ibid., 16. According to this model of human consciousness, salvation and worldly success were all but interchangeable. On the one hand, by seeing the reality that underlies Christological symbolism, "you will see that in Him by which you will be wholly captivated—filled with passionate admiration and love. And you will be thereby transformed" (37). On the

This promise of intelligibility was premised on the world (or the tract) at hand announcing itself, from the beginning, to be a representation. "It is not on the surface, but within, under, behind all facts and outward appearances, that are to be found those causes and principles, laws and relations, which link them together, and give simplicity to complexity, unity to multiplicity, and beauty to variety."[191] In being voluntarily attentive, the subject became the interpreter of a text that had already advertised itself as allegorical. Texts in turn offered assurance that apparent discontinuity—be it the developmental tensions within a tract storyline or the disorder of the material world—was, indeed, absolutely apparent. Surface details, in either case, would be resolved by the end of the story.

Reassurance that an overarching scheme of order was operative in the most worldly of situations—on a farm, at home, on a ship, in the street—precipitated the desire to interpret texts in relation to the reader's identity—on a farm, at home, on a ship, in the street.[192] The moment of sensing a preexisting totality—either within the narrative itself or in the world to which it referred—was a moment when evangelical media practices insinuated themselves into the very pores of social being, making certain sensibilities feel right and rendering particular feelings nonsensical. In this moment the "printed page" was

> A silent language uttered to the eye,
> Which envious distance would in vain deny;
> A link to bind where circumstances part;
> A nerve of feeling stretched from heart to heart,
> Formed to convey, like an electric chain,

---

other hand, this same subject will be able to "possess," for himself, "those methods of inquiry to which we owe all the discoveries of modern times, and especially, that perfection of the natural sciences, in their application to the arts of the industrial world, in the midst of which we live" (25). Such methods were akin to gold mining—one had to know how to read the signs on the surface in order to access the deeper meaning. Unlike the "indolent Mexican hunter, and rude Indian [who] had wandered for generations over that country of which the very dust was gold, and whose stones were jewels, and knew it not," the evangelical reader was like the "man of another race [who] came, with an eye that could see." To him who "digs," the "earth revealed those inexhaustible riches" (15-16).

191. Ibid., 16.

192. See, for example, Leigh Richmond, *The Dairyman's Daughter* (New York: American Tract Society, ca. 1830); *Interesting History of Mrs. Tooly* (New York: American Tract Society, ca. 1840); *The Blue Flag* (New York: American Tract Society, 1861); *Sabbath Occupations* (New York: American Tract Society, ca. 1840); and *Saturday Night: A Dialogue Between William Ready and Robert Wise at the Pay Table* (New York: American Tract Society, ca. 1840).

The mystic flash—the lightening of the brain—
And thrill at once, through its remotest link,
The throb of passion, by a drop of ink.[193]

This "mystic flash" was nothing less than the metaphysics of secularism becoming a meta-sequence, a revelatory moment that hastened "knowledge of the conscience and an ability to direct it."[194] By speaking to lone readers in their study, evangelical tracts provided those readers with the same incentive toward and pathways of self-examination. Tracts marked those readers with the terms of their own individuality—"the liberty of being *men* and *Christians*."[195] And finally, tracts attached them to an identity that was by definition universal.

Printed pages, then, were viral matters, replicating themselves in and through the individual.[196] "Where they have Bunyan, they use his language; as so with Baxter, Dodderidge, Payson, and others. Where they have but few books, the impression is deep."[197] This mimetic process, as described by one colporteur, generated a particular kind of subject. This subject, having recognized the validity of "Republican institutions" like the ATS as well as the "ability of the people to govern themselves," readily internalized the terms of evangelical piety as the means of self-control. "The Word of God," opined the *New-York Evangelist*, "contains the elements of individual freedom. It takes the conscience into God's keeping; and when this is done with any man, or any body of men, there is an end to bondage. There is no more room for ecclesiastical or political despotism."[198]

This "end to bondage," in addition to occluding its own dependence on an elaborate network of media incentives, also prepared antebellum readers for another kind of burden. For as R. Laurence Moore has pointed out, evangelical reformers, "determined to foster the habit of reading" at midcentury, "were a major force in creating a commercially exploitable reading public in America and determining its tastes."[199] To recognize the com-

---

193. Cited in Nord, "Religious Reading," 247.
194. Foucault, "The Subject and Power," 212-14.
195. Cook, *Home Evangelization*, 145.
196. On the biologization of language among Protestant media of a later vintage, see Pamela E. Klassen, "Textual Healing: Mainstream Protestants and the Therapeutic Text, 1900-1925," *Church History* 75, no. 4 (December 2006): 809-48.
197. Quoted in Nord, *Faith in Reading*, 146.
198. *American Colporteur System* (New York: American Tract Society, 1836), 8; "The Word of God the Security of Freedom," *New-York Evangelist* 17 (14 May 1846): 79.
199. R. Laurence Moore, "Religion, Secularization, and the Shaping of the Culture Industry in Antebellum America," *American Quarterly* 41, no. 2 (June 1989): 227.

patibility between evangelical media institutions and a host of so-called secular formations of American modernity—the market revolution being perhaps the most obvious—is once again to glimpse the strange materiality of secularism, an atmosphere in which human and divine economies became conceptually distinct yet practically equivalent.[200]

10. Feedback, Security, Secularism

Evangelical media practices did not simply generate the conditions of "secular America" but were themselves conditioned by the conceptual atmosphere of secularism. This atmosphere was not antithetical to religiosity. Instead, it was saturated with those feelings, attitudes, and practices that animated definitional categories about religion. And most significantly, this atmosphere assumed material weight in the deployment of those definitions at the level of the population. Consequently, representations of "true religion" were *more* than representations and *less* than didactic schemes to inculcate specific doctrines of evangelicalism. On the contrary, they were narrative performances of secularism. By not recognizing essential differences between religious and "secular progress," narratives as diverse as *Religion in the United States*, "Christianity and Secular Progress," and *The Rocket* recontextualized the analytical and political practices of evangelicalism. They shifted their referents from creeds and institutions toward one's life in general, as it related to family, friends, and the increasing presence of strangers. To become truly religious, according to these narratives, was not to turn away from the world but to cultivate a reasonable attitude within it and an attentive disposition toward it. To become truly religious, then, was to coordinate one's attitudes and behaviors with principles essential to the maintenance of civil society.

On the one hand, the discourse of evangelical secularism conjured an overarching metaphysics to which historical details or personal habits necessarily corresponded. On the other hand, it depended on the assumption that present conditions possessed a degree of discontinuity, be it traces of despotism or illiteracy. The fact that the present had yet to correspond, fully, to a universal code gave narrative performances of

200. Although evangelical publishers did not express a consistent message regarding capitalism, their practices were nonetheless compatible with an ongoing market revolution. On the ambivalent rhetoric of ATS literature regarding the rise of the market revolution, see Mark S. Schantz, "Religious Tracts, Evangelical Reform, and the Market Revolution in Antebellum America," *Journal of the Early Republic* 17, no. 3 (Autumn 1997): 425–66.

evangelical secularism an aggressive urgency, a sense that their version of reality was in the process of becoming. These narratives thrived on a circumscribed space of necessary instability—secularity conceived of as the temporary condition of obfuscation and the promise of overcoming it. As these narratives were disseminated with technological force, their "essential function" was to imagine and domesticate the negative, "to respond to a reality in such a way that this response cancels out the reality to which it responds—nullifies it, or limits, checks, or regulates it." As "something like an imperial discourse" in antebellum America, evangelical secularism helped set the terms that all arguments about religion had to adopt in order to become intelligible.[201]

To paraphrase N. Katherine Hayles on the subject of modernity, the principle of feedback, or "reflexivity," must be appreciated if one is to begin to grasp the rich and complex history of evangelical secularism.[202] To suggest the concept of feedback as a frame for understanding the powerful narratives of evangelical secularism is not simply to note the synergy within them—how, for example, Common Sense epistemology and republican politics catalyzed the authority of one another by appealing to principles of immediacy (positive feedback). Nor is it merely to call attention to the cumulative force of these narratives, what William Ellery Channing called the "action by joint forces." Most important, the frame of feedback suggests that the circulation of these narratives has added up to more than the sum of their parts. These interrelated narratives served to reinforce their own authority in the moment of their reception and beyond—their effects feeding back into the process from which they arose. Such appreciation of feedback shifts the focus from ideology to the ways in which ideas become living convictions—self-perpetuating and enabling rather than es-

201. Foucault, *Security, Territory, Population*, 47, 3, 276. Susan M. Ryan has done much to point out the ironies of evangelical reformers in terms of race, documenting, for example, the degree to which Indian missions were expressions of "benevolent violence" and an instance of good intentions gone intensely and devastatingly awry (*The Grammar of Good Intentions: Race and the Antebellum Culture of Benevolence* [Ithaca: Cornell University Press, 2003], 25-45).

202. Hayles defines reflexivity as "the movement whereby that which has been used to generate a system is made, through a changed perspective, to become part of the system it generates" (*How We Became Posthuman: Virtual Bodies in Cybernetics, Literature, and Informatics* [Chicago: University of Chicago Press, 1999], 8-9). In a similar fashion, Foucault writes that "discourses themselves exercise their own control," which is to say that a range of individuals come to assume the same range of proclivities, internal "procedures which function rather as principles of classification" ("The Order of Discourse," in *Language and Politics*, ed. Michael J. Shapiro [New York: New York University Press, 1984], 114).

sentially misguided. From the perspective of traditional mechanics, ideological regulation amounts to sustained repetition of a single sequence. From the perspective of feedback, however, such repetition is responsive to the point of becoming a meta-sequence, "or a sequence for determining other sequences, in which a goal is compared to some outcome and action is then taken to bring the next outcome closer to the goal."[203] To account for the principle of feedback is to account for the degree to which evangelical media practices have domesticated secularism as a matter of common sense.[204]

Tract society leaders were sensitive to how their narratives were not simply commodities but words that *virtually* assumed an agentive, even biological, force. "Ponderous presses seem to have become instinct with intelligence and Christian zeal," wrote Cook. "They seize the moistened paper with their iron fingers, draw it over the waiting type, stamp it with immortal truth, and place it on a wooden hand, which lays it gently upon the table, while it *seems* to say, 'There, I have given the truth more wings, that it may fly abroad and it may fill the earth.'"[205] Indeed, the process by which these pages were imagined, inscribed, cut, bound, distributed, and read by firelight was tremendously complex. It depended on all manner of new technologies that moved beyond mere mechanics into the sphere of automation: the science of statistics (the quantification and mapping of "spiritual destitution" for the purposes of extending the "system to every portion of the land"); stereotypography (the ability to copy and

---

203. Larry Hirschhorn, *Beyond Mechanization: Work and Technology in a Postindustrial Age* (Cambridge, Mass.: MIT Press, 1984), 27. There are two broad categories of feedback: positive feedback in which the output reinforces the input, and negative feedback in which the output serves to achieve a stable situation by increasing or decreasing the input depending on a predetermined variable. Evangelical narratives of secularism possessed elements of both positive and negative feedback.

204. Pointing to the "magnificent triumphs over matter, time and space, which the swift-coming future is to unfold," Bourne noted that "in 1765, Watt . . . demonstrated the expansive force of steam, and its value as a mechanical agent; and from that time to this, steam, as the great civilizer, has only demonstrated the possibilities of the human mind." Citing the Marquis of Worchester's *Century of Inventions* (ca. 1665 and reprinted in 1825), Bourne argued that the steam engine held out the promise of securing life itself, of, perhaps, even extending life beyond the grave: "An engine, so contrived, that working the *primum mobile* forward or backward, upward or downward, circularly or cornerwise, to and fro straight, upright, or downright" and "unanimously and with harmony agreeing, they all augment and contribute strength unto the intended work and operation; and, therefore, I call this a semi-omnipotent engine, and do intend that a model thereof shall be buried with me" (Bourne, "Science and Priestcraft," 80-82).

205. Cook, *Home Evangelization*, 65-67.

store plates for subsequent print runs), steam-powered presses, and the Fourdrinier papermaking machine.[206] All four innovations, it should be noted, were central in creating the conditions for mass mediation, increasing production exponentially and reducing the cost of paper dramatically. Furthermore, they each approached or operated according to the principle of feedback: statistical data continually conditioning decisions regarding distribution; stereotypography making possible repetition without difference; the steam press in its ability to regulate both its pressure and speed; and the Fourdrinier machine measuring and responding to the density of the paper rolling off its belt in order to regulate the input of fiber.[207]

To be sure, the technological prowess of evangelicals "reconfigured traditional understandings of church bodies, local communities, and families," but it also established circuits between individuals, between individuals and the social environment in which they encountered tracts, and finally, between stories about "true religion" and the metaphysics of secularism pulsing between the lines of those stories.[208] Both the principle and application of feedback was integral to the establishment of these circuits. The evangelical embrace of feedback, then, did not simply consist of plates, levers, governors, or ink. It also consisted of the particular manner in which evangelicals invested in the social as both an organizable space and horizon of possibility. It consisted of efforts to manage the practices of reading, or more precisely, to code the symbolic space in and through which words assumed their meaning. And it consisted of evangelicals narrativizing strange loops between epistemology and politics, religious and secular progress, the individual and the population.[209]

---

206. *Twenty-Seventh Annual Report*, 53; Nord, "Evangelical Origins of Mass Media," 6, 10, 11.

207. G. M. Jenkins, "Feedforward-Feedback Control Schemes," *Encyclopedia of Statistical Sciences*, ed. Samuel Kotz and Norman L. Johnson (New York: John Wiley & Sons, 1983), 3:57.

208. Joel L. From, "Moral Economy of Nineteenth Century Evangelical Activism," *Christian Scholar's Review* 30, no. 1 (Fall 2000): 46.

209. In a paper he delivered at the American Ethnological Society, Thomas Ewbank offered "hope for the negro," arguing that the "ultimate extinction of slavery" was premised upon the "complete subjugation of the earth and the application of all its resources to human happiness." Progress, he argued, was a "fundamental law," one whose materiality would be fueled by machines—most recently by the "expansion of aqueous vapor" and now by such things as printing presses. Ewbank's was a human commitment to "systematic arrangement"—figuring out and corresponding with the "laws that govern the affairs of the world." The need for "living-motors" would decrease in proportion to the development of "motive-agents." As "unlimited amounts of force" were "drawn out of inert matter," theology would give way to technology, or more precisely, industrial labor. The new age would "look out for 'signs' of emancipation different from these they [had] been accustomed to dwell on, and acknowledge the agency of physical science to hasten its approach—and in

Like the elaborate ritual life Tommo witnessed among the Typee, evangelical media practices were significant not because they enforced religious or secular behavior. On the contrary, they were significant because they spurred the imagination of one's identity and mediated one's actions in relation to newly minted concepts of religion and secularity. For at the end of the day, evangelical secularism was anathema to evangelical understandings of how the world was in essence. To be clear, this is not to accuse mid-century evangelicals of false consciousness. I do, however, want to stress the ironies of evangelical practice, that is, how their flight from the mediating grasp of subjective bias and political institutions generated something like the imperial discourse of secularism—*the atmosphere in and through which they recognized and conducted themselves as evangelicals*. And although evangelicals were not the only Americans who breathed in this atmosphere or dispersed it through their actions, they did develop a convincing ontology that made the recognition of secularism an unreasonable proposition. The mediations of secularism, however, were as pervasive as they were incomprehensible. Indeed, the very name, "secularism," may be too specific, too precise an analytic category to encompass the affective and effective qualities of modernity. America's God was, perhaps, more god-like than antebellum evangelicals or even contemporary historians have acknowledged. Or to quote Emile Durkheim on the difficulties involved in such acknowledgment, Durkheim the student of so-called primitive ritual: "To know what the conceptions that we ourselves have not made are made of, it cannot be enough to consult our own consciousness."[210]

---

doing so they will find themselves co-workers with nature, and therefore with God" (Thomas Ewbank, *Inorganic Forces Ordained to Supercede Human Slavery* [New York: William Everdell & Sons, 1860], 26–28, 5, 21, 32).

210. Emile Durkheim, *The Elementary Forms of Religious Life*, trans. Karen E. Fields (New York: The Free Press, 1995), 18.

CHAPTER 2

· ✳ ·

TOWARD A GENEALOGY
OF SPIRITUALITY

The fear of the sea and things that come from the sea is easily spoken. The other fear is different, hard to name, the fear of things at one's back, the silent inland presence.

DON DELILLO, *The Names* (1982)

Spirituality is just a word. Yet it is a word that has assumed such a dense measure of signification over the past two centuries that it has become almost meaningless. Complicating matters further is the fact that spirituality, the word, has gained increasing cultural currency since the 1960s. As numerous studies and surveys now attest, spirituality has become the dominant tradition within recent American religious history, a way for individuals to signal their authentic mode of piety within, against, or alongside religious institutions. Spirituality, according to a representative statement from one who is "spiritual but not religious," is free from parameters, "doctrine, tradition, [and] genuflecting," whereas religion "tells you what to do and when to do it, when to kneel, when to stand up, all of that stuff. Lots of rules." In *A Secular Age*, Charles Taylor cites this statement (from an interview conducted by Wade Clark Roof) as characteristic of "religion today."[1]

According to Taylor, spirituality in the postwar era owes much of its

1. Charles Taylor, *A Secular Age* (Cambridge, Mass.: Harvard University Press, 2007), 508; Wade Clark Roof, *Spiritual Marketplace: Baby Boomers and the Remaking of American Religion* (Princeton: Princeton University Press, 1999), 137. On the common depth of individualism "underlying the diversity of religious expression among the American middle classes," see Richard Madsen, "The Archipelago of Faith: Religious Individualism and Faith Community in America Today," *American Journal of Sociology* 114, no. 5 (March 2009): 1263-1301.

conceptual density to the secular, that is, to the circulating ideals of religious freedom and the rights of solitary conscience. Numerous Americans, he writes, are "heirs of the expressive revolution" who are "seeking a kind of unity and wholeness of the self, a reclaiming of the place of feeling, against the one-sided pre-eminence of reason, and a reclaiming of the body and its pleasures from the inferior and often guilt-ridden place it has been allowed in the disciplined, instrumental identity." Taylor, however, is reticent to criticize a key term of what he calls the "age of religious searching." Despite the inherent subjectivism of spirituality, argues Taylor, against those critics who dismiss it as wholly self-satisfied, this mode of piety entertains a "belief in a transcendent reality" and aspires to a "transformation which goes beyond ordinary human flourishing." Taylor is, of course, correct in situating spirituality as central to the contemporary secular imaginary (and rooted in nineteenth-century Romanticism). He affirms in a rather roundabout way what has become a stubborn matter of statistical fact—more Americans choosing to refuse association with religious institutions. They opt out, under the assumption that one can cultivate immunity from unseemly political demands and the thick haze of religious institutions past and present.[2]

Despite Taylor's gesture toward genealogy and claim to focus on the conditions of belief, certain scholars of American religion point out how Taylor posits particular terms, from the outset, that are exempt from critical interrogation—definitive forms that change over time, of course, but forms that remain essential to what it means to be human despite whatever content is presumed to inhabit them. These forms include transcendence, transformation (and by extension his definition of religion), and the fullness of interior being (unity, wholeness, feeling) that are the markers of "the spiritual life." Yet are not the pressures that make up the prehistory of the spiritual-but-not-religious types similar to those inflecting Taylor's criteria of religiosity and insistence that religion revolves around immediacy and firsthand experience?[3]

It is my contention that Taylor's marks of spirituality—the ethic of authenticity as well as the search for unity and wholeness—are not simply phenomena within religion but discursive effects of secularism (bound up,

2. Taylor, *A Secular Age*, 507–10.
3. See, for example, Jon Butler, "Disquieted History in *A Secular Age*," in *Varieties of Secularism in a Secular Age*, ed. Michael Warner, Jonathan VanAntwerpen, and Craig Calhoun (Cambridge, Mass.: Harvard University Press, 2010), 193–216, as well as Courtney Bender, "'Every Meaning Shall Have its Homecoming Festival," delivered at the Yale conference (April 4–5, 2008) that preceded the publication of the edited book.

for example, with ideologies of the market, the triumph of the therapeutic, sentimental individualism, and the progressive telos that accompanies each). In other words, the large-scale acceptance of these desires for the "more" has as much to do with the normalization of a religious-secular continuum (the *sine qua non* of secularism) as it has to do with any putative change in the form of religion.[4] Consequently, it may be well-nigh impossible to discern all of the ingredients that have gone into the making of spirituality — as some special province of religion, a religion that is true precisely because it is set apart from institutions, traditions, and mere human mandate. One can, however, begin with the word.

In the first half of the nineteenth century the term "spirituality" began to appear with increasing frequency among Protestants of all persuasions. More often than not, spirituality was used in reference to the immateriality of God.[5] It was among liberals and their institutions, however, that spirituality became increasingly associated with the human capacity for religion and not only a quality of the divine.[6] This capacious concept of spirituality bubbled up, through, and with various cognates of "spirit." The grammatical vectors included spirit-filled, spiritual religion, spiritual discernment, spiritual activity, spiritual perception, and in 1842, the faculty of Spirituality. It was in that year the American phrenologist Orson Fowler discovered a new organ "within the cerebral limits of Marvellousness," located "on each side of Veneration" in "the middle of the top of the head." Fowler labeled this previously unacknowledged organ Spirituality. According to Fowler, Spirituality enabled the rational appreciation of "spiritual influences" and "faith" in the "reality of spirits." A healthy specimen of Spirituality secured an "interior perception of TRUTH, what

---

4. On the "Protestant-secular continuum," see Tracy Fessenden, *Culture and Redemption: Religion, the Secular, and American Literature* (Princeton: Princeton University Press, 2007).

5. See, for example, Q.S., "The Spirituality of God," *The Christian Advocate* 4 (August 1826): 349–52.

6. The transition between the immateriality of God to a state of being appears in the etymological investigations of E. S. Goodwin, a Unitarian minister from Sandwich, Mass., in 1832. "*Spirituality*, in the abstract, is the realm [kingdom] of God, which before man can See he must 'be born of Spirit,'" wrote Goodwin. "In regard to the Divine Being, I would reverentially say, that this *state* is inseparable from himself." "In regard to finite beings," he continued, "*spirituality* can be contemplated only as what is called *realm* or *region* of *mind*; a *state* in which (apart from material association and external influence) thoughts, affections, volitions, and consciousness exist and reign. By *spirituality*, then, I understand that *state* or form of existence, in which thought, affection, volition, and consciousness abide and act; not as appertaining, particularly to any individual, but as what, in proper extent, is common to all beings possessing a spiritual nature" (E. S. Goodwin, "Meaning of שלם. Third Letter from Rev. Mr. Goodwin," *The Christian Examiner and General Review* 3, no. 2 (1832): 227–28).

is BEST, what is about to transpire, etc." Its "perversion," by contrast, resulted in a lack of reason due to "superstition" and "fear of ghosts."[7] Spirituality, for Fowler and his liberal predecessors, was a strange admixture of objectivity and spirit-seeing. It was about the possibility of disenchantment in an enchanted world. It was about fixing (as opposed to exorcizing) the object of spirit, identifying its code for the purposes of communicating with it.

This communicative desire is integral to what Leigh Schmidt calls the "invention of American spirituality." Schmidt provides a necessary and subtle correction to Taylor's conjectural history, showing how a style of piety, emergent in liberal Protestant circles, changed over time. Schmidt writes that this tradition of solitary communication with divinity or transcendent authority gained momentum in the early part of the nineteenth century. He convincingly argues that this tradition has prospered, perhaps more than the scholarly record would reflect, at the edges of the evangelical fold.[8] Moreover, he patiently demonstrates the compatibility of numerous practices of transcendental communication that have emerged over the last two centuries — not only with each other but also in relation to the progressive politics of liberalism. And although I do not share Schmidt's hope for the redemptive possibilities of this tradition, I am indebted to his case that spirituality was a formal process among antebellum liberals, largely detached from any specific doctrine.[9]

---

7. "On the Functions of the Organ of Marvellousness," *American Phrenological Journal* 3, no. 8 (May 1, 1841): 361. See also O. S. and L. N. Fowler, *New Illustrated Self-Instructor in Phrenology and Physiology* (New York: Fowlers & Wells, 1859), 172, 122.

8. This, of course, does not imply that evangelicals played no role in the emergence of spirituality as a practice. See the discussion of spirituality as an aspect of "pulpit eloquence" as well as the use of "spiritual religion" to signify "true religion" in, for example, Joseph Belcher, ed., *The Baptist Pulpit of the United States* (New York: Edward H. Fletcher, 1853), 312–13; Henry Clay Fish, *History and Repository of Pulpit Eloquence* 5, no. 2 (New York: Dodd, Mead, 1850): 366; *Spiritual Religion* (New York: American Tract Society, 1830). On "spirituality" as a transdenominational piety, a mode of absorbing "the various little differences that may arise," see "Be Spiritually Minded," *New-York Evangelist* 17 (November 12, 1846): 181. After the Civil War, spirituality had become an eminently practical matter among evangelicals, a shorthand for a pious life, like a pocket watch one could lose. "Now, if we leave the door open, only on a crack," warned a character in a story published by the American Tract Society, "the world will come in and steal away our spirituality, our peace, hope, and joy, and all that is worth the Christian's having" (S. G. Ashton, "I Can Not Feel My Sinfullness," *Sabbath at Home* 1, no. 3 (May 1867): 289.

9. Leigh Eric Schmidt, *Restless Souls: The Making of American Spirituality* (San Francisco: Harper San Francisco, 2005), 6. Schmidt's defense of "democratic freedom and cosmopolitan progressivism" is indebted to and reflects the anti-institutional sensibility associated with the conceptual emergence of spirituality (290). So while Schmidt's history is elegant and useful for its content and scope, it does not question the relationship between the sensibility of anti-institutionalism and the institutional logic of liberalism. Indeed, Schmidt openly mocks the

Schmidt, like Taylor, chides those scholars who fail to see the "larger context," the sincerity, and the creativity of "contemporary American spirituality." The "stunted quality" of such assessments, argues Schmidt, is due to an inability to appreciate the politics of spirituality and the fact that more is going on here than mere navel-gazing.[10] There is real engagement with the social world. Spirituality is never an empty form but ever an embedded practice. And I agree, perversely so.

In addition to being a mode of solitary communication with the divine, spirituality also involved a tremendous amount of epistemic traffic. Information to and fro. *Lonely missives to God constituting a mediasphere.*[11] This making of spirituality occurred within ostensibly religious venues such as Unitarianism as well as ostensibly secular ones like penny presses and etiquette books. As with any discursive formation, something was added to the air, registering its effects from a distance. But perhaps what is most interesting here is how spirituality was simultaneously a mode of haunting and a means of disenchantment. For in achieving corporeal status, the concept of spirituality was integral to the imagination and maintenance of a subject who was wholly rational, truly religious, who felt at home in an uncanny world.[12]

To say as much complicates the visions of a founding subject in the works of Taylor and Schmidt. It also questions those narrative frames that assume that religion has suffered the "whammy" of disenchantment in the

---

"cynical narrative" of Jeremy Carrette and Richard King, *The Selling of Spirituality: The Silent Takeover of Religion* (London: Routledge, 2005). This book, argues Schmidt, is overly taken with the relationship between "commercialization" and "modern interiority" (21). Schmidt also objects to its suggestion that "privatized spirituality" is "a capitalist, corporate, colonial, and consumerist tool" (320). For a critique of Schmidt and Wade Clark Roof and how their work on "spirituality" has been complicit in affirming definitions of autonomy, creativity, and liberty central to liberalism's self-understanding, see Kerry Mitchell, "The Politics of Spirituality: Liberalizing the Definition of Religion" (unpublished paper delivered at "The Politics of Religion-Making," conference held at Hofstra University, October 4-6, 2007). I am indebted to Mitchell's call "to recognize the nebulous character of spirituality as a primary datum and not an analytical shortcoming." Scholars of American religion, writes Mitchell, would be "better served by an attempt to understand precisely how the indeterminacy of spirituality, and its operative categories of self and freedom, function in the maintenance of social order" (13).

10. Schmidt, *Restless Souls*, 271.

11. Which is to say that the communication integral to spirituality was also matter of epistemics and effect, that is, the gritty, embodied, and mediated work of knowing the relations between God, self, and society. For a fascinating study of communication as a discursive formation, see Armand Mattelart, *The Invention of Communication*, trans. Susan Emanuel (Minneapolis: University of Minnesota Press, 1996).

12. See, for example, O. A. Brownson, "Spirituality of Religion—Goodwin's Sermons," *The Unitarian* I (1834): 410-13.

secular age, forced to retreat to the safe haven of personalized belief. For disenchantment, I contend, has been one of the most significant enchantments of the secular age, registering its effects from a distance and in the process conjuring a host of normative assumptions about how reality is in essence. Consequently, what is most remarkable about spirituality in the antebellum period is how it reflected the impossibility of distinguishing between disenchantment and enchantment even as this division was relentlessly pursued in its name.

Given the degree to which spirituality is involved in a complex game of truth—a game that happens not so much in relation to the political but is already wholly saturated with politics—it is necessary to subject spirituality and its conceptual constellation (reasoned objectivity, transcendental communion, solitary transformation, anti-institutionalism, etc.) to thick genealogical investigation. What, for example, is the substance of transcendence being conjured at any particular moment? What forms of self are being generated in order to be transformed? What constitutes a fullness that has yet to be achieved? What is the quality of reason that makes possible a divine realm that is responsive to the nature of the human, a divine realm that can be accessed, decoded, and applied for the purposes of a human flourishing that is assumed to be its logical and natural extension?

The following investigation is informed by these questions. It begins with three stories about the stakes of spirituality in antebellum America. Each of these stories broaches the sense of security involved in addressing, for the purpose of defending oneself from, the symbolic and affective logics of institutions. Each story deals with the desire for objectivity, the language of spirit, and a style of reasoning that served to convince white Protestants in the north, however uneasily, that they were immune to various forms of emotional suasion and excess.[13] Indeed, each story involves the theorizing of affect, a penchant to examine one's mood or sensibility as it fluctuates in relation to an outside, ever with the goal of patrolling that border.

1. Three Stories of Secularism and Spirituality

In June 1850 the Harper Brothers—James, John, Joseph, and Fletcher— launched their *New Monthly Magazine*. These four Methodists from Long

---

13. See, for example, Edward Deering Mansfield, *American Education, its Principles and Elements* (New York: A. S. Barnes & Co., 1851), 81.

Island, although not part of the media empire of evangelicals, were driven by similar dreams and means of mass circulation. At the cutting edge of technological investment, marketing, and distribution, the Harpers did not simply reach a national audience but turned circulation into a fine-tuned commercial enterprise. To be sure, the content of *Harper's* often veered into explicitly theological territory. But such musings, even as they retained an evangelical cast (an occasional reference to "our fallen state"), also leaned in more liberal directions, accounting for the radical immanence of God and the process by which the "One Great Soul" does "penetrate into our most interior spirituality."[14]

Mass media, suggested *Harper's* in 1851, was a benevolent, even liberating, force. It did not impose any specific political program upon the populace. It made accessible to "the great mass of the American people, an immense amount of useful and entertaining reading matter." It was, in the end, broadly democratic, inviting individuals to sharpen their analytical skills in service of making public opinion an "honest ruler." Because objectivity was a universal inheritance, it was also the consummate value of civilized progress, a way to resist the primitive but effective reach of priestly and other infidel institutions.[15] No less an authority than Jeremy Bentham had anticipated the special providence of a periodical like *Harper's* to shape public opinion. "Bentham, speaking of those old superstitious rites by which it was intended to exorcise evil spirits, says very truly, 'In our days, and in our country, the same object is obtained, and beyond comparison more effectually, by so cheap an instrument as a common newspaper. Before the talisman, not only devils but ghosts, vampires, witches, and all their kindred tribes, are driven out of the land, never to return again! The touch of Holy Water is not so intolerable to them as the bare smell of Printer's Ink.'"[16]

14. "Editor's Table," *Harper's New Monthly Magazine* 4, no. 23 (April 1852): 700.

15. "Advertisement," *Harper's New Monthly Magazine* 1, no. 1 (June 1850): ii. As was the case with evangelicalism, such notions of benevolence were often code for anti-Catholic sentiment. Indeed, *Harper's* was not averse to presenting itself as defending the Republic from Old World institutions steeped in monarchy, Romanism, and the crass materialism that threatened it. See, for example, "The Midnight Mass: An Episode in the History of the Reign of Terror," *Harper's New Monthly Magazine* 5, no. 28 (September 1852): 340–45. On anti-Catholic sentiment associated with the appearance of spirituality, see "Christ in History," *New Englander and Yale Review* 6, no. 24 (October 1848): 519 and "The Corruption of the Lord's Supper into the Latin Mass," *New Englander and Yale Review* 11, no. 43 (August 1853): 434. See also Jenny Franchot, *Roads to Rome: The Antebellum Protestant Encounter with Catholicism* (Berkeley and Los Angeles: University of California Press, 1994).

16. "Public Opinion and the Press," *Harper's New Monthly Magazine* 2, no. 8 (January 1851): 193. Bentham's quote comes from the "Book of Fallacies" in the *Works of Jeremy Bentham*, part 8 (Edinburgh, William Tait, 1839), 400.

In citing Bentham, *Harper's* was instructing its readers to assume responsibility for disenchanting themselves in order to see clearly the world they shared. This was not an uncommon refrain among those skeptical of institutional power and who stuck closely to the script of Enlightenment in America. Disenchantment, later to be identified as *the* descriptive marker of secular modernity, already signified a process of securing the boundary between (Protestant) facts and (Catholic) fancies, certainty and uncertainty, legitimacy and illegitimacy. Long before assuming its Weberian sense, disenchantment was an epistemic practice. To set free, from a magic spell, charm, or illusion.[17] To see one's situation clearly, or at the very least, to calculate one's circumstances for the purpose of improving them. Enchantment, by contrast, was a matter of external imposition—a psychological condition to be sure but also a political pathology when a population was stricken with extreme credulity.[18]

In antebellum America, Bentham was an oft-cited example of the disenchanted gaze. He had immunized himself from the charms of the public and was therefore able to address, with epistemic confidence, the apparent murkiness of the social environment. "There never lived a man," declared another periodical, "with such a mind for the analysis of what other men have always regarded as incapable of analysis. Thoughts were weighed by him as others weigh the atmosphere."[19] Bentham's heroic objectivity—depicted as his ability to address the ambient effects of other men's thoughts—translated the logic of Scottish Common Sense into an ethical stance. Its focus was on an entity—the public—that was neither tangible, visible, nor quantifiable yet nonetheless real. This was Common Sense with a distinct Romantic edge, or at the very least a mode of know-

17. Max Weber, "Science as a Vocation," in *From Max Weber: Essays in Sociology*, ed. H. H. Gerth and C. Wright Mills (New York: Oxford University Press, 1958), 139. To be clear, mysterious incalculable forces still came into play. Yet they were encountered with expectations of transparency, assumptions of calculability, and ambitions of certainty. Their existence was at best momentary. What this state of disenchantment portended, with its submission to future calculability and infinite progress, is in part an evacuation of moral reflection, a refusal to acknowledge the self as a relational entity. This state of disenchantment, driven as it was by a calculative and instrumental rationality, was utterly uncreative because it left no room for sustained unknowing and no possibility for the world to exceed one's representations of it. Thomas A. Carlson, *The Indiscrete Image: Infinitude and Creation of the Human* (Chicago: University of Chicago Press, 2008), 117.

18. See, for example, Rufus Blakeman, *A Philosophical Essay on Credulity and Superstition; and also on Animal Fascination, or Charming* (New York: D. Appleton & Co., 1849).

19. "Jeremy Bentham," *Brother Jonathan* 5, no. 14 (August 5, 1843): 408. See also "Jeremy Bentham," *The United States Democratic Review* 8, no. 33 (September 1840): 251–57, in which Bentham is praised for his "practical cast of mind" and "cherished modes of faith" (252).

ing that addressed the formative role of public opinion and consequently the more hazy ontic corners of antebellum life.

Harper's invocation of Bentham was an implicit acknowledgment of the progressive force of "public opinion." It was also an argument for the necessity of confronting—on a personal level—the ambient nature of the social in order to counter its charms. Here was a call to focus on those things that did not immediately come into focus. It was also an invitation to cultivate knowledge about the signs and ideas that were not indigenous to the individual yet were nonetheless integral. It was, finally, about the making of a rich interior sense of being amidst the circulation of social forces.

———

This style of reasoning received its most explicit and sustained articulation among liberal Protestants who adhered to the proposition that "we are saved when we become capable of salvation." Liberals championed piety as a highly reasonable affair, so reasonable, in fact, that it accounted for the inevitability of influence—divine, of course, but also social—rather than demonize it. "Man, by constitution and circumstances," wrote Henry W. Bellows, "is so mixed up with nature, with society, with history, with the universe, with Christ, and with God, that it is never easy to see or to say where he ends and they begin, what he is in himself, and what he is only in them." Bellows, the minister of the First Unitarian Church of New York City and editor of *The Christian Examiner*, called for his parishioners to cultivate their powers of "spiritual discernment." Such discernment was necessary in order to parse complex theological points and to achieve "discrimination and clearness" about how the self was both independent from God yet wholly inspired by him. All "moral progress" depended upon discriminating "influences from around and from above." The desire to make inert vibrant matters. As Bellows insisted, "we must put things in their places and keep them there."[20]

20. Daniel Walker Howe, *The Unitarian Conscience: Harvard Moral Philosophy, 1805-1861* (Cambridge: Harvard University Press, 1970), 198; Henry W. Bellows, "Spiritual Discernment," in *Re-Statements of Christian Doctrine* (Boston: American Unitarian Association, 1867), 20, 28. See also James Walker, "Spiritual Discernment" (1854-58), in *Reason, Faith, and Duty: Sermons by James Walker* (Boston: Roberts Brothers, 1877), 202-21, at 218. Religious liberalism is an admittedly vague term that stands in for a diverse and diffuse array of ideas and practices. Scholars have relied on general characteristics to differentiate those who neither proclaimed an evangelical sensibility nor practiced within evangelical settings. This generalist approach is perhaps called for, given how such individuals moved in, out, and across

For Bellows, objectivity was the key to "Christian character." The relationality of human existence was no obstacle to systematic assessment. Indeed, spiritual discernment was virtuous precisely because everything was so connected. "Man is a social being," insisted Bellows, so "mixed up with his fellow-men," that it was necessary to study the "nature of the social habits and sentiments which greatly influence our characters." How else might the individual even notice "the police that observe him" and "the indomitable will behind them" not to mention "all the vast political machinery that quiets and controls a great metropolis"? According to Bellows, the "social order which embosoms" the individual could be neither denied nor escaped. On the contrary, to recognize society's "powers" and "charms" was to actualize one's "*un*social or independent destiny—[one's] strict individuality, . . . personal accountableness, [and] capacity for an inner solitary life." Disenchantment, here, was to recognize certain forms of enchantment as a reasonable state of affairs and mediation as a fundamental principle of faith.[21]

The affective power of society, however, was admittedly hard to fathom, let alone discern, in cities infected by what Bellows called the "trading spirit." As the circulation of goods, services, and people increased exponentially under market conditions, the "virtues of merchants" became all-pervasive. According to Bellows, the "trading spirit" was both enveloping and disorienting. "The excessive anxiety written in the American countenance," wrote Bellows, is due to "the concentration of the faculties upon an object, which in its nature is unattainable—the perpetual improvement of the outward condition . . . the restless desire to be better off." Such was "the ambition of all classes of society." City dwellers, according to Bellows, were akin to being at sea. Their observations "vitiated by an unknown current," city dwellers were subject to atmospheric conditions that they could neither control nor see beyond. The "spirit of anxious

---

mainstream denominations. Differences between religious liberals and evangelicals revolved around the willingness of liberals to emphasize, explicitly, the creative and redemptive potential of solitude as well as the immanence of divinity. Religious liberals also tended to define social justice as a religious issue because the object of such justice was the *whole* of humanity. And in keeping with their appreciation of a common human nature, liberals also made gestures of tolerance toward other religious traditions, seeing them as creative permutations of a singularly religious sensibility. See, for example, Schmidt, *Restless Souls*, 12–14.

21. Henry W. Bellows, "Spiritualism and Formalism," *Re-Statements of Christian Doctrine* (Boston: American Unitarian Association, 1867), 391; Bellows, "The Influence of the Trading Spirit Upon the Social and Moral Life of America," *The American Review: A Whig Journal of Politics, Literature, Art, and Science* I (January 1845), 94; Bellows, "Spiritual Discernment," 22–23, 29.

gain" was "infect[ious]." It was open-ended, anonymously enforced yet specific to each individual, and therefore threatening. It had caused the urban population to lose themselves—grasping anxiously for something which loomed on the horizon. Here was a diagnosis of nausea, enchantment without recourse to the "objective tendency in our nature."[22]

Bellows's argument was of a piece with other writers who depicted urban environs as unsettling.[23] In Bellows's rendering, city dwellers were made doubly anxious by economic incentives and their inability to recognize such incentives as enabling fictions. "The customs of the city in which we are brought up," lamented Bellows, "seem to most persons of divine appointment." The problem according to Bellows was not enchantment per se but the wrong kind of enchantment. Against the false gods of the city, Bellows insisted on the necessity of "awe and dreadful love and wonder" in the presence of God rather than restless communion. "Human nature," insisted Bellows, was "worthy of unspeakable, immeasurable reverence, because God informs it, because it reveals God." We had no "right," declared Bellows, "to imagine that we have begun to know, much less to measure and fathom our glorious and all-hallowed Creator." According to Bellows, enchantment was a condition of salvific freedom. For if you were not startled, truly startled, by the "powers, charms, uses, origin, [and] value" of society, then you were useless, no better than "those tribes and races . . . that live most in the bosom of nature" and therefore have "the least knowledge of her powers."[24]

———

In September 1849 Bellows visited the home of Herman Melville to baptize his son, Malcolm. The Melvilles had begun to attend, intermittently, the First Unitarian Church of New York City that February. Two years later, Ishmael, the off-and-on narrator of *Moby-Dick*, offered his own take on the charms of the city and the "commerce" that "surrounds it with her

22. Bellows, "The Influence of the Trading Spirit," 95; J.H.M., "Bushnell's Discourses," *Christian Examiner* 46 (May 1849): 475.
23. See Karen Haltunnen, *Confidence Men and Painted Women: A Study of Middle-class Culture in America, 1830–70* (New Haven: Yale University Press, 1982), 36ff.
24. Bellows, "The Influence of the Trading Spirit," 95, 94; Henry W. Bellows, "Memorial Discourse," in *The Channing Centenary in America, Great Britain, and Ireland: A Report of the Meeting held in Honor of the One Hundredth Anniversary of the Birth of William Ellery Channing,* ed. Russell Nivins Bellows (Boston: Geo. H. Ellis, 1881), 25, 33; Bellows, "Spiritual Discernment," 28.

surf."[25] In the process of introducing himself in a chapter entitled "Loom-ings," Ishmael directs the readers' attention to a magnetic curiosity—all the inhabitants of Manhattan who have crowded its southern shoreline, gazing outward toward the ocean in "mystic revelry." As Ishmael tours New York City on a "dreamy Sabbath afternoon," he is struck by how the comforting routine of city dwellers was complemented by, perhaps even dependent upon, a "mystical" attention to what looms on the horizon. "Look at the crowds of water-gazers there," Ishmael demands. "What do you see?"

> Posted like silent sentinels all around the town, stand thousands of mortal men fixed in ocean reveries. . . . But look! here come more crowds, pacing straight for the water, and seemingly bound for a dive. Strange! Nothing will content them but the extremist limit of the land; loitering under the shady lee of yonder warehouses will not suffice. No. They must get just as nigh the water as they possibly can without falling in. And there they stand—miles of them—leagues. Inlanders all. . . . Tell me, does the magnetic virtue of the needles of the compasses of all those ships attract them thither?[26]

Note how this differs from the description of urban life offered by Bellows. The crowd, here, to the degree that they hover at the edges of the sea, is not threatened by mysterious forces. Indeed, they seemingly inhabit a ground of certainty without having to account for the mysterious forces before them. In countering what had then become a literary convention, Ishmael depicts an urban spectacle pervaded by a rote calmness—a space of contemplation rather than alienation, anxiety, or distraction. There is much "magic" and "wonder" here but very little disturbance. In their abil-ity to circumscribe their own anxiety, these landsmen do not recognize the "trading spirit." They look forward and not behind them. With nei-ther Bentham's "ghosts" nor Bellows's nausea to contend with, their only concern seems to be jostling for position at land's end. "How then is this?" asks Ishmael. "Are the green fields gone? What do they do here?" Ishmael

25. Hershel Parker, *Herman Melville: A Biography*, vol. 1, *1819–1851* (Johns Hopkins Univer-sity Press, 1996), 625, 659.

26. Such ontic anchoring was the raison d'être of a romantic primitivism that gazed upon the racial and ethnic other—here the ships full of exotic immigrant passengers—in order to se-cure their own identity at their expense. That such a gaze was instrumental in colonizing the white subject is suggested by Ishmael's use of "leagues," evoking the Iroquois who, over the previous decade, had been the subject of nationalistic appropriation by Henry Schoolcraft and had, by the time *Moby-Dick* was published in the fall of 1851, become the subject of Lewis Henry Morgan's *League of the Ho-dé-no-sau-nee, or Iroquois* (Rochester: Sage & Brother, 1851).

here invites reflection on the function of this "strange" ritual and the apparent tension between landsmen's cultivation of wonder and their various states of immobility.

Rather than avoid that which looms, landsmen seem to be fixated on it, perhaps even orienting themselves in and through the disorientation that loomings portend. Oddly enough, such willed wonderment on the landsmen's part functions to anchor them, both literally and figuratively, to the land, to themselves, to their social positions. For as Ishmael suggests, there is something peculiar about how landsmen engage in such sea-gazing "meditation," pursuing a vision that had the *potential to potentially* dislodge, even as they spend their "days pent up in lath and plaster—tied to counters, nailed to benches, clinched to desks." Moreover, by concentrating on that which looms rather than on a particular material object, they seem to push Common Sense empiricism beyond its carrying capacity. Yet in doing so they renew it and, most significantly, their sense of selves in a Romantic register. And it was there—at the "extremest limits" of the land—where Common Sense reached its affective limit, that it became most effective. For what was looming, most intensely, was not necessarily beyond the sea landsmen scanned. On the contrary, it was at their back, out of sight, enabling them to gaze at the horizon in a particular and wonderful way. A story of torment overcome, transformed into the mildest of conditions.

2. Silent Inland Presence

As in the previous chapter, I am interested in the feelings, styles, and ambitions that characterize the discursive practices of secularism. This chapter revisits moments when spirituality emerged as both a designated capacity of human being and style of liberal Protestant piety advanced, in large part, within institutions. Once again, I focus on the aesthetics of conviction among a white Protestant subculture at mid-century. This genealogy of spirituality begins by addressing yet another appropriation of Scottish Common Sense, the epistemic handmaiden of secularism and the dominant mechanism by which Protestants of various persuasions convinced themselves that they believed. Spirituality, I contend, emerged from the differential tension between evangelical and liberal appropriations of Scottish Common Sense.

Like their evangelical counterparts, "Liberal Christians" were attracted to the vision of human nature and formal guarantees of certainty offered by Common Sense. In both strains of Protestant piety, ethics became a matter of ontology; the "solemn duty" of the human was fulfilled by acting upon the solemn nature of the human. In both, the epistemic freedom of the human was called upon in order to overcome threats to that same freedom. In both, a logical circularity fueled technics of measuring the self, expanding the self, and evaluating its substance. And in both cases, it was this circularity—a sense, but also the process, of words and images imploding upon themselves—that made pieties born of Scottish Common Sense such appealing propositions.[27]

At the Romantic edge of antebellum Protestantism, Common Sense philosophy promised not salvation per se but the opportunity for the individual to see himself, God, the world around, and the relationship between them. Salvation, of course, would be a natural consequence of "spiritual discernment"—an assessment of self that was at once theological and sociological. So whereas self-examination was integral to Protestantism in general, liberals may be distinguished by their focus on the "cultivation of Christian character" against the backdrop of social as well as divine influence. "I am a man acted on by other men," wrote Unitarian minister William Ellery Channing, "I am influenced by all around."[28] Channing, here, was imagining what the social was, its meaning, and how it affected him. Because God was immanent, vitally so, he assumed that such information was important for both living in the world and living beyond it. The experience of the public was part of the unfolding of divinity, a communication about rather than with God.

After distinguishing the liberal approach to Common Sense reasoning from its evangelical counterpart, this genealogy of spirituality turns to the figure of Channing, the minister of Federal Street Church in Boston from 1803 until his death in 1842. Channing was an ambient figure in the making of spirituality—an elite advocate of the working class, a media celebrity for whom Francis Hutcheson had been the "medium of awakening," a firm believer in the immanence of God and the reality (and communicability) of the spirit-world, a proponent of mental science, friends to

27. As Bellows once remarked: "Man knows God only because he is made in his rational and moral image. God is as much dependent upon our moral and rational powers for worship, communion, and filial love, as we are dependent on his holiness and loveliness and paternal character for an object which is truly adorable" (Bellows, "Memorial Discourse," 25). See also William Ellery Channing, "Self-Culture," in *Works* (1889), 15.
28. Howe, *The Unitarian Conscience*, 198; *Dr. Channing's Note-Book: Passages from the Unpublished Manuscripts of William Ellery Channing*, ed. Grace Ellery Channing (Boston: Houghton, Mifflin and Company, 1887), 33.

both Ralph Waldo Emerson and the Scotch phrenologist George Combe. According to Bellows, Channing was a "modern prophet" whose "Christian rationalism" served to forge one of the key terms and styles of liberal piety. "None have been able to escape the power of his spirituality," remarked Bellows. Others noted Channing's "spiritual energy," his "intense Christian spirituality," and his call to "comprehend the spirituality of religion." In 1838 Channing issued his summary statement about the ends and means of Unitarian piety. In his sermon "Self-Culture," he espoused the possibilities of "acting on, determining, and forming ourselves" to a "mass" of working class Bostonians. "In this country," declared Channing, "the mass of the people are distinguished by possessing means of improvement, of self-culture, possessed nowhere else."[29]

Decades after its first delivery, Channing's sermon was still a template for translating a focused interiority into the basis for public virtue. Quoting Channing, for example, *The American Gentleman's Guide to Politeness and Fashion* (1857) insisted that it was a moral imperative to "discern not only what we already are, but what we may become."[30] In Channing's wake and, more explicitly, within the rhetorical environs of mental science and moral philosophy, "spirituality" became the conceptual tissue connecting the immaterial quality of God to an individuating capacity, to an epistemic virtue common to all humans.

Moving from the elite environs of Boston Unitarianism and its orbit of

29. Channing, "Self-Culture," 14; William Henry Channing, *The Life of William Ellery Channing* (Boston: American Unitarian Association, 1899), 33; Bellows, "Memorial Discourse," in *The Channing Centenary in America, Great Britain, and Ireland*, 22, 38; Channing, "Self-Culture," 15, 12, 14; Rowland G. Hazard, *Essay on the Philosophical Character of Channing* (Boston: James Munroe and Company, 1845), 6; "The Celebration at Meadville," *The Channing Centenary*, 324; "Celebration at Madison," *The Channing Centenary*, 339. So pervasive were the encomiums surrounding Channing that the Rev. J. M. Buckley of the Methodist Episcopal Church declared Channing to be a "champion of the purest spirituality in religion." See "Celebration at Brooklyn," *The Channing Centenary*, 160. On Channing's own call, see "Life a Divine Gift," in *Works* (1889), 974.

30. Henry Lunettes, *The American Gentleman's Guide to Politeness and Fashion* (New York: Derby & Jackson, 1857), 424. For reprintings and recastings of Channing, see D. Barton Ross, *The Rhetorical Manual, or Southern Fifth Reader* (New Orleans: J. B. Steel, 1854), 282–85; Joseph Barker, *The Evangelical Reformer, and Young Man's Guide* 3 (April 1839-May 1840): 153–54 (London); *The Intellectual Repository and New Jerusalem Magazine* 2 (1841): 221–26 (London); David B. Tower and Cornelius Walker, *North American First Class Reader; the Sixth Book of Tower's Series for Common Schools* (New York: Daniel Burgess, 1855), 210–14; *The Millennial Harbinger* 7 (1850): 39–40; *The Connecticut Common School Journal* 1 (December 1838): 40–41. For an unattributed delivery of Channing's sermon, see "Superiority of Men to Animals" in *The Works of Nathaniel Emmons, D.D., Third Pastor of the Church in Franklin, Mass, with a Memoir of his Life*, ed. Jacob Ide, vol. 6 (Boston: Congregational Board, 1863), 625–41.

moral philosophy and mental science, the narrative then visits the more crowded, perhaps more peripheral precincts of the Phrenological Cabinet, located at 131 Nassau Street in New York City and headquarters of Fowlers and Wells. Beginning in 1838, their *American Phrenological Journal* (hereafter cited as *APJ*) was the centerpiece of an organizational complex whose mission was for every American to "know thyself." Through media, marketing, licensing, and therapeutics, Fowlers and Wells promoted a hands-on approach to religion that generated the experience of freedom within a framework it persistently upheld. In 1842, the year of Channing's death, Orson Fowler, who had seriously considered the Congregationalist ministry, spearheaded a revision of the religious faculties in general, and the invention of "Spirituality" in particular. Fowler's actions were precipitated by experiments in magnetic manipulation conducted with his friend La Roy Sunderland, editor of *The Magnet* and traveling magnetizer. According to Fowler, Spirituality was what made religion true—a matter of knowing, on one's own, the hidden potential lying behind material things.[31]

By the end of this chapter I hope to have offered a glimpse into three related matters: (1) a field of statements about spirituality as they appeared, circulated, and congealed in liberal Protestant circles, (2) the strange logic of disenchantment that organized them, and (3) the manner of adopting one or more of these statements in order to know oneself as religious.

3. Common Sense Differences and the Epistemics of Spirituality

The compatibility of evangelicalism and liberal Protestantism—under the sign of secularism—hinged upon their deployment of Scottish Common Sense as a means of self-examination. Conversely, the differences between

---

31. For an excellent account of phrenology's use of religious language and idioms, see Lisle Dalton, "Phrenology and Religion in Antebellum America and Whitman's *Leaves of Grass*," *Mickle Street Review* 15:1-36. To be clear, the phrenological organ of Spirituality is not the exact equivalent of the style of piety that this chapter explores. The discovery and subsequent deployment of spirituality within an examination, however, were indicative of the affective power of the concept of spirituality. "On the Functions of the Organ of Marvellousness," *APJ* 3, no. 8 (May 1, 1841): 361; O. S. and L. N. Fowler, *New Illustrated Self-Instructor in Phrenology and Physiology* (New York: Fowlers & Wells, 1859), 172, 122. On Orson Fowler's friendship with La Roy Sunderland, "Miscellany," *APJ* 4, no. 6 (June, 1842): 167-68. On the centrality of magnetic experiments in antebellum America, see Ann Taves, *Fits, Trances, and Visions: Experiencing Religion and Explaining Experience from Wesley to James* (Princeton: Princeton University Press, 1999), 141-48.

liberal and evangelical piety revolved around how Common Sense reasoning was experienced as reasonable. Spirituality was made in and through these differences.[32] These differences were not strict but made up of different assumptions about human flourishing. These differences were also bound up in media and approaches to the question of mediation. For as the ethics of Common Sense circulated across and beyond evangelical lines, into more public venues, there were subtle transformations in the object and ends of self-examination.

For evangelicals, Common Sense was central to "self-examination," which in turn sustained their "elevated standard of piety." The "conscientious Christian," as opposed to the "superficial," could not allow a "single day to pass without an investigation of his moral character." Such vigorous attention, according to evangelical readings of Common Sense, was dependent upon direct access to one's own consciousness. Such access, in turn, would defend the subject from the affective power of the object. Enchantment, here, was a target. Common Sense philosopher Thomas Reid warned his audience about the Epicurean "doctrine" that "slender films or ghosts, *tenuia rerum simulacra,* are still going off from all things and flying about; and that these being extremely subtle, easily penetrate our gross bodies." It was only Francis Bacon's "strict and severe method of induction" that promised to cultivate a "habit of attention" so as to "form clear and distinct notions of [the mind's] operations in the direct and proper way, and to reason about them." It was "knowledge alone of the capacities of the mind, that can enable a person to judge of his own acquisitions." And it was their "proper exercise" that would fend off "magical" thinking and the tendency to "spiritualize the nature of" the "medium." What others have called "species, forms, phantasms," argued Reid, "we immediately perceive" precisely because they were anchored in the solidity of the object-world.[33]

32. Which is to say that the field of statements that concerned spirituality in the antebellum period was far from homogeneous. The density and range of signification was in part an effect of secularism. Compatible significations of spirituality include: an institutional agenda (E.F., "Spirituality," *The Universalist Quarterly* 9 [July 1852]: 293–94); the mark of utter human vitality (E.F., "Spirituality," 295); a badge of human authenticity ("On Spirituality," *The Knickerbocker* 17 [April 1841]: 282–84); a state of inspired creativity ("Miss Barret's Poems," *The American Whig Review* 1, no. 1 [January 1845]: 38–49); an endowment that distinguished the human from the animal ("On Sin," *The Western Messenger* 8 [May 1840]: 17, and "The American School of Art," *The American Whig Review* 16, no. 92 [August 1852]: 140); and finally, a vague synonym for piety ("The Life and Times of Richard Baxter," *North American Review* 35, no. 76 [July 1832]: 39).

33. *Advice to a Young Christian on the Importance of Aiming at an Elevated Standard of Piety* (New York: American Tract Society, 1843), 83; Thomas Reid, *The Works of Thomas Reid with an Ac-*

The Common Sense directive to know the self by knowing the self knowing the world was not confined to evangelicals. Nor was the appeal to Bacon. Indeed, an explicit agenda of antebellum publishers was to promote desires to induce, to decipher, the fundamental laws of being by way of the most trifling details of social life. Penny presses, for example, celebrated the virtues of objectivity and themselves as securing them. These newly affordable and daily newspapers, according to the editor of the *New York Herald,* followed "the true Baconian path" in properly interpreting the details of life in general.[34]

By mid-century there existed a range of massively mediated and mediating forms that sought to provide techniques and information useful in cultivating one's humanity: from daily articles in the penny press to hydropathic encyclopedias, etiquette primers, didactic fiction, encyclopedic self-help manuals, and compendiums of inspirational biography to pamphlets, printed sermons, broadsides, and bills. In home hygiene manuals, for example, symptoms and prescriptions were coordinated with vivid biological descriptions and figures. In stories of the self-made men of America, the self became both a particular and universal phenomenon. It was a site to be worked on in the here and now, a specificity to be assessed continually, so as to make it correspond to the nature of the human. Whether emphasizing reason, memory, mystical bliss, monetary success, health, sanity, and/or status, these texts were in the business of celebrating selves that could be. For to attend to details was to have figured out the underlying principles of the self to be made.[35]

---

count of His Life by Dugald Stewart (New York, J. & J. Harper, 1822): 1:317, 320; Reid quoted in Dugald Stewart, *Elements of the Philosophy of the Human Mind* (Cambridge: Hilliard and Brown, 1829), 1:17, 50–51.

34. Ronald J. Zboray, *A Fictive People: Antebellum Economic Development and the American Reading Public* (New York: Oxford University Press, 1993), 122ff.; Michael Schudson, *Discovering the News: A Social History of American Newspapers* (New York: Basic Books, 1978), 54, 27–28.

35. John G. Cawelti, *Apostles of the Self-Made Man* (Chicago: University of Chicago Press, 1965), 55f.; *Etiquette for Gentlemen; or, Short Rules and Reflections for Conduct in Society. By a Gentleman* (Philadelphia: Lindsay and Blakiston, 1852), 21, 188. The proliferation of materials that promised personal mastery of that which all individuals shared was in part fueled by the "secular" aspirations of an urban middle-class (Haltunnen, *Confidence-Men,* 82). On the mastery one's own biology, see *The Hydropathic Encyclopedia: A System of Hydropathy and Hygiene in Eight Parts,* ed. R. T. Trall, M.D. (New York: Fowlers & Wells, 1854). In a burgeoning market economy, mastery was inevitably linked to, if not equated with, new opportunities of self-education and material benefit—choosing an occupation, forging a business partnership, entering into marriage, cultivating psychic unity, hygiene, and/or social skills. See, for example, Edward Rogers, *A Manual of Useful Knowledge: Containing a Catechetical Treatise* (Utica: DeWitt C. Grove, 1851); Hannah More, *Letters to Young Ladies* (New York: Leavitt &

By mid-century, elaborate strategies for self-making proliferated as even the most mundane activities could be pursued with solemn induction. Take, for example, *Etiquette for Gentlemen; or, Short Rules and Reflections for Conduct in Society. By a Gentleman* (1852) which suggested that "[i]n the economy of modern society, life is composed of little things; and he that is best prepared to exhibit propriety in minute affairs, will be generally best fitted for the duties of his station." These and other maxims to "attend to your person, your clothes, and everything about your person" every "moment of your life" were conceived of as decidedly apolitical, a way to become social while securing, to your advantage, a relationship between self and other. And because one's engagement with social laws was inevitable, it made perfect sense to become adept in the ways of "moral magnetism" so as to strengthen oneself in light of "frequent and long associating with others." Such discernment, moreover, resulted not in a "system of morals" or "finished plan of conduct." Instead, it was sufficient unto itself. It was a style essential for integration into the orders of social life, a way for the "public exhibitions on the great theatre of human life" to run smoothly and, in effect, reproduce themselves. It was a style in which the individual could become entirely at "ease" with the performance of "Perfect propriety."[36]

The goal of "being natural" was achieved not by public assertion but by restraint. Epistemic patience was a mark of normality. Readers, for example, were warned not to transgress the bonds of "social connexion" nor to "mention politics at a dinner-table." *Accumulate insight before making any move. Know your social coordinates. Be careful in the performance of sincerity.* For only by first discerning a relationship between self and other could one then "respect" it and fine-tune one's performance in light of it. "Persons who enter society with the intention of producing an effect, and of being distinguished, however clever they may be, are never agreeable. They are always tiresome, and often ridiculous." Instead, young men were to "present themselves with a modest assurance" so as to better "observe, hear and examine" their own actions in public. Such calculating reserve was Lord Bacon's standard of civility: acting properly because one possessed secure knowledge about the self. "No man," Bacon was reported

Allen, 1853); R. T. Trall, *The Hydropathic Encyclopedia*; William Hosmer, *The Young Man's Book or Self-Education* (Cincinnati: Henry W. Derby, 1855); *How to Do Business: A Pocket Manual of Practical Affairs and Guide to Success in Life* (New York: Fowlers & Wells, 1857).

36. *Etiquette for Gentlemen*, 224, 132; Rogers, *A Manual of Useful Knowledge*, 152, 147; More, *Letters to Young Ladies*, 11.

to have said, "will be deficient in respect towards others, who knows the value of respect to himself."[37]

The wide-ranging beatification of Bacon suggests the extent to which something like secularism had become the grammar through which differences within the Protestant canopy were expressed.[38] It was as if Reid's suggestion that one should "measure a man's understanding by the opinion he entertains of [Bacon]" had become a matter of common sense for liberal Protestants in general and their public sphere in particular. Like evangelicals and ostensibly secular publishers, liberal clergy saw in Bacon the legitimacy of their own appeal to reason. According to William Ellery Channing, Bacon was of the "highest class of minds," notable for its "range" across "heaven and earth" and its "deep intuition into the soul." Unitarians adopted Bacon as an "active" "explorer of truth." In the light of Bacon's taxonomic skills, theology was revealed to be a matter of inductive science — classifying facts, ordering classifications, and revealing a universal order. In the light of Bacon's objectivity, piety was shown to hinge upon one's ability to recognize the self, at the end of the day, in relation to the "infinite materials" that surrounded it.[39]

The use of Bacon — made by Methodists, conservative Presbyterians, etiquette manuals, progressive Unitarians, Transcendentalists, and, later, séance spiritualists who claimed to be in direct communication with him — revolved around a broadly shared approach to life in general — doggedly empirical, boldly inductive, and skeptical (at least rhetorically) of abstractions. Yet even as a wide range of Protestants invoked Bacon as a paragon of social decorum and the virtuous embodiment of Common Sense, there were subtle differences in how the relationship between ethics and epis-

---

37. *Etiquette for Gentlemen*, 219, 128–29, 217. On the performative demands of sincerity, see Haltunnen, *Confidence-Men*, 93.

38. For the most part, Protestant writers forgave Bacon for his "minor" character flaws (Bacon was convicted of accepting bribes during his term as lord chancellor of England) in light of his insistence that philosophy was the handmaiden to religion. For evangelical defenses of Bacon, see Francis Bacon, *Thoughts on Holy Scripture*, compiled by the Rev. John G. Hall (New York: American Tract Society, ca. 1836) and "Bacon's Philosophy," *Methodist Quarterly Review* 29 (1847): 22–52; Rev. Samuel Hopkins, "Religious Character of Lord Bacon," *The Biblical Repository and Classical Review*, 3d series (1847): 127–42. On liberal defenses, see Edward Everett's "Character of Lord Bacon," *North American Review* 16 (April 1823): 300–337; "Review of Hobbes' *English Works*," *Christian Examiner* 29 (January 1841): 320–35; "Lord Bacon," *Christian Examiner* 72 (March 1862): 157–82. See, also, "Lord Bacon," *New Englander and Yale Review* 10 (August 1852): 335, 374, as well as "The Relation of the Study of Jurisprudence to the Origin and Progress of the Baconian Philosophy," *New Englander and Yale Review* 6 (October 1848): 543–48.

39. Reid, *The Works of Thomas Reid*, 25; Channing, "Remarks on the Life and Character of Napoleon Bonaparte," in *Works* (1889), 524–25; *Dr. Channing's Note-Book*, 38.

temology was construed.[40] And it was from within these different registers of ambition and fear that the epistemic infrastructure of spirituality emerged.

In contrast to those evangelicals who actively rejected enchantment as a perceptual error and dismissed specters as primitive illusion, Unitarians were drawn to Common Sense because they could legitimate the empirical reality of spirit. As Channing declared, "the spiritual in common life,—this is the great discovery." Channing was often celebrated for this discovery. Whereas Bacon had revealed the laws of the physical universe, Channing was said to have done the same for those undergirding human nature. *Assessing human behavior as one would measure the arc of the sun; becoming saved in achieving a God's-eye view of one's own actions.* This was "Channingism," the "reason of Bacon" joined with the "spirituality . . . of an Augustine."[41]

Channing's confirmation of the innate potential to see one's "spirit"

40. As Ahlstrom remarked, Scottish Philosophy was "in America the handmaiden of both Unitarianism and Orthodoxy" ("The Scottish Philosophy," 257). Indeed, many inter- and intradenominational fault lines formed over arguments about the proper definition and use of Common Sense reason. As E. Brooks Holifield argues, Bacon was pervasive in antebellum Protestantism even as his eponymous philosophy generated different definitions of what, exactly, constituted the empirical (*Theology in America: Christian Thought from the Age of the Puritans to the Civil War* [New Haven: Yale University Press, 2003], 178). See also Theodore Dwight Bozeman, *Protestants in an Age of Science: The Baconian Ideal and Antebellum Religious Thought* (Chapel Hill: University of North Carolina Press, 1977), 27, 72-74. Much criticism of the new-fangled liberalism, particularly among conservative Presbyterians, focused on the non-Baconian aspects of what was pejoratively called "Pantheism," "Rationalism," and/or "Transcendentalism." See, for example, Bozeman, 134-36, as well as Charles Hodge, "The Latest Form of Infidelity," *Biblical Repertory and Princeton Review* 12 (1840): 31-71. On the compatibility between Bacon and Transcendentalism, see Ralph Waldo Emerson, "Lord Bacon," in *The Early Lectures of Ralph Waldo Emerson, vol. 1, 1833-36,* ed. Stephen E. Whicher and Robert E. Spiller (Cambridge, Mass.: Harvard University Press, 1959), 320-36. Emerson speaks of Bacon as the "Lawgiver of science and the profound and vigorous thinker who has enlarged our knowledge in the powers of man, and so our confidences in them" (325-26). It is interesting to note that Emerson heralds Bacon's enumeration of the "Causes of Error" that arise from the individual relying too heavily on the dogmas and traditions of others ("the intercourse of society and especially from language") (331). For the Unitarian critique of Emerson on Baconian grounds, see Francis Bowen's *Critical Essays on a Few Subjects Connected with the History and Present Condition of Speculative Philosophy* (1842). On communication with the spirit of Bacon, see John W. Edmonds and George T. Dexter, *Spiritualism* (New York: Partridge & Brittan 1853).

41. *Dr. Channing's Note-Book*, 89; James H. Perkins, "The Relations of Nature, Reason, and Revelation," *The Western Messenger* 8 (June 1840): 85; David Swing, "Channing as Religious Reformer," in *The Channing Centenary*, 268. On Channing's Baconian ability to observe the natural world with a telescopic degree of precision, to see clearly abstract truths, and coordinate these truths into a unifying vision, see Rowland G. Hazard, *Essay on the Philosophical Character of Channing* (Boston: James Munroe and Company, 1845), 14.

clearly—to be objective—entailed particular ways of knowing the self in the world and being in the world with others. Enchantment, from Channing's perspective, could be properly managed—not overcome but mastered. Evangelical accusations of infidelity would not negate the necessity of having to measure the self in the face of inevitable influence from afar. According to Channing, for example, the goal of "spiritual activity" was "to unite the child-like teachableness, which gratefully welcomes light from every human being who can give it, with manly resistance of opinions however current, of influences however generally revered, which do not approve themselves to our deliberate judgment." Spiritual activity, in other words, involved two different vectors. For to be passively open to the divinely inspired order of the human was also to resist, through critical judgment, when it was necessary. An elision, abstract and anxious, of docility and freedom.[42]

4. Self-Culture and the Mechanics of Transcendence

Spirituality emerged within Unitarian precincts as both a diagnosis and antidote to enchantment, a way to produce the absolute and complete truth of the individual under difficult circumstances. Spirituality, here, was not simply a quality of God. It was also a faculty of human being. It was the capacity to be cultivated, the *sine qua non* of self-culture in which the "spirituality of God" came to embody a new, true, and proper way for humans to be "religious." "Our nature is perpetually developing new senses for the perception and enjoyment of God," declared Channing:

> The human race, as it advances, does not leave religion behind it, as it leaves the shelters of caves and forests. . . . On the contrary, religion opens before the improved mind in new grandeur. . . . The soul, in proportion as it enlarges its faculties and refines its affections, possesses and discerns within itself a more and more glorious type of the Divinity, learns his spirituality in its own spiritual powers, and offers him a profounder and more inward worship.[43]

42. Channing, "Self-Culture," 24. "Men must be subjected to some law," wrote Channing, "and unless the law in their own breast, the law of God, of duty, of perfection, be adopted by their free choice as the supreme rule, they will fall under the tyranny of selfish passion, which will bow their necks for an outward yoke." Cited in Howe, *Unitarian Conscience*, 157.
43. Channing, "Unitarian Christianity Most Favorable to Piety," 388; Channing, "Christian Worship," 411.

To commune with divinity was a means of cultivating one's own potential—one's senses, one's intellect. In Channing's lofty rhetoric of perfection, spirituality was much more than communication with divinity. It was a matter of "enlargement," at once a quality of God to be imitated, an individual capacity to be perfected, and a practice without end.[44] Perpetual mental exercise would allow individuals to provide terms for God and, just as importantly, to come to terms with themselves. The exercise of human reason became a pious end unto itself, the surest method to discover its divine source.[45]

Although the "solemn duty" of self-culture would eventually render the oversight function of institutions (including religious ones) obsolete, epistemic obstacles remained. Because "the passion for belonging to a mass is strong in us all," wrote Channing, it was increasingly difficult and necessary for Americans to "see with their own eyes,—speak with their own lips." Channing warned of a power to "crush and subdue; a power which robs men of the free use of their nature, takes them out of their own hands, and compels them to bend to another's will." For Channing and other Unitarians, such warnings were necessary because degrees of compulsion were an inevitable consequence of social life.[46] Indeed, the self could be continually cultivated *because* it was complicit in the society that surrounded it. Unlike evangelicals who assumed the inviolability of consciousness, those pushing the Romantic envelope within Protestant ranks insisted that the cultivation of self involved the diligent assessment of the fluidity between self and society.[47]

44. Channing, "Spiritual Freedom," 174; Channing, "The Religious Principle in Human Nature," 936. Channing recommended such inspection in the evening hours as part of a daily program that included devotional prayer in the morning and, in the evening, a "review not only of our blessings, but our actions," recounting "irregular desires and defective motives, talents wasted and time misspent" ("Daily Prayer," 495).

45. William Henry Channing, ed., "Address at the Formation of the Berry-Street Conference," *The Life of William Ellery Channing, D.D.* (Boston: American Unitarian Association, 1899), 220. See also the widely circulated tract *Reason and Revelation* by Abiel Abbot Livermore (Boston: American Unitarian Association, 1838).

46. Channing, "Self-Culture," 15, 24; *Dr. Channing's Note-Book*, 8, 28; Channing, "Remarks on the Life and Character of Napoleon Bonaparte," 550; Channing was skeptical of the "ignorant masses" when it came to matters of policy and governance, a position Tocqueville drew upon as he formulated his own ideas about the tyranny of public opinion. "Civil liberty is not enough," wrote Channing. "There may be a tyranny of the multitude, of opinion, over the individual. . . . Popularity enslaves." See also George Wilson Pierson, *Tocqueville and Beaumont in America* (Oxford: Oxford University Press, 1938), 421–23.

47. "Our knowledge of God, man, the universe, may be reduced very much to relations," insisted Channing. "Strip man of his relations, and what do we leave of him? He has no private, no public history—no purpose—no progress—no good" (*Dr. Channing's Note-Book*, 108).

The principle of relationality was essential to the cultures of liberal Protestantism. In an effort to avoid being "turned into a mere tool, copy, echo of the public will and the public voice," liberals invoked Common Sense for the purposes of making mediation into an object of immediate inspection. In doing so, they moved beyond a strict empiricism in order to make this 'beyond' subject to rational inquiry and classification. For that which transcended material assessment included not simply divinity but also the pneumatic materialism of society. According to Channing, one's salvation depended upon the kinds of experiential ties one (forged and) acknowledged—not only with God but also with the world around. "The world is a manifestation of God, is a sphere of human action, is a source of wisdom, only so far as its relations are discovered."[48]

Enchantment, here—the state of being subject to incalculable powers— was taken as a condition of life itself. There was an implicit acceptance of living life as a networked proposition—a matter of "spiritual circulation"— linked, for better or for worse, to everything and everyone else.[49] Extricating oneself from an infinite maze of relations was by definition impossible, a position Unitarians shared with the new mesmeric psychology. Yet Unitarians mounted a vigorous defense against a surplus of relationality in their quest to be free from the charms of others.

By the late 1830s mesmerism had made inroads into liberal circles by way of the lyceum circuit as well as through those who utilized mesmerism in the business of mental healing. By the mid-1840s over two hundred professional mesmerists were active within the Unitarian precincts of Boston.[50] Mesmerism posited the existence of invisible streams that

48. *Dr. Channing's Note-Book*, 109. On the "doctrine of Divine Influences," see James Walker, "Public Opinion," in *Reason, Faith, and Duty: Sermons Preached Chiefly in College Chapel* (Boston: Roberts Brothers, 1877), 239. On the "amazing adaptability of Scottish philosophy to liberal Christian philosophy," see "Introduction," in Sydney E. Ahlstrom and Jonathan S. Carey, *An American Reformation: A Documentary History of Unitarian Christianity* (Middletown, Conn.: Wesleyan University Press, 1985), 34.

49. *Dr. Channing's Note-Book*, 30.

50. Although Unitarians were never champions of mesmerism, they did admit that its "philosophical spirit" should be applied to "reported wonders and mysteries." Review of Chauncy Hare Townshend, *Facts of Mesmerism, for Reasons for a Dispassionate Inquiry into it* (Boston: C. C. Little and James Brown, 1841), in the *Christian Examiner* 31 (November 1841): 276-77. The approval of the *Christian Examiner* extended to the "Report of the Boston Committee on Animal Magnetism" contained in this volume. By the 1850s, however, in the midst of what they viewed as the institutional threat of spiritualism, Unitarians could also offer rather damning accounts of mesmerism based on what they saw as wild and misinformed appropriations. "Miss Martineu's Gospel of Atheism," *Christian Examiner* 50 and fourth series, 15, no. 3 (May 1851): 489-502. Such skepticism, however, still held out the possibility for animal magnetism to be useful in the treatment of nervous disorders.

circulated in, through, and between living individuals. Otherwise known as animal magnetism, these streams contained energies that marked both individual vitality and one's shared humanity. The explanatory currency of mesmerism increased as cases of involuntary experiences, memory loss, split personality, and somnambulism became increasingly common. Such abnormalities could be explained away by the "secret charm[s]" of social life—how one was affected by the perceptions of others and how one's perceptions affected those perceptions. "Some may call this Animal Magnetism Spiritualized," wrote one Boston Unitarian, "but if it is not a truth, then may I be ridiculed for believing it as I do most firmly."[51]

Such reluctance was in part an acknowledgement of the tension between docility and freedom so integral to the making of spirituality in the antebellum period. Magnetism, for example, was often maligned as a salacious and predatory science, a form of social manipulation that stripped victims of their power and worth. For in the heights of a magnetic trance, the mesmerist could manipulate the path of the surrounding force field so as to recalibrate his interaction with the patient. For others, however, mesmerism made credible the circulation of spirit among humans via telepathy, telegraphy, and telekinesis. Each referred to a movement of spirit that acted with intent and across distances. These movements could also be directed if not controlled by humans for benevolent purposes. In exposing the mechanisms by which effects were registered upon the individual from afar, magnetism could be a scientific explanation of how and why individuals acted the way they did in social settings.[52] In presenting a tangible picture of affect, magnetism made enchantment into a mundane condition of freedom or, at the very least, a slightly ominous yet inevitable prospect of human being.

Animal magnetism, while not exclusively liberal in character, did offer a version of agency that resonated with Unitarian piety. Within the frames of both magnetism and self-culture, moral agency was premised upon inscriptions whose processes were incalculable. Yet in both, these processes were subject to calculation—not directly but in pathologies of

---

51. Alan Gauld, *A History of Hypnotism* (Cambridge: Cambridge University Press, 1992), 185; Taves, *Fits, Trances, and Visions,* 125f.; "Journal of George Jaques, Dec. 1840-January 1846." Doc. 372, Joseph Downs Collection and Winterthur Archives, Winterthur Museum and Library, Winterthur, Del.

52. Taves, Fits, *Trances, and Visions,* 125f. Taves has discussed in lucid terms how mesmeric psychology was central to how a variety of Americans justified or criticized Protestant revivalism (and thereby positioned themselves in relation to Protestantism and religion in general).

social influence.[53] For Channing the mastery of social circulation was an urgent matter. "Greatness is inward sovereignty. He who is not shaped by innumerable influences,—but bends them all to the ends of the moral nature,—he is great." Only then would the individual achieve *a degree* of immunity from matters economic and/or political. The acceptance of social circulation was made plain here. But then it wasn't. "I believe," continued Channing, "we have a power over the soul by which we can take it *in a great degree* out of the power of external things" (my emphasis). The promise of both magnetism and self-culture, then, was premised on a degree of immunization from the always pressing and often unreasonable claims of social custom. So whereas too much enchantment was a problem, a degree of enchantment was inevitable.

As was often the case in the making of spirituality, bets were hedged even as sentiments compelled the mind ever forward. All signs portended calculability. Despite the vibrancy of matter, the mind was in charge—a sentiment captured by Channing's strained insistence that "outward things act upon us *not so much* according to their own natures as according to our own" (emphasis mine). A strange confidence in which there was little, if any time for contradiction. "We were placed in the material creation," declared Channing, "not to be its slaves but to master it, and to make it a minister of our highest powers."[54]

5. Spiritual Faculties and Capacities

Although faculty psychology had long been integral to American Protestantism, it was during the first half of the nineteenth century that liberals consistently, and sometimes rather literally, deployed Common Sense as a conduit between the mind of man and the mind of God. And not without reason. "We have faculties for the spiritual," wrote Channing in 1841, and a "power" of "spiritual perception." Rational knowledge of the mental faculties—conscience, memory, and perception in particular—even more

---

53. The tension between enchantment and disenchantment (as well as the conflation of these states) was an integral part of the psychological vocabulary of mesmerism. So whereas disenchantment signified the process of coming out of a mesmeric state, enchantment was a rather accurate portrayal of human ontology. See *Lectures on Atomic Theory*, 273-74, printed earlier in "The Methodology of Mesmerism," *The Massachusetts Quarterly Review* 7 (June 1849): 289.

54. *Dr. Channing's Note-Book*, 25, 91, 32; William Ellery Channing, "On the Elevation of the Laboring Classes," in *Works* (1889), 42.

so than revelation, secured the ground of theological inquiry as well as pastoral care.[55] For someone like Channing, mental exercise, rather than the convulsive conversions of evangelicals, was the proper means of piety.[56] Or as Bellows put it, "Men do not spontaneously study the separation of their own minds or separate their various powers by careful analysis. Yet these powers are separable and it is immensely instructive and disciplinary to separate them."[57]

Reasonable delineation of the constituents of one's own consciousness, however, was not simply difficult work. It was a form of natural grace. "The faculties of man," continued Bellows, were "divine seeds sown in the soil of his nature." Or as James Walker flatly declared, the "spiritual faculties and capacities" were not only the *foundation* of religion in the soul of man," but had been "attested and put beyond controversy by the revelations of consciousness." Walker, Unitarian Minister, president of Harvard University, and steward of the literary presence of Reid and Stewart in America, added that the "manifestation and development of these spiritual faculties and capacities" were "essentially" related to "our idea of a perfect man." By contrast, to allow external impulses to compromise the development of spiritual faculties was to "abuse" one's "noble nature" and was nothing less than sin itself. Because "sin" was "the mind affected in a particular way," salvation was an immanent and imminent proposition. Proper habits of mental cultivation, in other words, would keep sin at bay and lead to an integrated personality. They would also lead to a convincing picture of God.[58] And they would lead to social harmony in which each individual had assessed, calibrated, and streamlined his or her own mental operations.[59]

55. Channing, "Introductory Remarks," in *Works* (1889), 11; Rev. George Bradburn, "Utility of Phrenology," *Annals of Phrenology* 2, no. 2 (August 1835): 146-47.

56. Christopher G. White has shown how liberals appealed to mental sciences to explain the nature of religious experience, the vexing subject of assurance, and the dynamics of social life in *Unsettled Minds: Psychology and the American Search for Spiritual Assurance, 1830-1940* (Berkeley: University of California Press, 2009).

57. Bellows, "Spiritual Discernment," 26-27.

58. Bellows, "'The Word of God,'" 93-94; Howe, *Unitarian Conscience*, 198, 60; James Walker, *The Philosophy of Man's Spiritual Nature in Regard to the Foundations of Faith* (Boston: American Unitarian Association), 4; Walker, "Spiritual Life," 4; *Dr. Channing's Note-Book*, 96; Channing, "Unitarian Christianity," 388.

59. Howe, *Unitarian Conscience*, 256. Consequently, proper habits were also conducive to a particular kind of politics. For as Channing argued, the harmony of the faculties was the key to the "best administration of a state" and "public prosperity" despite claims made of behalf of "political science" ("Spiritual Freedom," 173). On this point, see Channing's equation of republicanism with the "highest spiritualism," by which he meant an institution that does not impose but "honors man as man" (*Dr. Channing's Note-Book*, 13).

In framing mental science as an extension, if not a distillation, of Common Sense theism, Unitarians were integral in establishing the tradition of moral science as the raison d'être of Protestant seminaries and colleges.[60] Taken up by those educators who sought to frame Christianity in general as a science of investigating the "law of life," moral science affirmed that the "perpetual and complete self-culture of every bodily and mental faculty is due in the right of our own spiritual being, and [it] is unworthy of any man to neglect any portion of his person which admits of improvement. The general maxim is,— SECURE A COMPLETE SELF-DEVELOPMENT." Moral science also revolved around the "controlling law" of the human that was "above" human nature yet located within each human. "Moral science," wrote Laurens Hickok, "must find its [determining] principle within the spiritual part of man's being." Once this principle was located, it was then possible to erect "a system of morals" by "extending" it through "systematic application."[61]

Moral science was not solely a liberal invention. It was, however, integral to the making of spirituality in liberal circles. For to practice the "morality" of self-culture was in turn to practice "true piety."[62] Moreover, to actualize "the spiritual and self-controlling of the rational in man" was also to "rise into the higher light of a purely philosophical consciousness, and become familiar with *a priori* principles and transcendental demonstration." Such was the movement beyond the "tribunal of Common Sense" in which "we pass from the facts of experience wholly out beyond it, and seek for the rationale of experience itself in the necessary and universal principles which must be conditional for all facts of a possible experience."[63]

Mental science, here, became an administrative means, a benevolent

---

60. "Psychology" was a term popularized by Dugald Stewart and defined by Thomas Reid as the systematic study of the "nature and operations of minds" (*The Works of Thomas Reid*, x). Mental Science became institutionalized in such works as Thomas C. Upham's *Elements of Intellectual Philosophy* (1827), popular among the Scotch Realists at Princeton Seminary, and Thomas Brown's *Philosophy of the Mind* (1827), edited by Levi Hedge and central to the educational sculpting of Unitarianism as a tradition.

61. Laurens P. Hickok, *A System of Moral Science* (Schenectady: G. Y. Van Debogert, 1853), 87–88, 60, iii–iv.

62. Unlike "superstition," the proper "spiritual discipline" would "invigorate [rather] than enfeeble the human system." Enfeeblement, here, was the mark of "barbarous" peoples, those hopelessly enchanted souls who had "abdicate[d] the authority of [their] own rationality" rather than submit to the "righteous authority" within themselves. Hickok, *A System of Moral Science*, 73–74, 82.

63. Laurens P. Hickok, *Rational Psychology; or, The Subjective Idea and Objective Law of All Intelligence* (New York: Ivison, Phinney, Blakeman & Co., 1867), iii, 13–14.

way to cultivate a reasonable piety in those who had known nothing but superstition and idol worship. In the 1850s, for example, English Unitarian Charles Dall used both Channing's celebrity and mesmerism to pursue missionary activity on the Indian subcontinent. Dall's moral science was premised on the potential for Indians to become truly religious, that is, to sever all material ties and to be bound only to the abstractions of God and their shared humanity. "Protestantism absolves man from all allegiance short of God in religious things, just as democracy absolves men from all allegiance short of humanity in secular things."[64]

6. The American Institution of Phrenology

The road to self-improvement is thus fairly and fully opened; and the *first* step to be taken is for every one who would walk therein to STUDY HIMSELF. Self-knowledge will show you just what you *are*, and the principle of balance already explained, what you should *become*, and that of the increase of organs, how to become what you should be. As, before you can repair a watch, you must ascertain what portion of it is out of order; so, before you can do the first correct thing towards self-improvement, except by accident, you must know exactly wherein you depart from the true standard of mental and moral perfection.

    o. s. FOWLER, *Education and Self-Improvement, Founded on Physiology and Phrenology: or, What Constitutes Good Heads and Bodies, and How to Make Them Good, by Enlarging Deficiencies and Diminishing Excesses* (New York: Fowlers and Wells, 1844)

To have honed in on the psychological dimension of piety as the basis for knowing and being in the world is to have already assumed that whatever faculties exist inside are not only shared by all but applicable to every nook and cranny of the world. There was a grandeur here, an articulation of the soul that moved beyond what Common Sense philosophers called pneumatology and toward a social science that was both theological and physiological. Such grandeur was integral to the distillation of Unitarian piety into spirituality. Such grandeur fueled the evolution of mental science into

---

64. C.H.A. Dall, *Human Brotherhood, The True Church of Jesus* (Calcutta: J. P. Bellamy, 1856), 4. Channing, Tuckerman, and Ware had all been involved in the establishment of the Society for the Promotion of Christianity in India (1825). For a discussion of the colonial imagination of Unitarians, see Spencer Lavan, *Unitarians and India: A Study in Encounter and Response* (Boston: Beacon Press, 1977). See, also, Peter van der Veer, *Imperial Encounters: Religion and Modernity in India and Britain* (Princeton: Princeton University Press, 2001), 44f.

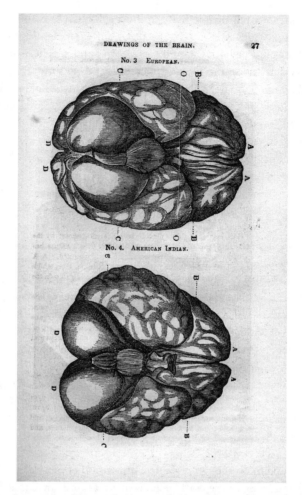

FIGURE 8 · A comparison between the European brain and the American Indian brain. "AA are placed at the frontal portion of the intellectual lobe, which AA, BB enclose, and which is much longer and fuller in the European than Indian Brain." From O. S. Fowler's *Memory and Intellectual Improvement Applied to Self-Education and Juvenile Instruction* (New York: Fowlers and Wells, 1847), 27.

a science of morals. And such grandeur, at least for our purposes, made spirituality recognizable as a formation of secularism, a liberal style of piety in which religion, politics, and epistemology congealed at the level of affect even as they became different components of the brain. So the different names became specific biological entities (and therefore subject to comparison and pathology) even as the institutional phenomena they served to categorize became utterly diffuse. A difference, for example, between Europeans and American Indians was the shape and size of their frontal lobe, itself the site of the intellectual faculties, otherwise known as the physico-perceptive group.

Phrenology was unapologetic in making empiricist assumptions that the brain itself was the surface of mental depth, the material expression of a spiritual essence. Moreover, the brain was a composite of different but interdependent faculties that could be measured in terms of size and proportionality. And finally, as an applied science of human nature, phrenology prescribed regimes of cultivating and/or curtailing growth. Phrenology was "useful as a system of moral and metaphysical philosophy" in which consciousness of the object-world—of seeing things as they really were—was not simply premised upon self-consciousness but was wholly conflated with it.[65] In this scheme, mental faculties or organs were sensual components of the thinking subject—for to examine oneself phrenologically was to think about each of the organs as instruments of reason and consequently to be able to trust in them because one has attained a degree of control over them.

Phrenology had made some inroads into the U.S. by the time the American Unitarian Association was founded in Boston in 1825. But it was not until the arrival of Dr. Johann Spurzheim (and later, George Combe) in the United States that the new human science gained a wide following. Spurzheim was a disciple of Franz Joseph Gall, the Viennese physician credited with the invention of phrenology. In September 1832 Spurzheim began a series of well-publicized lectures at the Boston Athenaeum. They became at first a minor sensation and, upon Spurzheim's untimely death that November, a major one that generated much interest in phrenology and spawned societies throughout the northeast.[66] Channing and other Unitarian leaders attended the funeral of the "noble-minded" Spurzheim.[67] Channing, in a remark that was laudatory despite striking a humorous

65. George Bradburn, "Utility of Phrenology," 133–34. For a Hegelian reading of phrenology, see Mark C. Taylor, *Hiding* (Chicago: University of Chicago Press, 1997), 13–15.
66. On this incident and the history of phrenology in America in general, see Madeleine B. Stern, *Heads & Headliners: The Phrenological Fowlers* (Norman: University of Oklahoma Press, 1971). As Harriet Martineau wrote at the time, "when Spurzheim was in America, the great mass of society became phrenologists in a day . . . all caps and wigs . . . [were] pulled off, and all fair tresses disheveled, in the search after organization" (*Retrospect of Western Travel* [London: Saunders and Otley, 1838], 3:201).
67. Channing, "Discourse on the Life and Character of the Rev. Dr. Tuckerman," in *Works* (1889), 595; "Death of Dr. Spurzheim," *The Boston Medical and Surgical Journal* (November 14, 1832), 226.

note at phrenology's expense, once wrote to a friend that Spurzheim had possessed a "singular insight into human nature" and that "phrenological writings" contributed "excellent views on the subject of the improvement of the human race. I have at this moment a phrenological head and brain on my table, and a young lady by the side of it, of a fine intellect and character, who has studied the science. She has been polite enough to find all the nobler organs in my head, so that I have no personal objections to the truth of the doctrine."[68]

In general, Unitarians displayed little objection to phrenology, as the liberal environs of Boston became "the phrenological emporium on this side of the Atlantic." The Boston Phrenological Society (BPS), founded by Spurzheim's business manager and publisher, became a space where Unitarian theology mixed freely with phrenological sentiment.[69] Leaders of the BPS included Unitarian ministers—George Bradburn, Joseph Tuckerman, as well as John Pierpont (who would turn from Congregationalism to Unitarianism in 1845). The BPS confirmed that phrenology "settles the question of religion" by demonstrating that humans were inherently religious, that religion was linked to the exercise of agency, and that the "religious philosophy" of phrenology was the spiritual essence of Christianity. Indeed, "true religion" implied the perfect manifestation of "the personality, the *I*" that could be encountered only if one were able to give God, himself, a phrenological examination.[70]

68. Anna Letitia Le Breton, ed., *Correspondence of William Ellery Channing and Lucy Aikin, from 1826 to 1842* (Boston: Roberts Brothers, 1874), 159. Channing also befriended the phrenologist George Combe as he toured America in the late 1830s. It is not surprising, then, that Channing's contemporaries aligned him with the phrenological cause despite Channing's stated reservations about reductive materialism (*Dr. Channing's Note-Book*, 99). In February 1835, for example, the Unitarian minister Joseph Tuckerman delivered a lecture to the Boston Phrenological Society in which he argued that "the Philosophy of that celebrated Divine [Channing] and the doctrines of phrenology were based on the same fundamental principles of the mind" (*Annals of Phrenology* 2, no. 4 [February 1836]: 502). In 1841 Channing was accused of being a phrenologist by *Tait's Edinburgh Magazine* ("Mr. Combe's Notes on the United States, During a Phrenological Visit, 1839-42," *Tait's Edinburgh Magazine* 8 [April 1841]: 242).

69. Silas Jones, *Practical Phrenology* (Boston: Russell, Shattuck, & Williams, 1836). The Boston Phrenological Society had inherited much of Spurzheim's collection of casts, masks, and skulls. Their 1835 catalog listed hundreds of specimens, including Jeremy Bentham, Samuel Taylor Coleridge, Francis Bacon, and Rene Descartes. See *A Catalogue of Phrenological Specimens, Belonging to the Boston Phrenological Society* (Boston: John Ford, 1835).

70. "Phrenology and Religion," *Annals of Phrenology* 2, no. 2 (August 1835): 153, 158-59. Moreover, phrenology was able not only to explain the evolution of the religious faculties within history but to compare and judge different religious traditions based on craniological evidence (155-57).

Within the BPS, there was a concerted effort to frame phrenology as both true religion and true science of the mind—"its laws are the laws of the human mind; that it has interpreted truly the revelations of God written in the constitution of man's spiritual nature."[71] In 1834, the BPS enlisted a sermon by James Walker into the phrenological cause, reprinting it with suggestive annotations. A year later, Walker himself declared that "an exact analysis of the mental faculties" was not itself sufficient to secure one's "spiritual well-being." Instead, he urged his parishioners to go beyond the cold taxonomies of mental science toward something that sounded much like phrenology. The individual aspiring to "spiritual well-being" must investigate how the mind "acts, on being variously affected and modified, as it is, by peculiarities of temperament and circumstances. . . . And this he must study in the living subject;—in himself." Despite the talk of vitality, the dead body on the table is you. For within your own mind lies the history of the "religious sentiments . . . which are to our profession what collected specimens of morbid anatomy are to the physician."[72]

By the mid-1840s the firm of Fowlers and Wells had turned phrenology into both a spectacle and a thriving publishing enterprise, due in part to their ability to appeal directly to Unitarian sympathies and prejudices.[73] The brothers Orson and Lorenzo Fowler, alongside the businessman Samuel Wells and his wife Charlotte Fowler, quite literally picked up where the BPS left off in the late 1830s.[74] They endorsed the idea that phrenology was "destined to form a new era in Christianity." Their stated goal was to "Phrenologize Our Nation," phrenology being "the crowning essence of true religion" and as such that which cut across Protestant dif-

---

71. Elisah Bartlett, M.D., "An Address delivered at the Anniversary Celebration of the Birth of Spurzheim and of the Organization of the Boston Phrenological Society, January 1, 1838," *American Phrenological Journal* 1, no. 5 (February 1, 1839): 149.

72. James Walker, "A Sermon preached at the dedication of the Second Congregational Church in Leicester," *Annals of Phrenology* 1, no. 3 (November 1834): 391-98; James Walker, *A Discourse on the Law of Spiritual Life* (Boston: American Unitarian Association, 1835), 11.

73. See, for example, the republication of Channing's sermon, "The Arrogance of Wealth—by Dr. Channing," in *American Phrenological Journal* 5:139-41. In addition to such praise, Fowler and Wells explicitly targeted Unitarians. See, for example, the "phrenological conversion" of a contemporary doubting Thomas—the anti-phrenologist S. Dean, a "Unitarian clergyman of acknowledged talents, and considerable critical acumen" (*American Phrenological Journal* 4, no. 7 [July 1842]: 176-78).

74. See "Lectures of Mr. George Combe, in Boston and New York, with a Brief History of Phrenology and its Present State in the Former Place," *American Phrenological Journal* 1, no. 4 (January 1, 1839): 118-28. See also "Phrenological Lectures and Examinations of Messrs. Fowlers in Boston," *American Phrenological Journal* 3, no. 9 (June 1, 1841): 430-32.

ferences.[75] Under the auspices of Fowlers and Wells, phrenology became a therapeutic brand, advertised, cross-marketed, and disseminated through both word and deed. In addition to their Boston and Philadelphia offices, their vaunted Phrenological Cabinet at the corner of Beekman and Nassau Streets in New York City served as a publishing house, phrenological museum, exhibit and store, a lecture booking service, and private examination room.

An exam cost three dollars. In addition to providing exams on-site, the Phrenological Cabinet also offered training sessions and private lessons for those who would then return home and offer their own examinations. These examinations would be based, of course, on the Fowlers and Wells code and would incorporate their busts, literature, and even instruments. There was an intense intimacy to the exam, a blend of psychoanalysis and scalp massage. The subject was initially sized up for any obvious signs of temperament or profession. After the initial assessment the physical exam began. Once the general shape and size of the skull was determined by measuring tape, the examiner would then sketch a rough diagram of the patient's head in order to compare the relative development of various regions — the domestic propensities located in the back of the head, the selfish propensities located on either side of the head above the ear, the faculties of reason located in the front of the head, and the moral sentiments located at the very top of the head.[76] These regions were in turn subdivided into individual faculties. A skilled examiner knew, for example, that Concentrativeness was under Self-esteem, behind Destructiveness, and over Adhesiveness and Inhabitiveness. The physical examination culminated in the measurement of each of these faculties using calipers, craniometers, fingers, and informed judgment. Each faculty was measured according to a 1 (very small) to 7 (very large) scale.

An exam was advertised as a prophetic revelation of what lay deep

---

75. "Boston Phrenological Society," *American Phrenological Journal* 2, no. 5 (February 1, 1840): 235; "The American Phrenological Journal for 1849," *American Phrenological Journal* 11 (1849): 10; "Progression a Law of Nature: Its Application to Human Improvement, Collective and Individual," *American Phrenological Journal* 8 (August 1846): 240. As will be discussed in chapter 4, phrenology also possessed an evangelical hue, due in part to Orson's interest in the Congregational ministry as well as his desire to appeal to evangelical desire to missionize in the name of "true religion." As the *APJ* instructed, readers were to missionize their neighbors by measuring their heads — this direct approach being the "best mode of convincing unbelievers of its truth" ("Rules for Finding the Organs," *APJ* 11 [1849]: 116). See also Stern, *Heads & Headliners*, 12.

76. "Rules for Finding the Organs," 116–17.

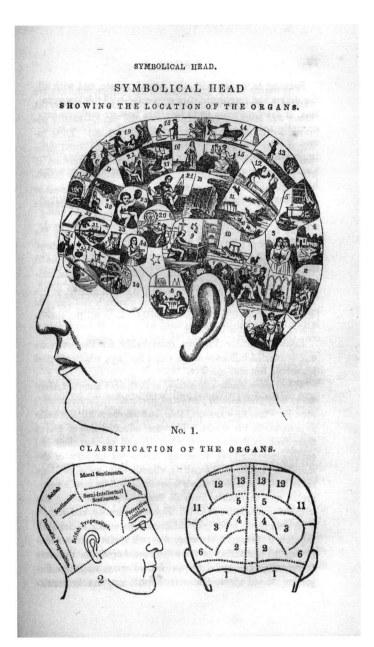

FIGURE 9 · Symbolical Head from L. N. Fowler's *Marriage: Its History and Ceremonies with Phrenological and Physiological Exposition of the Functions and Qualifications for Happy Marriages* (New York: Fowlers and Wells, 1848), 73.

within the recesses of self. Its effect was total self-knowledge. Its purpose, however, was not simply to catalyze attention but to "enable persons to adapt themselves to each other."[77] In that regard, a phrenological examination often diagnosed one's individuality, originality, and imagination even as it prescribed the need for submission. This submission was, of course, an intricate matter, involving the recognition of your own code as that of phrenology and then acting, somewhat independently, upon that code with the goal of overcoming weakness and developing strengths that you have recognized as essential to the self. "You are more original than imitative," wrote L. N. Fowler in 1848 while examining the head of James Terry. "Do not copy the manners of others but act out of your own nature without duplicity or affectation." Terry was praised for his ability to "read the character and motions of action of those with whom you associate." Yet Fowler also instructed Terry to "adapt yourself more agreeably to others, to be more pliable in society. Your are inclined to radicalism, for you think for yourself and your imagination being active you forget the present in thoughts of the future." As Fowler admitted, certain of Terry's organs "require[d] discipline" in light of the human standard set by phrenology. "Learn to have more balance and harmony, apply them to your own organization, and perfect your character as much as possible."[78]

As a tourist attraction, the Phrenological Cabinet competed with Barnum's American Museum for the attention and money of visitors. Admission was free. Once inside Clinton Hall, the visitor experienced a barrage of visual stimuli in accordance with the Fowlers' insistence that "to learn, we must first Observe, and to do this, must have Things to look at." The halls of Fowlers and Wells contained a "sea of heads"—"popes, and cardinals, and architects . . . Luther, and Huss, and Baxter . . . Clay, and Calhoun, and Clinton . . . Wellington and Napoleon, Burr and Hamilton" as well as "excellent moderns" such as "Channing." The Cabinet also displayed casts and skulls of Native Americans, idiots, and other vicious characters in order to reveal the necessary exceptions to the rule of human potential. A visitor to the Cabinet could purchase an array of items—books, celebrity busts, plaster casts, human as well as animal skulls, models of the brain with removable parts, life-sized anatomical drawings, and wired skeletons. By the mid-1850s, Fowlers and Wells were procuring, advertising, and selling patent rights with particular focus on technologies that

77. "Importance of a Phrenological Examination," *APJ* 20 (August 1854): 38.
78. "Phrenological Description of James Terry by L. N. Fowler, March 10, 1848." James Terry Papers, Winterthur Museum and Library, Winterthur, Del.

furthered their reform enterprise such as galvanic machines and breast pumps.[79]

The marketing of phrenology by Fowlers and Wells depended upon positioning phrenology as eminently practical and useful.[80] Taking aim at "philosophizing phrenologists," the *APJ* successfully translated the explicit anti-monarchialism of Edinburgh's *Phrenological Journal* into populist codings of republicanism and critiques of elite treatises of philosophy.[81] These elite treatises included, of course, those of Reid and Stewart, whom were periodically accused in the pages of the *American Phrenological Journal* of self-absorption, political ineptitude, and being incapable of offering a clear picture of what faculties, exactly, constituted the human mind and how they were related.[82] Such protestations, however, did not signal a rejection of Common Sense realism but rather a reframing of its fundamental insights into a more useful, hands-on, and nurturing epistemology.[83] "How important," exclaimed Fowler in the key of Common Sense, "that man should understand his moral nature and obey its laws!"[84] Common Sense, here, became an eminently practical endeavor, appealing to those who were not privy to the works of Reid or Stewart. So even though phrenology had been ridiculed by the likes of Dugald Stewart "and other men of undoubted talent and information," Fowler knew enough about public opinion to have positioned phrenology as an outgrowth of the Scottish Enlightenment.[85]

To this end Fowler sought to usurp the origin story of Common Sense, locating the birth of phrenology in Bacon's "extraordinarily" large head. Not only were his "perceptive and reasoning organs ... wonderfully developed," but they were organized and integrated. "In this wonderful man, all the conditions of phrenology meet, all its requirements are fulfilled,

79. Stern, *Heads & Headliners*, 59–60; "Man Measurement," *APJ* 26 (1857): 71; "Patent Office Department," *APJ* 21 (April 1855): 91.

80. As a "systematic science," phrenology was the surest means of choosing a compatible spouse, an occupation, an employee, or a personality best suited to one's "developments." Fowler, *Self-Instructor*, 176; Stern, *Heads & Headlines*, 38; "Man Measurement," 71.

81. Fowler, *Education and Self-improvement*, 146; Steven Shapin, "Phrenological Knowledge and the Social Structure of Early Nineteenth-Century Edinburgh," *Annals of Science* 32 (1975): 237.

82. "On the Comparative Merits of Phrenology, and the Philosophy of Reid and Stewart," *APJ* 3, no. 12 (Sept. 1841): 530, 534–35. See also G. N. Cantor, "A Critique of Shapin's Social Interpretation of the Edinburgh Phrenology Debate," *Annals of Science* 33 (1975): 208.

83. The *APJ* was incensed, for example, at the rudeness of Dugald Stewart, who refused to meet with Spurzheim ("Biography of Dr. Spurzheim," *APJ* 3, no. 1 [October 1840]: 4–5).

84. O. S. Fowler, *Religion; Natural and Revealed: or, The Natural Theology and Moral Bearings of Phrenology* (New York: Fowlers & Wells, 1844), 16.

85. See reprint of "Remarks on the Natural Laws of Man," *APJ* 3 (September 1, 1840): 32.

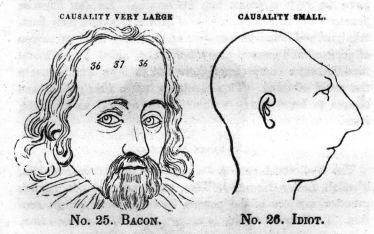

It is also very large in the accompanying engraving of Bacon, but small in that of an idiot.

CAUSALITY VERY LARGE   CAUSALITY SMALL.

36   37   36

No. 25. BACON.   No. 26. IDIOT.

It is large in Herschel, as seen in the expanse of his fore-head, and the prominances at this point; but retreats in Bur-ritt. In Franklin this organ was immensely developed [417], and his talents form an excellent sample of the cast of mind it imparts.

15

FIGURE 10 · Diptych of Francis Bacon and "Idiot" from O. S. Fowler's *Memory and Intellectual Improvement Applied to Self-Education and Juvenile Instruction* (New York: Fowlers and Wells, 1847), 169.

and of course there is no chance for the slightest equivocation." Given his "unusual endowment of ideality," Bacon was able to make metaphysical inquiry a matter of empirical observation. This was in keeping with the fact that the "uses" of calculation were "incalculably great." For in displacing the anticipation of nature with a map of nature, Bacon was able to discern the invisible structures that held things together and consequently the connections between what was on the inside of your head and everything else.[86]

86. "Analysis, Adaptation, Location, and Cultivation of Calculation," *APJ* 8 (1846): 251; "Observations Upon the Character and Philosophy of Lord Bacon," *APJ* 3, no. 5 (February 1, 1841): 193-96; Fowler, *Self-Instructor*, 131-32. On Bacon as antidote to the distractions of social life, see "Public Opinion and Taste," *The Christian Reformer, Or, Unitarian Magazine and*

The head of Bacon also signaled the condition of epistemic control to which phrenology aspired. Bacon, unlike Native Americans, Africans, and idiots, was a wholly realized agent. Having large reasoning organs and harmonious interactions between his intellectual faculties, Bacon was able to direct his own attention. Having subdued his animal organs to the necessary degree, Bacon had achieved a kind of humanity that was lacking (but not an impossibility) among primitive peoples. The juxtaposition between Bacon and an idiot, for example, served to exaggerate who and who had not received the gospel of phrenology. Unable to talk, feed, or think for himself, the idiot was hopelessly enchanted. He was overwhelmed by a mimetic compulsion, repeating "instinctively" all he heard and imitating the gestures and actions of others "with the greatest fidelity."[87] Such overwhelming instinct, of course, was precisely what phrenology sought to counter—the too-muchness of anything and everything surrounding an essential self.

According to phrenology, the specter of imbalance was at once a political and epistemic problem. The increasing public visibility of racial and ethnic others threatened the clean lines and smooth workings that lent support to the dense hierarchies of white privilege. This ideology was also ever threatened from within, given that phrenology posited that the mind was materially divided.[88] Exclusions, in other words, were a matter of political and cognitive necessity. A violence that went unacknowledged as it became integral to the imagined security and normalization of a white normality.[89]

7. Believing in Ghosts In Order Not To

As we have already seen, the emergence of spirituality as the human capacity for religion hinged upon the anxious elision of docility and free-

Review 4 (July 1848): 428. English Unitarians attributed to Bacon a science of fashion that addresses the "atmospheric" processes of mass media.

87. "Review of Lecture on Phrenology by Frank H. Hamilton, M.D.," *APJ* 4, no. 9 (September 1, 1842): 262–63. See also Thomas C. Upham's citation of Gall on idiocy in *Elements of Mental Philosophy* (New York: Harper & Brothers, 1845), 2:376.

88. Phrenological literature was heavily annotated with reports of doppelgangers, derangements, lunacy, and other mental disturbances. See, for example, "Cases of Spectral Illusions Confirmatory of Phrenology," *American Phrenological Journal* 1, no. 5 (February 1, 1839): 135–48; "Case of Mono-mania," *APJ* 1, no. 5 (February 1, 1839): 155–57; W.F., "Double Personal Appearances," *APJ* 22 (July 1855): 2–3.

89. On the drift of marking ethnic difference from the language of religion to the language of attention to the grammars of scientific assessment, see Franchot, *Roads to Rome*, 54–55, as well as Fessenden, *Culture and Redemption*, 111–36.

dom, enchantment and disenchantment. Indeed, the achievement of the latter in either case was dependent on the persistence of the former. In a similar fashion, the possibility of "self-losing" was integral to the metaphysics of phrenology, perhaps even more so than in Unitarianism and the scientific study of morals. For phrenologists, insanity and other forms of self-losing were corporeal diseases. Those who were mentally disturbed embodied pathological exaggerations of various faculties and were therefore of demonstrative value.[90] Far more disturbing than any single case of insanity was the universal susceptibility to insanity that phrenological understandings of the self implied. If the self was functionally divided into various faculties, then what, if anything, could be the principle or force of unification?

Upon assuming editorship of the *American Phrenological Journal* in 1842, Orson Fowler's first order of business was to address an apparent tension between an insistence on both the divisibility and unity of the self. As articles and references to animal magnetism increased in the pages of *APJ*, Fowler became more intimately involved in the experiments of itinerant mesmerist La Roy Sunderland. At Sunderland's side, Fowler witnessed firsthand the spectacular credibility that magnetism could provide phrenology.[91] Not only did Fowler begin to frame phrenology in terms of magnetic psychology, but he also used this frame to counter lingering concerns and accusations that phrenology left no space for free will. Resolving the tension between submission and agency, enchantment and disenchantment, however, was a delicate and perhaps even impossible task.

Whatever anxiety over self-losing had been present in the pages of the

90. Channing once warned: "We live in a world where, if we please, we may forget ourselves. . . . In the present life we have, as I have said, the means of escaping, amusing, and forgetting ourselves" ("The Evil of Sin," in *Works* [1889], 352). For Laurens P. Hickok, the self did not necessarily "remain and retain itself at the centre." For "so soon as there is a self-finding there is also" the possibility of "self-losing" (Hickok, *Rational Cosmology: or, The Eternal Principles and the Necessary Laws of the Universe* [New York: D. Appleton & Co., 1858], 253); John D. Davies, *Phrenology: Fad and Science, a 19th Century Crusade* (New Haven: Yale University Press, 1955), 89.

91. Orson Fowler, "My Proposed Course," *APJ* 4, no. 1 (January 1, 1842): 1–8. In this same issue Fowler began to make the case for the truth and utility of animal magnetism; "The Phrenological Organs Excited by Means of Animal Magnetism," *APJ* 4, no. 1 (January 1, 1842): 46–53. See also "Phrenology and Animal Magnetism," *APJ* 4, no. 8 (August 1842): 213–18. In 1847 Fowlers and Wells published *Fascination; or the Philosophy of Charming* by John B. Newman, M.D. This short book rebranded the theory and history of animal magnetism under the name of fascination, paying respect to the ideas of Franz Anton Mesmer but arguing that his understandings of magnetic phenomena were both derivative and overly obscure. "Mesmerism did not discover anything new," wrote Newman as he gestured toward others theories of magnetism then in circulation, including Sunderland's (13–14).

American Phrenological Journal, under Fowler's editorship there began to appear forceful affirmations of the magnetic state as the site of agency.[92] In adopting a hands-on approach to magnetism (as opposed to the more ethereal and often unacknowledged embrace of Unitarians), the multimedia company of Fowlers and Wells affirmed that "[o]ur existence commences in the process of magnetizing."[93] First and foremost, Fowlers and Wells argued that animal magnetism was the most effective and empowering antidote to various forms of mental imbalance. Indeed, under magnetic influence the encounter with the phrenological examiner became wholly therapeutic—a way for the individual to become his or herself. The examiner would first pass his hand from the top of the patient's head down the side of the face, neck, and arms. He would then seek to detect specific derangements of forces and disturbances of current within the patient. Once located, the "rectification of magnetic disorder" could proceed, as the examiner redirected the flow of magnetic force through and between organs. Consequently, induction of the magnetic state could recover autonomy by countering situations in which one's mental faculties were out of balance or when the psyche had been "overpower[ed] by allurement."[94] Again, enchantment serving disenchanted ends.[95]

On another level, the *APJ* celebrated magnetism as a way to reveal the truth of phrenological categories. Magnetism was a vehicle of scientific inquiry because it exposed, with empirical rigor, the array of functions within the mind and the boundaries between them. On both the lyceum circuit and in the Phrenological Cabinet, Fowler would magnetize specific faculties of a living subject in order to demonstrate their existence for all to see. "On magnetizing any organ," reported Fowler, "the spontaneous

---

92. Fowler's proposed course may also have been a response to the critical letters received by the *APJ* regarding their earlier treatment of phrenology's relation to fatalism and moral responsibility. For even in the attempt to clarify itself, the *APJ* offered sophisticated yet convoluted defenses of the "free agency of man." The "phrenological argument is, that man must be a free being, and that the freedom expressed in the term liberty, as applied to choice of, and motives between, is inherent in his nature of which he cannot be divested, and which is self-determined by the consciousness it endures. . . . Then man is necessarily free, [but] not from choice . . . but it is the necessity which makes the freedom" ("Moral Agency," *APJ* 2, no. 8 [May 1, 1840]: 374–75).

93. "Living Magnetism," *APJ* 5, no. 1 (January 1843): 14, 23.

94. "Magnetism as Remedial Agent," *APJ* 11 (1849): 185–86; Stern, *Heads & Headliners,* 71; La Roy Sunderland, *Book of Psychology: Pathetism, Historical, Philosophical, Practical* (New York: Stearns and Company, 1853), 26.

95. "This wonderful field of knowledge having been thus cleared of the hedges and specters with which it was encompassed by ignorance and fanaticism, may now be entered with safety" ("Living Magnetism," *APJ* 5, no. 1 [January 1843]: 8).

function of its faculty is thus stripped of all artificial influences, and exhibits itself in its naked, primitive state." When Philoprogenitiveness was activated, for example a patient on stage would begin "fondling as though they held a child." When Veneration, alone, was excited, "they uplifted their hands and repeated the Lord's Prayer."[96]

On still another level, Fowler used mesmerism as an evidentiary technic and way to justify his revision of Spurzheim's map of the faculties. "No sooner had an application of Animal Magnetism been made to Phrenology," wrote Fowler, that he had discovered both new organs and, more significantly, the function of the "space between the organs": "There was a considerable unappropriated space between the organs, and, on *this* account, the organs are not wholly surrounded by those dotted lines which form their boundaries." So even though each organ was an agent, each of the organs was part of a network. Differences between the organs constituted their purpose and served to either bind them together or not. Fowler's mesmeric insights precipitated new names for organs, new numbers and groupings, and consequently, a new "symbolical head" that displayed eighty-three organs in contrast to the thirty-five originally named by Spurzheim (and the thirty-eight that had been cited the previous year in the *APJ*).[97]

The magnetic condition governing the faculties was but a microcosm of how bodies interacted in space, how within society each human was "surrounded and pervaded by *its* own distinctive aura" and in "contact with" other "magnetic atmospheres" that "mutually act upon each other." Indeed, the intensity of interdependence was likened to a kind of viral logic.[98] Fowler's magnetized vision of faculty interaction was also an argument about the kind of agency one could expect to achieve within society. For whereas disorder between faculties compromised agency, their harmonious interaction signaled something akin to free will. Agency, there-

96. O. S. Fowler, *Religion; Natural and Revealed*, 51; "Phreno-Magnetism," *APJ* 5, no. 6 (June 1843): 275–78. Upon completion of the demonstration, the person who had been magnetized was then able to ascertain the state of his or her physiognomy. For to become magnetized was to gain access to the pathways of the magnetic forces "mov[ing] along the nerves" and coursing through the body's organs, a clarity of phrenological vision that was not possible in the "natural waking state" ("Living Magnetism," 18, 21–22).

97. "Phrenology and Animal Magnetism," *APJ* 4, no. 9 (September 1, 1842): 225–30; J. G. Spurzheim, *Phrenology, in Connexion with the Study of Physiognomy, To which is Prefixed a Biography of the Author by Nahum Capen* (Boston: Marsh, Capen & Lyon, 1833), 157.

98. W.F., "Animal Magnetism," *APJ* 13, no. 2 (February 1851): 39–41. "This doctrine of personal magnetic spheres, and of the volatile and penetrating electroid essences of other bodies, involves the *rationale* of contagious and infectious diseases" (40).

fore, and the singularity it implied, were matters of relationality. According to the *APJ*, agency arose not from any single organ but from the lines of force that unified them all. "In the act of thinking," declared the *APJ*, magnetic forces "move from the great pole in the centre of the brain. . . . We therefore think by the action of these forces." And what was at the center? Where did these forces come from? "Our *will* or the engineer which determines our actions," was the answer. Here, again, was the animating tension of spirituality. Ambiguity. Italicization. Hedging. And with only the slightest of hesitations. "Our *will* or the engineer."[99]

8. True Religion Before the Invention of Spirituality

As a self-described "religious science," phrenology advertised itself as "the only system of mental philosophy, which makes us acquainted with the precise character and number of the faculties of the mind which belong to" the "moral and religious nature" of the human.[100] Such appeals were aimed directly at those who already considered themselves religious, particularly those who remained skeptical about revivalism.[101] In offering their readers a "correct test and touchstone of true and false religion," Fowlers and Wells idealized a style of piety that was vaguely liberal and explicitly

99. "Living Magnetism," 24. As with the ideal symmetry at the core of republican theory, the "debate of the faculties" was a communal exercise of personal agency ("Debate of the Faculties," *APJ* 13:49-50; 73-75). And while the debates between faculties could become heated, phrenologists insisted that "the faculties be trained all to work *harmoniously* with each other, and never be allowed to *conflict* or *quarrel* with each other" (Fowler, *Education and Self-Improvement*, 157). Here were psychic and political economies that did not simply lead to the kinds of overlapping consensus envisioned by liberalism but that were themselves premised upon the impossibility of real (i.e., sustained) conflict. Debate, in other words, was ever harmonious. Otherwise, something would be amiss. The members of the BPS, not as galvanized by republicanism as Fowlers and Wells, were more forthcoming in their assessment of the debates between faculties. "The human mind is not a democracy," declared the Society. "The human mind is a hierarchy" ("Phrenology and Religion," *Annals of Phrenology* 2, no. 2 [August 1835]: 158).

100. "On the Abuse or Perversion of Certain Faculties in Religion," *APJ* 3, no. 11 (August 1, 1841): 517-21.

101. A phrenological exam could diagnose, simultaneously, one's aptitude for business and religion. For example, Thomas R. Hazard was praised for his ability to "execute business on an extensive level" and then told that his "religion consists in doing right and doing good more than in faith or religious feeling of any kind." This invitation to feel more religious was effective when framed, for example, alongside one's "mathematical talent" or ability to "engage in speculations in stock and real estate." It framed religious experience as something one could practice, develop, and perfect. "Phrenological Character of Thomas R. Hazard by Dr. Butler, 10.6.54" (Rhode Island Historical Society).

removed from the more emotional precincts of evangelicalism.[102] For it was only after a phrenological examination that "every individual" would "see at a glance the departures of his own religious opinions and practices from . . . the true standard of our nature, pointed out by Phrenology." This standard, in turn, conformed to the *"perfection* of Christian character" and resulted in "the true, spiritual worship of God."[103] And although Fowlers and Wells claimed to be above the sectarian fray, they took aim at fellow Protestants for descending into Catholic institutionalism, ceremonialism, and intolerance. Orson Fowler criticized those who would corset on the Sabbath, those who participated in revivals ("Revivals," wrote Fowler, "are to the mind what artificial stimulants are to the body"), as well as "those who *pretend* to be *liberal*." Indeed, Fowler criticized Unitarians and Universalists, already drawn to the tenets of mental science and magnetism, for not upholding their professed liberalism, which for Fowler meant embracing phreno-magnetism.[104]

The proper quality of liberal piety implied harmony between the moral sentiments.[105] According to phrenology, the moral sentiments were simultaneously the most human of all the faculties and, quite literally, the ones closest to God. In the early 1840s, before the invention of Spirituality, these included *Veneration* in the center of the top of the head, between Benevolence and Firmness; *Benevolence* was an inch in front of Veneration; *Marvellousness* was located on either side of Veneration; *Hope* was found on either side of the forepart of Firmness; *Conscientiousness* on the two sides of

102. Fowler, *Religion*, 76. Public demonstrations of phrenology, however, were not unrelated to the evidentiary effect of revivalism. When a clergyman from Clinton, N.Y., was magnetized in 1843, for example, an experiment was conducted. "The Instant his Combativeness was touched, he arose, clenched his hands, and squared off for a fight, and became unmanageable. In order to prevent his injuring some one, his Benevolence and Veneration were touched; and he burst forth into a most fervent strain of prayer; and yet wanted to fight, but restrained himself from considerations of its impropriety in a clergyman, and because praying and fighting did not harmonize well together" ("Phreno Magnetism," *APJ* 5, no. 1 [January 1843]: 42).

103. Fowler, *Religion*, 59–60. Fowler provided a phrenological map of Protestant denominations based on how the organ of Veneration (the very center of religiosity) was inflected by the other faculties. Universalists, for example, had an abundance of Benevolence, Calvinists an excess of Conscientiousness, and Quakers no shared trait other than their weekly proximity to one another (Fowler, *Religion*, 56, 59). See also the explanation of religious differences based on physiognomy in *APJ* 8:321–23.

104. Fowler, *Religion*, 88, 233, 69, 72.

105. For a more expansive view of true religion being a product of cerebral organization, see Universalist minister T. J. Sawyer's "Influence of Cerebral Organization on Religious Opinions and Beliefs," *APJ* 3, no. 10 (July 1, 1841): 433–51.

the back of Firmness, above and anterior to Circumspection.[106] Together, these faculties determined the degree to which the individual was a "moral, accountable, and religious being." Indeed, harmony between these faculties was the mark of salvation and the freedom that accompanied it.[107]

Upon closer inspection, however, much of the rhetoric surrounding the moral sentiments was about their overlapping functions of submission. "By the still, small voice of these sentiments," wrote Fowler in 1842, "man instinctively *feels* that he should be governed. He is intuitively conscious of his obligation to yield obedience to their mandates. He *feels* their dictates to be *imperious* and *sovereign*."[108] Veneration, for example, the primary religious faculty, granted one the ability for creaturely adoration and "create[d] the feeling of awe of God." As Fowler reported, "I have never seen the back part of Veneration magnetized without also seeing the subject clasp and raise the hands in the attitude of worship, assume a devotional aspect and tone of voice, and express a desire to pray, or else break forth in the worship of God, enraptured in contemplating him."[109] But Veneration was not simply about God but equally about the capacity to defer to "elders and superiors." Consequently, Veneration was a "conservative faculty" that valued the principles of order and "avoid[ed] sudden changes and radicalism."[110]

Veneration provided the means of surrendering properly—to God,

---

106. L. N. Fowler, *A Phrenological Guide, Designed for Students of Their Own Character* (New York: L. N. Fowler, 1844), 38–43.

107. Fowler, *Education and Self-Improvement*, 2; Fowler, *Self-Instructor*, 115. As the seat of sovereignty, the religious sentiments governed, guided, directed, and restrained all the other propensities. Moreover, the religious sentiments regulated the influence of all the other faculties and were thus considered the "imperial crown." They were "made and given to rule the mind," to "govern by divine right." Indeed, it was in and around the crown of the head that true freedom—agency being the divine inheritance of the human—was consummated. Rev. G. S. Weaver, *Lectures on Mental Science According to the Philosophy of Phrenology* (New York: Fowlers & Wells, 1852), 203, 205; Fowler, *Education and Self-Improvement*, 149f.

108. O. S. Fowler, *Fowler on Matrimony: or, Phrenology and Physiology Applied to the Selection of Congenial Companions for Life* (New York: Fowlers & Wells, 1842), 49. Conscientiousness instilled a love of duty, Benevolence included an element of sacrifice, and Marvellousness an element of epistemic deference. Fowler, *Phrenological Guide*, 39–43.

109. Because magnetism was the "means or medium" of influence, the magnetizer would "throw" a "charge" by the "laying on of hands" (in imitation of Jesus and his apostles) or else by willed manipulation of the magnetic pathways surrounding the patient. "Phrenology and Animal Magnetism. No. 2," *APJ* 4 (1843): 215-17.

110. Fowler, *Religion*, 45, 51; Fowler, *Education and Self-Improvement*, 235-37. Across the Atlantic, the faculty of Veneration was referred to more explicitly as "Submissiveness" and was considered the key to a "law-abiding disposition" (Townshend, *Facts of Mesmerism*, 58).

FIGURE 11 · Faculty of Veneration. Detail from "Symbolical Head, Illustrative of Organs," *American Phrenological Journal* 13, no. 1 (January 1851): 21.

of course—but also to the progressive history of religion. According to Fowler, Veneration allowed "mankind to worship" and was a human trait that "has appeared in all ages, among all tribes." It was the consummation of a long history of organizational development. "Thus saith Phrenology." Having originated as a vehicle of animistic sensitivity, the organ of Veneration had evolved by adapting to the "nature of things," which meant it had come to validate the political conditions of Protestant piety. As a "self-evident" politics, "the sentiment of worship of God," if "calculated" and "properly exercised," would "benefit mankind by promoting moral purity and general enjoyment." For in addition to producing adoration for God, Veneration also generated "reverence for religion" itself. In her effort to promote phrenology among children, for example, Lydia Fowler (Lorenzo's wife) first enjoins, "Children, you *must* cultivate this organ of Veneration, which is very important. . . . You *must* lay aside all rough, vulgar habits and manners." She then, and only then, adds without resorting to italics: "You must also cultivate veneration for God; you ought to pray to him, and love to do it."[111]

Such was the rhetoric of dependence accompanying descriptions of the moral sentiments in the early years of Fowlers and Wells—so much so that many accused phrenology of repackaging Calvinist determinism and the torment of original sin in a physiological guise. But Fowlers and Wells always bristled at such accusations, and by the late 1840s there was evidence of a strategic push to clarify how Veneration, despite imparting "a sense of weakness, a feeling of poverty and helplessness," would inevitably serve to fill "the throne of dominion within" and achieve "the acme of true hu-

111. Fowler, *Religion*, 51; Fowler, *Phrenological Guide*, 39; Fowler, *Education and Self-Improvement*, 235-37; Mrs. L. N. Fowler, *Familiar Lessons on Phrenology, Designed for the Use of Children and Youth* (New York: Fowlers & Wells, 1848), 2:106.

man greatness."[112] Such clarification on the part of Fowlers and Wells was years in the making.

9. Spirituality and the Decline of Wonder

Before the embrace of mesmeric technics, Fowlers and Wells had most closely aligned "true religion" with Veneration. But as animal magnetism was establishing "the spiritual, immaterial existence of mind in a state separate from matter," the publications of Fowlers and Wells introduced the organ of Spirituality—the active and engaged faculty of religion that infused the element of agentive consent into Veneration's apparent *habitus* of submission.[113] The freedom that Spirituality entailed and guaranteed, however, continued to be a matter of obedience—not to God per se nor even to the members of one's community—but to a mild and idealized version of the self.

In May 1841, the *American Phrenological Journal* reported "seeming contradictions" between how Spurzheim, Combe, and O. S. Fowler delimited the faculty of Marvellousness.[114] It declared that it was seeking to reconcile that fact that Spurzheim had used the term Marvellousness (and Combe, Wonder) for a disposition to revel in situations that were both ordinary *and* transcended the mundane in a dramatic way.[115] This was a cutting-edge report—"found to differ from high authority"—that presented itself as a consolidation and integration of earlier phrenological paradigms.[116] It was, however, a fundamental revision of what constituted the underlying mechanics of piety.

According to the report, firsthand evidence suggested "that there are two organs contained within the cerebral limits of Marvellousness as delineated by Dr. Spurzheim." There was the element of surprise or appreciation of novelty—mere wonder. And there was a more subtle belief in the reality of "spiritual influence." Mere wonder was necessarily directed at the ordinarily novel. "Numerous observations have convinced me," wrote

112. William B. Elliot, "The Primary Function of Veneration," *APJ* 11:143; Weaver, *Lectures on Mental Science*, 214–15.
113. "On the Abuse or Perversion of Certain Faculties in Religion," *APJ* 3, no. 11 (August 1, 1841): 517; Fowler, *Religion*, 106.
114. "On the Functions of the Organ of Marvellousness," *APJ* 3, no. 8 (May 1, 1841): 360–64.
115. Combe used the category of Wonder and remarked that the difference between it and Spurzheim's Marvellousness (or *Surnaturalité* in his French editions) was only nominal. George Combe, *Elements of Phrenology* (Boston: Marsh, Capen, & Lyon, 1835), 77–79.
116. "On the Functions of the Organ of Marvellousness," 360.

FIGURE 12 · Faculty of Spirituality envisioned as a communicative moment with God, with hands stretched, with Old Testament roots. Detail from "Symbolical Head, Illustrative of Organs," *American Phrenological Journal* 13, no. 1 (January 1851): 21.

the author (most likely Orson Fowler, given his magnetic experiments and earlier statements in the *APJ*), "that some persons have a strong love for the new, the wonderful and the mysterious." There was something to these feelings of surprise, admitted the author, but they had nothing to do with the functional definition of religion.[117]

The essence of Marvellousness was concerned solely with extraordinary things (coded here as invisible and/or immaterial). This essence gave "faith—faith in the existence and indestructibility of the soul—faith in its power over matter—faith in its capabilities of eternal happiness or misery—and faith in all surrounding and occult influences of the spirit from which it is an emanation."[118] In lieu of future tests and observations

117. Ibid., 361. Because Wonder was not about soul-matters, it should henceforth be grouped with the self-perfecting faculties of Imitation, Ideality, and Sublimity rather than with the moral/religious sentiments. On this point the author cited a previously published article by M. B. Sampson (363). See "On the Primary Function of the Organ of Wonder," *APJ* 1, no. 7 (April 1, 1839): 201-10. Sampson suggests that the organ be called "Admirativeness" (202). An inconsistency is apparent in this issue, with a subsequent statement that "Veneration, Hope, and Wonder, combined, give the tendency to religion" ("Elementary Principles of Phrenology," *APJ* 1, no. 7 [April 1, 1839]: 240).

118. "On the Functions of the Organ of Marvellousness," 363. Fowler's subtle recoding of Marvellousness had already begun in "Elementary Phrenology," *American Phrenological Journal* 2, no. 7 (April 1, 1840): 326.

made by "my friends or myself," the definition of Marvellousness was to be purified of mere wonder. Marvellousness was now "strictly a religious organ."[119] Its proper purview became the "world of spirits," that is, invisible, immaterial, and otherwise "spiritual" matters. And finally, the proper name of Marvellousness was now Spirituality.[120]

Throughout the mid-1840s the faculty of Marvellousness slowly morphed—first into the hybrid "Spirituality [Marvellousness]" and then into "Spirituality." Although the use of the lone term Marvellousness was increasingly rare after 1847, the older vocabulary was never fully transformed (due in part to the endless recycling of printing plates by Fowlers and Wells).[121] Regardless of name, this newly revamped faculty soon became the reigning member of the moral sentiments—the "leading element of true piety." Spirituality "quicken[ed] benevolence, veneration, hope, conscientiousness, and the whole moral group," guaranteeing their "ascendancy" over the rest of the faculties. Spirituality made possible a "*spiritualization* of our natures." As integral to both the formula and maintenance of true religion, Spirituality amounted to a "happifying," lasting, and liberating piety.[122]

The invention of Spirituality was a matter of epistemic opportunity. First and foremost, the "teachings" of Spirituality were "above reason, but will never conflict with it." As the perfect vehicle by which to "contemplate" your "spiritual relations," Spirituality taught that knowledge of self depended upon understanding the self's relationality to various spiritual pressures. For with the reinvention of Marvellousness as Spirituality, the truth of religion itself moved toward assessing one's place within a vast network of spiritual connections. Here was the white man's province

119. "On the Functions of the Organ of Marvellousness," 363. On the question of whether Marvellousness was a moral sentiment or imaginative faculty, see Mrs. L. Miles, *Phrenology and the Moral Influence of Phrenology: Arranged for General Study, and the Purposes of Education, from the First Published Works of Gall and Spurzheim* (Philadelphia: Carey, Lea, and Blanchard, 1835).

120. The newly revamped faculty of Marvellousness corresponded to an appreciation for the existence of magnetic forces. For just as the faculty of Veneration proved the existence of God, Marvellousness was now material evidence for the reality of an invisible magnetic economy. "Phrenology and Infidelity," *The Phrenological Almanac of 1845* (New York: O. S. Fowler, 1845), 58. For another iteration of this logic, see "Clairvoyance: Its Harmony with the Known Laws of Mind.—No. I," *APJ* 10 (1848): 28–30.

121. Even in the article entitled "Marvellousness—Its Definition, Location, Function, Adaptation, and Cultivation," *APJ* 9 (1847): 377–82, the term "Spirituality" is used throughout to designate this organ. In "Causality and Marvellousness," the term Marvellousness was used to designate the "love of the new and wonderful," that which Spirituality no longer signified (*APJ* 13, no. 6 [June 1851]: 131–32).

122. O. S. Fowler, *Education and Self-Improvement*, 234–35; Fowler, *Religion*, 111.

of calculability. With the vigorous activity of Spirituality, you became attuned to the porous boundaries of the self. You sensed spiritual influences. And you became adept at negotiating their inevitable presence. Agency, in other words, was born out of recognizing the validity of "spiritual influences" that necessarily inflected one's actions, decisions, and beliefs.[123]

Spirituality allowed you to recognize ghosts, to appreciate them intimately and without fear. Taking the measure of one's enchanted situation, in turn, was all but equivalent to agency. As Fowler declared elsewhere, if the moral sentiments were "to be productive of good," they "MUST IN ALL CASES, be enlightened, and guided by intellect, by science, by reason, by knowledge."[124] In other words, when Spirituality and the other moral sentiments interacted with the intellectual faculties, enchantment became subject to deliberate and sustained attention.[125] For ghosts were not to be feared but attended to, properly, on one's own terms and according to the promise of reason. "If you ask me whether I believe in the existence and appearance of ghosts," speculated Fowler,

> I say yes, with emphasis. Not that I ever saw one. Nor is it the testimony of others that imparts this confidence. *It is this principle.* I never saw an apparition. My organ of spirituality is too small ever to see one. But I believe this principle. It will not lie. I believe that the spirits of departed friends hover over us, and conduct our choice, our course. . . . If we are sufficiently spiritualized, we might hold converse with the spirits of our departed friends, with angels, and with God! I believe they might become our guardian angels, to tell us what we should do, and what avoid . . . they would become our spiritual conductors, carrying a torch-light by which we could guide our erring footsteps into the paths of success, of holiness, of happiness.

123. "Marvellousness—Its Definition, Location, Function, Adaptation, and Cultivation," 382; Weaver, *Lectures on Moral Science,* 217.

124. Fowler, *Religion,* 70. Both reason and religion were coded as white. For example, in assessing the "animal religion of the ignorant, superstitious negro of southern slavery," Fowler laments that he has "no intellect, to elevate, and enlighten, and direct" his religious impulses.

125. The intellectual faculties, like those of religion, were racially coded, Galileo's "philosophizing, penetrating, investigating, originating cast of mind," for example, being juxtaposed with the "inferior reasoning capabilities" of Native American women (Fowler, *Self-Instructor,* 159–60). Intellectual faculties were naturally compatible with Spirituality, given their propensity to "ascertain causes and abstract relations" and their appreciation for "first principles, or laws of things."

According to Fowler, the refurbished organ of Spirituality "spiritualized" man. It adapted *him* "to a world of spirits" and imparted "the element of *spirituality* to his nature." To become spiritualized, then, was to be rendered "a spiritual, immaterial, immortal being"—a process in which you knew everything because you knew yourself and your place within a network of spiritual forces.[126]

Such was the circularity of Spirituality, the faculty that made it possible to "converse with the spirits of our departed friends, with angels, and with God!"[127] In such conversations mere wonder was to be excluded. For while the invisible forces coursing through the material world were at times unwieldy and unpredictable, they were nonetheless an integral part of cultivating the self. One might even go so far as to argue that the faculty of Spirituality insisted upon a requisite amount of incalculability in order to calculate it. As an instinctual form of reason, Spirituality was not so much a negation of doubt as it was an evacuation of dread—a style of knowing rather than thinking in which little if any price was to be paid for access to the truth. Specters were by definition already domesticated; familiar faces rather than unseemly disruptions; wholly expected rather than unforeseen.[128]

The invention of Spirituality on the part of Fowlers and Wells was a defense of religion as an act of cognition and intentionality. When functioning healthily, Spirituality provided leverage upon the strictures imposed by Veneration. The perversion of Spirituality, in contrast, compromised one's "independent capacity of mind" and ability to control one's attention.[129] Spirituality allowed you to "*follow* your innermost impressions or presentiments in everything." It opened "your mind to the intuitive reception of truth." And it enabled you to become a "disembodied mind [that]

126. Fowler, *Religion*, 96, 105; O. S. and L. N. Fowler, "Phrenology and Infidelity," *The Phrenological Almanac* (1845): 58.
127. Fowler, *Religion*, 105.
128. Note the subtle transposition of deference, the *sine qua non* of Veneration. For even as the individual acknowledges his subjection to God, spiritual forces, or even the demands of social life, he does so on his own terms. Moreover, those terms were known in advance by way of Spirituality. Despite gestures to the contrary, Spirituality served to demarcate an interior process of agentive reason from an exterior life to which this agentive reason would then apply itself. In securing "a distinction between the psychic and the social," Spirituality allowed little if any room for their mutuality to be recognized. Consequently, one learned to acknowledge but not to recognize those forces that had already structured the reason to be actualized and the self to be cultivated. See Judith Butler, *The Psychic Life of Power: Theories in Subjection* (Stanford: Stanford University Press, 1997), 19.
129. Fowler, *Religion*, 106, 122.

sees by spiritual cognizance." Transcending both the body and material circumstances. Operating from above, all-seeing, part and parcel, as they say, to divinity. Transcendence never felt so good as when you became what you already were in essence.[130]

Because the organ of Spirituality was "feebly developed" and "miserably small in the American head!" (even among those Protestants with well-endowed Veneration), there was a sense of urgency pervading the advice to cultivate it. In order to work on Spirituality, for example, the patient was instructed above all to "meditate. Commune with your own soul and your God—not at times 'few and far between,' nor hurriedly, but daily and long."[131]

Such instruction served to transform, into a divine calling, the seamless self-regard that occurred when the patient treated his own being—systematically—according to the natural structures of human consciousness.[132] After an examination, for example, the patient received advice (written and/or verbal) and returned home with a personalized copy of the *Self-Instructor in Phrenology and Physiology*. The cover page was inscribed with the name of the patient, the date, and the signature of the examiner. It was a permanent record of the size of each of the patient's faculties. It provided detailed, cross-referenced advice as to how to proceed to develop oneself phrenologically, that is, how to either cultivate or restrain a given faculty in relation to an encyclopedic statement about each of the faculties. The exam, combined with the *Self-Instructor*, would "enable every individual to place his own fingers upon every element of his character; and . . . will correct these estimates, and teach men precisely what they really are."[133] Such activity allowed the individual to submit to himself, or more precisely, to his idealized location within a vast network, or even more precisely, to the metaphysical order that lies behind that network.

In the act of inscribing so-called universal categories upon each and every particularity of self, nothing at all remained outside.[134] Indeed, the

---

130. Fowler, *Self-Instructor*, 123; Fowler, *Religion*, 106.

131. Fowler, *Religion*, 101; "Marvellousness—Its Definition, Location, Function, Adaptation, and Cultivation," 380.

132. The goal was to make every person "his own phrenologist." Fowler, *Education and Self-Improvement*, 148; *Self-Culture*, iii, 118.

133. Fowler, *Education and Self-Improvement*, 145.

134. See, for example, the poem, "Verses Inscribed by a Phrenologist on a Skull," *APJ* 9 (1847): 359. In Edgar Allen Poe's riff on phrenology, it was the ease of resolving these tensions in and through a set of universal categories that was itself the most troubling. In his estimation, phrenology was perverse not because it resignified Calvinism in a physiognomic

very idea of outsidedness went unacknowledged.[135] For when all was said and done, Spirituality had guaranteed that there was nothing, religiously speaking, worth wondering about.

To be clear, I am not claiming that spirituality—an emerging style of piety within liberal circles—may be reduced to the invention of a particular faculty bearing its name coined by a particular media institution at a particular moment in time. It is, however, to argue that during a phrenological examination the category of religion became an object of intense focus, dissection, and revision. During an exam the piety of the patient became something much more (and much less) than faith in God or even belief in specific doctrines. During and after the exam piety became a matter of subtle and sustained attention to one's faculties. It necessitated a vigilant assessment of your interactions with others and the outside world as well as an alignment of your interior energies with the entirety of your physical constitution. Phrenology generated a style of liberal piety that allowed individuals to establish their own volition within a metaphysical scheme (and a social environment) of de facto relationality.

10. Everlasting Subject

Modernity begins when the human being begins to exist within his organism, inside the shell of his head.

MICHEL FOUCAULT, *The Order of Things*

The origins of spirituality are deeply obscure. Indeed, as a style of piety, it begins nowhere in particular. Yet the word did assume an ethical substance in and through an evolving network—of institutions, metaphysical schemes, theories of living, and practices of self-discovery and maintenance. As I have demonstrated, there was no single line of development, no single trajectory of influence from, say, Channing to the penny presses to phrenology. Rather, there was an ever-increasing density (as opposed

---

key but because it perpetuated excessive belief in the human ability to categorize. According to Poe, this was the faculty that went undetected by even the most perceptive phrenologists: "In the considerations of the faculties and impulses—of the *prima mobilia* of the human soul, the phrenologists have failed to make room for a propensity which, although obviously existing as a radical, primitive, irreducible sentiment, has been equally overlooked by all the moralists who have proceeded them" (Edgar A. Poe, "The Imp of the Perverse," *Graham's Magazine* 28, no. 1 [July 1845]: 1–3).

135. Max Horkheimer and Theodor W. Adorno, *Dialectic of Enlightenment*, trans. John Cumming (New York: Continuum, 1993), 16.

to nominal clarity) to the concept of spirituality as it resonated across all manner of ideological boundaries—from self-help and etiquette guides, to solemn arguments about religion and morals, to a range of psychological technics that resonated with theological doctrines and churches. It is precisely this density, this sense of repetition, that marks the power of secularism. In this chapter I have purposefully moved from theological musings of Unitarians to the airy rhetorical environs of mental and moral philosophy to the intimate inspection of one's head in hopes of glimpsing an affinity between them.

In 1843, Boston Unitarian and horticulturalist George Jaques declared in his journal that "the spiritual part of man is capable of infinite progress in improvement." This was part and parcel to his assumption that "good works from right-motives are the only rational foundation of a Christian Life." Jaques was committed to a program of self-examination and development in the service of society. His politics, in other words, was dependent upon a rigorous cultivation of self, a creative act that guaranteed "right-motives" in public. "I do not believe in hereditary religion or politics," continued Jaques. "I would no more adopt the opinions of my parents and ancestors *because* they were *their opinions,* than I would give myself the itch because some of them might have had it." A few months later, Jaques looked to the pages of *Fowler's Practical Phrenology* (1840). He then looked to the mirror to assess and adjust his character against an eternal standard of the human. "If Phrenology be true," wrote Jaques, "I am constantly inclined to underrate myself (self-esteem being the smallest organ in my head)." It was here that Jaques's "spiritual part" became bound up in phrenological categories of self-reflection and normality. And it was here that Jaques expressed a strange desire for transcendence—a desire to be monitored, to be systematically organized by a standard of truth that originated from outside him yet was essentially related to him.[136]

This chapter has addressed what might be called the politics of spirituality in the antebellum period. My focus has been on the relationship between spirituality and the moral pressures surrounding someone like George Jaques. Spirituality, I have argued, gained vibrancy as an epistemic virtue in and through a field of statements—from the directives of Unitarianism to cultivate oneself and to become spiritually discerning; to the burgeoning disciplines of mental and moral science where the "disordered actions of the brain" were attributed to "spectral illusions"; to the tech-

---

136. "Journal of George Jaques, Dec. 1840–January 1846." Doc. 372, Joseph Downs Collection and Winterthur Archives, Winterthur Museum and Library.

nics developed by phrenologists for measuring and massaging the moral sentiments.[137] In juxtaposing these statements, one begins to notice a pattern that revolved around (and was, perhaps, fueled by) the irresolvable tension between what Channing called, respectively, the "permanence of the I" and the fact that "we catch each other's feelings."[138] One also senses here the making of an essential and universal capacity, a promise of transcendence and transformation that was, first and foremost, a matter of mental cultivation. For those awash in a sea of strangers and even stranger circulations, spirituality offered a way to acknowledge the infectious quality of social life even as it secured the means of immunization.[139]

Unitarianism, mental science, moral philosophy, and phrenology—each of these belief practices seemingly moved beyond the empirical horizon of Common Sense in the service of sketching the contours of spirit.[140] For in assuming degrees of overlap between human and political bodies, these vectors of Common Sense framed mediation in such a way that it became integral to how one calculated the difference between self and world. Experiences of mediation were, in the process, rendered immediately accessible. Transparency was at stake for the purpose of renewing its promise.

Consequently, this chapter has dwelled upon the notion of perpetuity, or more precisely, how the concept of spirituality secured itself and the constancy of its own motion. The "spiritual activities" of liberal Protestants were, first and foremost, dramas of security. To conceive of the self as infinite possibility, as bearing a potential resemblance to God himself or his laws, did not necessarily lend itself to a substantive account of what did or should constitute the self. Indeed, what took precedence in each of these calls to cultivation was the formal delineation of self rather than the prescription of specific content. These calls were more about

137. Rufus Blakeman, *A Philosophical Essay on Credulity and Superstition; and also on Animal Fascination, or Charming* (New York: D. Appleton & Co., 1849), 67–68. For an extended inquiry into what I have been calling phantasmaphysics, see Jane Bennett, *Vibrant Matter: A Political Ecology of Things* (Durham: Duke University Press, 2009).

138. *Dr. Channing's Note-Book*, 104, 36.

139. Spirituality, I argue, was bound up in those statements that addressed one's relationship with strangers, that framed "the most intimate dimensions of subjectivity around comembership with indefinite persons in a context of routine action" (Michael Warner, *Publics and Counterpublics* [New York: Zone Books, 2002], 74–76).

140. "We have more evidence that we have souls or spirits than that we have bodies," declared Channing. "Farther, how irrational is it to imagine that there are no worlds but this, and no higher modes of existence than our own!" (Channing, "The Future Life," in *Works* [1889], 360).

recognized mechanisms than doctrinal content, a process without end.[141] Spirituality, however, even as a formal process, empty of content, would continue to become increasingly dense. A strange nature. From divine immateriality to epistemic virtue to mental faculty to an acknowledgment of and response to the spectral demands of modernity. And finally, a desire for disenchantment that corresponds to an intensification of enchanting conditions.

I began this chapter with a series of broad questions about spirituality and "religion today." What have been the mechanics of transcendence among those who have understood themselves as spiritual or who have employed the word spirituality? What kinds of transformations ensued from committing to a program of institutional immunity? What was the ethical substance and effects of the human flourishing involved? How did these effects in turn perpetuate particular social norms? There are no definitive answers. What remains are the questions, narrative, and footnotes. Dwelling rather than seeking.

—

The refashioning of Marvellousness in 1842 ushered in "the soul-ravishing truths about heaven and the spirit-land taught by Spirituality."[142] This was, perhaps, a logical conclusion of the kind of "spiritual discernment" advocated by Unitarians. It also marked a prehistory of those sentiments and attitudes that would later come together, publicly, under the banner of séance spiritualism. And although the words 'spiritualism' and 'spiritual-

141. On the prerogatives of keeping busy among Unitarians, see Howe, *Unitarian Conscience*, 113. Henry Ward Beecher was one of the most vocal and visible proponents of phrenology within the established precincts of liberalism. In imagining society in terms of a network, Beecher sensed both the disappearance of the human and the potential for epistemic renewal. "In society men are like threads," he wrote, "woven in and out, and composing a fabric of many colors. They tend to lose their personal distinctness. One wishes to separate himself from all influences about him, and see just what is left of himself" (Henry Ward Beecher, *Lectures to Young Men, on Various Important Subjects* [New York: M. H. Newman & Co., 1853], 363). This passage is also cited in Schmidt, *Restless Souls*, 86. Beecher's was at once an awareness of being bound up with an ethereal systematicity yet also a plea to engage in the hard and ceaseless work of distinction. The persistence of this tension was the key to transforming enchantment into disenchantment. Take, for example, Beecher's case for "industry" in all things and his taxonomy of "many grades of idleness" and "various classes of idlers," ranging from the "Lazy-man" to the fashionable and wily idler. Idleness was defined as not attending closely to one's business. Subsequently, "idle men's imaginations" were "haunted with unlawful visitants" (36).

142. "Spirituality—A Glimpse of Heaven," *APJ* 11 (1849): 344.

ist' did not come into common usage until 1852, much of the excitement over the "modern mysteries" of spirit communication was informed by something like the concept of spirituality I have been discussing.[143] Or more precisely, by the desire codified by Spirituality and its subsequent effects.[144]

During this same time in the pages of the *APJ* Spirituality became increasingly linked with the capacity for clairvoyance. For with a large organ of Spirituality, declared the *APJ* in 1851, one was able to see the truth of oneself by seeing the magnetic interconnectivity of each and every soul. And vice versa.[145] Years earlier Fowlers and Wells had noted books by or on Swedenborg, guardian spirits, and, in 1847, the visions of Andrew Jackson Davis.[146] By this time Davis had become known as the "Seer of Poughkeepsie." He was a traveling trance lecturer who had recently published his lectures as *The Principles of Nature* and visited the Phrenological Cabinet in New York City, where he underwent an examination by L. N. Fowler. Davis, wrote Fowler, was "naturally below mediocrity in the exercise of the feelings of devotion." Despite his small Veneration, Davis's "sense of the spiritual and its influences is strong." And to clarify that spiritual did not necessarily connote wonder, Fowler wrote that Davis's "love of the curious, novel, and marvelous, is moderate."[147]

By the end of 1847 Davis, alongside a group of Universalist ministers and professed Swedenborgians, had co-founded *The Univercoelum and Spiritual Philosopher*. Davis soon became the most visible authority on séance spiritualism, the widespread, well-publicized, and loosely organized incidents of spirit communication revolving around infamous knockings of

143. R. Laurence Moore, *In Search of White Crows: Spiritualism, Parapsychology, and American Culture* (New York: Oxford University Press, 1977), 13.

144. In addition to being a relay between phreno-magnetism and spiritualism, spirituality also foregrounds the exclusions within the emancipatory politics of liberalism so often ascribed to spiritualism. See, for example, Ann Braude, *Radical Spirits: Spiritualism and Women's Rights in Nineteenth-Century America* (Boston: Beacon Press, 1989).

145. "The Clairvoyant State Compatible with the Nature of Mind," *APJ* 11 (1849): 371–73. On this logic among séance spiritualists, see Louis Alphonse Cahagnet, *The Celestial Telegraph; or, Secrets of the Life to Come, Revealed through Magnetism* (New York: J. S. Redfield, 1851). "What magnetism rigorously demonstrates is the spirituality of the soul and its immortality; also, that souls separated from the body can in certain cases put themselves in communication with living beings, and Convey to them their sentiments" (1).

146. "Davis's Revelations," *APJ* 9 (1847): 230. See also "Notices of New Books" from that same issue, in which George Bush's *Mesmer and Swedenborg* is cited as well as A. E. Ford's translation of H. Werner's *Guardian Spirits: A Case of Vision into the Spiritual World* (1847).

147. L. N. Fowler, "Phrenological Description of Andrew J. Davis, The Poughkeepsie Clairvoyant," *APJ* 9 (1847): 352.

ARTICLE LX.

PHRENOLOGICAL DESCRIPTION OF ANDREW J. DAVIS, THE POUGHKEEPSIE
CLAIRVOYANT. BY L. N. FOWLER.

No. 51. ANDREW J. DAVIS.

(Given in New York, October, 1847.)

MR. DAVIS's head is of full size, being twenty-two inches in circumference, and well proportioned to his body. His mental or nervous temperament predominates; the motive, or bilious, is next in power, with only
a fair amount of the vital : consequently, the strongest tendencies of his
mind are intellectual, and his enjoyments are elevated, rather than animal or sensual.

His mind is highly active and very susceptible, and he is easily influenced or awakened by external objects or internal emotions. He has
great power of endurance, both mental and physical, and his system is
more free from disease or debility than that of most persons. His mind

FIGURE 13 · Andrew Jackson Davis from L. N. Fowler's "Phrenological Description of Andrew J. Davis, the Poughkeepsie Clairvoyant," *American Phrenological Journal* 9 (1847): 351.

Rochester in the spring of 1848. Visitations from the likes of Swedenborg, George Washington, and William Ellery Channing soon followed.[148]

Well before his partnership with Fowlers and Wells, however, Davis had endorsed phrenology, confirming that "Phrenology has been proved demonstratively to every erudite man of science, and is admitted to be true as regards its *foundation* and *general* phenomena."[149] After being published by Fowlers and Wells (an 1851 edition of *The Philosophy of Spiritual Intercourse*), Davis wrote that phrenological self-examination would continue in the afterlife (just as Unitarians had affirmed self-culture as an exercise in perpetuity).[150] Indeed, his works were suffused with a phrenological analytic—from offering an extended riff on the religious sentiments to writing of the "peculiar prominence on the top of the head" of Martians, "indicative of [their] high veneration" and two brains within.[151] Moreover, Davis praised phrenology for having introduced men to the hidden labyrinths of their own minds, more so "than any mental philosophy or religious system in existence."[152]

148. Eliab W. Capron and Henry D. Barron, *Explanation and History of the Mysterious Communion with Spirits, Comprehending the Rise and Progress of the Mysterious Noises in Western New-York Generally Received as Spiritual Communications* (Auburn: Finn & Rockwell, 1850), 68. In life Channing had insisted that "we have connection with all spirits," and that the "past is living in us when we think it dead." The consequence was both epistemic and salvific—a "clearer, more definite conception of the future state" because this state was "founded on the essential laws of the mind." He also declared "that spiritual beings in that higher state must approach and commune with each other more and more intimately in proportion to their progress" (*Dr. Channing's Note-Book*, 91, 110; Channing, "The Future Life," 360-61).

149. Andrew Jackson Davis, *The Principles of Nature, Her Divine Revelations, and a Voice to Mankind by and through Andrew Jackson Davis*, 8th ed. (New York: S. S. Lyon and Wm. Fishbough, 1851), 23. See also the phrenological themes in W. J. Fox, "Mental Slavery," *The Univercoelum and Spiritual Philosopher* 1, no. 16: 245-48; T. L. Harris, "Spiritual Advancement: The Precursors of Institutional Reform," *The Univercoelum and Spiritual Philosopher* 1, no. 24 (1848): 369-71; as well as George Bush's lecture on Swedenborg and Phrenology at New York University in 1846. The latter is noted in *The Phrenological Journal* 89 (October 1846): 384.

150. Andrew Jackson Davis, *The Philosophy of Spiritual Intercourse: Being an Explanation of Modern Mysteries* (New York: Fowlers & Wells, 1851), 62; Howe, *The Unitarian Conscience*, 256; see also Norton, "The Duty of Continual Improvement," *Christian Examiner* 2 (1825): 412-19, and James Walker, "The End Not Yet," *Sermons Preached in the Chapel of Harvard College* (Boston, 1861), 327.

151. Davis, *Principles of Nature*, 198. Noted in Catherine L. Albanese, *A Republic of Mind and Spirit: A Cultural History of American Civil Religion* (New Haven: Yale University Press, 2007), 211.

152. Andrew Jackson Davis, *The Great Harmonia: Being a Philosophical Revelation of the Natural, Spiritual, and Celestial Universe*, vol. 1 (Boston: Benjamin B. Mussey & Co., 1850), 103. Despite the fact that Davis had been "involuntarily persuaded" of phrenology's "modern metaphysics," he proposed going beyond phrenology in order to make explicit its rendering of the invisible and spiritual principle within each individual. Andrew Jackson Davis, *The Great Harmonia*, vol. 2 (1851), 130; Davis, *Principles of Nature*, 24.

Not surprisingly, Davis insisted on the absolute centrality of *"organized* individuals,"* which in turn led to family harmony, social harmony, national harmony, and universal harmony. Key to such organization, of course, were the faculties of religion. In order to participate in the "grand Drama of a progressive and Spiritual experience," one needed to coordinate their "faculty of Faith" and "organ of wonder" with the "reason-principle." Only then could one throw off the "yoke of theological despotism." Or as Davis declared, to not appreciate the truth of his Harmonial Philosophy was to possess "ill-directed veneration." According to Davis, piety was to be practiced in light of the mediated predicament of human beings. For as animal magnetism had made clear, every individual was at once in control yet ever susceptible to human influences, both past and present. According to Davis, the "highest development of true religion" happens when you recognized your place within a grand spiritual bureaucracy, what he called "the Institution of the GREAT HARMONIUM."[153]

Magnetic reasoning, argued Davis, was precisely what was required for such inquiry to proceed. It would engender a capacious sensitivity to the invisibility of the social—all those "electrical elements [that] flow down from the brain into the nerves, and into all the infinite ramifications of the nerves, and thence into the atmosphere which we breathe." It would also enable the individual to communicate with the spirit-world. "This reasoning is the *true* reasoning," argued Davis. As opposed to the crass supernaturalism of Catholics, the true reasoning proved "visible effects by imperceptible and invisible causes."[154] The imperative of such reasoning, however, was disenchantment. The "spirit of rationalism" would, in other words, address enchantment as both an epistemological and political problem. "No more shall the miracle-expecting multitudes among men sacrifice their reason upon superstition's altar."[155] The population was about to break "the degrading shackles of superstition and false imagination."[156]

153. Davis, *Principles of Nature*, 123-24, 101; Davis, *Philosophy of Spiritual Intercourse*, 165, 170-72; Davis, *Present Age*, 26, 29, 63; Davis, *The Penetralia: Being Harmonial Answers to Important Questions* (Boston: Bela Marsh, 1856), 317. "The social relations of men are [to be] investigated, classified, and harmonized," wrote Davis. "Prompted by justice, each man studies himself; his physical and spiritual qualifications, his fitness and relative attractions to the nearest, or most distant, neighbor" (*Philosophy of Spiritual Intercourse*, 172, my emphasis).

154. Davis, *Principles of Nature*, 22f; Davis, *Philosophy of Spiritual Intercourse*, 26. See also W. M. Fernald, "Catholicity or Rationalism—No Middle Ground," *The Univercoelum and Spiritual Philosopher* I, no. 11 (February 12, 1848): 161-64.

155. Davis, *Philosophy of Spiritual Intercourse*, 34; Albanese, *Republic of Mind and Spirit*, 210.

156. Davis, *Principles of Nature*, 6. Davis went so far as to cite Bacon in his desire to challenge "fictions sacredized, and sanctified by the spirit of Antiquity, and the powerful sanction of general consent" (*Great Harmonia*, 1:287).

Disenchantment, here, was not the vanquishing of ghosts. Rather, it was a matter of calculating them; a style of living with them, free from the bondage of ignorance, in a kind of egalitarian state.[157]

It was here, in the style of reasoning promoted by Davis, that a tension between docility and freedom resonated once more in the antebellum era.[158] A dialectic of disenchantment. "Spiritual perception," according to Davis, was a form of epistemic liberation precisely because it revealed the extent and intricacy of one's embeddedness in the "mighty network of Nature."[159] This insight was crucial to Davis's critique of the "dogma of moral freedom." "If you should study the science of man," wrote Davis, "you will observe that all liberty or freedom is *comparative*; not absolute. All will is *consequent*; not primary." The line separating humility and masochism here is rather thin, as agency happens in the continuous recognition of subjection—the fact that "society"—both present and past—was "to a considerable extent, accountable for his actions. . . . Man, I repeat, is not the creator of the inexorable laws of his being . . . He is their everlasting subject; hence, too, he obeys."[160] According to Davis, all humans "are, or may be, mediums," which amounted to an explicit acknowledgment that humans were by definition enchanted.[161] Consequently, it was imperative that everyone cultivate their spiritual cognizance in order to tend to the delicate balance between agency and submission, epistemic encounter and incorporation.[162]

As the concept of spirituality reached a logical conclusion in Davis,

---

157. Davis, *Philosophy of Spiritual Intercourse*, 121f., 83. Because spirits, too, were externally influenced, influence itself was not a threat to agency but rather integral to its consummation within a spirit network.

158. Within spiritualist circles more generally, the phrenological faculty of "Spirituality" became a privileged form of reason. See, for example, William T. Coggshall, *The Signs of the Times: Comprising a History of the Spirit-Rappings, in Cincinnati and Other Places* (Cincinnati: Author, 1851), 108. Coggshall here cites from the article "Spirituality—Recent Occurrences," published in James Buchanan's *Journal of Man* 1, no. 10 (February 1850): 489–506.

159. Davis, *The Great Harmonia*, 1:358.

160. Andrew Jackson Davis, *The Approaching Crisis: Being a Review of Dr. Bushnell's Recent Lectures on Supernaturalism* (New York: Author, 1852), 197–98, 201, 205. On this ambiguity, see Bret E. Carroll, *Spiritualism in Antebellum America* (Bloomington: Indiana University Press, 1997), 107f.

161. An ideal, perhaps, was the "homo-motor medium." The homo-motor medium was "exclusively and perfectly under systematic and regular control" yet one who also achieved "perfect individuality" in his or her communion with the spirit-world. Davis, *Present Age*, 154–55. Davis, in other words, recognized the existence of mysterious forces, forces that were permeating the individual, perhaps even producing him. Yet these forces were calculable, subject to a regular and reliable logic, which for Davis would not exhaust their divine quality.

162. Davis, *Present Age*, 367; Davis, *Philosophy of Spiritual Intercourse*, 202.

cultivation of self became a calling, continuous and everlasting. "The foundation of all thought," insisted Davis, "is incapable of self-compre-hension." Consequently, the self could not, finally, know itself because "no principle contains within itself the power of self-investigation."[163] In-vestigation had to be pursued by other means—in and through sustained attention to relationality. Comprehension was a matter of deferral rather than finality. It was a style of reasoning that depended upon a sense of mystery as an invitation to certainty, a sense of obscurity as a sign of po-tential transparency. Counterintuitively, Davis's initial denial of immedi-acy and clarity served a constructive purpose.

According to Davis, each individual had a "guardian spirit" who was "constitutionally and phrenologically *congenial* to the earthly charge." Moreover, this spirit was a "better, wiser, and more advanced" version of the person he or she guarded.[164] The effect of communing with a more perfectly self-aware version of the self was nothing short of transcendence. For while an aspect of self was not wholly in control, the self was resistant, at some level, to society. To the degree that it was immune, it was part and parcel to divinity. Such immunization involved a two-step process: acknowledging the powerful charms of the social as a primary means of domesticating them.

Davis's version of spiritual intercourse, like a phrenology examina-tion, promised the solitary individual that he or she could (not to mention should) live in relation to the universal standard of the human commu-nity. You could imagine that there was an almost infinite density to the internalization of this standard, an idealized composite of each and every human who had ever lived. There was pleasure in submission. *Epistemic virtue morphing into ontology. Inscribed upon the self by the self. A silent inland presence.* What Tocqueville called, perhaps in response to his friendly en-counter with Channing, the "perpetual exercise of self-applause."[165]

———

Which brings us back to the strange kind of Romanticism at work in the disposition of the landsmen—an opening of self to "mystical vibration[s]" that simultaneously grounds down. Ishmael's description of the "strange" ritual—pacing back and forth between the "limits of the land" and a ha-bitually demarcated interiority—is not as pointed as Tommo's portrait

163. Davis, *Principles of Nature*, 201.
164. Davis, *Present Age*, 72.
165. Tocqueville, *American Institutions*, 266.

of evangelical missionaries we witnessed in the previous chapter, but it nonetheless broaches similar questions about secularism: the aesthetics of conviction among those who had either moved away from evangelicalism, favored immanent conceptions of divinity, or otherwise drifted in and out of more liberal Protestant circles. Specifically, it captures something about the making of spirituality in antebellum America.

The landsmen's practice of pacing back and forth from the water's edge enables them to become comfortable in their chairs, to come to know themselves while clinched to their desks. "Surely," suggests Ishmael, the landsmen's imagination of the sea as a site of adventure and self-knowledge relates somehow to the "meaning" of their reticence and constraint before the ocean, not to mention the quality of self-knowledge they achieve. "And still deeper the meaning of that story of Narcissus, who because he could not grasp the tormenting, mild image he saw in the fountain, plunged into it and was drowned."

Narcissus looked into the water but did not wholly recognize his reflection. He was instead disturbed—at least initially. The image he saw was tormenting, indistinct. He sensed that his reflection had power over him, that its shimmering visage animated him rather than he it. "That same image," confides Ishmael, "we ourselves see in all rivers and oceans. It is the image of the ungraspable phantom of life." Yet Narcissus attempted to grasp it, to make it a matter of empirical clarity, and to establish his authority over it.

The story of Narcissus is about the death of an individual. It is also a story about a collective desire to punch through the images on the horizon and to grasp the "very being of what is represented."[166] And finally, it is a story that speaks of the emergence of spirituality, dramatizing how the looming orders of secularism take hold—indirectly, circuitously, searingly—in the lives of those who most benefit from them.

166. Michel Foucault, *The Archaeology of Knowledge and the Discourse on Language*, trans. A. M. Sheridan Smith (New York: Pantheon Books, 1972), 240.

CHAPTER **3**

⚭

A SHORT BIOGRAPHY OF **LEWIS HENRY MORGAN**

with Curious Asides on the

AFFECT OF SPIRITUALITY & THE EMERGENCE

of ANTHROPOLOGICAL COMPREHENSION

For such is the wonderful skill, prescience of experience, and invincible confidence acquired by some great natural geniuses among the Nantucket commanders; that from the simple observation of a whale when last descried, they will, under certain given circumstances, pretty accurately foretell both the direction in which he will continue to swim for a time, while out of sight, as well as his probable rate of progression during that period. . . . And as the mighty iron Leviathan of the modern railway is so familiarly known in its every pace, that, with watches in their hands, men time his rate as doctors that of a baby's pulse; and lightly say of it, the up train or the down train will reach such or such a spot, at such or such an hour; even so, almost, there are occasions when these Nantucketers time that other Leviathan of the deep, according to the observed humor of his speed; and *say to themselves*, so many hours hence this whale will have gone two hundred miles, will have about reached this or that degree of latitude or longitude.

Moby-Dick; or, the Whale (1851)

Man, when left to the guidance of his own inward persuasions, searches after the Author of his being, and seeks to comprehend the purposes of his existence, and his final destiny.

LEWIS HENRY MORGAN, *League of the Ho-dé-no-sau-nee, or Iroquois* (1851)

"How evident that in strict speech there can be no biography of an Indian-hater *par excellence*, any more than one of a sword-fish, or other deep-sea denizen; or, which is still less imaginable, one of a dead man. The career of the Indian-hater *par excellence* has the impenetrability of the fate of a lost steamer. Doubtless, events, terrible ones, have happened, must have happened; but the powers that be in nature have taken order that they shall never become news."

HERMAN MELVILLE, *The Confidence-Man* (1857)

1. Involuntary Preparations Going On

Lewis Henry Morgan loved Native Americans, perhaps because he owed so much to them. Having moved to Rochester, New York, in 1845, Morgan began taking notes, conducting interviews, and collecting artifacts at the Tonawanda Reservation in Genesee County. *League of the Ho-dé-no-sau-nee, or Iroquois* was published in 1851. Morgan's was a sympathetic treatment of the "spirit" binding together the diverse aspects of Iroquois existence—the cut of a dress, a civic ceremony, the belief in the souls of the dead still walking the earth, a longhouse, the boiled bark of straps and skeins. Subsequently, Morgan continued his ethnographic activities while accumulating a sizeable fortune as a lawyer for commercial railroads, director of the Iron Mountain Rail Road Company, and investor in iron mining operations in the Upper Peninsula of Michigan. Before and after his economic success, Morgan was integral to the professionalization of anthropology in America, producing such far-reaching studies as *Systems of Consanguinity and Affinity of the Human Family* (1871) and *Ancient Society* (1877). He lobbied legislatures on behalf of the New York State of Natural History, compiled extraordinary amounts of data on indigenous kinship systems, and lent his time and energy to burgeoning institutions like the American Association for the Advancement of Science and the Smithsonian Institution.

As this chapter will demonstrate, Morgan's mode of ethnographic inquiry was a decidedly effective formation of secularism. Throughout his career Morgan mapped, with ever-greater precision, a cohesive system that organized, animated, and perhaps even transcended the human world. In searching for the script of life itself, a universal code that determined particular ways and means of being human, Morgan's career resonated with the interpretive dilemma of Narcissus and the liberal pursuit of self-culture that I previously discussed in terms of the epistemic mechanics of spirituality. Here, again, in what may be called Morgan's "physiognomy of the country," one may witness the ambitions that made the Common

Sense conflation of knowing the self and knowing the world so appealing.[1] For in Morgan's case, expert knowledge of the other—of other humans but also of the spirit that bound them to each other—became a righteous mode of self-knowledge. Morgan, here, becomes representative of a kind of secular subjectivity, his decisions the product of a complex but not necessarily contradictory set of tensions.

In what follows I focus on the emotional cadences and epistemic moves of Morgan's emergent anthropology. I do so in order to broach, yet again, the circuitously affective ways in which secularism authorized itself in antebellum America. Morgan spent the entirety of his adult life searching for what he called the "Author of his being." According to Morgan, this search was a process of moral instruction, self-transformation, and "heart-felt piety which the mind cannot resist."[2] Morgan had identified with this private quest for wholeness and closure ever since he was a young lawyer in Aurora, New York. As the founding member of the "Grand League of the Iroquois" in 1843, a secret society of white men devoted to emulating native practices and communicating with the "Great Spirit," Morgan sought a kind of conversion denied to him by the contemporary condition of his society. "The great defect of Education," he once lamented, was "that we study everything but ourselves." In seeking to know himself as he truly was, Morgan envisioned himself as participating in the progressive narrative of civilization. "Mental and moral constitution," he announced, were to be his "primary objects" of inquiry.[3]

League of the Iroquois was part of the long transition from the study of a divinely sanctioned human society toward the investigation of human articulations of self and divinity as well as the relations between humans determined, in part, by those articulations. In moving away from traditional theological accounts of human artifice, *League* described

1. E.G.S., "American Ethnology," *The American Whig Review* 9 (April 1849): 385.
2. Lewis Henry Morgan, *League of the Ho-dé-no-sau-nee, or Iroquois* (Rochester: Sage & Brother, 1851; rpt., Secaucus: The Citadel Press, 1975), 223. For additional references to the author of being or existence, see *League*, 149, 155, 184, 223, 290, and Lewis Henry Morgan, *The American Beaver and His Works* (1868; New York: Dover Publications, 1986), 190, 283. See also "On Piety," *The Liberal Christian* 1 (March 6, 1824), 200: "He that is without the proper affections to the author of his being, or who does not study to cultivate them by those acts and exercises, which are the natural and necessary expressions of them, should indeed be ashamed to make any pretensions to integrity and goodness of character."
3. Lewis Henry Morgan, "An Address on Temperance, May 14, 1843," Box 21, folder 5: B153. Lewis Henry Morgan Papers, Department of Rare Books, Special Collections, and Preservation, University of Rochester.

the social relations of the Iroquois as effective in and of themselves. Yet Morgan also claimed that each Iroquois possessed an "individual independence and boundless freedom," a harmony of existence that civilized men no longer enjoyed. The author of their being—the Great Spirit—pervaded every gesture, every word, every action and exchange of their lives. For Morgan, the promise of correspondence was an ancient inheritance.[4] By Morgan's account, Iroquois identity was untroubled by their knowledge base, beliefs, morals, laws, customs, and art. Having achieved a high standard of "spiritual meditation," there was no tension between an essential self and the artificial demands of society. There was no tension given how the social had become an extension of the biological self, the biological an extension of the social. And it was the complexity of this seamlessness, these almost infinitely dense measures of relationality, that Morgan sought to understand for the purpose of emulation.[5]

In playing out the drama of spirituality, Morgan assumed existence to be a matter of enchantment. The world around impinged upon the ideas and actions of each individual even as it bound together those ideas and actions into a coherent whole. The consistent focus of Morgan's ethnographic project was the quality of this binding agent and the substance of its influence. Consequently, he approached the material world as a network of signs. These signs pointed beyond themselves to an overarching code that governed their relationality and effect. As Gillian Feeley-Harnik has persuasively shown, Morgan "was trying to grasp the *generative* power of speech by expanding what we understand by speech to include mute utterances articulated in other forms." Beyond these utterances lay the "vague language" of life itself, the animating spirit of material representations. This spirit was nothing less than the authority of being, subject to scientific inquiry, scrupulous documentation, and patient mapping.[6] As with liberal Protestants from the previous chapter, Morgan's was a firm acknowledgement followed by a commitment to overcome what he had

---

4. "That the laws of nature were unchangeable and perfect," declared Morgan, "was the most sublime discovery of ancient learning; and it teaches the obvious lesson to man, that he should imitate her perfection as his only guide, and adhere to her laws as his only safety" ("An Address on Temperance, May 14, 1843").

5. Morgan, *League*, 139.

6. Gillian Feeley-Harnik, "'Communities of Blood': The Natural History of Kinship in Nineteenth-Century America," *Comparative Studies of Society and History* 41, no. 2 (April 1999): 230. See also her "'The Mystery of Life in All Its Forms': Religious Dimensions of Culture in Early American Anthropology," in *Religion and Cultural Studies*, ed. Susan L. Mizruchi (Princeton: Princeton University Press, 2001).

acknowledged—a defensive attempt to theorize and nail down the conditions of enchantment.

Although Morgan did not use the term culture, his language of spirit and circulation anticipated the coinage of culture in the works of later anthropologists, most notably E. B. Tylor. Feeley-Harnik has argued that the culture concept emerged in the writings of Morgan as a way to negotiate theological and scientific approaches to the question of design and human origins.[7] Yet questions remain regarding what exactly was going into this so-called displacement of theology.[8] Consequently, this chapter will revolve around a series of questions: What epistemic desires, practices, and institutions conditioned the results of Morgan's negotiation? What metaphysical scheme enabled Morgan to subject the invisible relations of society to empirical verification? What led Morgan to the cutting edge of articulating the terms of anthropological comprehension?[9] What were the terms that allowed Americans like Morgan to explain themselves to themselves and then to apply this explanation toward creating the material conditions of their own future?

On one level, this chapter continues my exploration of secularism—here the formation of ethnographic inquiry and its relationship to notions of

---

7. Feeley-Harnik, "Mystery of Life," 145. Raymond Williams has argued that the idea of culture as a unified and unifying property was rooted in a sense of crisis pervading the nineteenth century and in the changing attitudes accompanying the Enlightenment and the Industrial Revolution; Williams, *Culture & Society: 1780–1950* (New York: Columbia University Press, 1983), 233. The question of religion and the religious grammars that informed the emergence of the culture concept have been largely confined to insights concerning the theological commitments of Protestant missionary reports and the Romantic sensibilities of mid-century England. See, for example, Christopher Herbert's argument that the leading paradigm of Anglo-European social thought in the nineteenth century was that of social control, a secular substitute for the rhetoric of original-sin theology within the English context; Herbert, *Culture and Anomie: Ethnographic Imagination in the Nineteenth Century* (Chicago: University of Chicago Press, 1991), 31–44, 157–58. Exceptions that focus on religious contexts within antebellum America include the works of Feeley-Harnik, Susan L. Mizruchi, *The Science of Sacrifice: American Literature and Modern Social Theory* (Princeton: Princeton University Press, 1998), and Alex Calder, "'The Thrice Mysterious Taboo': Melville's *Typee* and the Perception of Culture," *Representations* 67 (Summer 1999): 27–43.

8. While invoking the "DEITY" in his intellectual works, such instances smacked less of piety than they did of Morgan's drift toward the "solving name" of culture to anchor his elaborate theories of social signification. On the concept of a "solving name," see William James, *Pragmatism: A New Name for Some Old Ways of Thinking* (New York: Longmans, Green, and Co., 1907), 53.

9. On the question of comprehensibility, see Arnold I. Davidson, "Styles of Reasoning: From the History of Art to the Epistemology of Science," in *The Emergence of Sexuality: Historical Epistemology and the Formation of Concepts* (Cambridge, Mass.: Harvard University Press, 2001), 125–41.

spirituality, séance spiritualism, and evangelical textuality. At another level, this chapter places secularism in relation to what Susan M. Ryan argues was the penchant for Anglo-Americans to resist "seeing the violence undergirding" their claims of benevolence at mid-century.[10] I dwell on an apparent inconsistency between Morgan's code of ethnographic virtue and the logic of imperial conquest that he believed himself to be defying. For what began as a youthful defense of Iroquois land claims in the 1840s soon turned less benevolent as Morgan participated in business ventures that furthered native dispossession. By the mid-1850s Morgan was pursuing more practical and seemingly less sentimental endeavors—facilitating the acquisition of capital and land in the Upper Peninsula of Michigan and theorizing, benevolently, about the necessity of Indian acquiescence to civilized progress.

Morgan's search for the author of his being was marked by deferral rather than consummation. For Morgan, a sense of tension, an intimation of a secret about to be disclosed, was necessary for both personal and national growth. His compulsion to seek redemptive wisdom in the colonial encounter embodied an honest love for the remnant of native societies at mid-century. Yet Morgan's perpetual search for the code that authorized his being was intimately related to institutional strategies of Indian removal. Both Morgan's search and these strategies were premised on an initial perception of insufficiency, a sense of potentiality that could be experienced, with pleasure, repeatedly. Biography and imperial context, in other words, both turned on the perpetual desire to fulfill a destiny that had not yet arrived, to experience a just-out-of-reach sense of cohesion and wholeness. Transformation was inevitable. Legibility was manifest. A code preexistent. The future could be written because it was a foregone conclusion. Perhaps not Indian-hating *par excellence*, but the metaphysics of a distinctly American emotion.[11]

2. Secularism and the Authority of Being; with Reference to Cartographic Ambitions both Fictional and Otherwise

Captain Ahab was not an Indian-hater, yet his metaphysics betrayed more than a hint of imperial fervor. And a penchant for maps, both figurative

10. Susan M. Ryan, *The Grammar of Good Intentions: Race and the Antebellum Culture of Violence* (Ithaca: Cornell University Press, 2005), 25, 45.
11. On the relationship between secularism and colonialism in a global context, see Gil Anidjar, "Secularism," *Critical Inquiry* 33, no. 1 (Autumn 2006): 52–77.

and literal. Having lost his leg to Moby Dick, Ahab's monomania was, among other things, a particularly intense and fictionalized quest to locate the author of his being:

> What is it, what nameless, inscrutable, unearthly thing is it; what cozening, hidden lord and master, and cruel, remorseless emperor commands me; that against all natural lovings and longings, I so keep pushing, and crowding, and jamming myself on all the time; recklessly making me ready to do what in my own proper, natural heart, I durst not so much as dare? Is Ahab, Ahab? Is it I, God, or who, that lifts this arm?

For Ahab, the promise of self-presence seemed but a cruel joke. Even upon recognizing the limitations of his own reasoning, Ahab could not stop mapping the certainty to which he had become accustomed. He could not adjust. He steadfastly refused to be traumatized. The wound to Ahab's sense of self was not severe enough to steer him from his course. "Ahab is for ever Ahab," he mutters at the end.

As it is described throughout the novel, Ahab's monomania is fueled not simply by "the mechanical humming of the wheels of his [own] vitality" and the technologies that produce that vitality. His hatred also stems from the taunting impossibility of knowing his own code, of recovering (and therefore calculating) that part of himself that lies behind the surface, in the belly of the beast:

> All visible objects, man, are but as pasteboard masks. . . . If man will strike, strike through the mask! How can the prisoner reach outside except by thrusting through the wall? To me, the white whale is that wall, shoved near to me. He tasks me; he heaps me; I see in him outrageous strength, with an inscrutable malice sinewing it. That inscrutable thing is chiefly what I hate.

Whereas Ahab's initial encounter with Moby Dick had precipitated his existential crisis, it was perpetuated by his faith in nautical instruments to "pretty accurately foretell both the direction in which [the whale] will continue to swim for a time, while out of sight" in the manner of an explorer reading his "reliable" map of the "steadfast land" or a passenger reading a railway schedule. Hence the inordinate amount of time Ahab spends with his "large wrinkled roll of yellowish sea charts." Ishmael notes in an aside:

Now, to any one not fully acquainted with the ways of the leviathans, it might seem an absurdly hopeless task thus to seek out one solitary creature in the unhooped oceans of this planet. But not so did it seem to Ahab, who knew the sets of all the tides and currents; and thereby calculated the driftings of the sperm whale's food; and, also calling to mind the regular, ascertained seasons for hunting him in particular latitudes; could arrive at reasonable surmises, almost approaching to certainties, concerning the timeliest day to be upon this or that ground in search of his prey.

Ahab's was an intense coordination of measurements and calculations of those measurements. His "elaborate migratory charts of the sperm whale" were made possible by the fact that whales were guided by "some infallible instinct" and endowed with "secret intelligence from the Deity."

Alone in his cabin Ahab pondered his charts. The swinging pewter lamp, "suspended in chains" overhead, cast "shadows of lines upon his wrinkled brow, till it almost seemed that while he himself was marking out lines and courses on the wrinkled charts, some invisible pencil was also tracing lines and courses upon the deeply marked chart of his forehead." Ahab's desire to coordinate the particularities of his own quest with the accumulated knowledge of whale migrations has begun to inscribe itself upon him. In a moment that distills the affective logic of a phrenological examination, Ahab's private desire has itself become structured by the desire infused in the moldy maps before his eyes. There is a kind of freedom to be found in this moment of incorporation as Ahab chooses, with the intentionality and reason that such deliberation portends, to submit to the promise of limitless calculability.

—

"Since the above was written," notes Melville in a footnote, the scene of Ahab's subjection "is happily borne out by an official circular, issued by Lieutenant Maury, of the National Observatory, Washington, April 16th, 1851. By that circular, it appears that precisely such a chart is in course of completion." Melville was referring here to Matthew Fontaine Maury, a rising star within the Navy and the author of a widely used textbook, *A New Theoretical and Practical Treatise on Navigation* (1836). Maury had followed the seafaring example of his older brother, who had once been stranded for two years on Nukahiva, the same island that was the setting of *Typee*. In 1839 Maury was thrown from the top of a stage-coach, his tendon ripped from the lower part of the knee. No longer allowed to pursue

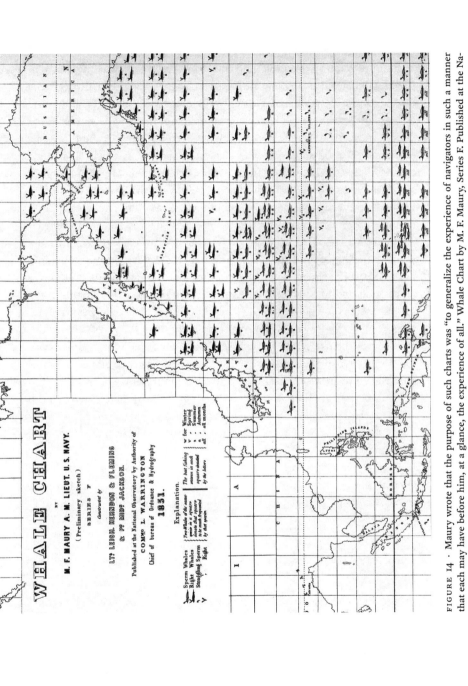

FIGURE 14 · Maury wrote that the purpose of such charts was "to generalize the experience of navigators in such a manner that each may have before him, at a glance, the experience of all." Whale Chart by M. F. Maury, Series F. Published at the National Observatory (1851).

active duty at sea, Maury shifted his focus to hydrography and other matters, including maritime law and lobbying the Navy to adopt steam as a motive power for ships and artillery.[12]

Fond of quoting the Bible and Shakespeare, Maury was the First Superintendent of the U.S. Naval Observatory (originally called the Depot of Charts and Instruments). Maury regarded "earth, sea, air, and water as parts of a machine, pieces of mechanism, not made with hands, but to which, nevertheless, certain offices have been assigned in the terrestrial economy." Such assignation was part and parcel to divinity. "It is good and profitable to seek to find these offices," continued Maury. For "when, after patient research, I am led to the discovery of any one of them, I feel with the astronomer of old, as though I had 'thought one of God's thoughts,'—and tremble."[13]

Maury's interpretive strategy was to read the diverse signs of earth and sea as pointing beyond themselves to a "perfect" "system of circulation. For as Maury declared, such a system invests the atmosphere and makes "the whole world kin!" As he instructed his readers, "look behind and study" the "exquisite system of machinery by which such beautiful results are brought about." Only then would "parts of the physical machinery" reveal themselves to be "expression of One Thought, a unity with harmonies which One Intelligence, and One Intelligence alone, could utter." Nailed to his desk with charts strewn, Maury envisioned himself to be deciphering the blueprint of an "engine" built by God himself. With characteristic bravado, Maury mapped "the secret paths of the seas" as a way to strengthen his moral character, elevate the mind, and "enoble[] the man."[14]

In the late 1840s Maury became fascinated with stories of sperm whales who were reported to have exhausted the reserve of harpoon lines by diving straight down, remaining submerged for hours on end.

12. Diana Fontaine Maury Corbin, *A Life of Matthew Fontaine Maury* (London: Sampson Low, Marston, Searle, and Rivington, 1888), 10f., 29, 36, 40; Helen M. Rozwadowski, "Technology and Ocean-Scape: Defining the Deep Sea in Mid-Nineteenth Century," *History and Technology* 17 (2001): 221–22.
13. Cited in Frances Leigh Williams, *Matthew Fontaine Maury: Scientist of the Sea* (New Brunswick: Rutgers University Press, 1963), 340.
14. Matthew Fontaine Maury, *The Physical Geography of the Sea and Its Meteorology* (1855), ed. John Leighly (Cambridge: Harvard University Press, 1963), 95, 70, 103, 200. "What a powerful engine is the atmosphere!," Maury exclaimed. "And how nicely adjusted must be all cogs, wheels, and springs, and pinions of this exquisite piece of machinery, that it never wears out or breaks down, nor fails to do its work at the right time, and in the right way!" (91–92). See also Williams, *Matthew Fontaine Maury*, 262, 341; Corbin, *A Life*, 159–60.

By 1849, Maury had moved beyond the mere measurement of salinity, winds, currents, and surface temperatures to the measuring of depth. Soon after he became famous for having issued a series of "Track Charts" as well as trade-wind charts, thermal charts, storm and rain charts, and whale charts, the latter of which were cited by Melville. More significant, perhaps, was the public sentiment that Maury's "modern science" was "fated to explode" the notion that the bottom of the ocean was "unfathomable."[15]

By 1853 Maury had made enough deep sea soundings to begin to produce a map of the Atlantic floor. As Maury's fame spread, he was contacted by Cyrus Field, an American financier interested in finding a viable Atlantic cable route. Having contacted Morse about the practicality of transmitting messages across the Atlantic, Field enlisted Maury's expertise in his venture. With the navigational skills of Lt. Otway Berryman, Maury soon announced the discovery of the so-called "Telegraphic Plateau" between Newfoundland and Ireland that would eventually allow for transatlantic telegraphy. After many failed attempts, the first trans-Atlantic messages were sent in August 1858 and accompanied by much fanfare. Despite the fact that the cable went mute later that October, Maury's quest to disclose the secrets of God's machine had become massively consequential. In addition to further naturalizing the subjugation of the ocean, his efforts contributed to the perception that telegraphic messages (and the industrial imagination that conditioned them) were located beyond the space of social relations.[16]

According to Maury, the telegraphic plateau "seems to have been placed there especially for the purpose of holding the wires of the submarine telegraph, and keeping them out of harm's way." Whereas other parts of the ocean floor were full of wreckage, skulls, and tumultuous "sights of ugly death," this particular patch of the ocean floor was likened to the stillness of death. It was a "vast cemetery" and, at the same time, a window into the origins of life. Dead shellfish of microscopic size had been recovered and brought to the surface. Their perfect form testified to the fact that "no current exists where they lie, that no shocks disturb them, that they rest in

15. Steven J. Dick, *Sky and Ocean Joined: The U.S. Naval Observatory, 1830–2000* (Cambridge: Cambridge University Press, 2003), 96; "Telegraph Supplement," *Harper's Weekly* 2, no. 88 (September 4, 1858), 10.

16. Williams, *Matthew Fontaine Maury*, 226; Dick, *Sky and Ocean*, 108; Rozwadowski, "Technology," 229; Philip E. Steinberg, *The Social Construction of the Ocean* (Cambridge: Cambridge University Press, 2001), 113.

a death-like stillness very well befitting so huge a grave."[17] Consequently, "once laid" on this plateau, "a telegraph cable is secure forever." Here was a colonization of the sea that exceeded similar efforts to secure civilization on the peripheries of empire. For Maury's painstaking inquiries also testified to the fact that the telegraphic plateau had been "mapped with more accuracy than the interior of the continents of Africa or Australia."[18]

3. Networks, Circulation, and Representations of Networks and Circulation in the Vicinity of Rochester

Cyrus Field's American Telegraph Company was largely financed by investments from Rochester, New York. Rochester had flourished in the first half of the nineteenth century, an urban center that witnessed the commercialization of agriculture and canals, as well as a manufacturing boom.[19] By the time Morgan arrived in Rochester in 1845 it was emerging as a node in an expansive networks of capital, transportation, communication, and liberal reform. Rochester had long been a site of media activity, with numerous journalistic offerings and propaganda sheets. When a telegraph connecting Rochester and Albany opened in June 1846, daily newspapers such as the *Democrat* and the *Advertiser* were quick to include "By Telegraph" columns.[20] By the early 1850s, with the accumulation of investment capital and infrastructure, telegraph lines were extending westward and Rochester was fast becoming "the telegraph capital of interior America."[21]

Heman Ely, a Rochester lawyer, was an early proponent of the telegraph industry and the head of the Lake Erie Telegraph Company, a consortium of Rochester telegraph companies that were working together to link the eastern seaboard and the entire Great Lakes region. In 1848 Ely shifted his

17. Cited in Rozwadowski, "Technology," 229, 220. "Telegraph Supplement," 10.

18. "Telegraph Supplement," 10. See also Daniel R. Headrick, "The Imperial Telecommunications Networks," in *The Tentacles of Progress: Technology Transfer in the Age of Imperialism, 1850–1940* (New York: Oxford University Press, 1988), 97–144.

19. Paul E. Johnson, *A Shopkeeper's Millennium: Society and Revivals in Rochester, New York, 1815–1837* (New York: Hill and Wang, 1978), 13; Blake McKelvey, *Rochester, the Water-Power City, 1812–1854* (Cambridge, Mass.: Harvard University Press, 1945), 285–86. During this time Rochester also became a hub of abolitionist activity and women's rights.

20. McKelvey, *Rochester,* 150, 315–16.

21. Saul Benison, "Railroads, Land and Iron" (Ph.D. diss., Columbia University, 1953), 66. With the New York passage of the general incorporation law in 1848, Rochester immediately benefited with three new insurance companies and two telegraph companies. McKelvey, *Rochester,* 331–33.

business interest to railroading. It was Ely's desire to establish lucrative lines of transportation between the iron reserves of the Upper Peninsula of Michigan and the industrializing hubs on the Great Lakes and eastern seaboard that would eventually draw Morgan into the railroad business. Ely's shift also marked a moment in which both telegraphy and railroads had begun to win over public sentiment (after some initial skepticism) as they increasingly coordinated their efforts to bring order and efficiency to their co-dependent networks.[22]

Morgan's Rochester was awash in representations of a world in circulation. Yet even the most triumphalist rhetoric about the intense relationality between people, machines, and information was laced with implications about the existence of a system of interdependence that did not itself depend upon any single person or agency.[23] "The electric telegraph is gradually spreading its network of nerves throughout the land," declared one popular journal. Eliding the difference between biology and communication, the telegraph was "creating a system so highly sensitive that literally a throb at its metropolitan heart will be felt almost simultaneously in every distant part." The effect was "immediate communication."[24] Similarly, as "iron roads . . . spread their network over the land," the "moral effects" and "political effects" were considerably felt. All manner of barriers were collapsing—time and space to be sure, but also those boundaries that once could be counted on to secure essential notions of human intentionality and control.[25] Yet still there was comfort and security to be found in notions of totalizing expertise, mutual dependency, and enclosure.[26]

By mid-century, descriptions of networks involved magnetic, electrical, and divine imagery in an effort to evoke new structures and experiences of sociality.[27] A law of social organization was emerging whose complex-

22. Benison, "Railroads, Land and Iron," 68; Robert Luther Thompson, *Wiring a Continent: The History of the Telegraph Industry in the United States, 1832–1866* (Princeton: Princeton University Press, 1947), 204.

23. See, for example, "Miscellany," *The American Whig Review* 12 (October 1850): 434. On being "entangled in an inextricable network of fate," see "The Mysterious Leg," *The Living Age* 13 (May 22, 1847): 355. On the imperial "network" of "Christian sanctity" spread over a "heathen wilderness," see "De Quincey's Writings," *The North American Review* 74 (April 1852): 439.

24. Untitled, *The Living Age* 12 (January 2, 1847): 7.

25. "The Railway Potentates—Mr. Hudson, Mr. Chaplin, Mr. Russell, Mr. Strutt," *The Living Age* 14 (September 25, 1847): 586–87.

26. "Railroads," *New-York Evangelist* 23 (October 1852): 178.

27. See, for example, "Terrestrial Magnetism," *Harper's New Monthly Magazine* 1, no. 5 (October 1850): 655. On the redemptive imagery associated with communication networks, see Armand Mattelart, *The Invention of Communication*, trans. Susan Emanuel (Minneapolis: Uni-

ity transcended "the lower principle of outward and mechanical arrangement." Such "organizing power" was often seen as inherently religious, premised as it was upon our "faith in unseen things and supernatural powers." Such power was vital, akin to the "life inbreathed by the Creator [into] the solid, bony frame, the network of nerves, the circulating blood, the beating heart." As the basis of a renewed "social unity," this power was on the horizon, destined to spread over "our vast unoccupied territory." As a kind of "state" that was "something more than an enlargement of the family," it guaranteed its own perpetuity. This principle of "national unity" was insubstantial, difficult to name, yet decidedly republican—a "combination of the members of the state [in which] all shall act for each, and each for all, and their concentrated powers flow through common channels for the common blessing."[28] Or as Morgan wrote in *League*, "Civilization is aggressive." And it was also "progressive—a positive state of society, attacking every obstacle, overwhelming every lesser group, and searching out and filling up every crevice, both in the moral and physical world."[29]

Throughout his career, Morgan was fascinated by networks—from kinship systems to railway geography to beaver dams. He was attracted to phenomena without any discernible center, whose essence was nonessential. He considered himself to be taking a realist approach to things, securing the stable flux of the object world by insisting that an order revealed itself, first and foremost, as spirit.

During Morgan's initial inquiries into the structural divisions of the Iroquois Confederacy, he discovered a system of relationality that "linked the nations together with indissoluble bonds." These ties were made up of blood, nomenclature, and ritual practices. And while this network was not the explicit focus on Morgan's first book, this data set became a foundational template for the rest of his career, culminating in *Systems of Consanguinity*. In *Systems*, Morgan surveyed substantive differences between the world's indigenous populations vis-à-vis how they designated and classified kindred. He made visits to American Indian reservations and solicited information from foreign missionaries. But as evidenced by hundreds

---

versity of Minnesota Press, 1996), 85f. See also "The London *Times* on American Intercommunication," *The International Magazine of Literature, Art, and Science* 4, no. 4 (November 1851): 461-67.

28. "National Unity," *New Englander and Yale Review* 6 (October 1848): 588, 578, 585, 579, 583, 582.

29. Morgan, *League*, 444-45.

SYSTEMS OF CONSANGUINITY AND AFFINITY.   77

TABLE I.—SYSTEMS OF CONSANGUINITY AND AFFINITY.

Families.	Classes.	Branches.		Dialects.	Author of Schedule.	Pronoun My.
SEMITIC .	ARABIC .	Southern . .	1	Arabic	C. V. A. Van Dyck, D.D. .	Suffix i.
			2	Druse and Maronite . . .	Hon. J. A. Johnson . . .	" i.
	HEBRAIC .	Middle. . .	3	Hebrew	Prof. W. Henry Green . .	" i.
	ARAMAIC .	Northern . .	4	Neo-Syriac or Nestorian . .	Austin H. Wright, M.D. . .	" e.
			5	Armenian	John De Artin (Native Arm.)	Im.
ARYAN			6	Erse or Irish	D. Foley, D. D.	Mo.
	CELTIC .	Gadhelic . .	7	Gaelic or Highland Scottish,	Rev. Duncan McNab . . .	Mo.
			8	Manx	John Moore	My.
		Cymric . .	9	Welsh	Evan T. Jones, Esq. . . .	Fy.
	IRANIC .	—	10	Persian	Rev. George W. Coan, D. D.	Suffix ăm.
	INDIC .	—	11	Sanskrit	{ Prof. W. D. Whitney } 2 S. { Fitz Ed. Hall, D.C.L. }	Mama.
	TEUTONIC .	Scandinavian	12	Danish and Norwegian . .	Hon. W. Raasloff	Post { minn { mas. { min { fem.
			13	Icelandic	Prof. I. Sigwrdson . . .	" { mim { mas. { min { fem.
			14	Swedish	Edward Count Piper . . .	Min.
			15	Anglo-Saxon	Lewis H. Morgan	
			16	English	" " "	My.
		Low German .	17	Holland Dutch	Gerard Arink, M. D. . . .	{ My { mas. { Myne { fem.
			18	Belgian	Father P. J. De Smet, S. J.	{ Myn { mas. { Myuen { fem.
			19	Platt-Deutsh	Lewis H. Morgan	{ Me { mas. { Mene { fem.
		High German	20	German	Joseph Felix, Esq.. . . .	{ Moin { mas. { Meine { fem.
			21	German-Swiss	Herr C. Hunziker	{ Mein { mas. { Meine { fem.
	ROMAIC .	Modern . .	22	French	Lewis H. Morgan	{ Mon { mas. { Ma { fem.
			23	Spanish	Senhor Miguel Maria Lisboa	Mi
			24	Portuguese	" " "	{ Min { mas. { Mia { fem.
			25	Italian	Prof. Paul Marzolo . . .	{ Mio { mas. { Mia { fem.
			26	Latin	Lewis H. Morgan	{ Meus { mas. { Mea { fem.
	HELLENIC .	Ancient . .	27	Classical Greek	" " "	{ Emos { mas. { Emē { fem.
		Modern . .	28	Modern Greek	Glossary of Prof. Sophocles .	
		Lettic . . .	29	Lithuanian	Prof. F. Bopp	
	SLAVONIC .	—	30	Polish	Augusta Plinta, Esq. . . .	{ Moj { mas. { Moja { fem.
			31	Slovakian or Bohemian . .	Prof. Kanya	{ Moj { mas. { Moja { fem.
			32	Bulgarian	Elias Riggs, D. D. . . .	Post mi.
			33	Bulgarian	Rev. Charles F. Morse . .	" ni.
			34	Russian	By a Russian	{ Moi { mas. { Maja { fem.
URALIAN	TURKIC .	— —	35	Osmanli-Turk	Rev. Andrew T. Pratt . .	Suffix m.
			36	Kuzulbashe	Rev. George W. Dunmore . .	Post mun.
	UGRIC . .	Finnic . . .	37	Magyar	Prof. Paul Hunfalvy . . .	Suffix m.
			38	Esthonian	Hon. Chas. A. Leas . . .	Minn.
			39	Finn	{ Dr. Urjo Koskinen } 2 Sch. { Mr. G. Selin }	Suffix ni.

FIGURE 15 · Affinities between major language systems revolving around the use of the first-person possessive. From Lewis Henry Morgan's *Systems of Consanguinity and Affinity of the Human Family* (Washington: Smithsonian Institution, 1871), 77.

of tables and charts, the formalities of systematicity remained consistent across geography—an evolving structure made up of fated inevitability and linguistic choice.

Via tabular results linking grammar and blood, Morgan discovered correlations that pointed to the metaphysics of progress and pointed back, "with sensible clearness," to "'the hole of the pit whence [we have been] digged' by the good providence of God." This silent space was wholly determinative of the logic of kinship relations, past, present, and future. Consequently, Morgan's charts were utterly symbolic, signifying a family origin whose effect upon "modern times" had yet to be determined. "In their importance and value," wrote Morgan, his tables reached "far beyond any present use of their contents which the writer may be able to indicate"[30]

Morgan had difficulty naming the animating systematicity on display in his tables. Resembling the family obligations of the primitive tribe, it was that which "places" each person where that person ought to be. This was similar to a point made by J. H. McIlvaine, a Presbyterian minister and close friend who had spent over two decades trying to bring Morgan into the Christian fold. Having read the manuscript of *Systems* before publication, McIlvaine reasoned that Morgan

> had not perceived any material significance or explanation of the immense body of entirely new facts which he had discovered and collected. He could not at all account for them. In fact, he regarded this system, or these slightly different forms of one system, as invented and wholly artificial, so different was it from that which now prevails in civilized society, and which evidently follows the flow of the blood. During all these years, he had not the least conception of any process of thought in which it could have originated, or of anything which could have caused it so universally to prevail. He treated it as something which must throw great light upon pre-historic man, but what light he had not discovered.[31]

McIlvaine here suggested that a deficiency in Morgan's analysis lay in his refusal to assign ultimate authority of human evolution to God's hand.

Morgan's point, however, was perhaps too liberal for McIlvaine to appreciate, given the latter's evangelical cast of mind and professorship at the evangelical bastion of Princeton. For Morgan's search for the author of his being did not culminate in the solving name of God but, in fact, depended upon the numerous vectors of relationality that intersected each person. Biology into politics; filiation into affiliation. Consistent with the epistemic virtue of spirituality surveyed in the previous chapter, Morgan

30. Lewis Henry Morgan, *Systems of Consanguinity and Affinity of the Human Family* (Washington: Smithsonian Institution, 1871), vii, 8; *League*, 81; "An Address on Temperance, May 14, 1843."

31. Joshua H. McIlvaine, *The Life and Works of Lewis H. Morgan, LL.D, an address at his funeral* (1882). Reprinted in *Rochester Historical Society Publications* 2 (1923): 51–52.

envisioned each of us as surrounded by a "widening circle of kindred." Whether we know it or not, he declared, "millions of the living and the dead, all of these individuals, in virtue of their descent from common ancestors, are bound to the '*Ego*' by the chain of consanguinity."[32]

4. Religion and Morgan's Scene of Writing

Six years after the publication of *Systems*, Morgan offered a sweeping theory about the origin and development of kinship networks. In *Ancient Society*, Morgan argued that the "history of the human race [was] one in source, one in experience, and one in progress." Consequently, he was able to track the "germs" of inheritance and property relations from savage "arrow head[s]" to "the smelting of iron ore" to "the railway train in motion, which may be called the triumph of civilization."[33] *Ancient Society* was uncontroversial in confirming the matriarchal structure of primal societies and the affinity between patriarchy and the higher development of civilization. In keeping with the scholarly trajectories of early ethnography, Morgan's scheme possessed a masculine charge in detailing the succession of technics and institutional networks over biological reproduction.[34]

As the culmination of Morgan's anthropological career, *Ancient Society* is notable for how it handles the category of the "religious." In mapping the shift from family ties to those of the state and commerce, Morgan acknowledged the potential importance of "the science of comparative religion" yet claimed that it was inessential to his present project. Because "the growth of religious ideas is environed with such *intrinsic difficulties*," Morgan reasoned, the history of religion "may never receive a perfectly satisfactory exposition. Religion deals so largely with the imaginative and

---

32. Morgan, *Systems*, 11.
33. Lewis Henry Morgan, *Ancient Society* (1877; Tucson: University of Arizona Press, 1985), xxx, 553.
34. Morgan characterized the six periods of evolutionary history in terms of technological advancement—knowledge of fire, invention of bow and arrow, invention of pottery, domestication of animals and irrigation, use of iron tools, and phonetic writing. In doing so, Morgan followed a general model of social and technological progress derived from Scottish Common Sense, particularly Adam Smith's evolutionary stages of hunting, pasturing, farming, and commerce. Morgan also celebrated the United States as a zenith in human evolution—the development of monogamous families, a territorially based state, and institutions that guaranteed private property and its transfer. Elisabeth Tooker, *Lewis H. Morgan on Iroquois Material Culture* (Tucson: University of Arizona Press, 1994), 11.

emotional nature, and consequently with such *uncertain elements of knowledge*, that all primitive religions are *grotesque* and to some extent *unintelligible*. This subject must "fall [outside] the plan of [my] work."[35] Religion, or at least its natural history, was an interpretive abyss for Morgan. Religion operated according to passion, not empiricism or reason. Consequently, it was neither part of civilization's plan nor, for that matter, could it be a part of his book. Best to avoid religion until all the facts were gathered, organized, and secured. In the last line of *Ancient Society*, Morgan claimed only to offer an "incidental suggestion" when it came to matters of religion. He invoked the authority of an anonymous, depersonalized system—"the plan of the Supreme Intelligence."[36] This disembodied intelligence was God-like in its effects yet substantially human.[37]

In his insistence that religion was not a viable category for analyzing or naming the cause underlying a series of phenomena, Morgan was not only or simply affirming the authority of Baconian science. He was also justifying his life-long refusal to use religion as a category of self-understanding. For in both his private life and his professional vision, religion was that which all too often disrupted the smooth workings of social life and personal identity—a pit of passion, a regressive path that we would all do well without. Morgan, for example, never joined the Presbyterian Church, whose members included both his wife and his closest acquaintances.[38] When pressed by his friend McIlvaine about his relationship to religion,

---

35. Morgan, *Ancient Society*, 115, 5–6 (my emphasis).

36. Ibid., 554.

37. There, perhaps, is no better phrase that signifies what I am talking about when I talk about secularism. Consequently, I am hesitant to call Morgan's desire (borrowing a phrase from Karl Löwith), "a mistaken Christianity that confounds the fundamental distinction between redemptive events and profane happenings" (Löwith, *Meaning in History: The Theological Implications of the Philosophy of History* [Chicago: University of Chicago Press, 1949], 203, 30). Rather than view Morgan's career as simply evidence for Judeo-Christian eschatology becoming a secular theodicy that excused all manner of violence and injustice, I am interested in locating the source of that violence (physical as well as epistemic) in the frustrations that arise from what Hans Blumenberg suggests is the subjunctive mood that pervades modernity. Consequently, Morgan's epistemological desires were overextended to the degree that they could no longer be sufficiently consummated. Hans Blumenberg, *The Legitimacy of the Modern Age*, trans. Robert M. Wallace (Cambridge, Mass.: MIT Press, 1983), 69, 61.

38. On Morgan's Protestantism, see Carl Resek, *Lewis Henry Morgan: American Scholar* (Chicago: University of Chicago Press, 1960), 50–51; Thomas R. Trautmann, *Lewis Henry Morgan and the Invention of Kinship* (Berkeley and Los Angeles: University of California Press, 1987), 64–70; and Gillian Feeley-Harnik, "'Mystery of Life,'" and "'Communities of Blood.'" These valuable contributions are noted throughout the chapter and contrast with Leslie A. White's defense of Morgan's scientific perspective in "Morgan's Attitude toward Religion and Science," *American Anthropologist* 46, no. 2 (1944): 218–30.

Morgan replied that "I do not claim to have freed my mind from all skeptical doubts, but my heart is with the Christian religion."[39]

On the one hand, Morgan distanced himself from the religious defined in terms of institutional formalities and the soft coercions of tradition. On the other hand, his ambivalence was a product of, as opposed to a reaction to, the charged environment of religion in which Morgan lived and worked. By the time Morgan reached early adulthood, the "burned-over district" of upstate New York had witnessed both intense Protestant revivalism and new religious movements such as séance spiritualism. Charles Grandison Finney, for example, had preached in Morgan's family church in the 1830s and had continued to visit the area well into the 1840s. In the great revival of 1830-31 Finney had galvanized the citizens of Rochester with his "new measures"—epistemological and political prescriptions that confirmed the ability of each individual to obtain salvation and to transform society in such a way as to secure the optimal conditions for everyone to exercise, on their own time and in their own way, the natural capacity to save themselves.[40] In response, many people in Rochester became involved in foreign missionary work and tract societies. Finney was a thorough-going Arminian who railed against the tyrannical implications of Calvinism and the "dogma(s) of Papacy." God did not operate in secret. On the contrary, all was revealed to everyone through the evidence of the senses.[41]

39. McIlvaine, *Life and Works of Lewis H. Morgan*, 56. Morgan publicly advocated temperance but never did so on behalf of any religious organization. Although he admitted that revivals had contributed to the cause, the "virtue of total abstinence" was not an "element of . . . religion," as it had been decreed by the "celebrated Impostor," "Mahomet." On the contrary, the case for temperance must be made without recourse to "fanciful speculations." Morgan's case rested on his argument that temperance was a "moral law" as well as a law of economy and health. "Ardent spirits" taxed the Republic with unnecessary crime and legal expenses. "Our national vice" also had debilitating effects on the "human machine." On his duty to "enlighten . . . public opinion," Morgan cited no less an authority than the phrenologist George Combe, whose *Notes on the United States of North America, During a Phrenological Visit* had recently been published. See "Address on Temperance, May 5, 1843," and "Address on Temperance, delivered by Scipio, Dec. 10, 1843," Box 21, folder 7: B174f, B183, Lewis Henry Morgan Papers, University of Rochester.

40. Trautmann, *Lewis Henry Morgan*, 64-65; McKelvey, *Rochester*, 278-79, 282. As Paul Johnson argued over thirty years ago in *Shopkeeper's Millennium*, a book worthy of reconsideration in light of contemporary debates over secularism, the lasting effects of Finney's "new measures" fueled both the consolidation of state power (most notably in the rhetoric of transparent labor relations) and the consolidation of religion as an eminently private affair.

41. Charles Grandison Finney, *Lectures on Revivals of Religion*, ed. William G. McLoughlin (Cambridge: Harvard University Press, 1960), 107-9; Charles G. Finney, *Lectures on Systematic Theology Embracing Lectures on Moral Government, Together with Atonement, Moral and Physical Depravity, Regeneration, Philosophical Theories, and Evidences of Regeneration* (London:

The evangelical vectors of intentionality and empirical immediacy were not absent from Morgan's later inquiries. Indeed, one would be hard-pressed not to see in Morgan's ethnographic project traces of Finney's insistence on the legibility of spirit and the capacity of each and every individual to read the marks of this spirit upon themselves. But rather than make the case for the influence of religion upon Morgan's secular science, I am more interested in exploring how Morgan's method and object of inquiry were surfaces of an emergent secularism. For what is remarkable about the budding anthropological comprehensibility in Morgan's life is how he defined religion, distanced himself from its formal iterations, yet participated in a particular distillation of it. To that end, one must account not only for the evangelical character of Morgan but also how and why that character was compatible with other formations of Protestantism.

The relationship between spiritualist metaphysics and Morgan's desire to recognize the terms of his own agency has received little scholarly attention, perhaps given the perception that evangelicalism and spiritualism were oppositional theologies.[42] Yet evangelical notions of legibility and "voluntary attention" (the title of McIlvaine's book discussed in chapter 1) were strangely present during the spiritualist boom of the late 1840s and early 1850s.

News of spirit communication emanated from the Fox family home in the village of Hydesville, about twenty miles from Rochester. John and Margaret Fox and their two daughters, Kate and Margaretta, were members of the Methodist Episcopal Church. One evening in March 1848, the family heard a "slight knocking in one of the bedrooms" that made each feel if they were being charged by a galvanic battery. The family looked but could not find the source of the knockings. The knockings continued, day after day. One night, the youngest daughter began to snap her fingers in imitation of the knockings. The knockings began to imitate her imitations. The knockings responded, accurately, to Mrs. Fox's command to count to ten. The knockings correctly identified the age of each child. The

William Tegg and Co., 1851), x–xi. On the connection between the emotional economy of revivals and the rise of social science, see Finbarr Curtis, "Locating the Revival: Jonathan Edwards's Northampton as a Site of Social Theory," in *Embodying the Spirit: New Perspectives on North American Revivalism*, ed. Michael J. McClymond (Baltimore: Johns Hopkins University Press, 2004), 47–66.

42. Feeley-Harnik broaches Morgan's proximity to spiritualism but dos not explore its metaphysics vis-à-vis the making of Morgan's object of inquiry. Feeley-Harnek does, however, provide an apt description of its hybridity: a "paradoxically organic transcendent materiality" ("'Communities of Blood,'" 256, 223).

source of the knockings then identified itself as a "spirit of a man," thirty-one-years old.[43]

Eventually, Margaret "asked the question: 'Will the noise continue if I call in the neighbors?'" This was exactly what the knocking wanted. "The answer was by rapping in the affirmative." As the "mode of communication . . . gradually improved" and included the letters of the alphabet, *it* soon spread to Rochester. P. T. Barnum arrived in June 1849 and enlisted the Fox sisters for public viewing. Soon they were performing three shows a day ("receptions") with opportunities to purchase a private "sitting." When a public investigation was held at the newly opened Corinthian Hall in November 1849, it was reported that there were a host of spirits who welcomed such investigations because they wanted to be made "more public."[44]

Although many dismissed spirits as "humbuggery," many accounts confirmed the phenomena of spirit communication through appeals to reason and science. Indeed, among the advocates of spiritualism there was a clear project to banish the "*super*natural" from the public sphere. Their goal was to provide "a reasonable and natural explanation" of spirit communication.[45] In his discussion of the "Rochester knockings," Andrew Jackson Davis offered a "spiritual" explanation in order to demystify them and argued that they were in no way unique. "The 'noises,'" he wrote, were "like the tickings of the telegraph when thoughts are transmitted from one end of the wire to the other. Intelligence was openly demonstrated as producing and conducting the sounds." According to Davis, the recent outbreak of spiritual intercourse would provide an epistemic space to contemplate one's relationality and the authority of one's being. "The mind of man is really a new discovery," proclaimed Davis. "It seems to live

43. Eliab W. Capron and Henry D. Barron, *Singular Revelations: Explanation and History of the Mysterious Communion with Spirits, Comprehending the Rise and Progress of the Mysterious Noises in Western New-York, Generally Received as Spiritual Communication* (Auburn, N.Y.: Finn and Rockwell, 1850), 12–13.

44. Capron and Barron, *Singular Revelations*, 12–13, 42–43, 48–49; Earl Wesley Fornell, *The Unhappy Medium: Spiritualism and the Life of Margaret Fox* (Austin: University of Texas Press, 1964), 25; P. T. Barnum, *The Humbugs of the World* (New York: Carleton, 1866), 82–85; C. Hammond, *Light from the Spirit World: Comprising a Series of Articles on the Condition of Spirits, and the Development of Mind in the Rudimental and Second Spheres* (Rochester: W. Heughes, Book and Job Printer, 1852), 250.

45. *The Rochester Advertiser* dismissed "humbuggery" in May 3, 1850. Cited in McKelvey, *Rochester*, 290. Capron and Barron, *Singular Revelations*, 5–6. Publication of the second edition of this book in 1850 was facilitated by Fowlers and Wells.

a new life—being as it is a wondrous vital battery—with every particle a magnet."[46]

The remainder of this chapter offers a roughly chronological narrative of how Morgan came to fix his anthropological purpose, drawing as he did from the Common Sense philosophies of Lord Kames and Adam Smith, evangelical theories of textuality, spiritualist aspirations to spectral legibility, and of course, capitalistic ventures in iron mines and railroads. To disentangle these different yet compatible threads is to begin to unpack the dense measures of experience that constituted Morgan's applied practice of spirituality.

Again, it would be too much to argue that Morgan's ethnographic practice was actually evangelicalism or spiritualism in disguise. Yet it would be not enough to argue that Morgan's work was influenced by religious ideas. Neither position is incorrect in that his social theory was a transposition of a "Supreme Intelligence" animating the workings of this world. Yet Morgan's work did not simply secularize; rather, it synthesized, in a politically powerful way, what evangelicalism and spiritualism shared—namely, a reasonable approach to the ambient energies of modernity as legible, liberating, and potentially salvific.

5. A Common Sense Education

Morgan attended Union College, an ecumenical venture established in 1795 in Schenectady, New York. At Union Morgan's education was anchored in readings from and lectures about Scottish Common Sense philosophy.[47] Morgan attended many lectures by Union's president, the Rev. Eliphalet Nott, the former pastor of the First Presbyterian Church of Albany, inventor of the Nott stove, and one of the leading stove manufacturers of the day. In his insistence upon the confluence of biblical studies and natural science, Nott used Lord Kames's *Elements of Criticism* as basis for his president's lectures. Nott presented the ideas of Kames in a critical fashion, reading them in light of his own faith, affirming the basic assumptions of Common Sense epistemology even as he refuted Kames's arguments about the unbridgeable difference between ethnic groups. Nott

46. Andrew Jackson Davis, *Present Age and Inner Life; A Sequel to Spiritual Intercourse* (New York: Partridge and Brittan, 1853), 52, 57, 60, 62.
47. Resek, *Lewis Henry Morgan*, 9; Trautmann, *Lewis Henry Morgan*, 22.

had little patience for Kames's polygenesis, given his own commitment to nonsectarian and global Christianity. As Nott stated in one of his lectures, "Man was made to be religious, to acknowledge and reverence God, and to be conformed in his moral conduct to the Law of God. You have only to consult your hearts to be convinced of this. The proof is there inscribed in characters which are indelible." According to Nott, religion was a universal potential in each person to decipher, personally, "the author of his being"[48]

As a source of Morgan's spirituality and ethnographic reasoning, Nott argued that religion was a matter of epistemic virtue, the ends and means of its own purification. "The time is yet distant, it is believed, *when nothing will be left in religion to be purified; nothing in the remedial system to be improved; nothing in political institutions to be reformed, and nothing in the physical sciences to be acquired.*" But there was much work to be done. Hence, Nott's call to "know" the "elements" and "name" the "processes" that "Omnipotence employs." Nott's faith in the inevitable discernment of these processes was often couched in metaphors of haunting and the future revelation of "some race of kindred spirits." "Spirits," declared Nott, "whose acuter vision or more powerful glasses enable them to look down on us, regardful of our progress, [are] eager to communicate their sympathies, and impatiently waiting for the time when our improved instruments shall enable us to recognise their signal, and to give back by telegraph from our sidereal watch-towers the signs of recognition."[49]

Such digressions into haunting were *in keeping with* Kames's notion of disenchantment and his discussion of taste—those supplemental emotions, passions, and appetites that needed to be harnessed in order to make reason reasonable.[50] Taste, for Kames, was a "rational science" and intended to identify, "with certainty," those judgments that were "incorrect" and "whimsical."[51] Kames's brand of Common Sense created a defensive boundary around untruth and delusion. Sure of what was excessively real,

48. Lord Kames, *Elements of Criticism, with Analyses, and Translations of Ancient and Foreign Illustrations*, ed. Abraham Mills (New York: Connor & Cooke, 1836), 21; Eliphalet Nott, *Counsels to Young Men on the Formation of Character, and The Principles which Lead to Success and Happiness in Life* (New York: Harper & Brothers, 1840), 32, 72, 180, 225, 261.
49. Nott, *Counsels to Young Men*, 282–84.
50. Thomas Cooley, *The Ivory Leg in the Ebony Cabinet: Madness, Race, and Gender in Victorian America* (Amherst: University of Massachusetts Press, 2001), 23.
51. Kames, *Elements of Criticism*, 13–14.

Kames had no doubt about what was not, so much so that he drew up plans to eradicate the possibilities for delusion.[52] Kames, for example, instructed his reader in the best ways to approach those "instances [when] an unexpected object overpowers the mind, so as to produce a momentary stupefaction." In order to promote rational judgment Kames produced a taxonomy of novelty, wonder, and surprise. Such "designing wisdom," he wrote, allowed the mind of the reader to recognize "new objects" when they first made an appearance. And it would prevent the mind from becoming "totally engrossed with them," so as to "have no room left, either for action or reflection."[53] Wonder, according to Kames, was a positive good only in the service of its eventual effacement. For the experience of novelty was but a catalyst for accumulating knowledge for the self and about the self.[54]

Nott's curious blend of spiritualist sentiment and Common Sense reasoning resonated with Morgan. In pursuing the Kamesian directive to overwhelm that which was mysterious with empirical scrutiny and semantic resolve, Morgan expressed increasing concern over what he feared was the dissipating "energy of the nation."[55] As fault lines emerged over slavery, economic reform, and temperance, Morgan found assurance in Kames's emphasis on taste as the engine of social reform. Moreover, Kames's focus on the social effects of knowledge prefigured the kind of investigation that Morgan would soon conduct among the Iroquois. For amidst rumors of war with Mexico and increasingly hostile debates over sectionalism, Morgan would look to the remarkably civil affairs of the Iroquois as a covenantal ideal. By reading the empirical surfaces of Iroquois social organization, Morgan sought to discover the secret of their former success—a cohesive substance that was present everywhere yet fully concentrated nowhere. According to Morgan, this tangible spirit of Iroquois

---

52. Martin, *Instructed Vision*, 54.

53. Kames, *Elements of Criticism*, 133, 136.

54. Taste, in addition to domesticating the apparently fantastic, was also the hinge in a process that was both personally enriching and socially benevolent. When properly cultivated, taste "invigorate[d] the social affections" and "moderate[d] those that [were] selfish." Civilization depended, first and foremost, on good taste and the sociality that flowed from it. As Kames declared, his was an attempt to generate social sympathy, "to form a standard of taste, by unfolding those principles that ought to govern the taste of every individual" (Kames, *Elements of Criticism*, 15). See also Lord Kames, *Elements of Criticism* (London: G. Cowie and Co., 1824), 6.

55. Lewis Henry Morgan (signed "Aquarius"), "Thoughts at Niagara," *The Knickerbocker* 22, no. 3 (Sept. 1843), 195.

organization could be possessed in the present in order to make manifest the promise of American destiny.

———

Drawing upon missionary accounts and assuming a proto-ethnographic perspective, Common Sense works by Lord Kames, Adam Ferguson, and Adam Smith were notable for their insistence that humans could only be understood in terms of their sociality.[56] Such insistence was central to Morgan's emerging style of ethnographic reasoning. In *Theory of Moral Sentiments* (1759), for example, Smith made the case for the social component of possessive individualism. Anticipating key ideas in *Wealth of Nations* (1776), Smith envisioned an emotional economy "led by an invisible hand" and fueled by the human "love of system." He argued for the existence of an innate human capacity for "fellow-feeling." "By the imagination," wrote Smith, "we place ourselves in his situation, we conceive ourselves enduring all the same torments, we enter as it were into his body, and become in some measure the same person with him, and thence form some idea of his sensations, and even feel something which, though weaker in degree, is not altogether unlike them." Smith named this capacity for emotional mimesis "sympathy." According to Smith, a mirror is "placed in the countenance and behavior of those he lives with, which always mark when they enter into, and when they disapprove of his sentiments; and it is here that he first views the propriety and impropriety of his own passions, the beauty and deformity of his own mind."[57]

Despite the self's inherent ties to others, sympathy was a kind of relationality that also, and perhaps paradoxically, guaranteed the inviolability of that self. Social experience here became a privileged site of moral cultivation. As in the burgeoning discourse of spirituality, self-examination was premised upon the immanence of social relations yet was initiated in

56. William Y. Adams, *The Philosophical Roots of Anthropology* (Stanford: CSLI Publications, 1998), 23–25. To be sure, a self-serving and patronizing hue colored this insistence. As Adam Ferguson remarked in *An Essay on the History of Civil Society* (1767), the "American tribes" were an opportunity for self-knowledge and civil reform. "It is in their present condition that we are to behold, as in a mirror, the features of our own progenitors; and from thence we are to draw our conclusions with respect to the influence of situations" upon the progress of civil society (Ferguson, *An Essay on the History of Civil Society* [Philadelphia: A. Finley, 1819], 147).

57. Adam Smith, *The Theory of Moral Sentiments* (1759), ed. D. D. Raphael and A. L. Macfie (Oxford: Clarendon Press, 1976), 9–10, 110.

order to transcend them. For as Smith argued, even within sympathetic congress individuals remained individuals. "Fellow-feeling" was virtual and not real in the empirical sense but only a co-production of an imaginary bond. "It is the impressions of our senses only," Smith insisted, "not those of his, which our imaginations copy."[58] Smith here was advocating a kind of self-voyeurism, premised upon an initial incorporation into society as a means of gaining epistemic leverage upon the self. The goal was to perceive the author of one's being as a social phenomenon—an "impartial spectator" who judged the self from a position exterior to the self yet was anonymous in its lack of particularity.[59]

The concept of sympathy stretched empirical inquiry to its breaking point (suggested as much by Smith's numerous qualifications—"as it were," in some measure," "not altogether unlike"). In American evangelical circles, for example, sympathy came to be understood as a "CONTAGION OF FEELING."[60] As a natural pathogen, sympathy could be understood only through its effects. Sympathy was nothing yet it was everything. Elusive as the air we breathe, sympathy was also the essence of morality, communication, history, memory, and the future. Sympathy was total and totalizing, not unlike some versions of God.[61]

Smith privileged the imagination as the site where authentic human bonding occurred, carrying individuals beyond their material self-interest into mutual solidarity. Morgan, however, would seek something much more—to rationalize and quite literally measure these imaginary bonds.[62] To that end, sympathy made comprehensible Morgan's object of ethnographic inquiry.[63] His desire to see the world in terms of a systematic whole and to pursue it systematically, a lesson that Morgan had internalized by the time he graduated from Union College in 1840, would propel his practice of spirituality, that is, his life-long interest in the problems and prospects of social relationality.[64]

---

58. Ibid., 9–10, 184–185.

59. Ibid., 114–17, 134–35. See also Jennifer Pitts, *A Turn to Empire: The Rise of Imperial Liberalism in Britain and France* (Princeton: Princeton University Press, 2005), 43.

60. "Sympathy," *Christian Parlor Magazine* I (April 1845): 380.

61. See reprint of "Sympathy" in the *New-York Evangelist* 16 (June 19, 1845): 100. See also the 1819 review of "The Theory of Moral Sentiments . . . by Adam Smith," *North American Review* 8, no. 23 (March 1819): 380.

62. Terry Eagleton, *The Idea of Culture* (Oxford: Blackwell, 2000), 38–38.

63. Morgan cites *Theory of Moral Sentiments* in "Letters" of 1847 (460); Herbert, *Culture and Anomie*, 92.

64. Morgan's interest in the operative principle of human populations resonated with the evangelical reliance upon a Newtonian-inflected account of the social, pieced together from different threads of the Scottish Enlightenment. As Hutcheson wrote, anticipating much of

Shortly after his graduation from Union, Morgan addressed what might be called the zoological aspects of sympathy. In an article that appeared over two issues of *The Knickerbocker* Morgan applied Common Sense reasoning to refute what an anonymous contributor called "that indescribable and mysterious principle of [animal] instinct."[65] Animals, insisted Morgan, "have the senses, natural affections, and propensities, in common with man." Morgan admitted that instinct was "higher than mind; partaking something of Deity itself." Nonetheless, the rationality of animals—a deliberative and intentional process—could be "unraveled." Drawing on the work of Buffon, Morgan claimed "that animals have a language by which they apprehend each other. Concert of action and division of labor would be impossible without it." This was the code of sympathy, which Morgan insisted was a product of reason and not impulse. So rather than affirm that animal behavior was essentially "mysterious," Morgan likened it to the collective actions of African and Indian tribes—at times secretive and "unmeaning" but eventually known through its remarkable materiality.[66]

As he would do throughout his career, Morgan dabbled in the language of theology in order to distance himself from it. Here, he simultaneously redefined secrets of animal relations as manifest in the natural world, susceptible to contemplation and subject to sustained description. These relations were not divine in and of themselves. On the contrary, they signified an overarching principle of definitive organization, what Morgan would later call a "spiritual essence, or . . . the principle of intelligence." Morgan displayed both impatience with theology but also a desire to fold whatever was distinctive about theology into the directives of science. Just as he claimed that the "principle called *Instinct*" was actually "the principle of *Mind*," there was an implication that whatever Deity had been called in the past, new, more accurate appraisals were on the horizon, names for the "Author" of our being that would be devoid of their mystifying taint.[67]

This "spirit" was manifest in every particular piece of "Nature" yet could only be discerned through relationality, that is, in the act of com-

---

Smith's work on the moral sentiments, "our Affections were contrived for good in the whole.... Mankind are thus insensibly linked together, and make one great *System*, by an invisible Union." Hutcheson cited in Joel L. From, "The Moral Economy of Nineteenth Century Evangelical Activism," *Christian Scholar's Review* 30 (Fall 2000): 41.

65. "Thoughts on Immortality," *The Knickerbocker* 22 (November 1843): 395.

66. Lewis Henry Morgan (signed "Aquarius"), "Mind or Instinct: An Inquiry Concerning the Manifestations of Mind By the Lower Orders of Animals," *The Knickerbocker* 22 (November–December 1843): 417, 419, 507-9, 511, 515.

67. Morgan, "Mind or Instinct," 513-15; *American Beaver*, 256.

paring such phenomena as birds changing their flight patterns or beavers assembling to build their dams. Beavers, for example, assemble every June or July "in order to form a society." This society, in turn, could be dissected, compared across generations and species, and known.[68] Characteristic of Morgan's practice of spirituality, his was not simply an engagement with providential design but also an immersion into an immanent frame of reference. Apprehending others apprehending themselves in the service of apprehending himself. And so on and so forth. Ontology becoming an audacious epistemic practice.

6. Inindianation; or Gordian Knots Resolved

"Nearly all Indian-haters have at bottom loving hearts; at any rate, hearts, if anything, more generous than the average."

HERMAN MELVILLE, *The Confidence-Man* (1857)

Morgan's Common Sense education all but elided the difference between knowing the world and becoming himself. The codependency of epistemology and ontology would become a recurring pattern throughout Morgan's career. One of Morgan's more curious performances of social sympathy occurred at the beginning of 1843 when the underemployed lawyer initiated significant changes in the "Order of the Gordian Knot" in Aurora, New York. Morgan was already a member of this secret literary society, which at that time had several chapters around the state. In the summer of 1843 Morgan renamed the Aurora chapter the Order of the Iroquois. Modeled on the Freemasonry of Morgan's father, the order sometimes met in the woods and other times in an abandoned Masonic lodge. Given the lingering anti-Masonry in the air, Morgan was insistent on keeping the minutes and signs of the order from public view. "The public has no claims upon us whatever. We are not engaged in pursuits which need justification."[69]

The order served to complement rather bourgeois lives with imagined authenticity. One of Morgan's first orders of business was to insist that members attend meetings in complete Indian regalia. Members met monthly in the woods, donned Indian names and costumes, and

68. Morgan, "Mind of Instinct, 416.
69. Cited in Philip J. Deloria, *Playing Indian* (New Haven: Yale University Press, 1998), 88.

read poetry to each other in hopes of forging a new national literature and a new nation.[70] As its membership grew, Morgan took the lead in reorganizing the fraternal order along the lines of Iroquois political structures. Morgan's efforts followed a Smithian political script of forging emotional bonds with idealized Indian types "entitled to our sympathy."[71] On one level, the order claimed to be the protectorate of the remainder of the Iroquois and their history. On another level, the order was to revive the spirit of Iroquois civility and "taste," given how "nothing that may be properly called Iroquois can now be found among us." Given their "eternal silence," "nothing is left for us but to utter our regrets." Yet "these matters" demanded "investigation" "in their relation to ourselves."[72]

As the "Grand Sachem" between 1844 and 1846, Morgan believed that the order would become a model for sympathetic energies between Anglo-Americans, premised as it was on "feeling and respect for the unfortunate Indian."[73] With the end of "the era of Indian occupation," a "shade of obscurity deepen[ed] over the Indian footsteps." But according to Morgan, there was still hope, the possibility of benevolent action. "We can but faintly conceive" the pre-contact life of the Iroquois," Morgan conceded. He could, however, "fully appreciate" their "spirit."[74] Their impending absence, in other words, was to be preserved on the bodies and in the words of white men. Consequently, each member of the order underwent "Inindianation," a ritual Morgan designed and scripted. Because the Iroquois were "our type and progenitor," Morgan explained, they were "the mirror upon which our order must draw its image. Their deeds upon the warpath, at the council fire and at the festival are the materials with which we must work and an intimate knowledge of them is manifestly impor-

70. Ibid., 73. I am indebted to Deloria's account of Morgan's costumed dramas in the 1840s as representative of the contradictions inhering in the ethnographic project of participant observation. See also Mark C. Carnes, *Secret Ritual and Manhood in Victorian America* (New Haven: Yale University Press, 1989), 94–104.

71. "Address on Temperance, Dec. 10, 1843."

72. "An Address by Schenandoah," Box 21, folder 6, B435-38, Lewis Henry Morgan Papers.

73. Lewis Henry Morgan (signed "Aquarius"), "Vision of Kar-is-ta-gi-a, a sachem of Cayuga," *The Knickerbocker* 24 (September 1844): 245; Tooker, *Lewis H. Morgan on Iroquois Material Culture*, 73–74. On Morgan's involvement in the Grand Order, see Robert E. Bieder, "The Grand Order of the Iroquois: Influences on Lewis Henry Morgan's Ethnology," *Ethnohistory* 27 (Fall 1980): 349–61.

74. "Address by Skenandoah on the Geography and Trails of the Hodenosaunee," Box 21, folder 26, B238a, Lewis Henry Morgan Papers.

tant."[75] Inindianation, among other things, was a ritual counter to the "overwhelming influence of civilization."[76]

Before the initiate takes on the "solemn vows of the Cayuga" and receives "chords of brotherly love" from the Great Spirit, the Sachem (Morgan) informs the "pale-face" initiate that he has been taken captive. The Sachem then hints at an original, forgotten identity:

> Our scouts have again been upon the war-path and have brought in this young captive: who has wandered so long among the Pale-faces as to have lost nearly any trace of his parentage and descent from our ancient Nation; but the unceasing vigilance of our Indian band has enabled us to penetrate the obscurity which hung over his [illegible] in o[rder] to discover within him those elements of character that distinguish him as one worthy of joining us.[77]

Playing the part of the Sachem, Morgan portrays the essence of Iroquois character as universal and universally accessible, a "magnanimous" identity that must be urgently cultivated in the service of a civilized future. It was key to what Morgan would later call "spiritual independence." "The Indian," declared Morgan, "is a republican and this is more truly a fact than may at first appear."[78] The American identity to be donned by the captive, then, was not simply exceptional but conflicted. It was a truly human identity, deep inside, achieved when the captive submitted to those who had already discovered it within him.[79]

Inindianation ritualized a kind of submission that members of the order could acknowledge and affirm as metaphor, a performance of their reason and agency. Here was the dream of civilization played out by white men for white men. The inevitability of Native American extinction was transposed into a redemptive myth of cosmopolitan progress. Sacrifice was necessary because it allowed members of the order to don identities that they found most appealing. For even as the Great Spirit intoned during the ritual, "Long ago I saw in the future their destruction and I was

75. Cited in Deloria, *Playing Indian*, 80.
76. "An Address by Schenandoah."
77. "Grand order of the Iroquois. Seneca nation. Turtle tribe. Special form of initiation, 1845," Box 21, folder 19, Lewis Henry Morgan Papers.
78. "An Address by Schenandoah."
79. This was in keeping with Morgan's sense that in the "ever merging destiny of the different races of human beings, the white man is now triumphant" ("Copy of an address read by Schenandoah, April 17, 1844," Box 21, folder 8:443, Lewis Henry Morgan Papers).

very sad. Now I gaze upon the last remnant and know that they must quickly disappear."[80]

Within the theatrical space of Inindianation, the very act of communing with the Great Spirit served to expiate whatever guilt (or sense of ideological contradiction) lingered in the hearts of the young white professionals.[81] For in addition to the security of newly consummated identities, the order was a direct response to the call of the Great Spirit to preserve the context of Iroquois life in the texts of their curators. "O sooth their broken spirits," instructs the Great Spirit. "Soften their hard road, make peaceful their long sleep. Defend their noble natures. Save from oblivion their names, their customs, and their deeds; that they may be known forever in your books."[82] Or as Morgan declared to his "brothers" in the voice of Skenandoah, "The New Iroquois will explore their institutions; and the secrets of their rise and fall, their virtue and their renown, shall be embedded in our historical literature."[83]

In 1844 Morgan began to follow through on the Great Spirit's request. Under the pseudonym Aquarius, Morgan wrote "Vision of Kar-is-ta-gi-a, a Sachem of Cayuga." The conceit of Morgan's piece was his receipt of a spirit communiqué from an Iroquois warrior. Karistagia broached the culpability of "this white race" yet confirmed a shared humanity, an essential state of relationality from which to discover the author of one's being. This discovery, in turn, would disavow any imperious politics that conditioned the possibility of Morgan's desire. As in the ritual of Inindianation, Morgan was enacting a call for sympathy with the grieving and "unfortunate Indian." And in writing an overly sentimental portrait of Indian grief, Morgan justified such grief because it was being presently recognized and would subsequently be remembered. A celebrated and promoted legacy was sufficient to overcome the injustice of the past. For despite the necessary encroachments of the white population, there was peace and justice

---

80. "Grand order of the Iroquois. Form of Inindianation adopted, Aurora, Aug. 9, 1844," Box 21, folder 10, Lewis Henry Morgan Papers.
81. This logic is replicated in the ritual when the Great Spirit quells the voices of anger and revenge that are given a hearing. "A curse upon ye pale faces," sings the "First Chorus" of spectral Indians. "Will not one be left to weep amid the ashes of your desolation. Then, avenged with a terrible vengeance, will the shades of the red warriors rest quiet in their graves." Yet after this litany of curses the Great Spirit returns from "the happy hunting grounds beyond the setting sun." He does so not out of vengeance but in order to calm, recalling his earlier prophecy about the inevitable disappearance of his children. Box 21, folder 10, Lewis Henry Morgan Papers.
82. "Grand order of the Iroquois. Form of Inindianation adopted, Aurora, Aug. 9, 1844."
83. "Address by Skenandoah on the Geography and Trails of the Hodenosaunee."

to be found in the future, aided of course by the reform of government policies and friends such as Morgan.[84]

7. A Faith So Purely Spiritual

"How know I what involuntary preparations may be going on in him for things as unbeknown in present time to him as me—a sort of chemical preparation in the soul for malice, as chemical preparation in the body for malady."

The Confidence-Man (1857)

Soon after Morgan's reorganization of the Order of the Iroquois, its agenda became more self-consciously scientific. The shift from secret society to scholarly association coincided with Morgan's friendship with a young Seneca he met while browsing in an Albany bookstore in 1844. Ely Parker (Ha-sa-ne-an-da) enlisted Morgan and the order to lobby on behalf of the Seneca in their legal battle to remain on the Tonawanda reservation. The Ogden Land Company was seeking to remove the Seneca to Kansas based on what it claimed to be a binding legal agreement and what the Seneca claimed to be an illegitimate treaty forced upon them.[85] Morgan and other members of the order traveled to Washington D.C. to lobby President Polk and John Quincy Adams, then chairman of the House Indian Affairs Committee. Yet the land dispute remained unresolved (until 1857). A frustrated Morgan returned home, in search of long-term solutions to the plight of his Iroquois brethren.[86]

Soon after their meeting, Morgan arranged for Parker's initiation into the order and secured funds for Parker's education at Cayuga Academy, Morgan's alma mater. In Morgan's estimation, Parker was an ideal representative of the past and future of the Iroquois, versed in the traditions of spirit yet appreciative of the materiality of scientific inquiry and techno-

---

84. "It is gratifying to know," wrote Morgan, "that one of those Indian nations whose political existence has been extinguished to make room for a more fortunate race, is now in the enjoyment of an ample pension from the State, which has reaped all the harvest in these treaties, and that by its judicious employment they may be saved from destitution" ("Vision of Kar-is-ta-gi-a," 238–39, 245).

85. For a cogent account of this legal dispute that began in 1837, see Daniel Noah Moses, *The Promise of Progress: The Life and Work of Lewis Henry Morgan* (Columbia: University of Missouri Press, 2009), 54f.

86. Moses argues that *League* was written as part of Morgan's attempt to secure a position as a subagent in the Federal Office of Indian Affairs. *Promise of Progress*, 145–47.

logical progress. Indeed, much of Morgan's data presented in *League of the Iroquois* was a product of his conversations with Parker and only a handful of field trips, arranged and supervised by Parker. Parker functioned as a medium of Iroquois traditions, providing access, translating their spirit into terms that Morgan believed were empirically sound. In other words, Parker made sense of the ambiguous ontological status of Indians, reconciling their impending absence and their stubborn presence. As such, Parker was slightly unreal, a fleshy sign of an American destiny that had yet to be achieved. And it was precisely this sense of overcoming ambiguity, of making right the intractable situation of native populations, that made the Iroquois such a rich screen for Morgan's ethnographic projections.[87]

Morgan's science framed Indians as spectral entities. So, too, would spiritualist séances. Statements such as this became quite common in just a few years time:[88]

> *These* Indians are a noble band, robed in richest costume, and radiating a light before which many a white spirit's halo pales and darkens. They are fit recipients of the pure, the refined, the glorified. Kind and hospitable entertainers of all whom we love, and of all who seek us in kindness, these lovers of hills over which they once roamed in freedom,—lovers of the graves of their fathers, and of the spot where their own bones repose,—these are our doorkeepers and our watchmen.[89]

As has been noted by numerous scholars, spiritualism was suffused with posthumous visitations from native spirits.[90] For those seeking a "connection with the unfortunate and now fast disappearing tribes of the 'aborigi-

87. Elizabeth Tooker, "Isaac N. Hurd's Ethnographic Studies of the Iroquois: Their Significance and Ethnographic Value," *Ethnohistory* 27 (Fall 1980): 359. Deloria has noted the paradox of Morgan's insistence that the Indian race was rapidly disappearing, given his dependence upon the vital information given to him by Parker. Deloria makes an eloquent case for Morgan's anti-humanist impulse, a denial of the reality of Indians in favor of a guilt-expiating and self-serving vision of Indianness (*Playing Indian*, 90).

88. See Renee L. Bergland, *The National Uncanny: Indian Ghosts and American Subjects* (Hanover: University Press of New England, 2000).

89. Cited in Allen Putnam, *Natty, A Spirit: His Portrait and His Life* (Boston: Bela Marsh, 1856), 93.

90. Werner Sollors, "Dr. Benjamin Franklin's Celestial Telegraph, or Indian Blessings to Gas-Lit American Drawing Rooms," *American Quarterly* 35 (1983): 459–80; Robert S. Cox, *Body and Soul: A Sympathetic History of American Spiritualism* (Charlottesville: University of Virginia Press, 2003), 189–211; Molly McGarry, *Ghosts of Futures Past: Spiritualism and the Cultural Politics of Nineteenth-Century America* (Berkeley and Los Angeles: University of California Press, 2008), 66–78.

nal' people of the American continent," Indians returned not for revenge but for the purpose of conveying to whites the truth of the spirit-world.[91] Figures such as Black Hawk, Osceola, King Philip, Red Jacket, and Logan returned to confess their superstitious past and to provide testimony for the reasonableness of spirit communication. Throughout the 1850s, genocide was transformed into sacrifice. Returning Indian spirits testified to their newly acquired and exemplary form of Christianity. The spirits taught "the just, equitable, and reasonable doctrines of compensation, retribution, progress, individual responsibility, eternal self-consciousness, and equally eternal affection between the spirits who love each other."[92]

———

In the fall of 1846 Parker arranged for Morgan to become a member of the Seneca nation. Parker organized an elaborate initiation ceremony that took place over a number of days at Tonawanda.[93] This ceremony was a consummation of Morgan's conversion in the key of Common Sense. It was also a moment in which Morgan convinced himself of his independence by acknowledging his ontological dependence upon the "Indian race" and the Great Spirit. Morgan's initiation, while exhibiting the patronizing benevolence of imperial venture, must also be seen from the perspective of spirituality. For it is here, in this moment of Morgan's career, that one begins to see the intense links between his professional and personal ambitions. *A lone piety becoming politically charged.*

As he and Parker collected materials for *League*, Morgan came to understand Iroquois religion as an apolitical and eminently private affair that hinged upon the individual's freedom *of* conscience. The Iroquois embodied the truth of religion itself. Morgan would eventually detail the "mod-

91. In a typical visitation, the Indian spirit arrives with a "calumet of peace." His message is a mild rebuke of past actions. But rather than calling for reparations, he assumes that mutual hostility can be mutually overcome when understood from the perspective of cosmic inevitability—for the purpose that whites "may learn a lesson *even* from the red man" (emphasis original; Logan, "Logan's Speech," *The Spiritual Telegraph* 4 [1854]: 235-370). See also Josiah Brigham, *Twelve Messages from the Spirit of John Quincy Adams, Through Joseph D. Stiles, Medium* (Boston: Bela Marsh, 1859), 430.

92. Emma Hardinge, *Modern American Spiritualism* (1870; New Hyde Park: University Books, 1970), 481-82, 520. For a description of spiritualist communication with Indian spirits as disclosing "landscapes of white fantasy" and masking "acts of domination and conquest in a racialism transmuted into religious terms," see Catherine L. Albanese, *A Republic of Mind and Spirit: A Cultural History of American Metaphysical Religion* (New Haven: Yale University Press, 2007), 248-53.

93. Moses, *The Promise of Progress*, 66-69.

ern beliefs" of Iroquois, criticizing previous accounts of their religion as
either legitimating violence or overly coercive.[94] "The beliefs of our primitive inhabitants," explained Morgan in the key of secularism, guaranteed
their independence. *"A faith so purely spiritual,* so free from the tincture of
human passion, and from the grossness of superstition" (emphasis mine).
According to Morgan, "the spirituality of their faith" was buttressed by
their devotion to the Great Spirit. The "individual independence" of each
Iroquois was in turn guaranteed by the "liberality of their institutions."[95]

Iroquois spirituality had yet to be corrupted by the "power of gain" and
the "great passion[s] of civilized man."[96] "A people in the wilderness,"
wrote Morgan, "shut out from revelation, with no tablet on which to write
the history of passing generations, save the heart of man, yet possessed
of the knowledge of one Supreme Being, and striving, with all the ardor
of devotion, to commune with him . . . is to say the least, a most extraordinary spectacle." It was no less sublime, continued Morgan, than "the
spectacle of the persecuted Puritan, on the confines of the same wilderness, worshipping that God in the fullness of light and knowledge, whom
the Indian, however limited and imperfect his conceptions, in the Great
Spirit, most distinctly discerned." For Morgan, the "sound theology" of
the Iroquois was equivalent in stature to that of any "man, shut out from
the light of revelation, and left to construct his own theology." This do-it-
yourself piety, suggestive of Morgan's own, was fluid, literary, and attuned
to the spiritual depths of material surfaces. As Morgan wrote, such piety
promised to disclose "some part of the truth, as shadowed forth by the
works of nature." The Iroquois were spiritually advanced in that regard.
They were cognizant that freedom was a product of willing submission.
And they were sensitive to the fact the Great Spirit of Hä-wen-né-yu oper-

94. On the false religion of native populations, see "Past and Present of the Indian Tribes,"
The American Review I, no. 5 (May 1, 1845): 503.
95. Morgan, *League,* 179, 181, 138.
96. Ibid., 131. Within the Grand Order, an emergent site of American anthropology, Morgan's concerns and priorities tended to hold sway over the investigations of other members.
But significant differences did exist that shed light on Morgan's determination to depict an
Iroquois society animated by the spirit of human freedom as opposed to providence. Isaac
Hurd, for example, made significant contributions to Morgan's knowledge of Iroquois ceremonies. Hurd, who would go on to Auburn Theological Seminary and the Congregationalist ministry, was not nearly as triumphal as Morgan when it came to idealizing the Iroquois.
According to Hurd, the Iroquois lacked the "sweet and soothing influence of a religion to
purify the heart of its evil inclinations, and to elevate the soul to a sense of its real character,
and nature." For Morgan, however, the lack of a rigid religious infrastructure among the
Iroquois demanded emulation. Cited in Bieder, "The Grand Order of the Iroquois," 358. See
also Tooker, "Isaac N. Hurd's Ethnographic Studies."

ated on the universe through subordinate spirits who in turn gently and indirectly furnished "springs of action, rules of intercourse, and powers of restraint."[97]

Such epistemic sensitivity to the animating power of material circumstances was not only an Iroquois achievement. Through Morgan's efforts, it was also a goal shared by the emerging discipline/institutions of American anthropology. "The study of man, physiologically and psychically, is confessedly the noblest which can claim human attention; and the results of such study must lie at the basis of all sound organizations, social, civil, or religious. It involves a consideration of all his wants, his capabilities, impulses and ambitions—*the manner and extent in which they are affected by circumstances*" (emphasis mine).[98]

By mid-century, ethnological inquiry was shifting away from the unabashed colonialism of "frontier ethnology." A gentler attitude, if not more insidious effect, took hold as investigators accumulated knowledge about what was believed to be the noble yet vestigial populations destined for extinction. Affinities were sought as native peoples were heralded for the simplicity and decency of their social lives despite their savage peculiarities. Henry Schoolcraft, for example, a colleague of Morgan's who had once defended policies of removal, would come to believe through his ethnographic work that "no nation of the widely spread red race of America has displayed so high and heroic love of liberty, united with the true art of government, and personal energy and stamina of character, as the Iroquois."[99]

In 1848 Morgan expressed great enthusiasm for an antiquarian museum to be located at the University of the State of New York. As he proceeded to procure objects, Morgan articulated what he believed to be the social value of such a collection in a series of reports to the Board of Regents. The museum would gather "specimens of human ingenuity" that would "unlock the social history of the people from whom they come." The museum "would enable the Red Race to speak for itself through these silent memorials." And finally, the museum would "mark" the "extinction" of the Iroquois once their destiny was "fulfilled."[100] Morgan affirmed that material artifacts were not simply reflections of Iroquois history or social

97. Morgan, *League*, 224–25, 150, 180.

98. E.G.S., "American Ethnology," 385.

99. Henry R. Schoolcraft, *Notes on the Iroquois; or Contributions to American History, Antiquities, and General Ethnology* (Albany: Erastus H. Pease and Co., 1847), iii.

100. Morgan quoted in Tooker, *Lewis H. Morgan*, 45, 15, 164, 206–7.

life but contained within them the sympathetic energies of human invention. Such energies were "silent" and "unwritten," yet they spoke "more eloquently than all human description." The "intrinsic value" of "artificial remains" was tied to their legibility, that is, their place within an identifiable network. The protocol that organized their relationality, however, was contained ever deeper within.

8. From Voluntary Attention to Anthropological Comprehension

Morgan's desire to unlock the secrets of Iroquois materials evolved within a Protestant theological context. On one level, his curiosity resonated with an emergent spiritualist subculture and other liberal strands. On another level, it revolved around his close friendship with the Rev. J. H. McIlvaine, fellow member of the order (a warrior in the New Confederacy of the Iroquois). In 1848 McIlvaine, a philologist and student of Sanskrit, assumed the ministry of the First Presbyterian Church of Rochester, where Morgan's wife, Mary, was a member but Morgan was not. Conservative in respect to various doctrinal debates within Presbyterianism, McIlvaine's writings on voluntary attention and symbolism bore directly upon Morgan's budding ethnographic eye.[101]

Before arriving in Rochester, McIlvaine had addressed the issue of how to voluntarily attend to the "mysteries of the Word of God." His argument was an intervention, a way to split the difference between literal and allegorical readings of the Bible. Both readings, he argued, ignored the sociality of language. According to McIlvaine, the words of the Bible were "pregnant with spiritual truth—truth alike for all times and place, universal for man." Literalists were blind to the "spiritual sense in these narratives," reading them only for content to be weighed against the measure of reason. Those who regarded scripture "as nothing but allegories and parables" may produce persuasive and beautiful arguments, but they were destined to become lost. Their readings of scripture were but readings of their own mind.[102]

---

101. See Trautmann, *Lewis Henry Morgan*, 60–73; Feeley-Harnik, "'The Mystery of Life in All Its Forms,'" 152.

102. J. H. McIlvaine, *The Tree of the Knowledge of Good and Evil* (New York: M. W. Dodd, 1847), 11–13. Such a reader "casts himself loose upon a wide and dangerous sea without chart, or compass, or rudder. He is liable to be continually driven and tossed upon an infinite chaos of his own imaginations, over which the Spirit of God, has never brooded" (13).

Voluntary attention meant tending to a deeper semiotics. It also meant to work through, in a sophisticated manner, how the surfaces of human life pointed beyond themselves and in turn were made meaningful by this beyond. The meaning of the Bible, consequently, was its vital and animating presence within human history and social life. Words, according to McIlvaine, possessed a residue of signification that contained elements of gesture, action, emotion, and the location in which they were uttered. They were imbued with a "life-giving power . . . unspeakably greater than anything that can be found in mere words." According to McIlvaine, to read the Bible properly demanded an appreciation for this residue — conceived of as God's indwelling spirit—in both language and the world at large. Although McIlvaine did not intend for his work to be a treatise on symbolism, he did make gestures toward the necessity of the symbolic decoding of texts other than the Bible, including the history and sociality of humans: "For a symbol is a body-ing forth or representation to the senses of ideas and emotions as these are found in the mysteries of life. Every act of man, therefore, as a significant expression of the ideas and feelings from which it springs, is a symbol." According to McIlvaine, a "spiritual life" lurked within each and every sign, a mysterious yet coherent whole that guaranteed that apparent contradictions were just that—compatible at the level of a deeper semiotics.[103]

Although McIlvaine's theological understandings of the problems and prospects of social sympathy were not equivalent to Morgan's, they do illuminate the particular kind of Protestant sensibility that would inform Morgan's future inquiries.[104] By the late 1840s, for example, Congregationalist Horace Bushnell, even more than McIlvaine, was pushing theology in the direction of anthropological comprehensibility.[105] Bushnell was explicit about the intimate relationship between the "natural language of the sentiments" and spirit.[106] In "Preliminary Dissertation on the Nature of Language," a sermon owned by Morgan's wife, Mary, Bushnell de-

---

103. McIlvaine, *Tree of the Knowledge*, iv, 9, 3–5, 22.

104. McIlvaine attempted to outline a Protestant as opposed to "infidel" social science, the former being a project that for McIlvaine had always included Morgan despite Morgan's own claims to the contrary. J. H. McIlvaine, "Organization the Fundamental Principle of Social Science," *The Presbyterian Quarterly and Princeton Review* 5 (1876): 628–53.

105. Horace Bushnell, "Preliminary Dissertation on the Nature of Language as Related to Thought and Spirit," in *God in Christ* (Hartford: Brown and Parsons, 1849).

106. Horace Bushnell, "Unconscious Influence," in *Sermons for the New Life*, 2d ed. (New York: Charles Scribner, 1858), 192.

clared that words were "only shadows of truth."[107] Like McIlvaine, Bushnell understood the intrinsic ambiguity of language as evidence of God's mysterious presence in history and the world at large. He took to task "our ethnologists" who fail to appreciate the radical multiplicity of human language as an expression of the mystical singularity of God. "There is a logos in the forms of things," Bushnell explained. The "outer world, which envelops our being, is itself language, the power of all language," written by the "universal Author" and "EXPRESSED every where."[108] Bushnell's insistence that social relations registered their effects from a distance was explicitly theological.[109] Yet Bushnell's interest in the rules that governed the processes of human relationality was also conceptually analogous to ethnographic works that would appear during the second half of the century. Such works would soon posit culture as a transcendental signifier, a metaphysical entity that primitive groups had consistently misidentified but that could now be properly "understood only by a few."[110]

From the perspective of secularism in antebellum America, the threshold of anthropological comprehensibility was crossed by way of a lone assumption made with numerous inflections. Conservative and liberal Protestants alike, alongside phrenologists, spiritualists, and self-styled ethnologists, posited the uniformity of a symbolic system that made all human differences part of the same epistemic arena. Here was the will to read a code that confirmed, in the act of reading, that everything was connected and connectable. The "uniformity" of "man's constitution,"

---

107. Bushnell, "Preliminary Dissertation." 73. Mary Morgan catalogued Bushnell's *God in Christ* in March 1849; see Thomas R. Trautmann and Karl Sanford Kabelac, *The Library of Lewis Henry Morgan and Mary Elizabeth Morgan* (Philadelphia: The American Philosophical Society, 1994), 129.

108. Bushnelll, "Preliminary Dissertation," 15, 30.

109. "Far down," wrote Bushnell, "in the secret foundations of life and society, there lie concealed great laws and channels of influence, which make the race common to each other . . . laws which often escape our notice altogether, but which are to society as gravity is to the general system of God's works" ("Unconscious Influence," 195). See also Daniel Walker Howe, "The Social Science of Horace Bushnell" *The Journal of American History* 70, no. 2 (September 1983): 306.

110. E.G.S., "American Ethnology," 393. Bushnell's Romantic description of divinity anticipates both the strange materiality of "culture" and E. B. Tylor's discussion of how "savages" attribute "something of the nature of a soul or spirit" to material things. "This something," wrote Tylor, "usually resembles in form and dimensions the material object it belongs to, is often perceptible to the senses of sight and hearing, sometimes seems solid enough to be touched, but is more usually impalpable and capable of being passed through by solid objects as well as of passing through them" (Tylor, "The Religion of Savages," *Fortnightly Review* 6 [1866]: 73).

declared an authoritative article on the subject, was "attended by a like uniformity of natural consequences, as resulting almost of necessity in corresponding uniformity in his beliefs and conceptions, and their modes of manifestation."[111]

By 1847, Morgan had begun to speak of the "animating spirit" of the Iroquois state—"so systematic in its construction and so liberal in its administration." This spirit did not originate in any single place but was a matter of circulation and "reciprocal influences" between individuals, the population, and institutions. In conceptualizing social life as a significant and semiotic whole, this spirit was also a precursor to the notion of culture that would dominate anthropological inquiry for the next century.[112]

9. The Spirit of Secularism

As Morgan organized *League* around a concept of "animating spirit," news of the Fox sisters broke. Claims of strange knockings spread from Hydesville to Rochester and beyond. Within the liberal Protestant tradition, spiritualists adhered, perhaps even aggressively, to an immanental cosmology. Spirits aided in the progress of events on earth.[113] They were vehicles for and source of the "interchange of social sympathies, between man and man, in everyday life."[114] As sympathy became translated into the language of metaphysical religiosity, it was no longer considered solely in terms of an instinctual capacity of the human. It was also beyond the person, beyond the body. It was a social phenomenon, occult yet ever subject to reason.

Indeed, many spiritualist tracts framed themselves as explanations of the economy and characters of the spirit world. For Rochester residents Isaac and Amy Post, Adam Smith's "invisible hand" was an object of metaphysical inquiry. The Posts were members of the Spiritualist Church in Rochester, located about one block from Morgan's home. After hosting

111. E.G.S., "American Ethnology," 394.
112. Skenandoah [Lewis Henry Morgan], "Letters on the Iroquois," *The American Whig Review* 5 (March 1847): 447. See also Morgan, *League*, 127–28. On the early history of American anthropology, see Curtis M. Hinsley, *Savages and Scientists: The Smithsonian Institution and the Development of American Anthropology, 1846–1910* (Washington, D.C.: Smithsonian Institution Press, 1981).
113. C. Hammond, *Light from the Spirit World*, 250.
114. Davis, *Present Age and Inner Life*, 52; Cox, *Body and Soul*, 26, 34.

the Fox sisters in their home, Isaac became an accomplished medium in his own right.[115] "Nothing so much elevates the soul as a correct spirituality," declared the spirit of Quaker founder George Fox. Another spirit conveyed to Post how good it was "to live in this age of the world; spirits disembodied can so readily give of their knowledge to their embodied friends, although I was stranger to thee, yet I find no difficulty in forming an acquaintance, with that love that words cannot express." Or as Benjamin Franklin surmised in the introduction to Post's collection of communiqués, "It seems to me when spirit laws are understood, every one will rejoice to be governed by them."[116]

Spiritualism sought nothing less than a material confirmation of an invisible order. A parallel development—psychometry—put this confirmation into practice. Psychometry was the science of detecting the life-record of inanimate objects and measuring the accretions of human meaning they have collected. Psychometry was a social psychology and an important nexus between spiritualism and Morgan's ethnographic sensibility.[117] Mid-century psychometrists like Joseph Buchanan, dean of the Eclectic Medical Institute of Cincinnati, undertook elaborate investigations into the material reality of the unseen that were designed to provide empirical evidence for the process of social animation.[118] Psychometry enfolded phrenology into a science of spirit-seeing. But instead of focusing solely on the body, psychometry had applied the insights of mesmerism to the "laws of social intercourse" and the "moral atmosphere" surrounding each individual.[119]

115. Feeley-Harnik, "Communities of Blood," 254.

116. Isaac Post, *Voices from the Spirit World, Being Communications from Many Spirits, by the Hand of Isaac Post, Medium* (Rochester: Charles H. McDonell, 1852), 81, 131, xi.

117. See, for example, W. S. Courtney, "Clairvoyance and Psychometry," *The Spiritual Telegraph* 3 (1854): 275-79.

118. See, for example, Joseph R. Buchanan, *Manual of Psychometry: The Dawn of a New Civilization* (1885), 4th ed. (Boston: Frank H. Hodges, 1893). Buchanan was an early proponent of mesmerism, phrenology, and spirit communication. He was a pivotal figure in promoting the "Cincinnati rappings" in the fall of 1850. See William T. Coggshall, *The Signs of the Times: Comprising a History of the Spirit Rappings, in Cincinnati and other Places* (Cincinnati: Author, 1851), 27f.

119. "The fact of the impressibility of the brain, upon which rests the demonstration of a true and thorough Anthropology," wrote Buchanan, will "do more to humanize the world, than any other effort for its moral and intellectual enlightenment which has yet been made" (*The Neurological System of Anthropology, as Discovered, Demonstrated and Taught in 1841 and 1842* [Cincinnati: Office of *Buchanan's Journal of Man*, 1854], 197, 199, 1). See also J. R. Buchanan, "Sympathetic Impressibility," *Buchanan's Journal of Man* 1 (October 1849): 353-68. In 1841, Buchanan, discovered an "acute sensibility" for appreciating "subtil influences" in the organ of Spirituality. And like the Fowlers, Buchanan was explicit about the heightened

In making sympathy a tangible yet immaterial substance, Buchanan equipped his "Anthropology" with the capacity to scan not only the (always already) interconnected horizon for secret relations but also, more importantly, with the capacity to reveal their meaning. In *Natural History of Man*, a work published in the same year as *League*, spiritualist John Newman relied on principles of sympathy to locate humans—their biology as well as "life-power"—on the evolutionary scale between plants and the angels they would soon become. For spiritualists like Newman, sympathetic ties between humans were simultaneously empirical and invisible. The workings of everyday life—both its social and biological dimensions— corresponded directly to the mirror of the spirit-world. According to Newman, it was only now, because of this reflective quality, that the "thinking portion of mankind" had been properly directed toward an "investigation of themselves."[120]

Spiritualists, without apology, appealed to empirical inquiry and practical application.[121] Their piety revolved around the experience of sympathetic ties with spirit, with an eye toward measuring them in relation to oneself.[122] A revolution of religion was inevitable as humans became *"more reasonable."* In fomenting this revolution, spiritualists viewed their activities as eminently scientific. "What is religion?," asked Davis in prodding his audience to separate from doctrinal ritual and to cultivate their interior capacity to discern the authority of being. As opposed to the religions of the past that possessed "no principles of systematic interpretation," such reasoning would enable spiritualists to apprehend the "exquisite harmony" of the world, discriminate "between right and wrong," and achieve "happiness." Moreover, such reason would allow the individual to recognize existence as an "equilibrium of forces" and to locate them-

---

sense of perception that Spirituality catalyzed—"attention turns away from gross matter, and it acquires an extraordinary power of recognizing mind, until at length even disembodied mind is distinctly perceived." J. R. Buchanan, "Psychometry," *Buchanan's Journal of Man* 1 (February 1849): 55; J. R. Buchanan, "Spirituality—Recent Occurrences," *Buchanan's Journal of Man* 1 (February 1850): 489.

120. John B. Newman, *The Natural History of Man; Showing his Three Aspects of Plant, Beast, and Angel* (New York: Fowlers & Wells, 1851), 13.

121. Spiritualists claimed that spirit communication had solved murders, tracked down thieves, discovered lost papers, cured gambling addictions, helped rescue those who were buried alive, steered ships away from inclement weather, helped detect water springs, minerals, and oil treasures. Harding, *Modern American Spiritualism*, 520f.

122. On spiritualism and sympathy, see Cox, *Body and Soul*. See, also "Case of Sympathy," *The Spiritual Telegraph* 3 (1854): 68.

selves amidst "reciprocal relations."[123] Self-knowledge would be the result of knowing metaphysical order incarnate.[124]

10. On Epistemics, Empire, and the Diffusion of Both

Morgan's ethnographic pursuit—a search for the author of being—was a curious blend of evangelical and spiritualist sensibilities. In January 1852, Morgan delivered a lecture to a Rochester audience grown accustomed to revivals, telegraphy, trance lectures, and other occult spectacles.[125] At the beginning of *Diffusion Against Centralization*, Morgan noted the passing of the day when "the mass of the people were excluded" from "the cultivation of practical or speculative knowledge." He, in turn, praised the "broad-cast" of "accumulated stores of knowledge" and the creation of a "community of property" that is not material but is made up of the "circulation" of "the thoughts of gifted men."[126] According to Morgan, there was an unseen something in the American air. This "energy of the nation," this "mass of the people," was spiritual, "composed of Franklins, Marshalls, Washingtons" who "need no commemorative column[s]" but "live 'through the still lapse of ages,' with perpetual freshness in the minds of men."[127] This was an energy, like the Great Spirit had been for the Iroquois, that guaranteed both personal liberty and a strong yet non-

123. Andrew Jackson Davis, *The Approaching Crisis: Being a Review of Dr. Bushnell's Recent Lectures on Supernaturalism* (New York: Author, 1852), 207; Davis, *Philosophy of Spiritual Intercourse*, 163–65. Like Morgan, Davis posed scientific theories of human evolution as the purification of communication between humans across space and time. The first human species, according to Davis, had been born with an innate, prevocal ability to "read the import of each other's thoughts." But with the onset of vocal expression, and later written language, came "misunderstanding." It was only now, argued Davis, that humans were overcoming centuries of misunderstanding, recovering their universal sensitivity to the silent and unwritten thoughts of one another. Spirits, of course, were leading the way in this advance, providing insight and opportunities for earthly inhabitants to communicate with one another, telepathically, with recourse only to their "common reason" (*Approaching Crisis*, 104f).

124. Agency, here, was consummated when the self became a node, attracting and channeling the circulating energies between earth and heaven: Davis writes of the "man [who] 'prays without ceasing'—he prays that holy and glowing prayer which the angels love to gaze upon—that living prayer which sanctifies his own soul" (*Philosophy of Spiritual Intercourse*, 36).

125. Sollors, "Dr. Benjamin Franklin's Celestial Telegraph," 471–74.

126. Lewis Henry Morgan, *Diffusion Against Centralization: A Lecture Delivered from The Rochester Athenaeum and Mechanic's Association* (Rochester: D. M. Dewey, 1852), 7, 18.

127. Ibid., 7, 10, 14, 20, 21, 25, 35, 47, 50; Aquarius [Lewis Henry Morgan], "Thoughts at Niagara," *The Knickerbocker* 22, no. 3 (September 1843): 195–96.

intrusive social fabric. By 1852, this American spirit had become a matter of "American policy," coursing through institutions, laws, all forms of commerce, and therefore the farms and factories that provided materials for trade. The diffusion of this energy would protect "personal liberty" and guarantee the evolution of "representative democracy." Such diffusion would counteract the "despotic" forces of centralization that consolidated "power, wealth, trade, education and refinement in the hands of the few."[128] Morgan's lecture was an attempt to conjure what he had studied since graduating from Union College—the animating spirit of any great nation. Invoking "the atmosphere of liberty," Morgan conjured what E. B. Tylor and others would later define as the concept of "culture."

For Morgan this unseen something possessed sympathetic agency of its own. It possessed the logic of pure circulation. Like the white whale, this *something* lies beneath the waves:

> There is a vast under-current of society moving along with irresistible power, and with an eternal flow, which is destined to swallow up all things arrayed against it.—This current is the *unwritten thoughts* of the people . . . which are imbibed from surrounding influences, the thoughts which pass by oral delivery from mind to mind. They are neither in books, nor constitutions, nor statute laws; they are written in the bosom of humanity.

The material effects of this "under-current" were interrelated and included the diffusion of knowledge in the forms of public schools, the free press, and public lectures, the diffusion of respectability in the forms of fair labor practices, the diffusion of property in the forms of the market economy and class mobility, the distribution of land, the diffusion of trade embodied in the "unwritten laws" of "commerce" that infused their "spirit into every mind [they] enter," and, finally, the diffusion of benevolent sentiments via the principle of religious toleration.[129]

Morgan's lecture, in articulating the politics of his ethnographic agenda, made clear his commitment to the metaphysics of secularism. The animating energy of the United States, in the service of "personal liberty," had "abolished this pernicious and unholy union of Church and State." Moreover, it had catalyzed such freedom by unleashing "the motive power" of the market. For although religion had long constituted "one of the most

128. Morgan, *Diffusion Against Centralization*, 18, 26, 30, 37, 38, 40.
129. Ibid., 11, 16–17, 19–21, 23, 27, 31, 38, 47.

enduring bonds of civil society," the separation clause had served to iso-late the truth of religion—the sense of moral responsibility. In antebel-lum America, the inertia of religious traditionalism was in the process of being purged. Denominationalism was the guarantor of voluntarism. And vice versa. "Religious power" was becoming ever more diffuse, its truth becoming ever more accessible at the level of personal choice.[130]

Religious freedom was a natural consequence of trade routes and riv-ers, "ploughed out by the fiat of Omnipotence." There was a seamlessness to it all. "Commerce," Morgan assured his audience, "wins its victories without a battle, and establishes an empire without a magistrate." Ac-cording to Morgan, commerce would guarantee the widest distribution of wealth and property and, consequently, the independence to determine what to do with it. Such independence, although once the province of native societies, an independence that had initially motivated Morgan's desire to pursue ethnographic inquiry among the Iroquois, could now only be accomplished at a price—by the dismantling of their communal notions of property and extended kinship networks. For in the future an expanding network of "religious affinities" would forge "a more endur-ing bond of union than legislative enactments, or constitutions, or even patriotism itself."[131]

As Morgan's drama of spirituality played out behind the lectern at the Rochester Athenaeum, the benevolent intentions he often expressed as-sumed an explicitly imperious hue. For even as Morgan distanced himself from any taint of religious tradition, going so far as to use the rather un-dignified lower case "c" when writing "christian" (after having capital-ized such words as "Commerce" and "Republic" throughout the written text), his lecture was nothing less than an apology for and sacralization of the state.[132] Here was the public version of what Morgan had previously expressed to politicians in Albany. The spread of civilization, while at once dependent upon the preservation of Iroquois spirit, was also dependent upon the "displacement" of the Iroquois themselves. "When this change is effected, they will cease to be Indians," wrote Morgan. "The pursuits of peace having diffused themselves over the whole republic, one universal and continuous hum of industry will rise from ocean to ocean."[133]

130. Ibid., 47-49.
131. Ibid., 40, 42, 46, 49; Moses, *Promise of Progress*, 134.
132. Morgan, *Diffusion Against Centralization*, 40, 43, 42, 46.
133. Morgan, "Report to the Regents of the University, Dec. 31, 1849." Cited in Tooker, *Lewis H. Morgan*, 207.

11. Industries of Indian-Hating

"After some months' lonely scoutings, the Indian-hater is suddenly seized with a sort of calenture; hurries openly towards the first smoke, though he knows it is an Indian's, announces himself as a lost hunter, gives the savage his rifle, throws himself upon his charity, embraces him with much affection, imploring the privilege of living a while in his sweet companionship. What is too often the sequel of so distempered a procedure may be best known by those who best know the Indian."

The Confidence-Man (1857)

After publication of *League* Morgan achieved a degree of local fame and practiced law in Rochester. He continued his inquiries into sympathy, presenting a paper in 1857 on the laws of Iroquois descent. This paper was the seedbed of his later works, *Systems of Consanguinity* and *Ancient Society*, as Morgan soon spent much time collecting ethnographic data on native populations. He met with the Sioux delegation in 1858, conducted fieldwork with the Chippewa, and began a comparative study of Seneca and Chippewa societies. As Morgan gathered evidence for his argument against polygenesis, he also laid the groundwork for becoming Commissioner of Indian Affairs in the Department of the Interior. In 1860 Morgan became a member of the state assembly of New York. He became increasingly concerned with what he saw as exploitation of native populations under existing Federal agricultural policies. And although he never achieved higher political office, Morgan's position on the unity of the human species was evident in letters to government officials lobbying them to allocate factories and industrial opportunities to Indians for the sake of their well-being.[134]

Morgan's adult life was suffused with the heated rhetoric surrounding the Indian Removal Act of 1830 that authorized the government to exchange land west of the Mississippi for Indian lands in the east. Forced removal of the Cherokee and other tribes in the 1830s only made the search for a benevolent solution to the Indian "problem" that much more urgent.[135] In carving out his own position on the issue in the 1840s and 1850s, Morgan rejected the rhetoric of coercion and violence and sought to bring native populations into the American fold. Such enfolding, however, often carried with it a different kind of imperiousness, what Melville

---

134. Benison, "Railroads, Land and Iron," 140, 160, 169–67, 192, 181–83.
135. Lucy Maddox, *Removals: Nineteenth-Century American Literature and the Politics of Indian Affairs* (New York: Oxford University Press, 1991), 16.

would diagnose in 1857 as a "metaphysics of Indian-hating" that wrapped itself in sympathy.[136] For as the calls of extermination became less strident by mid-century, there arose a kinder but no less passionate attitude toward native populations, a love so nostalgic, so self-assured that its effects were indistinguishable from those of hate.

The metaphysics of Indian-hating could, of course, assume different inflections. In *The Conspiracy of Pontiac*, published the same year as both *League* and *Moby-Dick*, Francis Parkman recorded the "final doom" of those "destined to melt and vanish before the advancing waves of Anglo-American power." According to the logic of Parkman and numerous others who held positions of influence over the Indian question, natives were at once to be celebrated and condemned. They were to be loved for their noble savagery, their pure spirit of individualism, their essential humanity. They were guilty, however, of having chosen their own fate, for having stubbornly refused a narrative of civilized progress. As such, living Indians were signs of their own inexorable end, specters to be honored by recognizing them as already gone.[137]

Others offered more sanguine assessments and detailed maps of how the project of assimilation could and should proceed.[138] Thomas J. Farnham, for example (husband of Eliza Farnham, writer, phrenologist, and penitentiary reformer), wrote of the "spirit of liberality" that should govern relations with natives. "The most successful means of civilizing their mental state," wrote Farnham, "is to teach them a language which is filled with the learning, sciences, and the religion which has civilized Europe, that they may enter at once, and with the fullest rigour into the immense harvests of knowledge and virtue which past ages and superior races have prepared for them."[139] Farnham's voice was representative of a liberal position on native populations and shared much with Morgan's logic. These were sincere and respectful efforts at unity. Yet such statements remained

136. On the evangelical strain, see Roswell Dwight Hitchcock, *An Address on Colportage: before the American Tract Society, at their forty-first anniversary in Boston, May 30, 1855* (New York: American Tract Society, 1855).

137. Wai-chee Dimock, *Empire for Liberty: Melville and the Poetics of Individualism* (Princeton: Princeton University Press, 1989), 117-18. Dimock argues that the dominant imaginary of Indianness at mid-century revolved around a "punitive representation of self," a form of agency that exercised itself in fits of negation as opposed to any constructive contemplation. Dimock also offers a fascinating reading of Captain Ahab in terms of this representation of self.

138. See, for example, Thomas J. Farnham, *Mexico: Its Geography, Its People, and Its Institutions: With a Map, Containing the Result of the Latest Explorations of Fremont, Wilkes, and Others* (New York: H. Long and Brother, 1846).

139. Thomas J. Farnham, *Travels in the Great Western Prairies, The Anahuac and Rocky Mountains, and in the Oregon Territory* (New York: Wiley and Putnam, 1843), 46, 64.

gestures of empathy because the self-consciousness of one's good intentions took precedence over any practical assessment of the historicity of
unification.[140]

Consequently, in their generosity, Morgan's designs were not without
their ironies. Although Morgan claimed to have made "the Indian" the
lifelong "object of [his] benevolence and protection," he was also a practical man. The progress of civilization was inevitable. Indians, he wrote,
"cannot hold out against the onward tide of population" and "must prepare to be incorporated into the great brotherhood of American nations as
equal citizens; perhaps even be engrafted on our race. I sincerely hope this
may be the result."[141] Such engrafting was mutually beneficial, enabling
the civilized American to locate the "profound antiquity" in themselves
and the Native American to cultivate the civilization within. For Morgan,
civilization was not simply inevitable but was also the means by which all
Americans—whether Anglo or native—would disclose the truth of themselves to themselves. It was only the latter, however, who had the privilege
of living authoritatively in the spirit-world.[142]

As Morgan pursued his scientific efforts of disclosure, he became increasingly involved with Rochester lawyer, engineer, and businessman
Heman Ely. Morgan had begun doing legal work in 1845 for the Ely family, owners of one of the largest flour mills in Rochester. In 1848, as new
opportunities arose, Ely shifted his business interests from telegraphy to
railroads and mining reserves in the Upper Peninsula of Michigan. Speculation had begun in earnest in 1819, with Lewis Cass's suggestion to John
C. Calhoun, then Secretary of War, to fund an expedition of the Great
Lakes area for mapping topography and gathering knowledge of Indian
tribes. Cass was acting governor of the Michigan territory and would
eventually become an honorary "warrior" of the Grand Order of the Iroquois. Cass was then intent on persuading these tribes to halt trading with
the British, to convince them to furnish land to other displaced tribes of
the Six Nations, and to eliminate Indian land titles "with a view to land
purchase."[143]

---

140. See, for example, Farnham's comments in *Travels in the Great Western Prairies, The Anahuac and Rocky Mountains, and in The Oregon Territory*, vol. 1 (London: Richard Bentley, 1843),
viii.
141. Quoted in Resek, *Lewis Henry Morgan*, 30–31.
142. The spectralization of native wisdom was compatible with the evangelical propensity to
use the noble savage trope in affirming their own identity as truly religious. Samuel Irenaeus
Prime, "A Lone Indian Feeling After God," *The Christian Parlor Magazine* 1 (October 1844):
163.
143. Benison, "Railroads, Land and Iron," 87, 6, 10.

In 1821 Cass planned the first of many federally funded expeditions, enlisting Henry Schoolcraft to investigate potential mining profits in the Upper Peninsula. Upon his return from the expedition Schoolcraft was already forecasting the "final extirpation" of the Chippewa. In 1826 representatives of the Chippewa signed the Treaty of Fond du Lac granting the United States "the right to search for, and carry away, any metals or minerals from any part of their country."[144] In 1836 Schoolcraft brokered a treaty between the Chippewa that annexed over sixteen million acres of their land in the Upper Peninsula. Another treaty in 1842 ceded fifteen million acres.[145] In 1845 Schoolcraft, too, became an honorary member of Morgan's Grand Order, naming himself "Alhala, a Wise-man of the Acqinushionee."[146]

Mineralogists working in the Upper Peninsula soon declared that "enough iron has already been discovered" between Green Bay and Lake Superior "to warrant the assertion that the supply is inexhaustible." As the first successful shipment of iron from the Upper Peninsula occurred in 1846, the land became increasingly valuable—in the construction of railroads, steam engines, and locomotives—whereas the Chippewa who inhabited it were decidedly less so.[147] For only after natives had been replaced with more savvy entrepreneurial regimes would "enough iron" be available "to construct a railroad around the world and then freight it for a thousand years."[148]

The major obstacle confronting investors such as Ely's Rochester group was how to transport the newly discovered riches back to the east. Each group of investors needed to patch together land and existing railways in

144. "Treaty with the Chippewa, 1826," in *Indian Affairs: Laws and Treaties*, vol. 2, ed. Charles J. Kappler (Washington: Government Printing Office, 1904), 269. See also the ethnographic treatment of this event in Thomas L. McKenney, *Sketches of a Tour to the Lakes, of the Character and Customs of the Chippeway Indians, and of Incidents connected with the Treaty of Fond du Lac* (Baltimore: Fielding Lucas, Jr., 1827).

145. Benison, "Railroads, Land and Iron," 22–23. See also Francis Paul Prucha, *The Great Father: The United States Government and the American Indians* (Lincoln: University of Nebraska Press, 1984), 1:261–62.

146. Moses, *Promise of Progress*, 52.

147. Over the next decade the remaining Chippewa and other native tribes were "persuaded" to migrate southward into Wisconsin or else convert to Catholicism. Removal of Chippewa continued through the early 1850s, the goal being their "ultimate incorporation into the great body of our citizen population" (Luke Lea, "Report of Commissioner of Indian Affairs," in *Annual Report of the Commissioner of Indian Affairs* [Washington, D.C.: Gideon and Co., 1851], 4, 13).

148. Citations from Benison, "Railroads, Land and Iron," 51, 95. On the inexhaustibility of iron in this region, see also *The Iron Resources of Michigan, and General Statistics of Iron* (Detroit: H. Barnes, 1856), 18.

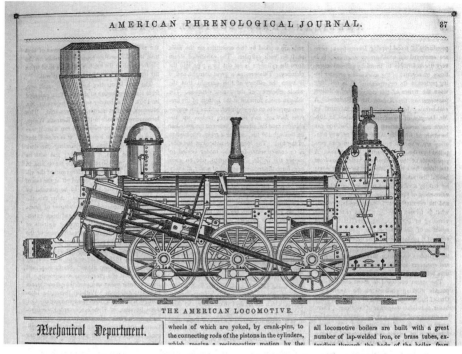

AMERICAN PHRENOLOGICAL JOURNAL. 87

THE AMERICAN LOCOMOTIVE.

Mechanical Department. | wheels of which are yoked, by crank-pins, to the connecting rods of the pistons in the cylinders, which receive a reciprocating motion by the | all locomotive boilers are built with a great number of lap-welded iron, or brass tubes, extending through the body of the boiler from

FIGURE 16 · The American Locomotive "approaches near to the spiritual and physical combination of the human machine." *American Phrenological Journal* 13 (February, 1851): 37.

order to secure a viable route and to make a mining business profitable. In 1850 the United States Congress began issuing land grants to railroad companies, intensifying competition among investors by ceding former Chippewa land as a means of generating economic infrastructure. From 1852 to 1857, an overwhelming number of plans, petitions, and bills were put before Congress and public officials in an effort to receive a land grant. Petitions to receive 'free" land in the Upper Peninsula spoke of the need for all Americans to "unconditionally unreservedly surrender and yield obedience" to the "commercial business of the country."[149]

In 1855 Morgan began to do legal work for Ely's Rochester investment group, becoming both legal counsel and investor in the Lake Superior Iron Company and the Iron Mountain Railroad Company. "The amount of ore is vast beyond all estimation," gushed Morgan in July 1855; "it would

149. Benison, "Railroads, Land and Iron," 102–4. During the 1850s such land grants exceeded 22 million acres.

stagger the belief of anyone who had not seen it."[150] With the sudden death of Ely in 1856, Morgan took a more active role in the Iron Mountain Railroad Company. Much (but not all) of his time would be taken up with resolving the different land claims surrounding Federal land grants and with outmaneuvering other competing railroad companies. Morgan lobbied Congress for land grants and became involved in attracting investors for speculative rail lines. He also invested in another potential route—the Bay de Nocquet and Marquette Railroad Company. Through the late 1850s he managed teams of surveyors, geologists, engineers, and Indian guides who streamlined the excavation, transportation, and distribution of iron and copper ore to Eastern markets. Morgan was in his element, a node within a vast evolutionary scheme of human history. "It would be a singular satisfaction could it be known to what tribe and family we are indebted for this knowledge" of "smelting iron," wrote Morgan at the end of his life. "The process of smelting iron ore was the invention of inventions," he remarked. "The accelerated progress of human intelligence dates from this invention."[151]

In helping to open up the continent to commerce Morgan became a modestly rich man, rich enough to have time later in life to manage his investments and continue his ethnographic and zoological research during his time in Michigan. In 1868 he published an account, dense with detail, about the relationships between the anatomy, structures, and lifeways of beavers in the Upper Peninsula. This despite the fact that the beavers had been "surprised" when a "[r]ailroad was . . . constructed through [their] rugged wilderness." Nevertheless, such commercial activity was what made possible *The American Beaver and His Works*, providing a "rare opportunity . . . to examine the works of the beaver, and to see him in his native wilds."[152] As he had done in *League*, Morgan wrote of the spirit animating the "industrious mute[s]" as it manifested itself in their networks of dams. The "preserving labors of the beaver," wrote Morgan, in addition to being "suggestive of human industry," were ciphers of a metaphysical order. "The life of the[ir] spiritual essence" was equivalent to their Common Sense. "When a beaver stands for a moment and looks upon his work, evidently to see whether it is right, and whether anything else is needed, he shows himself capable of holding his thoughts before his beaver mind." According to Morgan, beavers were in correspondence with the "principle

150. Quoted in Resek, *Lewis Henry Morgan*, 59.
151. Benison, "Railroads, Land and Iron," 102, 119–20, 124. Morgan, *Ancient Society*, 43, 538.
152. Morgan, *American Beaver*, 7–8.

of life" itself, exemplified by their social harmony and epistemic capacity to be "conscious of [their] own mental processes." And it was precisely this principle that Morgan sought to enact during his career. For in keeping with the drama of spirituality, to know the self was to know the self knowing the world. As a means of securing one's identity both in time as well as across it, such knowledge was to be cultivated at all costs.[153]

12. The Melodrama of Calculability

"He is self-willed; being one who less hearkens to what others may say about things, than looks for himself, to see what are things themselves. If in straits, there are few to help; he must depend upon himself; he must continually look to himself."

The Confidence-Man (1857)

In *League of the Iroquois*, Morgan had written that "man, when left to the guidance of his own inward persuasions, searches after the Author of his being, and seeks to comprehend the purposes of his existence, and his final destiny."[154] As this chapter has shown, Morgan's own search drew upon Common Sense philosophy and the concept of sympathy as well as the currents of evangelicalism and spiritualism that swirled around his scene of writing. From a discursive perspective, Morgan lived out the compatibility of Baconian science, evangelicalism, and spiritualism. He represented the world at every turn in his career as a matter of presence and calculability, relying upon those representations in order to assure himself of his own presence and calculability. Morgan's drama of spirituality—his struggle to articulate and practice a bounded selfhood amidst a world that was admittedly and radically relational—was more than either a displacement or replacement of religion. It was also a placement and, to some degree, enforcement of specific definitional boundaries—religion as a solitary epistemic endeavor; religion as an interior assessment of external forces; religion as a means of "spiritual independence." It is not surprising, then, that Morgan, who increasingly employed the frame of evolution to narrate the origins of human history, would end up discovering that the "Author" was a version of himself writ small in the heart of his native

153. Ibid., 6–8, 256, 190, 283.
154. Morgan, *League*, 149.

informants—both human and animal—and writ large in the workings of technological modernity.

Although Morgan's search possessed a self-serving quality, it nevertheless "may be regarded as not wholly without the efficacy of devout sentiment."[155] For in challenging the doctrine of polygenesis as expressed in the racial hierarchies of Samuel Morton, Josiah Nott, and Louis Agassiz, Morgan opposed the idea that different races had been created separately. In his affirmation of a transcendent yet non-theological totality—an atmospheric substance that linked together all parts of Iroquois life—Morgan was making an argument for the universal spirit of human society. On behalf of Iroquois humanity, he was also seeking communion with that binding element, a spirit pervading their life and deeds, a spirit that in and of itself conferred humanity upon them. Yet in making Iroquois humanity the finite object of his inquiry, the implication of Morgan's work was that Iroquois existence was wholly spectral. For as Morgan patiently compiled the signs of their "animating spirit," he assumed those signs to be reflections originating from beyond themselves. Each of those signs suggested a stand-alone order that anchored its meaning in real reality even as the sign was not real in and of itself. The humanity of the Iroquois, then, occurred not in the here and now but at an overarching and unified level of significance. Their humanity, after all, being largely an abstraction.

Morgan's drama of spirituality, steeped in liberal sensibility, ended the same way it had begun—on a decidedly imperial note. For throughout his career—from his reading of Lord Kames's taxonomy of wonder to his discovery of a universal system of kinship—the only outside that Morgan acknowledged was that which signified the inside. The secret relations of self and world were defined, from the outset, by their potential to be disclosed. Morgan's empathy, in keeping with Common Sense standards of objectivity, was properly scientific. A simultaneous identification with and distancing from the other. Consequently, the status of Morgan's identification with either Indians or beavers remains unclear, as does the success of his search for the authority of being itself.

Which brings us back, full circle, to Morgan's curious dismissal of religion as an obfuscating category of interpretation. In his final work, *Ancient Society*, Morgan once again distanced himself from the formalities of theology, providing empirical and statistical terms for the felt yet invis-

---

155. Herman Melville, *The Confidence-Man: His Masquerade* (London: Longman, Brown, Green, Longmans, and Roberts, 1857), 218.

ible bonds of human affiliation. Committed to the project of transparency, Morgan felt it necessary to offer some "incidental suggestion[s]" when it came to religion.

One such "suggestion" occurs when Morgan declared the origin of primitive kinship to lie "concealed in the misty antiquity of mankind beyond the reach of positive knowledge." Another occurs when he "reflects" upon the "new property career of mankind" and is struck by the "powerful influence property . . . now begin[s] to exercise upon the human mind, and of the great awakening of new elements of character it was calculated to produce." Although such an unintelligible situation could potentially derail the "natural," "necessary," and "progressive" accumulation "of experiential knowledge," Morgan performed, uneasily, a confidence that Americans could avoid the descent into the primitive grotesque. "Since the advent of civilization," wrote Morgan,

> the outgrowth of property has been *so immense*, its forms *so diversified*, its uses *so expanding* and its management *so intelligent* in the interests of its owners, that it has become, on the part of the people, an *unmanageable power*. The human mind stands *bewildered* in the presence of its own creation.[156]

The litany of "so immense . . . so diversified . . . so expanding . . . so intelligent" suggests a momentary lapse of interpretive ground. With an emerging industrial economy (of which Morgan was both participant and observer), with the market's relentless calculations of time and space, its tendency to partition and coordinate and to shine light into every dark recess, a shadow was cast.[157] Yet despite Morgan's admission that the current situation could produce situations that were beyond the reach of positive knowledge, *Ancient Society* did not flinch nor did it veer from its quantifying agenda. "Nevertheless," wrote Morgan, "the time will come . . . when human intelligence will rise to the mastery over property, and define the relations of the state to the property it protects. . . . The interests of society are paramount to individual interests, and the two must be brought into *just and harmonious relations*." Rather than recalibrate what in fact constituted positive knowledge, Morgan guaranteed future possibilities of clarification and control.[158]

In feigning bewilderment in the face of market forces as an explicit pre-

---

156. Morgan, *Ancient Society*, 502, 544, 3, 552 (my emphasis).
157. Martin Heidegger, "The Age of the World Picture," in *The Question Concerning Technology and Other Essays*, trans. William Lovitt (New York: Harper and Row, 1977), 133-35.
158. Morgan, *Ancient Society*, 552.

condition for his commitment to order, transparency, and legibility, Morgan expressed a particular version of secularism at mid-century. Despite the acknowledged and excessive calculations of property, Morgan insisted upon his potential to calculate those calculations. He equated the security of the state with the best interest of the individual despite the fact that property had begun to determine those interests, not to mention possess interests of its own. And lest we forget, Morgan insisted that knowledge and politics be set apart, quite literally, from the religious.

As an occult cartographer in the vein of Captain Ahab and Matthew Fontaine Maury, Morgan sought to chart what lay behind the varied and interconnected signs of spirit. For to recognize your embeddedness in the "secret relations" of the material world was prerequisite for disclosing them. This secret code of material existence, however, was not only manifest in singular points—the cut of a dress, a civic ceremony, circulations of capital, the boiled bark of straps and skeins behind museum glass—but also wholly immanent, part and parcel of the territory to be mapped as well as the mapmaker. By definition, it had no center and could not be located or contained in essence. Morgan's drama of spirituality was fueled by the faint impossibility of ever arriving at a space in which humans could discern and represent their own humanity to themselves and by themselves. Because the code was immanent, a matter of almost infinite distribution, there was a possibility that it could never be completely deciphered. Yet it was Morgan's recognition that much eluded his calculation that perpetuated his desire to map the relational ontology of human being, what he would eventually call "the great chart of human progress."[159]

By the end of his life Morgan's search for the "Author" of his being

---

159. Ibid., 341. The epistemics involved here (that is, the hard work of coming to know anything at all) resembles Foucault's description of *Homo economicus* as the representative man of nineteenth-century liberalism and centerpiece of the market revolution. Foucault argues that *Homo economicus*, as theorized by Adam Smith, was akin to your garden-variety Calvinist. Complete knowledge (whether it concerned God, salvation, or the totality of social relations) was a logical impossibility. Psychological assurance, however, was not. *Homo economicus*, like the man walking the streets of Geneva, did not simply participate in an indefinite field of forces. His security and freedom were wholly dependent upon the fact that this field was wholly indefinite. For both, the workings of the invisible hand implied a totality of relations yet prevented any single individual, including the sovereign, from seeing this networked whole. All knowledge in this situation under capitalism was circumstantial save for the knowledge of (the disciplined) self. "So," concludes Foucault, "we have a system in which homo economicus owes the positive nature of his calculation precisely to everything which eludes his calculation" (Michel Foucault, *The Birth of Biopolitics, Lectures at the College de France, 1978–79*, ed. Michel Senellart, trans. Graham Burchell [New York: Palgrave, 2008], 278).

had become thoroughly melodramatic. Rather than seriously engage the shadows produced by the outgrowth, uses, and management of material life, Morgan chose instead the well-worn rag of enacting doubt. This had always been the key to his success. Mystery and secrets existed, almost exclusively, in their potential to be revealed. Yet having staged and seemingly resolved the crisis of knowledge (the raison d'être of melodrama being that the resolution is already present in the staging), Morgan's career-long performance—from playing Indian in a rented Masonic Lodge to "father" of American anthropology and guarantor of human origin to savvy railroad lawyer and mining investor to faux bewilderment in the face of market forces—calls attention to the possibility that secrets, in strict speech, are never equal to the sum of their disclosure.

CHAPTER 4

THE TOUCH OF 𝔖𝔢𝔠𝔲𝔩𝔞𝔯𝔦𝔰𝔪

Change in the action of the mind, must be the basis of all reform; and whatever is done to enlighten the intellect or stimulate the better affections, is so much gained towards the great end which every philanthropist must have in view of this unfortunate class.

ELIZA FARNHAM, *Annual Report of the Matron of Mt. Pleasant State Prison for Females*, October 10, 1844

By producing in the minds of convicts an impression that their welfare is cared for, that they are not hopelessly lost, and that their efforts at reformation will be met by a kindly and an encouraging spirit, new aspirations after goodness are produced in them, new thoughts awakened, and new and better lives aimed at.

Report of the Inspectors of the Sing Sing Prison, January 1845

1. The Left Thigh of the Honorable Judge Edmonds

As a former legislator, lawyer, confidant to Presidents Martin Van Buren and Andrew Jackson, state senator, president of the New York Prison Association, and state Supreme Court judge, John W. Edmonds was a representative American—at least according the monumental *Portraits of Eminent Americans Now Living* published in 1853.[1] As Edmonds approached the end of his career as an administrator of state power, he turned toward the ad-

---

1. One of Edmonds's more memorable roles occurred in 1837, when he served as Jackson's attaché in an effort to gather information about Native Americans living on the borders of Lakes Huron and Superior for the purpose of removing them. John Livingston, *Portraits of Eminent Americans Now Living* (New York: Cornish, Lamport & Co., 1853), 2:801.

ministration of another kind of power. In two collections of spirit-world communiqués from Emanuel Swedenborg (d. 1772) and Francis Bacon (d. 1626), Edmonds announced the discovery of a "great truth which is marking the nineteenth century." The ontological status of this "truth" was decidedly ambiguous. On the one hand, Edmonds declared that it possessed a "most intimate connection with our religious faith." He cited the most recent population statistics found in *American Almanac* and concluded that the "revelation" of spiritualism would be the "common platform on which all might congregate and unite in one common adoration of the God of all." On the other, Edmonds also portrayed spiritual "intercourse" as a worldly phenomenon in that it possessed dramatic scientific and political import.[2]

Integrating the epistemological prescriptions of Scottish Common Sense and the social ethics of republican virtue, Edmonds emphasized that everyone "should investigate for himself, and not depend upon what others tell him" about spiritual intercourse. According to Edmonds, the "truth" of spirit communication was equally and universally available to all. It "sought no private haunts." It "enveloped itself in no useless mystery, but came out boldly before man, challenging his closest [public] scrutiny. It sought no blind faith, but demanded always, and under all circumstances, the exercise of calm reason and deliberate judgment. . . . It sent forth no preachers, it sought no proselytes, [and] aimed at building up no sect." Edmonds distanced spiritualism from the enthusiasm of revivals and the politics of revealed religion. Because spiritualism hinged upon man's "conduct, which he can control," and not upon "his faith, which he can not," the "truth" of spiritualism transcended the mere interests of "private citizen." As such, this "truth" was abstractly democratic and self-consciously secular, set apart from the particularities of personality and irrational bias. The means of cultivating the progressive capacities of the individual was instead "a matter of public interest" that would be debated and subsequently accepted by all Americans. Spiritualism, Edmonds argued, was nothing less than a vehicle for modernizing the psyche and reforming the body politic.[3]

Edmonds's drift toward spiritualist conviction began slowly, among

2. John W. Edmonds and George T. Dexter, *Spiritualism*, vol. 2 (New York: Partridge & Brittan, 1855), 19.

3. John W. Edmonds and George T. Dexter, *Spiritualism*, vol. 1 (New York: Partridge & Brittan, 1853), 8, 1, 9, 12, 53, 64, 69, 71, 15-18, 73.

strangers, with visits to local séances. Upon hearing rappings that sounded like those emanating from "the bottom of a car when traveling on a railroad," Edmonds "invoked the aid of science" in order to rule out the possibility of fraud. Edmonds then scheduled a series of interviews with mediums and clairvoyants. Their teachings, to which "no pure Christian could take exception," were marked by the rhetoric of scientific precision. But even though the microphysics of spiritual intercourse had swayed Edmonds intellectually, he had yet to experience, for himself *and through himself*, the workings of the spirit-world. That is, until the evening of February 17, 1851, when, as Edmonds recalled, he "was alone by myself," in bed and reading a novel by Walter Scott. The experience that followed, according to Edmonds, "seemed to come for the express purpose of reaching an impression of *collusion* that was lurking in my mind. It came when I was awake and in full possession of my senses" (emphasis mine).

After Edmonds had gone to bed, he reported to have "felt a touching on my left thigh, which I at first thought was the twitching of the muscles which all will at times experience. It continued, however, so long, and with such regularity of intervals, that I began to think it could not be from that same cause. I accordingly put my hand down by the side of and upon my thigh, and the touching ceased." Edmonds then felt something "on the top of my hand and across my fingers, as if that which touched my thigh had passed across my hand." Elusive, electric, and prone to withdrawal, the touching sensation itself could not be touched. Yet Edmonds could not ignore what he felt to be a passionate desire to communicate with *him*, to apply its knowledge in the consummation of *his* character, and to incorporate *him* into its system.[4]

In addition to its mechanical aura and technological directive (*technologia*, from the Greek meaning "systematic treatment"), Edmonds's encounter also possessed an erotic charge. The touchings "continued for twenty or twenty-five minutes, during which time I resorted to various expedients to test the reality of what I felt." "Determined to ascertain whether [the twitching] was intelligent," Edmonds held a lamp to his thigh but could detect nothing. "While I was asking, the touching ceased, and when my question was put, my thigh was twice touched with distinct intervals." "These touchings" then "made their appearance on the front of my thigh" and "right foot. . . . After that there came a stream of touchings from my left big toe, all the way up my leg to the upper part of my thigh. They were

4. Edmonds, and Dexter, *Spiritualism*, 1:18-19.

very numerous, and so rapid as to form almost a stream, yet each touch was quite distinct. . . . The touchings then appeared at my left side, near my loins, very gently and at intervals until I fell asleep."[5]

Edmonds then consulted a "rapping medium" about these and other kinds of encounters—pats on the neck, "as if by a gentle female hand," and other hands reaching into his pocket. The medium told Edmonds that his midnight encounter "was not, as I had supposed, my own imagining, but a direction that it would be well for me to heed." The medium then provided, by way of spirits, evidentiary testimony—a "communication" that knew too much about Edmonds to be denied. "I was startled, for here was to me evidence from which I could not escape, that my most secret thoughts were known to the intelligence that was dealing with me. There was no avoiding the conclusion." It was as if Edmonds had been accessed rather than the spirit-world.[6]

Edmonds insisted that his experience of being "repeatedly touched" by an "invisible power" was part of a widespread phenomenon. "There is not a neighborhood in the United States," declared the former judge, "where similar things have not occurred, and can be testified to by persons whose testimony would be received in any human transaction." Manifestations of spiritual intercourse had become so prevalent at mid-century because they were now "being developed" through the industry of "human progress." Edmonds, moreover, took great pains to remind his reading and lecture audiences that to adhere to the "truth" of spiritual intercourse was to be part of national movement as well as a global one in which the United States would assume the economic and industrial lead.[7]

In mingling the grammars of technology and spirit communication, Edmonds had begun to feel the pressures of antebellum society within the psyche and under his skin. Like many Americans, he was also struggling to come to terms with and provide terms for the increasing presence of technology in daily life.[8] As Edmonds and others sought explanations for structures without seams and feelings without visible sources, they turned to the language of occultism and its tropes of hidden intentionality.

5. Ibid.

6. Ibid., 21.

7. Ibid., 23, 51, 36

8. Andrew Jackson Davis, for example, welcomed such incursions as signs of spiritual intercourse, claiming that "railroads and steamboats are made and managed by spirit." Furthermore, technological innovation, rather than threaten the status of human nature, actually brought to light its pure potentiality and confirmed that *"human spirit travels faster than electricity"* (Davis, *The Philosophy of Spiritual Intercourse* [New York: Fowlers & Wells, 1851], 49, 31).

Such narratives, I argue, were rather accurate portrayals of life increasingly subject to telegraphy, steam presses, and the roaring wheels of a railway car.

This chapter traces one specific narrative of spectrality as it passed through the women's ward at Sing Sing State Penitentiary in New York—a major node of the evangelical reform network—on its way to Edmonds's left thigh. A ghost story, itself becoming a ghostly matter. The source of the "touchings," I argue, was discursive. They had everything to do with systematic treatments of the human and Edmonds involvement with them at Sing Sing. And finally, these "touchings" possessed a distinctly erotic feel, indicative perhaps of the democratizing impulse of secularism.

———

In 1844, Edmonds assumed the presidency of the Prison Association of New York (PANY) and appointed Eliza Farnham to be matron of Sing Sing Woman's Prison (also called Mt. Pleasant State Prison for Females). Farnham was a self-declared "free-thinker" who, at the age of twenty-eight, possessed both literary aspirations and deep commitments to social reform. Farnham had been tapped by Edmonds for her liberal sympathies and, more immediately, to quell a "rebellion among the convicts" who "had deliberately refused to conform to the rules" and had "turned the prison into a pandemonium."[9] As reported by Sing Sing inspectors in January 1844, the rebellions of "the most depraved and abandoned of the sex" were coded in political, epistemic, racial, and gendered terms. "They are mostly persons whose whole lives have been spent in the unrestrained indulgence of their passions, and they struggle long, and violently, and too often successfully, against every effort to teach them the lesson of self control. Many of them are blacks, from the stews and brothels of our large cities, lost to all sense of shame, and impervious to all good impressions. Violent battles are frequent in the prison, and knives have been known to be drawn among them."[10]

9. Georgiana Bruce Kirby, *Years of Experience: An Autobiographical Narrative* (1887; New York: AMS Press, 1971), 190–91. One source of this "open rebellion" was overcrowding. Another was the "process of corruption" in which young girls, often convicted of nonviolent crimes, were subject to the "curse" of "contamination." And yet another was blasphemous behavior, as when four prisoners "took an oath upon the Bible . . . solemnly devoting themselves to the devil, as his children, and to obey his commands!" (Prison Association of New York, *Second Report of the Prison Association of New York* [New York: Prison Association of New York, 1846], 37–38).

10. PANY, *Second Report*, 36–37.

Farnham brought with her to Sing Sing a "systematizing" approach to penology based on the doctrines of phrenology—the science of reforming the body by knowing the behavioral categories of the mind. Farnham, like Edmonds, would soon become involved in spiritualism and its "rational idea of salvation." As she later declared, the religious truth of spiritualism was premised upon "its clear revelation of our great needs, and its ample resources for satisfying them." But already Farnham's secular imaginary hinged upon the disclosure of secret meanings and the actualization of hidden potentials. It did not reject religion but, on the contrary, sought to reveal the heretofore undisclosed relationship between the cranium and human morality (conceived broadly as both behavioral tendencies and psychological dispositions). Like the elaborate spiritualist cosmologies it would come to inform, phrenology was a means of self-mastery.[11] Like spiritualism, phrenology sought to disclose the organic connection between human matter and human spirit, going so far as to map it on the surface of the skull according to the blueprint "of nature, universal in its operations." But rather than focus on securing the presence of the afterlife, phrenology offered reformers of various stripes a technology to secure a different kind of potential presence, that of the State. As Farnham insisted, phrenology was necessary in producing "respectable and useful citizen[s]."[12]

In her first report to PANY, Farnham announced her intention of "reducing the convicts to a sound state of discipline" through "the systematizing of details." This "was to be effected by means which had not hitherto been tried, viz. by substituting kindness for force, and other restraints, imposed through the mental constitutions of the prisoners." The goal, in short, was to invite inmates to "enjoy" the gift of "their liberty" by impressing upon them "the importance of self-government." Before Farnham's arrival, prisoners had been subject to various tortures, including mouth-gags, pulleys, stocks, and chains. Inmates who did not obey were handcuffed, wrapped in a blanket, and chained to the floor. At Sing Sing, Farnham re-

11. E. W. Farnham, *A Lecture on the Philosophy of Spiritual Growth, delivered at Plates Hall, May 18, 1862* (San Francisco: Valentine and Co., 1862), 12, 19.

12. O. S. Fowler, *Religion: Natural and Revealed: or, the Natural Theology and Moral Bearings of Phrenology and Physiology* (New York: Searing & Prall, 1844), 105; M. B. Sampson, *Rationale of Crime, and its Appropriate Treatment; being a Treatise on Criminal Jurisprudence Considered in Relation to Cerebral Organization with Notes and Illustrations by E. W. Farnham* (New York: D. Appleton & Co., 1846), 66, 123. On phrenology as a form of social physics, see George Combe's discussion of Quetelet and the fact that he was "anxious to apply . . . his own statistical inquiries" ("Miscellaneous Papers," *The Phrenological Journal* 85 [October 1845], 293).

placed such tortures with a program of therapeutic kindness. She induced and seduced prisoners to model their behavior according to phrenological scripts—a strategic and sustained effort to generate atmospheric pressures within the confines of the women's ward. As a woman named Squires attested, a twenty-nine-year-old inmate at Sing Sing convicted of manslaughter, Farnham's methods had catalyzed true reform, whereas before her arrival, "women were absolutely corrupted by being here." Squires recalled, "When I first came here the punishments were very severe. I had a sister die from the severity of the punishment; she having been tied up by her wrists for a long time." Others, reported Squires, had been tied up "until the blood gushed from their fingers' ends." Farnham, by contrast, "has attempted to make us comfortable."[13]

In 1846, following much conflict and controversy, Edmonds and Farnham finally secured the resignation of Sing Sing's resident chaplain, Methodist minister John Luckey. In doing so, they secured a phrenological approach to the management of the penitentiary atmosphere. It is my contention that this shift in institutional emphasis—from bodily disciplines in a Methodist key to emotional cultivations in the key of phrenology—was not as stark as either the participants or the press reported at the time.[14]

To be sure, this coup was carried out against an evangelical establishment and a somewhat conservative chaplain, even by the standards of mid-century evangelicalism. But more significantly, it was carried out in the name of what Farnham called a "true spiritual life." Before immersing herself in spiritualist circles in the 1850s and becoming acquainted with "the idea of the spirit-life, independent from the body," Farnham defined the truth of religion as simply the practice of "being very good." Conscious of her own large faculty of Veneration, Farnham defined the truth of religion that she brought with her to Sing Sing as a form of "spiritual vision." Consequently, she sought to "bring the creative power which the All-wise has delegated, to earth." Only then would life "glorify itself in deed, and in truth; and, divinely born, the human soul shall know and reverence itself, as the effect of a Divine cause, working through pure and holy instruments of true womanhood and righteous manhood." In this sense, true

13. PANY, *Second Report*, 38–39; PANY, *Third Report of the Prison Association of New York*, Part 2 (New York: Prison Association of New York. 1847), 59.
14. On phrenology as a form of "secular Methodism," see Roger Cooter, *The Cultural Meaning of Popular Science: Phrenology and the Organization of Consent in Nineteenth-Century Britain* (Cambridge: Cambridge University Press, 1984).

religion continued to be deployed within the walls of Sing Sing, the majority of whose inmates were "superstitious as well as ignorant."[15]

This chapter is concerned with the effects of secularism as they played out within the institutions of the American state. I argue that Farnham's management style of "gaining a personal influence over every individual" within the prison was not so much antithetical to evangelicalism as it was compatible. Despite her skepticism for organized religion, particularly as it manifested itself in enthusiastic and "orthodox" faiths, Farnham's "purely and truly natural" religious sentiment resonated with evangelical piety in formal structure as well as substantive effect.[16] Carrying the Arminian strain of evangelical piety to its logical conclusion, Farnham (with the support of Edmonds) folded voluntarism into what phrenologists considered the "all controlling necessity" of human reason. Farnham and Edmonds also rehearsed the millennialism of evangelicals in a decidedly phrenological key. Together, they transposed providence into an utterly human(e) project by insisting that sin was something to be overcome through individual effort. Driven by millennial visions of American progress, their phrenological reforms were a mix of Common Sense empiricism, republicanism, and the desire to integrate the two. Their agenda, to the extent that it anticipated their spiritualist beliefs, also refracted an unspoken trajectory of the evangelical public sphere, namely a *collusion* between the means of subjectivity and the ends of state formation.

2. Secularism, Spiritualism, and the Rights of Women

It is well known that at the coronation of kings and queens, even modern ones, a certain curious process of seasoning them for their functions is gone through. . . . Certain I am, however, that a king's head is solemnly oiled at his coronation, even as a head of salad. Can it be, though, that they anoint it with a view of making its interior run well, as they anoint machinery?

    Moby-Dick; or, the Whale

By mid-century, Americans such as Farnham and Edmonds were becoming conversant in occult grammars of piety that assumed the potential for correspondence between material existence and the world of spirit. These

---

15. Eliza W. Farnham, *My Early Days* (New York: Thatcher & Hutchison, 1859), 247, 170-71, 75, 15, viii; PANY, *Second Report*, 38.

16. PANY, *Second Report*, 39; Farnham, *Early Days*, 73-74, 311-12. On Farnham's anti-institutional bias, see her *Woman and Her Era* (New York: A. J. Davis and Co., 1864), 1:19.

metaphysical orientations came of age in upstate New York, marked by the increasing popularity of the mystical writings of Swedenborg, the outburst of spirit communication among Shakers in the late 1830s, the healing sessions of Andrew Jackson Davis (the "Seer of Poughkeepsie") in the 1840s, and, finally, the publicity garnered by Maggie and Kate Fox in 1848 with their claims of strange knockings in the basement of their Hydesville home. Spiritualist cosmologies deemphasized the notion of sudden conversion in favor of a more progressive notion of spiritual paternalism. Fearing the prospect of external restraint that was not divinely sanctioned, spiritualists chose instead to believe in the validity of spiritual constraint that issued from a "Supreme Legislator" dedicated to republican values and laissez faire principles. "Especially in America," wrote Davis in 1851, "there are many indications of the presence and influence of spiritual beings or agencies, possessing intelligence and manifesting extraordinary power over material objects and substances."[17]

Within the "republican" government envisioned by spiritualists, "ministering angels" used neither rhetoric nor "coercion" but openly "impressed" moral order "upon their constituents." In their version of republicanism, spiritualists did not necessarily adhere to the whole of what later thinkers would define as "secular" politics. They did, however, conceive of a public sphere set apart from the secrecy of monarchs, the delusion of superstition, and the passions of sectarianism. Communications between citizens, like those between the living and the dead, were matters of transparency, openness, and immediacy. Decoding the language of dead souls was but the first step in making the body politic legible to all individuals exercising their innate capacity for sympathetic reason. This sense of democracy, according to someone like Edmonds, could be cultivated by the investigative efforts of humans and not by blind faith. "This is not a superstitious age, but one of materiality and SCIENCE," declared Davis. "Theocracy of the senior nations of the earth is giving away—is melting like a mountain of ice before the sun—and true REPUBLICANISM is fast becoming the mighty spirit of existing empires!"[18]

For spiritualist leaders and those who would soon become them,

---

17. Davis, *Philosophy of Spiritual Intercourse*, 46. See also Bret E. Carroll, *Spiritualism in Antebellum America* (Bloomington: Indiana University Press, 1997), 61, 63.

18. Emma Hardinge, *Modern American Spiritualism* (1870; New Hyde Park: University Books, 1970), 11; Robert Hare, *Experimental Investigations of the Spirit Manifestations, Demonstrating the Existence of Spirits and Their Communion with Mortals* (New York: Partridge and Brittan, 1855), 88–89, 113; Davis, *Philosophy of Spiritual Intercourse*, 9.

epistemic independence and republican virtue were themselves divine. Divinity, in other words, was not restricted to a divine realm. Or as T. L. Harris argued in 1854 at a conference in New York, spiritualists worshipped "a God of freedom, a God of republicanism, a God of liberty, a God of equity, a God of science, a God of art, a God of poetry, a God of beauty, a God of heroism, a God of moral worth, a God of universal benevolence, and a God of universal inspiration. That God lives."[19]

Harris's riff was not uncommon among antebellum spiritualists—spiritualism was true. It was a religion born of the secular age. It was, in the end, about the transparency and immediacy that would result from sustained attention to mediation. But what were the reverberations that went unacknowledged? What were the politics of this unknowing? What were the epistemics? To what degree was spiritualism an extension of the "systematic benevolence" of evangelicals in pursuit of a divinely sanctioned republicanism? What was the relationship between the self-conscious sacralization of the State *and* the state of everyday life? What do practices that ascribed spectral presence to other bodies—organic and social—have to do with the rhythms of the secular age?

———

As Ann Braude has noted, antebellum spiritualism was infused with the impulse to radical reform and was integral to a burgeoning women's rights movement. As a "staunchly individualistic form of religious practice," writes Braude, spiritualists believed that "individuals could serve as vehicles of truth because each embodied the laws of nature in his or her being. Such individualism laid the foundation for Spiritualism's rejection of male headship over women—or indeed any individual over any other—whether in religion, politics, or society." Such anti-authoritarianism has led Braude and subsequent commentators to view spiritualism as a vehicle of human rights and progressive reform at mid-century, a space in which women not only endured, religiously, but assumed a public and therefore influential and empowering voice. As "a rebellion against death and a rebellion against authority," spiritualism appealed to middle to upper class women and their need to affirm themselves as moral guardians who could influence the fate of their families and society alike. Female mediums, for example, recoded the meaning of purity, passivity, and domesticity—

19. T. J. Ellinwood, "The New York Conference," *The Spiritual Telegraph* 3 (1854): 333.

dominant stereotypes of mid-century womanhood—as markers of religious and political authority.[20]

The case of Eliza Farnham was representative of this nexus between women's rights, the impulse to reform the "standards of the masculine life," and a burgeoning spiritualist subculture. Having become active in spiritualist circles, Farnham argued that the "spirituality of the Feminine" was part and parcel to the "Superiority of Woman." The agency of women was pure precisely because it "belongs to her interior," where man's was more often a product of "position, fortune, connections, or something which attaches more to his outer than to his inner life." According to Farnham, it was women, not men, who were the inheritance of the human. Masculinity was a deviation, at odds with how things were in essence. Men, in fact, were grudgingly aware that women had "more individuality" than they did. Out of resentment and the need to suppress this truth, a man would claim "she had no soul of her own; as if she were designed to be moved by another's will, and had neither the ability nor the right to think and decide for herself." Consequently, "Man must be regenerated by true and deep religious experiences, (Religion is feminine), or by the love and influence of Woman."[21]

In what seems like an irresolvable paradox, Farnham was at the forefront of promoting liberal ideals of subjectivity even as she actively sought the submission of others to these ideals. The "truth" of her phrenology, for example, defined intentionality as the sole ground of moral and legal responsibility. Moreover, this "truth" transcended politics, making the success of phrenological reform a foregone conclusion. Yet agency was explicitly premised on degrees of subjugation. "In our belief of this science [of phrenology] there is nothing *voluntary*; nothing which we could *at option* choose or refuse. It is the result of *all controlling necessity*."[22]

Before her arrival at Sing Sing, Farnham had written of the complexities of agency, an acknowledgement that would become the basis for her reforms at Sing Sing as well as her later turn to spiritualism. "What is freedom?," asked Farnham in 1843. In premising her case for the security of the nation state upon the notion of separate spheres, Farnham argued that women possess an inherent "authority which man can never wholly

20. Ann Braude, *Radical Spirits: Spiritualism and Women's Rights in Nineteenth-Century America* (Boston: Beacon Press, 1989), 6, 56, 2, 39, 82–83.

21. Farnham, *Woman and Her Era*, 1:13, 2:44, 94, 127, 296.

22. Charles Caldwell, *New Views of Penitentiary Discipline and Moral Education and Reform* (Philadelphia: William Brown, 1829), 11.

controvert" nor "wrest from her." In contrast to the performative author-ity of men in public, the rights of women had a "more permanent foun-dation" that was, in fact, superior to those of men. "To be equally free is not to be free to do and enjoy the *same* things, but to be equally free in what the author of our being has appointed us to enjoy or accomplish." True freedom, in Farnham's estimation, was a product of submission to a higher cause—the maintenance of family bonds and the reform of society. "Can a true woman ever be happier," declared Farnham, "than when she is surrounded by those whom her efforts—her sacrifices if you will—have made happy?"[23]

There was an interesting tension at work in Farnham's words and re-form activities. This tension revolved around the freedom to submit. On the one hand, this tension constituted the sense of hauntedness that was the emotional core of spiritualism. This mood in turn precipitated a com-plex process in which the conditions of enchantment morphed, by way of masochistic fantasy, into the sense of triumphal will. On the other hand, it was this tension—and the process of overcoming it—that animated the penitentiary reforms of the eighteenth and nineteenth centuries. Prison-ers, through a rigorous program of self-reflection, were to triumph over their own criminal faculties. In the remainder of this chapter, I dwell upon the resonance between metaphysical strains of Protestant piety and what Foucault identified as the emergence of biopolitics in the art of peniten-tiary governance—the application of force, from a distance, upon the ac-tions of individuals. *Without hardly having to touch the skin.* For in her cultivation of that which was both within *and* beyond the criminal body, Farnham deployed the truth of spirituality in order to catalyze the dor-mant potentiality of American citizenship.

3. The Penitentiary Movement and Republican Machines

The penitentiary movement within the United States began, in earnest, at the end of the eighteenth century.[24] With the construction of numer-ous facilities, the public spectacle of punishment began to move behind

23. Mrs. T. J. Farnham, "Rights of Women: Reply to Mr. Neal's Lecture," *Brother Jonathan* 5, no. 8 (June 24, 1843): 236–37.
24. W. David Lewis, *From Newgate to Dannemora: The Rise of The Penitentiary in New York, 1796–1848* (Ithaca: Cornell University Press, 1965); Thomas L. Dumm, *Democracy and Pun-ishment: Disciplinary Origins of the United States* (Madison: University of Wisconsin Press, 1987).

closed doors. The express goal was not necessarily punishment of the criminal body but rather the reform of the individual soul. Inseparable from Revolutionary politics, penitentiaries were considered localized and experimental theaters of American democracy. The first experiment occurred at the Walnut Street Jail in Philadelphia. The reforms instituted by the Philadelphia Society for Alleviating the Miseries of Public Prisons set precedents and patterns for numerous penitentiaries that were built in the first decades of the nineteenth century. As Benjamin Rush, founding member of the society, announced, the purpose of penitentiary reform was part of a large-scale effort to "convert" Americans "into republican machines. This must be done, if we expect them to perform their parts properly, in the great machine of the government of state." The application of democratic principles upon the bodies of citizens, according to Rush, would, in turn, enable citizens to apply this knowledge "mechanically" (i.e., continuously) to themselves and others.[25]

Rush's heady optimism was the outgrowth of a curious blend of millennialist and Enlightenment impulses. His fierce wishfulness converged around the increasing specification of the individual.[26] As physician, reformer, and signer of the Declaration of Independence, Rush's revolutionary agenda was always tinged with a loose Presbyterian faith. "Republican forms of government are the best repositories of the Gospel," he wrote in 1791. "They are intended as preludes to a glorious manifestation of its power and influence upon the hearts of men."[27] Rush's multivalent

25. Francis C. Gray, *Prison Discipline in America* (London: John Murray, 1848), 26; Benjamin Rush, "Of the Mode of Education Proper in a Republic," in *The Selected Writings of Benjamin Rush*, ed. Dagobert D. Runes (New York: Philosophical Library, 1947), 92.

26. "The American War is over," conceded Rush in 1787, "but this is far from being the case with the American Revolution. On the contrary, nothing but the first act of the great drama is closed. It remains yet to establish and perfect our new forms of government; and to prepare the principles, morals, and manners of our citizens" (Rush, "On the Defects of the Confederation," in *The Selected Writings of Benjamin Rush*, 26).

27. Cited in Mark A. Noll, *America's God: From Jonathan Edwards to Abraham Lincoln* (New York: Oxford University Press. 2002), 51. Motivated in part by theologies of trans-Atlantic revivalism of the eighteenth century, Rush's "republican spirituality" was premised upon the operations of spirit. Rather than mere salvation, Rush made the state of enchantment into an object of inquiry and a viable means to educate the population and manage the State. A sense of being haunted, in other words, made it possible to "order the religious impulse in humanity" by way of what Rush called "religious empiricism." Fond of digestive metaphors, Rush envisioned the turning of men into republican machines as a matter of stimulating political digestion. See, for example, his "The Influence of the Physical Causes Upon the Moral Faculty" (1786) in *Selected Writings*, 181–211. Rush here was taking the Scottish Common Sense perspective upon emotion to its logical conclusion. Not only were the passions the vehicle by which reason partook in religious matters (that which often catalyzed moral action, for ex-

statements were emblematic of how Quakers, northern evangelicals, and village *philosophes* often worked side by side on boards of managers and within the penitentiary itself. The fact that they found common cause in pursuing such a bold strategy of democratic inclusion—the transformation of criminal into citizen—was not surprising. All three communities imagined themselves as fully, freely, and systematically enacting the scripts of Common Sense empiricism and republicanism.

As Mark A. Noll has noted, Rush was the most "eloquent advocate for the Christian republican synthesis," an ideological constellation that paved the way for the triumph of evangelicalism by the eve of the Civil War. As early as the mid-eighteenth century, the currents of Common Sense and republicanism had begun to form what Noll has referred to as "America's God." Although Noll limits his analysis of the synergistic interaction between epistemology and political economy to the activities of evangelicals, his work nonetheless points to the scale and reach of this synthesis into everyday life and across denominational boundaries. In other words, the interplay between religious sentiments and secular vocabularies within the penitentiary movement should not be taken as a litmus test for confirming the extension of Protestant Christianity into the operations of the state. Rather than being seen as a corruption of social motive by the religious or as a misappropriation of Christian eschatology for secular purposes, the penitentiary movement is best understood as an excession of political rationality. It is also an example of how secularism made its way under the skin.[28]

---

ample), emotions themselves became propositions that were utterly reasonable—calculable and subject to mechanization. On the role of emotions within Scottish Common Sense, see John Corrigan, *Business of the Heart: Religion and Emotion in the Nineteenth Century* (Berkeley and Los Angeles: University of California Press, 2002), 295f. On the relationship between religion, politics, and emotion in the life of Rush, see John M. Kloos Jr, *A Sense of Deity: The Republican Spirituality of Dr. Benjamin Rush* (Brooklyn: Carlson Publishing, Inc., 1991), 21ff.

28. Noll, *America's God*, 65. Although Foucault does not broach the topic of secularization or the making of religion under certain regimes of veridiction, he does gesture toward the Christian character of practices of governmentality that emerged in the eighteenth and nineteenth centuries. Such practices as statistics, criminology, and medicine were envisioned as doing *more* that simply improving the subject. They also served to establish "an average considered as optimal on the one hand, and, on the other, a bandwidth of the acceptable that must not be exceeded." Foucault argues that the reorganization of political power is rooted in the conservative tendencies of the Christian pastorate in the late Middle Ages and early modern period. The techniques and procedures of a religious elite within both Catholicism and early Protestantism were transitional in the generation of new forms of power. Individualization was achieved by subjection within an "economy of souls" brought to "bear upon the whole Christian community and on each Christian in particular." Foucault adds that within "this context, the word *salvation* takes on different meanings: health, well-being

There is a performance going on here. A desire to make manifest—spectacular really—the promise of American democracy under the most difficult of circumstances. Penitentiary reformers were, self-consciously, dramatizing their technology as civilizing.[29] And indeed, penitentiaries were an impressive attempt to manage, systematically, bodies and information pathways within their walls as well as across them. For in addition to being a spectacle for the eyes of the citizenry, the penitentiary represented the latest innovations in architecture, financial management, political philosophy, statistics, and the division of labor. This particular extension of the "modern state," as Foucault has shown in his studies of the emergence of governmentality in the European context, was not devoid of theological residue. "This form of power," writes Foucault, "applies itself to immediate everyday life which categorizes the individual, marks him by his own individuality, attaches him to his own identity, imposes a law of truth on him which he must recognize and which makes individuals subjects." The penitentiary movement, for example, was founded on the practice of simultaneously promoting the progressive capacities of the individual and the nation. As with developments in other areas of society, it was a subtle agenda in which individuals were not made to conform but instead invited to partake in the same range of possible selves. Incentives that were ambient.[30]

(that is, sufficient wealth, standard of living), security, protection against accidents. A series of 'worldly' aims took the place of the religious aims of the traditional pastorate, all the more easily because the latter, for various reasons, had followed in an accessory way a certain number of these aims." Foucault here implies a thesis of secularization that revolves not around internal social differentiation but around intensification, that is, the deeply ironic effect of exacerbating precisely those conditions of unknowing that would be overcome by the triumph of reason and communicative transparency. For as I have argued, ghostly possessions continued as this discursive order was taking hold, congealing, becoming a matter of second nature. Michel Foucault, *Security, Territory, Population: Lectures at the Collège de France, 1977Ð1978*, ed. Michel Senellart, trans. Graham Bell (New York: Palgrave, 2007), 6, 184, 192; Michel Foucault, "The Subject and Power," in *Michel Foucault: Beyond Structuralism and Hermeneutics*, 2d ed., ed. Hubert L. Dreyfus and Paul Rabinow (Chicago: University of Chicago Press, 1983), 215.

29. The representative status of this kind of technology, it should be noted, attracted the attention of European observers like Gustave de Beaumont, Alexis de Tocqueville, and Harriet Martineau, who looked to American penitentiaries (and the profits they generated in taxing businesses that employed inmates during the day) for perspective on the meanings and means of democracy. Gustave de Beaumont and Alexis de Tocqueville, *On the Penitentiary System in the United States and its Application in France* (1833; Carbondale: Southern Illinois University Press, 1964); Harriet Martineau, *Retrospect of Western Travel*, vol. I (London: Saunders and Otley, 1838).

30. Foucault, "Subject and Power," 212. When asked what "the secret" was of his disciplinary success at Sing Sing, the warden Elam Lynds replied: "It would be pretty difficult to

On their visit to survey penitentiaries in the United States in 1831, Gustave de Beaumont and Alexis de Tocqueville noted that only one in twelve prisoners was female. But this would soon change. As republican virtue became ever more regulated and with women increasingly marginalized from market activities, women were increasingly convicted of crimes against the public order—drunkeness, vagrancy, petty theft, etc. Having been designed primarily for male convicts, the prisons and penitentiaries of the East were not hospitable places for what many considered to be "fallen women." Following the path forged by English reformer Elizabeth Fry, by the 1840s many American women had become involved in the plight of female convicts—through pan-Protestant aid associations as well as employment at the penitentiaries themselves.[31]

Beaumont and Tocqueville wrote, with a hint of irony, that the powerful cure enacted within penitentiaries had itself become contagious. Many Americans, they believed, had come to "occupy themselves continually with prisons" and had "caught the *monomanie* of the penitentiary system, which to them seems the remedy for all the evils in society." In other words, the increasing valorization of instrumental rationality among reformers did not necessarily result in a more rational political order. As Tocqueville would later note, the authority of public opinion outside the walls of the penitentiary was invisible and often "irresistible," a power that was both physical and moral, acting "as much upon the will as upon behavior."[32] Such power was, for lack of a better term, ghostly. It was both immediate *and* mediating. Within the penitentiary, the explicit management of opinion was a matter of gaining knowledge of the prisoner's conscience in order to direct it (opinion here signifying the vitality of collective rationality within a closed context). Outside the penitentiary, too, the cultivation of the categories through which individuals thought about themselves thinking about the world was a looming process. For in both cases there is a coming together, enacted by no one in particular yet felt at once by everyone.

---

explain it entirely; it is the result of a series of efforts and daily cares, of which it would be necessary to be an eyewitness. General rules cannot be indicated" (cited in Beaumont and Tocqueville, *Penitentiary System*, 162).

31. Estelle B. Freedman, *Their Sisters' Keepers: Women's Prison Reform in America, 1830–1930* (Ann Arbor: University of Michigan Press, 1984), 11, 14, 18, 22.

32. Beaumont and Tocqueville, *Penitentiary System*, 80; Alexis de Tocqueville, *Democracy in America*, trans. George Lawrence, ed. J. P. Mayer (New York: Anchor Books, 1969), 256, 254.

4. The Atmosphere of Secularism

In addition to the writings of John Locke and Jeremy Bentham, the shift in emphasis from punishment to rehabilitation was initiated by those reformers steeped in the practices of Quakerism and Evangelicalism. Eastern State Penitentiary in Philadelphia (est. 1821), for example, translated Quaker beliefs regarding the blessings of the inner light into an elaborate model of solitary confinement and religious instruction. The Auburn State penitentiary (est. 1817) in New York, on the other hand, was managed according to the "silent rule" beginning in 1824. At Auburn and its institutional cousin, Sing Sing State penitentiary (est. 1825), prisoners were kept in isolation only at night. During the day prisoners worked together, side by side, even as they were instructed not to talk or look at their fellow inmates.[33] Within both the Auburn and Pennsylvania systems, individual criminals had become a social experiment, a problem to be solved. In the Auburn system, however, a mix of ardent reformers and aggressive evangelicalism sought to produce the proper psychic and bodily pathways for criminals to feel their feelings and think about thinking.

Within the Auburn system the private was aggressively delimited in the best interest of both the individual convict and the general populace. It was a peculiar kind of atmosphere, a representation of the public sphere that was, in essence, absolutely private. It was a seemingly passive environment in which each convict was called upon to actively participate and "preserve an unbroken silence." As the rules at Auburn (and later Sing Sing) stated, convicts "are not to exchange a word with each other . . . they are not to exchange looks, wink, laugh, or motion to each other." Communication between inmates only stoked the fires of their sinful hearts and was thought to be a form of "contamination" and "contagion." "Their whole demeanor," therefore, "must be in accordance with the most perfect order, and in strict compliance with the discipline of the prison." Each prisoner, then, as he moved silently through the workday, was connected not so much to the other prisoners but, on the contrary, through the same haze of disciplinary assumptions about their sinful natures. Or as Beaumont and Tocqueville suggestively noted, "The prisoner in the United States breathes in the penitentiary a religious atmosphere that surrounds him on all sides." It is a dense but familiar air. The prisoner is "more

---

33. Prison Association of New York, *First Report of the Prison Association of New York* (New York: Jared W. Bell, 1844), 42.

amenable to its influence because his own early education *predisposes* him toward it" (my emphasis).[34]

To dwell upon the question of *predisposition* as it was broached by reformers is to encounter again the systematicity of evangelical secularism. In 1825, for example, the Rev. Louis Dwight, who had resigned as the treasurer of the American Bible Society, formed the Boston Prison Discipline Society and tirelessly promoted the Auburn system across the country. The Auburn system represented the harnessing of pure potential, "like the application of the steam engine in navigation." It marked a moment when the productions of second nature (citizens and, by extension, steam) overcame the limitations of nature (criminals and, by extension, wind). In the process of overcoming the merely juridical application of law, the Auburn system would become "an incalculable good to the world," wrote Dwight, applicable not only to prisons but colleges and private homes as well.[35]

In 1825 the Auburn system was literally transported to Sing Sing, New York, when Captain Elam Lynds, the warden at Auburn, marched a hundred convicts to a marble quarry on the Hudson River and constructed a penitentiary in four years time.[36] Sing Sing State Penitentiary opened in 1829 and was but one node within an increasing network of penitentiaries that operated according to the theo-politics of evangelical conversion. By the mid-1820s the Auburn system had become the preferred model among reformers who noted its capacities to capitalize on the "power of association," to establish "the spirit of submission," and to conform to "the habits of society"[37] As at Auburn, Sing Sing reformers were "actuated by motives of public policy and Christian benevolence." Consequently, they sought to chart and manage the ways, means, and expression of sin within a public setting. The motivation to contain "contaminating influences" within the penitentiary reflected a particular orientation toward sin that drew from the epistemological and political fundaments of evangelical secularism—

34. Beaumont and Tocqueville, *Penitentiary System*, 81, 38, 84, 122; John Luckey, *Life in Sing Sing State Prison as Seen in Twelve Years' Chaplaincy* (New York: N. Tribbals, 1866), 16.
35. Dwight cited in Andrew Skotnicki, *Religion and the Development of the American Penal System* (Lanham, Md.: University Press of America, 2000), 44; William Jenks, *A Memoir of the Reverend Louis Dwight* (Boston: T. R. Marvin, 1856), 6.
36. Luckey, *Life in Sing Sing State Prison*, 12. Lynds, known for his cruelty and his disdain for soft-minded religionists, was relieved of his wardenship within the first two years of Sing Sing's operation.
37. Beaumont and Tocqueville, *Penitentiary System*, 121, 59; Gray, *Prison Discipline*, 26.

theistic Common Sense and republicanism.[38] Sin was identifiable. It was containable. It was an opportunity for the individual criminal to convert him- or herself into a "republican machine." Sin, in other words, was always already a matter of public import, so much so that the demarcations of private and public fail to do justice to the complexity of the penitentiary situation.

Rather than leave the criminal in total physical isolation, reformers attempted to create the conditions in which the criminal felt himself to be alone with his God within a group setting. During the day each workshop was surrounded by a hidden gallery from which guards closely monitored the actions of each prisoner.[39] The goal was to maintain constant and anonymous surveillance of the criminal in order to allow him to become more aware of what exactly was being surveyed, that is, his sinful body. The criminal, it was theorized, could not then help but recognize his unique but common degeneracy. Upon recognizing the layers of anonymous surveillance—for even the keepers in immediate contact with the prisoners were under surveillance—the criminal would then seek to identify with, submit to, and find comfort in a form of power that was felt incessantly but ever incomprehensible.

With eyes wide open, submission to God's will was also an act of incorporation into the machinery of republican virtue. Chaplains, for example, given their access to the daily confessions, health, and desires of individual prisoners, were able to gather and organize information that tracked the relationships between a prisoner's crime and his or her age, residence, race, education, marital status, and personal habits. Even as chaplains provided prisoners with "private admonition, counsel, and instruction," they were providing regulatory agencies with statistical data that these agencies could then redeploy and use to revise methods of admonition, counsel, and instruction. In other words, the most personal traits of each prisoner were used in such a way as to create a totalizing picture of the prison population that would in turn become the leverage upon these personal traits.[40]

---

38. Gershom Powers, *A Brief Account of the Construction, Management, & Discipline &c. &c of the New York State Prison at Auburn* (Auburn: U. F. Doubleday, 1826), 18; PANY, *First Report*, 42.
39. Beaumont and Tocqueville, *Penitentiary System*, 60.
40. Prison Discipline Society, *Second Annual Report of the Board of Managers, Boston, June 1, 1827* (Boston: Perkins and Marvin, 1829), 61–71; Prison Discipline Society, *Third Annual Report of the Board of Managers, Boston, 1828* (Boston: Perkins and Marvin, 1830), 64–5; Prison Discipline Society, *Eighth Annual Report of the Board of Managers, Boston, May 28, 1833* (Boston: Perkins and Marvin, 1833), 160–63.

5. Democracy is Coming to the U.S.A.

Even as the Auburn system rose to ascendancy, its disciplinary ideals often fell short of the mark. Throughout the 1830s major problems were detected in this corner of the evangelical public sphere.[41] In 1842, confronting a dire financial crisis, Governor William H. Seward and the Board of Inspectors reappointed Elam Lynds as the principal keeper at Sing Sing, overlooking his reputation for violence in hopes of achieving financial solvency. Under Lynds's leadership both staff and salaries were cut. So, too, were monies allotted to the provision of food, clothing, and medicine. Instances of flogging increased dramatically. In 1843 Seward called upon the Rev. John Luckey, a Methodist minister, to once again make Sing Sing "consistent with the principles of Christianity." Luckey was quick to act. Stressing the importance of religious instruction and the Sabbath school, Luckey created a prison library in order to provide religious books "designed to inculcate correct moral principles."[42]

Most significantly, Luckey organized prison officials against Lynds's "reign of terror" and appealed to the president of the Board of Inspectors, John Edmonds, to redress the situation. Luckey was successful in convincing Edmonds to reconsider the board's original decision, and in January 1844 Lynds "was informed that his services would be dispensed with." With the help of Edmonds, Luckey had gotten exactly what he wished for—the resignation of Lynds and a renewed emphasis on the evangelical strategy of locating and leveraging the specter of criminality. From Luckey's perspective, the reinstatement of the "mild system" at Sing Sing was the consummation of the original impetus behind the Auburn system as articulated by Dwight and others.

Luckey's evangelical triumph, however, paved the way for his eventual marginalization.[43] Edmonds, having been invited to tour Sing Sing

41. Reports of beatings, torture, suicides, shortages of food, heat, and clothing, as well as internal strife among officials began to tarnish the reputation of Sing Sing almost immediately. By the end of the decade both Auburn and Sing Sing were under investigation by the state of New York for both physical and financial improprieties. In 1839, even Louis Dwight had questioned the viability of Sing Sing as an institute of reform. Prison Discipline Society, *Fourteenth Annual Report, Boston, May 1839* (Boston: Prison Discipline Society, 1839), 42–43.

42. Lewis, *From Newgate*, 215. Against the wishes of Lynds, Luckey was also instrumental in loosening the strictures of solitary confinement at Sing Sing. In addition to allowing for letter writing and outside visitors, prisoners were granted access to spelling books during the week in order to furnish "them with opportunities for intellectual and moral improvement" (Luckey, *Life in Sing Sing State Prison*, 28).

43. Luckey, *Life in Sing Sing State Prison*, 22–24, 158, 33–34, 31.

with Luckey on numerous occasions during the Lynds debacle, became increasingly involved with the everyday operations of both the men's and women's wings of the penitentiary.[44] By the end of 1844 Edmonds had successfully called for the establishment of the Prison Association of New York (PANY), an organization whose charge was "the supervision of the internal organization and management of prisons in which convicts are confined, embracing the moral and physical influences to be exerted on the prisoners during their confinement." Even as it paid homage to the past successes of the Auburn system, PANY challenged some of its most cherished ideals, including the assumption that penitentiaries should be financially self-sufficient and, most significantly, that inmates should not be allowed to communicate with one another. The "silent rule" of the Auburn system, argued representatives of PANY, was "impracticable" and "not at all in unison with the benevolent breathings of the age."[45]

On the one hand, PANY seemed to represent a more intense effort to realize the Auburn system's goal of identifying the specter of criminality within each convict. On the other hand, the "new style of discipline" recommended and sanctioned by PANY was "emphatically national in its character" and represented a subtle but profound shift in its point of application. Whereas the initial impetus of penitentiary reform had revolved around the notion of crime being a matter of socialization, PANY emphasized the criminal's recognition of him- or herself as socializable. Only through such self-consciousness could the criminal be converted into a "useful citizen":

> The most powerful influence to awaken in the abandoned self-control and self-respect, is an expression of confidence in [the criminal's] capacity to regain character and an honorable social position. . . . The wrong-doer must be treated, *and must see that he is treated*, from the moment of his arrest till his release, with humanity; *he must be convinced* that the interests of his fellow-men demand his exclusion from society *until* his character is amended. (my emphasis)[46]

44. John W. Edmonds, *A Letter from John W. Edmonds, One of the Inspectors of the State Prison at Sing Sing, to General Aaron Ward, in Regards to the Removal of Capt. Lynds, as Principal Keeper of that Prison* (New York: Wm. G. Boggs, 1844), 10, 25. Edmonds also became increasingly skeptical of the use of physical violence even in the most desperate cases. As *The Prisoners' Friend*, a journal co-edited by soon-to-be spiritualist John Murray Spear, recalled in 1847, Edmonds "began with the keepers, by instilling into their minds the principles of the great 'Law of Kindness'" ("Biographical Sketch," *The Prisoners' Friend* [June 9, 1847], 89).

45. PANY, *First Report*, 7; Lewis, *From Newgate*, 226.

46. PANY, *Second Report*, 32; PANY, *First Report*, 30-31.

This process of recognizing, for oneself, the potential within was dependent upon a willing submission to the social, ideally construed and represented. Rather than localizing individual sin as the hinge of conversion, new methods began to focus increasingly on the cultivation of a different specter that was both within *and* external to the criminal body—that of the dormant potentiality of citizenship.

At the first meeting of PANY, the ends of penitentiary discipline remained the same. The site of its application, however, shifted from the emphasis on sin to its overcoming in a public arena, from producing conversion to the production of a liberal democratic subject. "This system of instruction is the most powerful instrument of discipline within our reach," read the inaugural report of PANY. "And why should it not be so? There is nothing new in this. It is but applying to the prison the principles upon which our families and our country are governed." Such principles, according to Edmonds, were "old in Scripture but new in human practice." They constituted "the great truth . . . all-pervading in its application to human concerns." Anticipating his invocation of the "great truth" of spiritualism, Edmonds's Emersonian pronouncement shifted responsibility for conversion, at least implicitly, from God's grace to the capacities of the individual to become an "Author of Nature." This was the metaphysical difference, an eroticization of evangelical reform strategies that prompted the "Kingdom of Heaven" to become the "blood with which the heart swells and the extremest capillary beats."[47]

6. Eliza Farnham's Government of Souls

The reorganization at Sing Sing did not occur without resistance. John Luckey, having successfully rallied PANY to oust Elam Lynds, was about to meet his match in the figure of Eliza Farnham. Amidst the Lynds controversy, Edmonds had attended a lecture by Farnham in New York City

---

47. PANY, *First Report*, 29-30; "Reform in Public Schools," *The Phrenological Journal* 30 (1832): 351. Political rationality, then, was not only still operative but at times could seem much more excessive than what had come before. PANY, for example, suggested that "factories be erected" in the vicinity of the prison so as to employ recently discharged convicts. PANY also promoted the use of "Auxiliary Societies" to "regulate" the public "breathings," themselves, "controlling . . . public opinion in the immediate vicinity of the prison" in order to make a community more sympathetic to newly released convicts as well as to the penitentiary workers among them. PANY, *First Report*, 51; Prison Association of New York, *Third Report of the Prison Association of New York*, part I (New York: Prison Association of New York, 1847), 32-33.

where she spoke on the importance of women in social reform activities. Shortly thereafter, Edmonds interviewed Farnham and appointed her matron of the Female Department of the State Prison at Sing Sing. Farnham, who had just returned from an extensive stay on the Illinois frontier, was, as noted above, a self-styled "free-thinker." She claimed that by the age of sixteen she had already familiarized herself with "the works of Paine, Volney, Voltaire, and nearly the whole school of infidel writers." Such "infidelity" was also comprised of a deep interest in the science of phrenology. Although Farnham was skeptical of the "orthodox" and enthusiastic piety of evangelicals, she considered phrenology to be a necessary revision of evangelical approaches to criminal reform and the cultivation of character.[48]

During her first year and a half at Sing Sing, Farnham completed editorial commentary for the republication of *Rationale of Crime, and its Appropriate Treatment* by the English phrenologist M. B. Sampson. Justifying her own notes and additions, Farnham wrote that it was "emphatically on the popular mind in republican America that such a work must exert its chief influence." Sampson's book insisted that environmental conditions and physical make-up were the best means of redressing insanity and criminal behavior. Because the human mind was divided up into various faculties controlled by specific areas of the brain, if any of these faculties was over or underdeveloped or if the balance between them was somehow skewed, criminal behavior could result. Too much or too little development of any faculty—whether it was a tendency toward benevolence, determination, combativeness, or veneration—was the result of a weak constitution and/ or deplorable social conditions. Crime, then, may have been that which transgressed God's wishes, but more importantly it violated the potential harmony between mind, body, and the human community. Proper balance and relationality—between the component parts in the head as well as between the mind and the social environment—were to be rigorously pursued.[49]

When Farnham arrived, the library collection consisted of Bibles and

---

48. Eliza W. Farnham, *Life in Prairie Land* (New York: Harper & Brothers, 1847), 234; Eliza W. Farnham, *The Ideal Attained* (New York: C. M. Plumbe & Co., 1865), 390–91.

49. Sampson, *Rationale of Crime*, xiii, 11; George Combe, *The Constitution of Man Considered in Relation to External Objects* (Boston: Marsh, Capen, & Lyon, 1837), 291, 301; George Combe and C.J.A. Mittermaier, "Miscellaneous papers regarding Mittermaier's *On the Application of Phrenology to Criminal Legislation and Prison Discipline*," *The Phrenological Journal and Magazine for Moral Science* 16 (1843): 15; reprinted in *The American Phrenological Journal* 5 (July 1843): 305–27.

seventy-five copies of Richard Baxter's *A Call to the Unconverted*. At the time, Baxter's *Call* was one of the most popular books published by the American Tract Society (and a staple of evangelical literacy programs since John Eliot had deployed an Algonkian translation for use in his "praying towns"). Farnham restocked Sing Sing's shelves with an eclectic array of titles "of a moral tendency": George Combe's *Constitution of Man*, Hannah More's *Domestic Tales*, Charles Dickens' *Oliver Twist* and *Nicholas Nickleby*, as well as *Life in Prairie Land*, Farnham's recently published account of her travels on the Illinois frontier. Farnham encouraged literate prisoners to study maps and travel literature in addition to their spelling books. She installed "large lamps" in the hallways and allowed convicts to take books back to their cells in the evening. She read aloud excerpts from evangelical tracts, poetry, *Littell's Living Age*, and Combe's *Constitution*, informing prisoners that their own bodies, and specifically their heads, played a major role in their "secular and religious instruction." In the setting of the chapel, Farnham read aloud from these texts, "hoping to lead the women's thoughts into healthier channels, and to awaken good resolutions." Many prisoners were "moved to tears over some scenes, and would take occasion to tell one or another of us how determined they were to lead different lives when they left the prison." Farnham also lectured on the "Discovery of Columbus" and the "Conquest of Mexico," encouraging prisoners to align their own moral progress with the evolution of the American nation-state.[50]

Despite the fact that Farnham jettisoned "dry evangelical book[s] . . . bent on converting [prisoners], and saving their souls from hell," she believed phrenology to be a practical supplement to Luckey's theological agenda. Urging prisoners to lead "better lives in this" world, Farnham maintained at least two of the central doctrines of evangelical reform: (1) that criminality was both "an act of insanity as well as a sin," and (2) that the penitentiary would reflect and promote the ideal atmosphere of civil society.[51]

Both Farnham and Luckey concentrated their efforts on something that was not strictly empirical—for Luckey the spectral entity of sin within the body, and for Farnham a dormant materiality that existed in its potenti-

50. Kirby, *Years of Experience*, 192f.; Combe and Mittermaier, "Miscellaneous Papers," 13; Prison Association of New York, *Third Report of the Prison Association of New York*, part 2 (New York: Prison Association of New York, 1847), 56.

51. Kirby, *Years of Experience*, 199–200; Sampson, *Rationale of Crime*, 58; "Review of Dr. Attomyr's Theory of Crimes, based on the Principles of Phrenology," *The Phrenological Journal and Magazine of Moral Science* 16 (1843): 259.

ality at the nexus between body and environment. For Luckey, silence, modified solitary confinement, and sudden conversion had served to secure knowledge of sin on the part of the individual criminal. Farnham, however, proposed "years of well-directed treatment" to "appeal to, and stimulate" higher sentiments such as justice with the objective of calling them "into abiding activity." "If the criminal is to be reformed at all," she wrote, "he is to be reformed for society, not solitude." Rather than rely upon God's all-seeing eye or even the creation of divine artifice by way of isolation and surveillance, Farnham relied on her ability to convey to criminals "that the strength of [their evil] desires [was] governed by physical laws, in the same manner as the strength of . . . other organs of the body." Rather than jettison the promise of eternal life, Farnham's innovations served to aestheticize salvation. Heaven became a place not only on earth but a space physically located behind the eyes and bound up in the sensory surfaces of the body.[52]

Although Luckey may have sympathized with the decreasing number of violent incidents and lashings under Farnham's watch, he remained suspicious of her phrenological prescriptions.[53] First and foremost, Luckey objected to what he viewed as a replacement of lessons about sin and salvation with lessons about the imperfections of human physiognomy and the capacity to overcome them. In addition to its displacement of providence and original sin, Luckey also thought phrenology to be misguided in its extreme emphasis on environmental influence. Farnham, by contrast, insisted on the need to make inmates aware not simply of their criminal habits but, more importantly, of their higher moral faculties in order that they could then take possession and control of them. As Farnham admitted, she sought to impart to criminals "a knowledge of the peculiar constitution of their own minds" in relation to others and to turn sin into something that was readily understood. For "as soon as the source of their evil desires is brought clearly within their comprehension," wrote Farnham, those desires could be overcome. Through individual effort one could clear away all "mystery, doubt, and uncertainty."[54]

Farnham's program of benevolence was marked by the racial hierarchies indigenous to the evolutionary schemes of phrenology. So even

52. Sampson, *Rationale of Crime*, 16–17, 135, 66; "'Phrenology' Its Scientific Claims; Its Investigation," *American Phrenological Journal* 8 (January 1846): 7–8.
53. The simmering tension between Farnham and Luckey came to a head, as it were, when Luckey discovered that Farnham had used his office for a sitting studio for the phrenological sketches that were to be included in *Rationale of Crime*. Lewis, *From Newgate*, 243–44.
54. Sampson, *Rationale of Crime*, 13, 66.

C. P.

C. P., a half-breed Indian and negro woman, under confinement for the fourth time. She has been twice imprisoned
for petit, and once for grand larceny, and once for assault and
battery with a knife. During one of her terms of confinement
she attacked her keeper with a carving-knife, and he was compelled to fell her with a loaded cane. When excited she exhibits the most uncontrollable fury, and is always disposed to
be offensive, aggressive, and more or less violent.

In her head destructiveness is enormously developed, with
large secretiveness and caution, and very defective benevolence
and moral organs generally.

FIGURE 17 · The Defective Moral Organs of C. P. from M. B. Sampson's *Rationale of Crime,
and its Appropriate Treatment; being a Treatise on Criminal Jurisprudence Considered in Relation
to Cerebral Organization with Notes and Illustrations by E. W. Farnham* (New York: D. Appleton
& Co., 1846), 158.

though the women under Farnahm's charge—by and large African Americans and first-generation immigrants—were deemed capable of achieving their humanity, their potentialities were not necessarily equivalent. For an inmate like "C.P., a half-breed Indian and negro woman," the obstacles to epistemic independence and republic virtue were all but insurmountable. "In her head," wrote Farnham, "destructiveness is enormously developed, with large secretiveness and caution, and very defective benevolence and moral organs generally."[55]

Despite such tragic acknowledgements, in Farnham's emphasis on communal activities and common spaces, she continued to rehearse a vision of white middle-class sociality for the women under her charge to emulate and internalize. Within these spaces, the interiority of each woman was both inviolable *and* porous. For according to the "studied design" of Farnham, conditions were such that the "spiritual life" of each prisoner was consummated in her ability to be influenced. To be subject to such influence did not compromise one's interiority. On the contrary, to be subject served to promote the further cultivation of the inner life.[56] Here again was the liberal concept of spirituality, with all of its sociological directives and racial codings, being systematically applied to a space of confinement that otherwise was a stand-in for the closed space of the public sphere.[57]

7. Born on the Fourth of July

Farnham's interest in phrenology had sparked, in her words, "an intense curiosity to penetrate the innermost centre of the stained soul, and observe the mysterious working of that machinery by which so fatal a result was produced." Such curiosity was occult, peering beneath the corrupt surface of the soul in order to isolate its essential "machinery." "I earnestly wished to penetrate," wrote Farnham, "to where the awful secret could be disclosed to me." Contrary to Luckey and his evangelical colleagues, Farnham sought knowledge, first and foremost, of the "machinery" that

55. Ibid., 158.
56. On the relationship between space and subjectivity under Farnham's leadership, see Janet Floyd, "Dislocations of the Self: Eliza Farnham at Sing Sing Prison," *Journal of American Studies* 40 (2006): 311–25.
57. As historian Bret E. Carroll has noted, the spiritualist cosmology, in its layers of increasing authority, resembled "the rigidly structured and tightly controlled prisons and asylums that had begun to dot the American landscape in during the 1830s and 1840s. . . . All spirits," as well as living persons "were essentially inmates in a cosmic asylum" (Carroll, *Spiritualism in Antebellum America*, 82).

produced the sin—an imbalance between the "higher sentiments" and the "tendencies to crime" that had not been recognized by "society and legisla-tors." Rather than pursue the strict individuation of sin, Farnham insisted that the "secret" rhythms (both good and bad) between soul, body, and social environment must be acknowledged publicly. Sin, in other words, became a matter of political concern, political responsibility, and politi-cal application. For the soul to "work" successfully meant for the soul to "work" socially. Given Farnham's admission that "humanity appeal[s] to me in masses more than by individuals," the alignment of individual sin and God's grace held less appeal for her than did the alignment of the masses to itself.[58]

Farnham's approach did, for all intents and purposes, displace God's sovereignty as final arbiter of sin and salvation. But rather than simply exchange theology for anthropology, God's law for natural law, Farnham sought to initiate a reciprocal loop between them, drawing upon the blue-prints of mesmerism in order to encourage prisoners to undertake inves-tigations of themselves as social creatures.[59] According to Farnham, the republican desire to forge reciprocal links between personal morality and social well-being could be consummated by managing the transmission of energy between criminal bodies. Through the principles of phreno-magnetism, Farnham had already arrived at what spiritualists would soon identify as the "vast nervous network of communication." Like the incho-ate concept of culture being developed by Lewis Henry Morgan less than three hundred miles away, Farnham's object of attention was a sympa-thetic medium, an economy of emotional forces that when managed cor-rectly could "excite" the virtues proper to republican governance.[60]

On the one hand, Farnham's was a therapeutic ethos that aggressively acted upon the environment within the penitentiary. Rather than coerce

58. Farnham, *My Early Days*, 350–51; Sampson, *Rationale of Crime*, xvi, xx.

59. Farnham's drift into the rhetorical terrain of mesmerism was not unique among peni-tentiary reformers with a vested interest in phrenology. See, for example, Charles Caldwell, *Facts in Mesmerism and Thoughts on its Causes and Uses* (Louisville: Prentice and Weissinger, 1842).

60. William Henry Channing, "The Judgment of Christendom," *The Spirit of the Age* 1 (Oc-tober 27, 1849): 264. "Many have been led astray by their anxiety to find a *medium* through which . . . influence is communicated," wrote the magnetist La Roy Sunderland. "What is the medium of *Cohesion?*," he asked. "What is the medium of any feeling which is excited in one mind by what is seen or heard, or merely *thought* of, by the person feeling it? You receive a letter from a distant friend, giving you joyful intelligence. Your joy is excited instantly. Where does *the fluid* come from that excites you in this case?" (La Roy Sunderland, "The Agent in Animal Magnetism," *The Phreno-Magnet and Mirror of Nature* 1, no. 10 [November 1843]: 296).

criminals into reforming themselves, Farnham sought to recreate a "natural" climate in which "continual influences" would "fall pleasantly upon and around them like dew upon the sickly seedling." Rather than force "theology on the prisoners," Farnham sought, somewhat paradoxically, to stimulate "improved conduct" that would be "the offspring of genuine and sound internal motives." It was a decidedly forward-looking strategy that would "keep the minds of the prisoners from dwelling on the evil past." On the other hand, Farnham's was a political ethos in accord with the directives of PANY. It assumed that the principles deployed within Sing Sing were "the same principles of government which we apply to the management of our families and the state."[61] Either way, Farnham understood sympathy not merely as a theory of moral sentiments but as a means to gain leverage upon the emotional economy of those under her watch.

In 1844, Farnham planned the first Fourth of July celebration at Sing Sing. Over the next few years these celebrations were emblematic of Farnham's strategy of aesthetic and political cultivation, or, more precisely, her phrenological plan for politicizing the skin. The fact that the inaugural celebration occurred on the "anniversary of our nation's independence" spoke to its inner logic. And although Farnham curiously did not attend the inaugural celebration, it set the tone for subsequent festivities.[62]

Such celebrations were, first and foremost, a ritual identification of hidden qualities of aesthetic appreciation and reason among the inmates. Through the "charming" activation of sight, smell, taste, sound, and the "sense" of democracy, wrote Farnham, "the lash may be removed as gently and effectually as the icy drapery of winter is melted away in the genial atmosphere of Spring." In addition to being identified as natural *and* national, such qualities of American citizenship were also defined by what they did not entail, that is, violence and coercion. Edmonds took the 1844 holiday as an opportunity to promote the ideal of democracy as "the power of knowing and choosing between good and evil." On the morning of the Fourth, Edmonds "sent the required number of bouquets, among which were two, much larger than the others, which were to be given to the

---

61. Sampson, *Rationale of Crime*, 78, 19; Kirby, *Years of Experience*, 199, 194; PANY, *Second Report*, 43.

62. PANY, *Second Report*, 59. At mid-century, various reform groups marked the Fourth of July as a special "occasion of friendly assemblage of those devoted to some movement for the improvement of the human condition." The significance of such "occasions," as was noted at the time, was enhanced by the technology of transportation networks—"The railways, which extend their iron arms in every direction, afford opportunities of multiplying and varying these charming occasions" ("The Fourth of July," *The Prisoners' Friend* [July 14, 1847]: 110).

most amiable among the prisoners." "I should like to have the selection made by the females themselves," wrote Edmonds, "thus I shall be able to discern, how well they understand what it is that forms the character which we most love and regard." As the prisoners learned to appreciate the capacity of their tastebuds, their ears and sense of rhythm, their noses as well as their eyes, they were also enjoined to cast votes and to cultivate a taste for democratic participation despite the fact that the final vote tally was "subject to the approval of the matrons."[63]

According to Farnham, for the criminal to acknowledge herself as a sensual creature was not enough. She also had to be encouraged to apply that knowledge to the self and her social conditions. "The ways of virtue," wrote Farnham, "must be made pleasant if we would have the wanderer accept our invitation to walk therein." Inmates, in other words, could learn to exact a nurturing force upon themselves. Consequently, the reorientation of the senses toward their natural capacity for empirical investigation was something that *both* "flow[ed] from the natural choice of a better constitution" *and* was pursued vigorously by the reformers. "Those sentiments which have lain dormant or been crushed by outrage and defiance," wrote Farnham, "must be gently summoned into being, and tenderly and patiently nursed by continual influences."[64]

The comportment of the keepers as well as the sensual stimuli imported into the prison were the levers of Farnham's version of reform—"a studied design . . . calculated in many ways to exert an important and salutary influence on the prison." Rather than rely upon a relentless focus on sin and an overwhelming incursion of God's grace, Farnham employed the law of similars and the law of infinitesimals. "The universal and invariable law," Farnham declared, is "that propensity continually appeals to propensity, sentiment to sentiment, and intellect to intellect." "It is the language of the moral sentiments alone," insisted Farnham, "in the officer or superior, that can call the same faculties into action in the dependent or inferior." Additionally, flowers, song, music, wall hangings, food, as well as the virtual casting of votes were not regular occurrences but served as incentives to reform, momentary "potentizations" that corrected existing imbalances between the propensities and the sentiments. In hopes of cultivating the specter of citizenship within each convict, Farnham organized a "natural"

63. "Influence of Flowers," *The Prisoners' Friend* (July 7, 1847): 105; "Visit of the Hutchinson Family to Sing Sing Prison," *The Prisoners' Friend* (April 29, 1846): 66; PANY, *Second Report*, 60; Kirby, *Years of Experience*, 208.
64. "Report on the Mount Pleasant State Prison," *The Prisoners' Friend* (April 21, 1847): 66; Sampson, *Rationale of Crime*, 78.

sensory environment in which each object and each individual was connected to every other within a closed semiotic circuit. It was a specific strategy for defining and "channeling" the power of "good resolutions" within a public setting. Ideally, this power would make its way into the body through the sensory organs. It arrived with no verbal epithet and it left no bodily mark. And it would act "by such slow degrees that [persons] would scarcely realize the change."[65]

When Farnham finally succeeded in rescinding the "silent rule" in January 1846, Luckey and his allies within Sing Sing took their complaints to the state legislature. Luckey's wife, Dinah, for example, leveled a four-point charge against Farnham. Having worked under Farnham in the women's wing, Dinah reported:

1st. The use of improper books

2nd. Mal-adjustment of discipline

3rd. Unlawful use of convict's time and labor

4th. An indifference to the interest of the State

It was, perhaps, this latter charge that female inmates had become self-serving, inclined to "work for any one rather than the State," that carried the most weight. Invested in a rather narrow definition of the state, the politicians sided with the Luckeys and their supporters within the evangelical reform community. Disturbed by the "general feeling [that] seemed to prevail" in which "convicts would work for any one rather than the State," Farnham's critics viewed the new arrangements at Sing Sing as "immoral and irreligious."[66]

PANY and its president, John Edmonds, however, supported Farnham. In July 1846, Edmonds and PANY gathered testimony to strengthen Farnham's case against the interests of his former ally. They understood quite well, instinctively even, that Farnham's methods were in tune with the most refined strategies of state centralization occurring outside penitentiary walls. As Farnham wrote in her defense, "My system of government may be designated as one of moral influences, adapted, as far as practicable, to the character and condition of each individual under it. . . . If he be surrounded with the right influence to produce and sustain this state

65. PANY, *Third Report*, part 2, 49; Catherine L. Albanese, *Nature Religion in America: From the Algonkian Indians to the New Age* (Chicago: University of Chicago Press, 1990), 133–34; Sampson, *Rationale of Crime*, 78–79; Kirby, *Years of Experience*, 193, 209.

66. Kirby, *Years of Experience*, 199; Gray, *Prison Discipline*, 67; PANY, *Third Report*, part 2, 49–52; Lewis, *From Newgate*, 245.

of things, the greater his liberty [and] the more rapid will be his moral growth." Inmates, too, attested to Farnham's personal touch in carrying out her agenda of totalizing reform. The fact that such testimony eventually led to Luckey's dismissal is wholly ironic, given how he and his allies had framed their charges against Farnham as a kind of anarchic negligence. They had utterly failed to appreciate that Farnham's goal of "secur[ing] more perfect submission" within the penitentiary was guided by "the maxim that 'that is the best government which governs least,'" a maxim she insisted was "equally applicable to such institutions as to States."[67]

8. Some Kind of Agency

Farnham resigned from Sing Sing in 1848. Despite the fact that many of her reform programs were rescinded, the disciplinary model that she put into practice would continue to resonate, both politically and personally. The reforms instituted by Farnham at Sing Sing anticipated emerging versions of civil society that hinged upon the logic of environmental determinism rather than the linear logic of cause and effect.[68] Such reforms operated according to principles of mediation and were based on detailed understandings of the pervasive power of the social and how that power affected the individual. Farnham did not impose strict models for action and belief upon the prisoners at Sing Sing. Instead, she attempted to domesticate human potential. Farnham created *specific* conditions in which proper action and belief would inevitably spring and *specific* channels through which they could inevitably be expressed. As Luckey was the first to note, her reforms were the expression of a particularly modern cosmological orientation—a way of conceiving the relationship between self, society, and invisible universe that was decidedly more fluid, more dense, and more active than the one vocalized from the Methodist pulpit. "From what we have seen of the greater spirituality of Woman," Farnham later wrote, "we are prepared to see her exhibit not only a greater feeling for, and trust in God and His goodness, than man exhibits, but also in the

---

67. PANY, *Third Report*, part 2, 60–63.
68. See, for example, Horace Bushnell, *Views of Christian Nurture* (Hartford: Edwin Hunt, 1847); Lewis Henry Morgan, *League of the Ho-dé-no-sau-nee, or Iroquois* (Rochester: Sage & Brother, 1851; rpt., Secaucus: The Citadel Press, 1975); E. Pershine Smith, *A Manual of Political Economy* (New York: Putnam, 1853); Henry Hughes, *Treatise on Sociology, Theoretical and Practical* (New York: Lippincott, Grambo, and Co. 1854).

more occult forces and laws upon which visible phenomena rest—the unseen part of the Supreme Will."[69]

At Sing Sing, Farnham had put a mesmeric spin on the phrenological dictum that "virtuous conduct" could be achieved through "beneficial" action upon "the activity of . . . mental faculties and organs."[70] Farnham had convinced Edmonds and PANY that the individual was always already subject to a network of forces that was external to that individual's "moral sentiments." Consequently, Farnham operated on the assumption that reform could best be realized through the strategic organization of that network. By intervening in the relationality between objects in the physical environment, she sought to energize liberty in the present, whereas Luckey had sought to exorcise the sins of the past. And whereas Luckey sought to create the proper conditions for a convict to be alone with his or her God, Farnham's plan was to organize a "natural" sensory environment in which each object and each individual was connected to every other through circuits of sympathy.

As Farnham noted in her memoir, *Life in Prairie Land*, within her Illinois community she had discovered an enlightened form of piety in the "religious feelings" of evangelicalism. "The pure and exquisitely beautiful sermons of our pastor, to which I had before listened with an intellectual pleasure merely, had now a higher import, a loftier mission to my mind. The sublime truths were interesting on other accounts than the chasteness and simplicity of the language in which they were presented. In truth I believed I had attained what I had always heard talked of as a great mystery, an incomprehensible blessing, viz., a religious state of mind." Farnham carried this religious state of mind with her to the Perkins Asylum for the Blind, where she continued to advocate the centrality of "influence" in the practice of reform. Her reform activities were later celebrated by the *American Phrenological Journal*, which included an analysis and picture of Farnham's head. Farnham's "efficient" character was noted, as was her "breadth of affection." Her head indicated her "ability to grasp and conquer subjects requiring steady logical power."[71]

Farnham's translation of evangelical political economy into a mesmerically inflected phrenological idiom set the stage for her eventual interest in spiritualist cosmologies of benevolent agents, her participation in

69. Farnham, *Woman and Her Era*, 2:110.

70. Combe and Mittermaier, "Miscellaneous Papers," 5.

71. Eliza W. Farnham, *Life in Prairie Land*, 209, 261; Lewis, *From Newgate*, 250; "'Heads Differ in Shape' Or, Phrenology by the Portrait," *American Phrenological Journal* 25 (June 1857): 133.

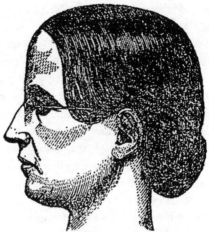

Fig. 8.—Mrs. E. W. Farnham.

FIGURE 18 · Eliza Farnham from "'Heads Differ in Shape' Or, Phrenology by the Portrait," *American Phrenological Journal* 25 (June 1857): 133.

the spiritualist subculture, her friendship with Orson Fowler and Andrew Jackson Davis, and finally her lectures on spiritualism in California. As she assured a San Francisco audience, a kingdom of god was at hand. "Spiritual growth makes the human career a perpetual revolution!" According to Farnham, spiritualism was the pinnacle of human evolution. It stood in contrast to a "barbarous, uncultured condition," the strict materialism of science, and an emasculated evangelicalism whose "most effective weapons [were] feeble-minded or cowardly ministers, and extremely pious old ladies of either sex."[72]

The fact that both Farnham and Edmonds would soon become public advocates for spiritualism was indicative of the power of secularism, or rather, of the powerful advertisements for its own inevitability.[73] The collaboration between Farnham and Edmonds at Sing Sing in the 1840s was part of a larger influx of spiritualist ideas into institutions of reform and

72. Farnham, *Lecture on the Philosophy of Spiritual Growth*, 14–16.
73. As Joel Tiffany argued in his case for spiritualism as the most refined science of social engineering, "the spiritual atmosphere [w]as a means of transmitting influences from mind to mind . . . all the manifestations of public excitement, or sympathy, are referable to these principles, and by carefully attending to them, we can learn how to create, and how to destroy these excitements" (J. Tiffany, *Lectures on Spiritualism, Being a Series of Lectures on the Phenomena and Philosophy of Development, Individualism, Spirit, Immortality, Mesmerism, Clairvoyance, Spiritual Manifestations, Christianity, and Progress, Delivered at Prospect Street Church, in the City of Cleveland* [Cleveland: J. Tiffany, 1851], 147–49).

coincided with the increased attention to the "spiritual welfare" and or "spiritual health" of prisoners in prisons and penitentiaries of the northeast.[74] Such attention promised to secure the capacity for self-control, self-respect, and self-culture—a three-pronged process of cultivating the individual mind and social conscience. The truths of spiritualism, as Farnham suggested, were "in harmony with what I believe of human capacity and spiritual power."[75] Under the sway of spiritualism, "you feel that in a certain very comforting sense, the universe is an ally of yours—a servant if you need—that all its forces, so far as you can appropriate and live by them, are yours—all that you can take awaits you."[76]

But rather than stress the emancipatory politics of these reform "efforts at social reorganization," I want to conclude by broaching a more disturbing possibility—that the efforts of Farnham and Edmonds were representative of how ideas of the human and its horizon of belief and action were being defined and deployed within an increasing technological society.[77] The mechanization of factory floors, the spread of rail lines and telegraph wires, the extension of trade and postal routes, not to mention nascent strategies of advertising, fundamentally altered the ways in which individuals imagined and experienced the boundary between self and world. "The powers of steam," declared the *American Phrenological Journal* in 1851, "surpasses all the wonders ascribed by our old legends to the genii of the spirit world."[78] The management of words, images, and bodies, from a certain perspective, expanded the reach of the public sphere and the possibilities for democratic dialogue. But as networks of information, commerce, and transportation expanded the range of possible actions and beliefs, the range itself became circumscribed by the strategic convergence of those networks.

As Tocqueville noted after his tour of American penitentiaries, "an immense, protective power" was looming on the democratic horizon, a

---

74. PANY, *Third Report*, part 2, 146, 187, 265, 272, 284, 370. On the "spiritual, moral, and intellectual instruction" of prisoners, see "State of New-York in Assembly, No. 241, November 27, 1847" and "No. 255, October 14, 1847," in *Documents of the Assembly of the State of New-York, Seventieth Session, Volume 8, No. 227, to No. 264, inclusive* (Albany: Charles Van Benthuysen, 1847), 13, 19. On more recent deployments of such attention, see Winnifred Fallers Sullivan, *Prison Religion: Faith-Based Reform and the Constitution* (Princeton: Princeton University Press, 2009).
75. Farnham, *Ideal Attained*, 391.
76. Farnham, *Lecture on the Philosophy of Spiritual Growth*, 12.
77. W.F., "Our Plans for Social Reform," *The Univercoelum and Spiritual Philosopher* 1, no. 15 (March 11, 1848): 233.
78. "The Steam-Engine," *American Phrenological Journal* 14 (July 1851): 14.

"new" thing that did not conform to the categories of "despotism" or "tyranny." Having once believed human conscience to be the lever of democratic reform within the penitentiary, Tocqueville now wrote of a "network" of "complicated rules that are both minute and uniform" that was almost impossible to locate or define. It "does not break men's will, but softens, bends, and guides it; it seldom enjoins, but often inhibits, action; it does not destroy anything, but prevents much from being born; it is not at all tyrannical, but it hinders, restrains, stifles, and stultifies" the potential for disorder.[79] And although such power may have been figuratively and literally untouchable, it nonetheless left its mark.

According to Tocqueville, democracy in America was not nearly as emancipatory as the people within it often told themselves and each other. As new opportunities that felt freely chosen emerged in concert with new modes of discipline, everyday life became a matter of disturbing enchantment, or what one contemporary observer described as the experience of the self as a "component" of "society" and a "link" in "carrying out the objects of commerce." "So curiously dove-tailed is the artificial system of human society," noted *American Whig Review* in 1845, "so complex is the reticulation by which the wants and wishes of our race are supplied and gratified, that scarcely any branch of art can be seriously affected in its progress without producing a sensible influence among a multitude of others, immediately or remotely connected with, or related to it."[80]

As I have insisted throughout this book, the effects of "systematic organization" at mid-century were ironic in that they undermined the conceptual mix of Common Sense empiricism and republican politics that fueled the desire for systematic organization. As the pace of technological modernization accelerated at mid-century, so too did strange "touches" that were experienced as bodiless and unlocatable. For Farnham and Edmonds, this mood became a means of organizing a population within the walls of Sing Sing State Penitentiary and others far removed. Indeed, it was the consummation of an American agency. Consequently, the ghost stories I have related in this chapter have served my larger purpose — foregrounding the potentiality of this subjunctive mood and how this sense of haunting structured emotional responses and epistemic practices.

Which brings us back, full-circle, to the bedroom of the honorable John Edmonds and the gentle twitchings that were "so rapid as to form almost a

79. Beaumont and Tocqueville, *Penitentiary System*, 87; Tocqueville, *Democracy in America*, 691–92.
80. "Post Office Reform," *American Whig Review* 1 (February 1845): 199.

stream, yet each touch was quite distinct." As Edmonds struggled to ascertain the source of his twitching, he came to the conclusion that "my most secret thoughts . . . have been freely spoken to" during spiritual intercourse "as if I had uttered them. Purposes which I have privily entertained have been publicly revealed; and I have once and again been admonished that my every thought was known to, and could be disclosed by, the intelligence that was thus manifesting itself." For Edmonds, the boundary between private and public was in no way absolute but mediated by organized and organizing forces. Such forces, according to Edmonds, were decidedly occult. Yet they were also susceptible to human knowledge. "Like the steam-engine and the magnetic telegraph, they are marvelous only to those who do not understand them."[81]

9. Repeatedly Touched on Different Parts of My Person

Rather than narrate the story of reform organizations such as Sing Sing as either one of economic and rehabilitative success or a slow declension into custodianship, a more disturbing picture comes into focus when one views their economic, rehabilitative, and custodial roles as inseparable in practice. The drama within Sing Sing, not to mention its lasting effects, disturbs treatments of religion as simply a process of individual or institutional meaning-making. It also disturbs understandings of religion that locate religion primarily within the cognitive and/or bodily domains, whether those domains are construed as sites of intentionality and/or evolution.[82] And finally, this picture neither confirms nor denies that the modern state is, in fact, religious. It does, however, suggest that the version of American modernity instituted by Farnham and Edmonds was, for all practical purposes, haunted.

Edmonds often looked back upon his time as president of PANY, his encounters at Sing Sing a reoccurring theme within the séance circle. In

81. Edmonds and Dexter, *Spiritualism*, 1:19, 75, 74, 77–78.

82. As I write these words, the methods and rhetoric of cognitive science are rapidly making claims upon the study of religion. See, for example, Ann Taves, *Religious Experience Reconsidered: A Building-Block Approach to the Study of Religion and Other Special Things* (Princeton: Princeton University Press, 2009). Taves's account is measured in comparison to more hyperbolic claims of cracking the code of religious experience. For a critical assessment of the claims of cognitive science, see Finbarr Curtis, "Ann Taves's *Religious Experience Reconsidered* is a sign of a global apocalypse that will kill us all," *Religion* 40 (October 2010): 288–92. See also my musings in "Always put one in the brain" (2008), *The Immanent Frame*, http://blogs.ssrc.org/tif/2008/10/09/always-put-one-in-the-brain/ (accessed November 25, 2010).

November 1853, for example, Edmonds observed a statue of a naked man whose "arms were tied above his head to a ring in the wall, and his face was turned over his left shoulder with a mingled expression of terror and defiance. Behind him stood a large, burly man, with his right hand as if to strike, and holding in it a cat-o'-nine-tails." After noting how this statue "represented a scene which once occurred in the State Prison," Edmonds then insisted on narrating the scene, in its entirety, in order to "convey more distinctly the idea of how far our earthly actions penetrate into our spiritual life."[83]

In the footnote Edmonds recalled that during his first year at Sing Sing he felt a professional obligation "to witness, personally, what this whipping with the cat-o'nine-tails was, so that I might judge of it for myself." "One day," however, when Edmonds was "passing through the main hall of the prison," he "accidentally stumbled on" a "group assembled around the whipping ring, and a prisoner tied up to it, as represented in the statue." Although the lashing had not yet begun, Edmonds intervened despite the prisoner's initial lack of repentance. Edmonds then took this prisoner under his wing. As Edmonds proudly recalled, "During the residue of his confinement in that prison he was one of the most orderly, submissive, and obedient men there; and in my efforts to reform the government of the prison, I frequently referred to his case as an instance of what might be done by judicious kindness instead of brute force."[84]

Edmonds's footnoted vision is significant, I argue, not because it invites psychoanalytic speculation as to what his spiritual vision was *really* about but for its insight into the relationship between the kind of civil sphere Edmonds and Farnham cultivated at Sing Sing and the one they imagined themselves to be living within. As Peter J. Hutchings has argued, "the formation of the criminal subject is deeply involved in the formation of secular subjectivity in the nineteenth century which involves the recasting of religious doctrines of sin and guilt in the form appropriate to a contractual, secularly based state where religion has been displaced by law, but where law is strongly marked by religion."[85] Hutchings's account of criminology is persuasive. It does not, however, focus on individual practices that were involved in this shift from theology to anthropology. As this chapter has argued, the "recasting" of subjectivity in light of secular assumptions about politics was not simply a political matter. It was also a

83. Edmonds and Dexter, *Spiritualism*, 2:309-10.
84. Ibid.
85. Peter J. Hutchings, *Incriminating Subjects: The Criminal Specter in Law, Literature, and Aesthetics* (New York: Routledge, 2001), 2.

yearning, a disturbance, *something that could be felt*—the experience, perhaps, of the soul becoming the prison of the body.[86]

For Edmonds and Farnham, as well as prisoners, the realization of autonomous judgment—an essential quality of American citizenship—was wholly masochistic. In each case the pleasure of moral autonomy depended upon recognizing the self as subject to an anonymous and immaterial network of surveillance. Or as Edmonds would later enthuse, "it [has been] demonstrated that our most secret thoughts can be known to and be revealed by the intelligence which is thus surrounding us and commuting with us. . . . Each can see and judge for himself." Edmonds's example suggests how the "eroticization of pain is merely one of the ways in which the modern self attempts to secure its elusive foundation."[87]

Edmonds's vision also challenges the historian to account for the strange ways in which "secular" subjectivity denies more than just its religious lineage but is itself dependent upon a blithe dismissal of its own porosity, its own dependence upon being "systematically treated." A republican version of political subjectivity, as experienced by Edmonds late one February evening, was marked by the pleasure of subjection. His pleasure became more refined on subsequent journeys into the spirit-world; his agency less pronounced as he sought to affirm something about himself that was not himself. For Edmonds, spirits promised blissful incorporation into the machinery of republicanism and offered a compelling vision of what it was like to live on the edge of "human progress." On this edge, the occult dynamics of American modernity could be glimpsed not through submission to a transcendent God but through submission to a multi-layered, kinetic, albeit quite stable social order.

To dwell upon Edmonds's eroticization of spiritual intercourse is not simply to point out that the predictions of secular progress had failed to materialize by mid-century but also to recognize that attitudes promoting moral agency as a public virtue had themselves achieved visceral currency. Under the narrative auspices of life, liberty, and the pursuit of happiness, spiritualists viewed themselves as cohering around a "national religion." Furthermore, they looked to the spirit-world to manage the inner workings of government, to maintain the conditions of democratic dialogue, and to cultivate the public sensorium.[88]

To conclude that the spiritualist dream of "automatic docility" was

---

86. Michel Foucault, *Discipline and Punish: The Birth of the Prison* (New York: Vintage Books, 1995), 29–30.
87. Asad, *Formations*, 119–20; Edmonds and Dexter, *Spiritualism*, 1:63.
88. Tiffany, *Lectures on Spiritualism*, 238.

either sacred or profane or some combination of the two does little to address the strange interplay of evangelicalism, occultism, and ideologies of the state in antebellum America.[89] When Edmonds and Farnham successfully replaced an evangelical program with a phrenological plan of governance and instruction, they retained and extended the systematic benevolence of evangelicals in the key of secularism. In their desire to align body and mind—both their own as well as those under their charge—they enacted the kind of public sphere evangelicals sought to create: a population of individuals free to act and think according to the same set of first principles.

To attend to this alignment is to begin to understand what exactly was twitching in Edmonds's left thigh and, more significantly, to begin to unpack the power and scope of what may be called, with all its disturbing ironies, a divinity born of the secular age.

89. Foucault, *Discipline and Punish*, 169.

EPILOGUE

· ✕ ·

What Do I Love When I Love

MY MACHINE?

A STATEMENT OF AMERICAN POLICYCAPTAIN AHAB ORDERS.

WILLIAM BURROUGHS AND BRION GYSIN, *The Exterminator* (1960)

1. Captain Ahab and the Question of Agency

Moby-Dick; or, the Whale is a book about what happens, or better yet, what could happen, when humans leave themselves to their own devices. Narrating life aboard a mid-century whaling ship — after it has already sunk — Melville's novel is a disturbing fiction. On the one hand, the navigational systems of the *Pequod* yielded an intelligence never consummated in or commandeered by any one single actor or element aboard the whaling ship. On the other hand, the crew of the *Pequod*, the vanguard of industrial and economic progress at the time, were drawn irresistibly, and in many ways inexplicably, to confront the mysterious force that was the white whale. On every page of *Moby-Dick*, the "springs and motives" of human action are relentlessly explored but never wholly explained. In coupling the mechanical "spring" with the psychological "motive," Ishmael complicated the question of who was driving what, or vice versa, in the seemingly endless pursuit of Moby Dick (not to mention his own seemingly endless asides). One could say that he refused to even answer it.

Ahab, however, provides a sense of closure to the question. "Swerve me?," he poses to the night air. "The path to my fixed purpose is laid with iron rails, whereupon my soul is grooved to run. Over unsounded gorges, through the rifled hearts of mountains, under torrents' beds, unerringly I rush! Naught's an obstacle, naught's an angle to the iron way." In a strategy that is born of genius and desperation, Ahab celebrates inevitability

©Mystic Seaport, Collection #1955.545, Capt. John Bolles, ca. 1860

FIGURE 19 · Captain John Bolles, Ambrotype, ca. 1860. Photograph courtesy Mystic Seaport Museum (1955.545).

for its own sake, the security that accompanies pure, endless repetition. Ahab's soul, like the railway car, would reach its destination precisely because all angles had been made straight. Obstacles obliterated. Maps at the ready. Every question answered. Legibility followed by truth.

Ahab's rationality was all but equivalent to his monomania — a desire to know despite the "unearthly conceit that Moby Dick was ubiquitous" and "immortal." On the one hand, Ahab comes "to identify with [Moby Dick]." Upon the whale's white canvas Ahab "visibly personified" not only "all his bodily woes, but all his intellectual and spiritual exasperations." The atmosphere aboard the *Pequod* had confused Ahab, overwhelming him to the point of becoming an agency within him: "You could almost see that thought turn in him as he turned, and pace in him as he paced; so completely possessing him, indeed, that it all but seemed the inward mould of every outer movement." This atmosphere has come to "possess" Ahab, creating the reality before him from within the interior space of an imagined independence. And it is Ahab's imagined independence that is at stake when he attempts to come to terms with that part of himself that is not utterly transparent.

Ahab's scheme was "delirious but still methodical." For, on the other hand, his systematic attention to the atmosphere aboard the *Pequod* was voluntary, the site in which Ahab became Ahab. Such attention allowed Ahab much leverage over his crew, the ability to silence even the "barely hinted imputation of usurpation, and the possible consequences of such a suppressed impression gaining ground." Consequently, Ahab exhibits a "heedful, closely calculating attention to every minute atmospheric influence which it was possible for his crew to be subjected to." "To accomplish his object," writes Ishmael, "Ahab must use tools; and of all tools used in the shadow of the moon, men are most apt to get out of order." The air thickens. Things begin to loom on board the *Pequod*. Ahab reaches for his sextant or telescope. Things become calculable, yet again. He was lost but now he is found.

On repeat.

Scene after scene Ahab is depicted as losing any point of reference other than the ceaseless and self-conscious mirroring of the self to the self. This theme is given dramatic treatment as Ahab reads the design on a piece of Ecuadorian gold he has used to commandeer the crew's attention and loyalty: "There's something ever egotistical in mountain-tops and towers," mutters Ahab, "and all other grand and lofty things; look here,—three peaks as proud as Lucifer. The firm tower, that is Ahab; the volcano, that is Ahab; the courageous, the undaunted, and victorious fowl, that, too, is Ahab; all are Ahab; and this round globe is but the image of the rounder globe, which, like a magician's glass, to each and every man in turn but mirrors back his own mysterious self."[1]

---

1. Ahab's demand for certainty is accompanied by the impossibility of satisfying it. Hence the "delirious and methodical scheme." Ahab's will to disenchantment in the face of its impossibility is not unrelated to the needs and the frustrations of many of the figures discussed in this book. Ghosts haunt but in doing so catalyze various projects of disenchantment. Over and over again. It is a process that depends not on the exorcism of ghosts but upon the

FIGURE 20 · Captain James Russell Swift, Ambrotype (mid-nineteenth century). Photograph courtesy Mystic Seaport Museum (1979.30.2).

———

Secularism, as I have argued, is more than an ideology. It is a moral force, a connective tissue, a widely shared and massively intricate set of political

inevitability of their exorcism. Hans Blumenberg notes something similar when discussing the necessary commitment to disenchantment that accompanies secularization. "It is not so much the modern age's pretension to total competence as its obligation to possess such competence that might be described as a product of secularization" (*The Legitimacy of the Modern Age*, trans. Robert M. Wallace [Cambridge, Mass.: MIT Press, 1983], 66).

and epistemological assumptions. And like anything in excess of ideology, secularism defies logic, particularly its own. Consequently, it may be well-nigh impossible to measure the powers of this normalizing process in which the truly religious and the truly secular emerge as compatible, if not wholly continuous within a field of legitimate human flourishing. It is, however, possible to tell a story about the resonance of secularism's metaphysics across space, time, and ideology.

The coinage of the word "secularism" has been attributed to George Jacob Holyoake's 1851 address to the London Hall of Science and his founding of the "Society of Reasoners," later renamed the "Secular Society." Holyoake called upon men to "throw away all other orthodox and heterodox creeds, and adopt *Secularism*." This was the *"common ground* on which all could work for humanity." Secularism, under the auspices of British Free Thinkers, came to be defined by its nonreference to God and seclusion from things divine. It denoted a space, time, and modality of being set off from the authority of religious or monastic orders—those notorious centers of secrecy and clerical intrigue.[2] Secularism was not only a description of history (secularization as inevitable) but also a moral imperative (charging its adherents to enact a particular kind of change over time). In both instances it promised emancipation in the form of rationalization, the differentiation of individuals and institutions within society, and the harmonic interaction between these component parts.[3] The very act of investigating the logic of these processes was itself a declaration that humanity was prepared to take the reins from the religious, leaving itself to its own devices in the management of past, present, and future meanings.

This notion of secularism, so closely allied to the nineteenth-century rhetoric of "progress" and "civilization," was the province of an Enlightened and white majority, describing and prescribing a transparent world set apart from primitive enchantments, mystery, and things that went bump in the night. For according to Holyoake and the spiritualist leaders who often spoke at the London Hall of Science, ghosts were no longer

2. On the "kingdom of secularism," see Christopher, "Religion, Atheism, and Art," *The Reasoner and Theological Examiner* 11, no. 8 (1851): 118; "Modern System Makers," *The Reasoner* 13, no. 4 (1852): 51. See also George Jacob Holyoake, "Principles of Secularism Defined," in *The Principles of Secularism* (London: Austin and Co., 1870), 11–13. "Secularism," however, was in use before as a pejorative for the more excessive reactions to modernity's false promises. See, for example, "Dr. Arnold's Miscellaneous Writings," *The North American Review* 62, no. 130 (January 1846): 181. See also Owen Chadwick, *The Secularization of the European Mind in the Nineteenth Century* (Cambridge: Cambridge University Press, 1975), 91.

3. Janet R. Jakobsen with Ann Pellegrini, "World Secularisms at the Millennium," *Social Text* 64 (Fall 2000): 4.

threatening because they had become objects of scientific experimentation and rational scrutiny.

At this time spiritualists circulated a survey in America, Europe, Asia, Africa, and "the islands of distant seas" for the purposes of gaining clarity on "rational religion." In 1854 the United States Congress received a petition with over fifteen thousand signatures attesting to the existence of an "occult force." The petition sought to convene a congressional investigation into "the power and intelligence of departed spirits operating on and through the subtile and imponderable elements which pervade and permeate all material forms." As spiritualism spread across American and Europe, the signatories were confident that "spiritual science" was on the verge of ascertaining "the truth, the whole truth, and nothing but the truth." Congress, however, thought otherwise, rejecting the petition with the wry suggestion that "it be referred to the committee on foreign relations."[4] The central question posed to the government went unanswered: what exactly was haunting antebellum America?

Invoking the London Hall of Science and the 1854 memorial to Congress, I remain uninterested in securing the ideological space where religion ends and politics begins, or vice versa. The more one tries to hold on to the categories of the religious and the secular, the less meaning they possess. I am, however, interested in the wholly contingent character of a differential that has become all but essentialized. Consequently, it has been a strange parallel—between the publicity of Enlightenment reason and increased intimacy with ghosts—that has informed my own approach to secularism in antebellum America. In each of my chapters I have chronicled particular strategies for dealing with spectral entities, how certain values were attributed to them, and what individuals did in light of them. I have approached secularism not as the literal exorcism of ghosts but rather in terms of the technics used to assess ghosts, the patterns of living with them, and the stories told about them.

Composed as a series of ghost stories, *Secularism in Antebellum America* has dwelled upon moments in which the truth of religion was consolidated within the Protestant public sphere. As I have shown, the synergy between Common Sense epistemics and republican politics generated a conceptual constellation—true religion, systematic organization, spirituality, sympathy, culture, and kindness—that fed into the materiality of saved souls, self-cultured individuals, ethnographic subjects, penitentiary

4. "Presentation of the Memorial," *Spiritual Telegraph* 4 (1854): 518–32.

inmates, and the like. These concepts, in harnessing the first principles of a secular imaginary, were phantasms that functioned "at the limits of bodies."[5] They took hold at the capillary level as evidenced in evangelical reading practices, the measurement of human skulls for therapeutic purposes, the costuming of the body in the regalia of Native Americans, the spiritualized approach to incarceration, and as we shall soon see, in the erotic desire to become mechanized. Consequently, it has been in the pathos of antebellum bodies that I have located the complex interplay between the agency of secularism and the agency of individuals.

The material role that secularism has played in producing particular styles of human being is a looping process. Yet this dynamic materiality is precisely what secularism denies in its appeals to a natural and unmediated freedom as well as to a politics of noncoercive consensus. For the diffusion of secularism across different sites was accompanied by a defense of its anonymity as well as by ample opportunity to imagine one's freedom in relationship to it. Yet the freedoms of the secular age necessarily depend upon how subjects are generated by way of words that loom on the horizon and that have nothing, initially, to do with those subjects. These words possess ontological status. They assume social force in the form of concepts. These concepts, in turn, become instantiated in technics, practices, and words relating to them. And so on and so forth.

Having made the methodological wager that the freedoms executed by humans are never pure, *Secularism in Antebellum America* is not merely a story about the drama of individuals carrying out their lives vis-à-vis the religious. It is also an analysis of those processes that made these dramas possible. To say as much is to argue that religion, both then and now, does not exist strictly in *essence* but also in *effect*. For in the age of distributive networks, the conceptual truth of religion persistently drifted across

5. Such concepts, in other words, were atmospheric, assuming the form of a barely detectable force whose strange materiality worked "against bodies, because they stick to bodies and protrude from them, but also because they touch them, cut them, break them into sections, regionalize them, and multiply their surfaces; and equally, outside of bodies, because they function between bodies according to laws of proximity, torsion, and variable distance" (Michel Foucault, "Theatrum Philosophicum," in *Language, Counter-memory, Practice: Selected Essays and Interviews by Michel Foucault*, ed. Donald F. Bouchard [Ithaca: Cornell University Press, 1977], 166–70). See also Brian Massumi, *Parables of the Virtual: Movement, Affect, Sensation* (Durham: Duke University Press, 2002). Massumi writes that "the problem with the dominant modes in cultural and literary theory is not that they are too abstract to grasp the concreteness of the real. The problem is that they are not abstract enough to grasp the real incorporeality of the concrete" (5).

denominational borders and social boundaries. It also seeped into bodies and, for better or for worse, created new conditions for practice and belief.

2. Automatic

God is, perhaps, not so much a region beyond knowledge as something prior to the sentences we speak; and if Western man is inseparable from him, it is not because of some invincible propensity to go beyond the frontiers of experience, but because his language ceaselessly foments him in the shadow of his laws.

MICHEL FOUCAULT, *The Order of Things*

In his vengeful desire to vanquish the white whale, Ahab leaves little room, initially, for considering how he too is subject to the conditions of the atmosphere. Yet as the *Pequod's* journey unfolds, Ahab has moments of doubt. He becomes anxious over his own performance, or more precisely, becomes aware that he is following a script. He bemoans his own "leakiness" and "mortal inter-debtedness," lamenting that "I would be free as air; and I'm down in the whole world's books." Before the final confrontation with Moby Dick, Ahab has already resigned himself to the fact that "the secret of our paternity lies in the grave, and we must there to learn it." Declaring that "I am the Fates' lieutenant; I act under orders," Ahab taunts the wind with his doublings, which is all that remains.

> Who has ever conquered it? In every fight it has the last and bitterest blow. Run tilting at it, and you but run through it. Ha! a coward wind that strikes stark naked men, but will not stand to receive a single blow. Even Ahab is a braver thing—a nobler thing than *that*. Would now the wind have a body; but all the things that most exasperate and outrage mortal man, all these things are bodiless, but only bodiless as objects, not as agents. There's a most special, a most cunning, oh, a most malicious difference!

Unable to come to terms with this difference, Ahab chooses to dismember his dismemberer in an act of desperate negation. Hoping "to be free as air," Ahab orders the ship's carpenter to build him a virtual body that would be up to the task. "Shall I order eyes to see outwards?" he asks himself. "No, but put a sky-light on top of his head to illuminate inwards." Complete self-disclosure. The vision Ahab desires, however, is so unreflective that the life he seeks is actually his own death. In his all-consuming passion to decode the meanings of self and external world, Ahab has succumbed, willingly, to the pleasures of automation.

In antebellum America, procedures for eliding the reality of secularism were bound up with ghosts who could be named and often knew the names of those they haunted. Such hauntings were often a form of closure, a way to acknowledge the inherent uncertainty of the world yet affirm one's own ability, however tentatively, to know that a stable system exists, behind it all.[6] Having been initiated "by some irregularity in the system," this process of closure began at the moment when the self "bec[a]me[] conscious of subjection to higher powers." This moment would, in turn, precipitate a distinct recognition, exposing the mechanics of subjection as both an invisible and indirect action that had "a kind of sleight o'hand and mystery about" it.[7] What is important here is not simply the sense of incursion but the sensation involved in its overcoming. For secularism may be glimpsed, however fleetingly, in those styles in which asystematic features of the world were detected, in those moments when felt impingements were transformed into confident facades.[8]

A central theme underlying my book has been how the conceptual space of religion figured into the making of an American modernity circa 1851. Accompanying my account of secularism has been a sense of closure, of social and psychic life occurring within an immanent frame. This has been strategic, for I am interested in thinking about secularism as an autopoietic system, an environmental agency that inflected how individuals made certain choices vis-à-vis the religious and how those choices served

6. Timothy Mitchell, "The Stage of Modernity," in *Questions of Modernity*, ed. Timothy Mitchell (Minneapolis: University of Minnesota Press, 2000), 26. Mitchell argues that the "metaphysics of modernity" may be glimpsed when the difference between representation and reality is staged as a matter of surface and depth. "The effect of this staging," he writes, "is to generate a new world of multiple significations and simulation. But its more profound effect is to generate another realm that appears to precede and stand unaffected by these proliferating signs; reality itself." See also Mitchell's *Colonizing Egypt* (Berkeley and Los Angeles: University of California Press, 1991).

7. As John Barton Derby remarked in 1835, there was "a kind of sleight o'hand and mystery about" the federal government. The citizen rarely, if ever, "feels its *direct* action," he mused. "And it is only by some irregularity in the system, that he becomes conscious of subjection to higher powers than his own paternal state government" (Derby, *Political Reminiscences, including a Sketch of the Origin and History of the "Statesman Party" of Boston* [Boston: Homer & Palmer, 1835], 171). As Derby implies, one could feel the presence of the state in the figure of the village postmaster.

8. J. A. Etzler, *The Paradise Within the Reach of All Men, Without Labor, by Powers of Nature and Machinery . . . in Two Parts* (Pittsburgh: Etzler and Reinhold, 1833).

FIGURE 21 · Steam Engine Regulator. "The apparatus is so adjusted, that when the engine is working at its proper speed, the governor shall produce just so much friction of the brake strap on the wheel, as will balance the friction of the pulley." "Rail-road News," *Scientific American* 7 (November 8, 1851): 57.

to reconstruct the structures of that system. Yet in framing secularism in terms of recursivity, of structures looping back upon themselves and the individuals who precipitated them, I also frame practices as recursive sites in which the accelerating convolution of a self-environment complex is ordered and given momentary pause.[9] This is a process whereby each day seems like a natural fact.

9. N. Katherine Hayles, *How We Became Posthuman: Virtual Bodies in Cybernetics, Literature, and Informatics* (Chicago: University of Chicago Press, 1999); Bruce Clarke and Mark B. N. Hansen, eds., *Emergence and Embodiment: New Essays on Second-Order Systems Theory* (Durham: Duke University Press, 2009), 6, 24. My approach to secularism shares much in common with discussions of modernity that note the "hyperacceleration of technoscientific incursions into the human" and a shift in critical focus from "the identities of subjects to the

Consequently, my goal has been to historicize the operational closure of secularism and to better appreciate living within its immanent frame. In doing so I have avoided the metaphors of false consciousness even as I have entertained the possibilities of social and technological determination. Rather than reduce individuals to undifferentiated cogs that are treated systematically by the protocols of modernity, I have instead dramatized an openness that paradoxically accompanies the closure of autopoiesis. I have focused on how the particularity of individuals is integral to systems of their own making. I have assumed throughout that the replicative capacities of secularism are accompanied by and, indeed, dependant upon, the responses of individuals to the structures they live within. I do not lament the effacement of human agency but instead assume that autonomy is never solitary, that humans may make decisions that are entirely their own despite the fact that the range of available choices has nothing, essentially, to do with them.

My goal, then, has been to look at how the ranks of antebellum Protestants inhabited the norms of a secular imaginary and by extension their own desires. Such habituations were often uneven, involving moments in which the self-sufficiency of the proprietary self was disturbed, at least momentarily.[10] I have chronicled how such disturbances were buffeted by procedures for eliding the power of secularism. The practices on either side of the disturbance—before and after—served the purposes of regulation. Together, looping back and forth between inevitability and outcome, they secured a founding subject whose experiences were deemed originary

---

networks of connections among systems and environments." The effect of a phrenological exam, for example, was not unrelated to the reading of a hand-delivered tract. At stake in both was nothing less than the life and presence of the individual who allowed himself to be taught to read himself by a phrenologist or who welcomed a colporteur into his home. A similar quality of self hung in the balance as you read either your own cranial structure in front of the mirror or read a tract by candle light. Both served to create and maintain the affective conditions of secularism. For both encouraged individuals to meet the expectations that circulated around them. And both enabled individuals to correspond with the protocols of secularism, at home and on their own terms.

10. Anxiety over the threatened dissolution of the boundaries of self, writes Terry Eagleton, has been endemic to the "human subject in the period of modernity." Once "subjectivity has become for the first time the foundation of the entire system of reality, that which brought it all to be in the first place and sustains it divinely in existence," a dialectical reversal necessarily ensues. For despite an overdetermination of sovereignty, the "ultimate foundation" of self "cannot be represented within the system it grounds, and so it slips through the net of language leaving the merest spectral trace of itself behind" (Terry Eagleton, "Self-Undoing Subjects," in *Rewriting the Self: Histories from the Renaissance to the Present*, ed. Roy Porter [London: Routledge, 1997], 266).

rather than mediated.[11] Yet such security was never absolute. For some kind of agency persisted in these efforts to negotiate and deploy a pressing social atmosphere or otherwise explain feelings of being acted upon from a distance. These efforts were indices of secularism's dynamic power. But they were also signs of human intentionality. For even as efforts to achieve integrity on the part of antebellum Americans were haunted by the very language that sanctioned their integrity, there existed a certain kind of struggle. A lingering fear of unfathomability, perhaps even deceit.[12] For as the archive of antebellum experience attests, a strange unease still simmers even as emancipatory rhetoric is voiced and progress insisted upon.

In framing this study around the emotions of haunting (a range that includes dread, wonder, sympathy, paranoia, and manic confidence), I assume, from the outset, that the subject is a fold of intellect and sensibility, whose freedom is unquantifiable not because it is limitless or evolving but because it does not exist in essence.[13] To have privileged the haunted strains of antebellum experience is to focus not necessarily on "lived religion" but rather on the living conditions of religion in a secular age. How, I have asked, does a so-called religious life come together at the intersection of contingent forces that are all but invisible to the subject in question? What are the experiential conditions of piety? What possibilities can and cannot be experienced at any particular moment in history? How and

11. Michel Foucault, "The Order of Discourse," in *Language and Politics*, ed. Michael J. Shapiro (New York: New York University Press, 1984), 125–26. "Against the great incessant and disordered buzzing of discourse," writes Foucault, there exist struggles to "remove from its richness the most dangerous part" and to "organize its disorder according to figures which dodge what is most uncontrollable about it." See also Foucault's description of the anthropological sleep, a dogmatic form of Enlightenment critique that (1) defines the human in terms of what it has already experienced and (2) defines everything that can present itself to experience as utterly human. This sleep is "so deep that thought experiences it paradoxically as vigilance, so wholly does it confuse the circularity of dogmatism folded over upon itself in order to find a basis for itself within itself" (Michel Foucault, *Order of Things: An Archaeology of the Human Sciences* [1966; New York: Vintage, 1994], 341–43). Thomas Carlson, in his Heidegerrian riff on such Common Sense circularity, writes of an ontotheological stance that "interprets being in terms of objectivity and defines truth in terms of the certainty achieved by the thinking human subject. The human subject secures such certainty in and through the representation of objective being as constant presence and calculability—to the point of reducing the world itself to a view or picture, a 'worldview,' produced by that subject alone, who thus becomes the ground and measure, if not already the maker, of all that is" (Thomas A. Carlson, *The Indiscrete Image: Infinitude and Creation of the Human* [Chicago: University of Chicago Press, 2008], 40).

12. "Self Reliance and Self Distrust," *Brother Jonathan* 3 (October 15, 1842): 202–3.

13. On the allure of conflating religious experience with an essential self, see Robert H. Sharf, "Experience," in *Critical Terms for Religious Studies*, ed. Mark C. Taylor (Chicago: University of Chicago Press, 1998), 94–116.

to what effect was "true religion" deployed in very specific and affective ways?[14]

To approach the subject as haunted is to appreciate how intentionality, agency, and other markers of identity are bound to the protocols of the subject's porosity, that is, in its positionality within a network of discursive forces. I have sought, in other words, to prise open how religion becomes a convincing sentiment and plausible structure of being for those living within the orders of a nonspecific Protestantism at mid-century. For just as religion has never been solely the invention of the scholar (contra Jonathan Z. Smith's infamous formulation), religion has never been merely an invention of human actors making decisions in light of their ultimate concerns.[15]

My lens of haunting has entailed a focus on subjectivity that jettisons metaphors of domination or control in order to view subjectivity as effect within a field of circulation. The individual, from this perspective, is not compromised by *what* influences *him or her*, but rather *is* the site of influence—a flow that generates momentary instantiations of a bounded interiority. "The individual," Foucault reminds the historian,

> is not to be conceived as a sort of elementary nucleus, a primitive atom, a multiple and inert material on which power comes to fasten or against which it happens to strike, and in so doing subdues or crushes individuals. In fact, it is already one of the prime effects of power that certain bodies, certain gestures, certain discourses, certain desires, come to be identified and constituted as individuals. . . . The individual is an effect of power, and at the same time, or precisely to the extent to which it is that effect, it is an element of its articulation.[16]

To rehearse Foucault's notion of subjectivization is to call into question a dominant paradigm of American religious historiography that continues

---

14. To ask such questions about the affective presence of religion is to point out not simply that the predictions of Enlightenment have failed to materialize but, on the contrary, that its definitional categories and attitudes regarding "religion" have. They have materialized in the form of public discourses about religion, scholars' assumptions regarding their object of study, and, most importantly, in the styles through which many Americans identify and understand themselves as religious. These discourses, assumptions, and understandings have, I contend, delimited certain perspectives on how exactly such a history unfolded and have limited opportunities to recognize the spectral materiality of secularism.

15. Jonathan Z. Smith, *Imagining Religion: From Babylon to Jonestown* (Chicago: University of Chicago Press, 1982).

16. Michel Foucault, "Two Lectures," in *Power/Knowledge: Selected Interviews & Other Writings, 1972–77*, ed. Colin Gordon (New York: Pantheon Books, 1981), 98.

FIGURE 22 · Portrait of Unidentified Man with Telescope (nineteenth century?). Possibly a sea captain. Photograph courtesy Mystic Seaport Museum (1990.123.1)

to operate according to the same epistemological and political principles that gave rise to the discipline in the mid-nineteenth century.[17] Such modes of historicism that posit the founding function of the subject become an

17. Such narratives insist, from the outset, that the intentionality of the subject can be either actualized or compromised. There is little middle ground. For once this zero-sum game of

authorizing solvent for the continuity of the secular age—delimiting the prospects for understanding how individuals come to know the world and how they organize themselves in light of such knowledge.[18] To say as much is not to deny that creativity or resistance happen but rather to insist that they happen in and through all those concepts that lend them structural integrity—experiential immediacy, interiority, intentionality, belief, etc.

In my treatment of this conceptual atmosphere and the subjects within it I have resisted conflating consciousness with agency. For whatever is decisive about action occurs within a field of possibilities that is already extant. Although respectful of the commitments of historical actors and their self-consciousness of religious commitment and/or denominational affiliation, I have not reduced religious conflict to matters of theology and/or doctrine. I have instead focused on the different ways individuals come to know themselves and to imagine themselves as part of a larger social world. In other words, by extending the locus of conflict to sites exterior to the self, the mediating metaphysics of secularism comes into fleeting focus. For there is ever more to action than consciousness and ever more to consciousness than intentionality.

3. Fucking Machines

Trained as a Universalist minister, John Murray Spear began to gravitate toward spiritualist circles in 1851, having already been an active proponent of abolitionism, prison reform, and women's rights.[19] By 1852, Spear had

---

agency is put into play by the historian, his or her narrative often goes on to accumulate evidence of human innovation, unpredictability, and dissent.

18. On "continuous history" as the "indispensable correlative of the founding function of the subject," see Foucault, *Archaeology of Knowledge and the Discourse on Language*, trans. A. M. Sheridan Smith (New York: Pantheon Books, 1972), 12–13. As Talal Asad writes, "the discursive move in the nineteenth century from thinking of a fixed 'human nature' to regarding humans in terms of a constituted 'normality' facilitated the secular idea of moral progress defined and directed by autonomous human agency" (*Formations of the Secular: Christianity, Islam, Modernity* [Stanford: Stanford University Press, 2003], 24).

19. Spear, at the age of ten, had been sent to work at the Dorchester Cotton and Iron Works just south of Boston, a place where he also attended Sunday School. Spear was called to the Universalist ministry at the age of twenty-four, became pastor of a Universalist church in New Bedford, where whale oil was imported that greased the rails and lit the lights of an ongoing industrial revolution. Spear soon became active in the causes of abolitionism, women's rights, and prison reform. In terms of the latter, Spear became the editor of the *Prisoners' Friend* and was known for the detailed descriptions of suffering he elicited from inmates on his many visits to penitentiaries. Driven to experience and communicate the pain of others, Spear once volunteered to be locked up in order to better understand their state of subjec-

become a full-fledged trance medium. Having been chosen as the earthly liaison for the "Association of Beneficents," Spear began to deliver spirit communiqués from the likes of Thomas Jefferson, Benjamin Franklin, and Benjamin Rush concerning the metaphysical principles underlying the construction of a new and radically egalitarian social state.[20] In November 1852, Franklin began to describe the details of a perpetual motion machine that would demonstrate the reality of the spirit world and "produce immense changes on your earth, such as words cannot describe." In 1853 Spear and his earthly associates began constructing a "new motive power" atop High Rock in Lynn, Massachusetts. This contraption of metal, magnets, and copper plates would provide the proper conditions for spirit intercourse and "infuse new life and vitality into all things, animate and inanimate."[21]

Not only would the "new motor" clarify, once and for all, the relationship between the human and divine, it would also "discover and scientifically control the mystery of the life principle."[22] The new motive power

---

tion. For biographical details, see Neil Burkhart Lehman, "The Life of John Murray Spear" (Ph.D. diss., Ohio State University, 1973), as well as John Benedict Buescher, *The Remarkable Life of John Murray Spear: Agitator for the Spirit Land* (Notre Dame, Ind.: University of Notre Dame Press, 2006).

20. This new state was modeled on the human body—it replicated in its own perfection the "mechanism of man" and its inherent concentricity. Consequently, the new state "should embrace among its generals the whole subject of intercommunication, embracing the railroad, the telegraph, the post-office, and all that machinery which will serve best to bind a common people together." Mass mediation, here, was the engine of a new form of governance that was "purely voluntary" because it was "exceedingly religious." John Murray Spear, *The Educator: Being Suggestions, Theoretical and Practical, Designed to Promote Man-Culture and Integral Reform with a View to the Ultimate Establishment of a Divine Social State on Earth*, ed. A. E. Newton (Boston: Office of Practical Spiritualists, 1857), 428, 442, 474-75.

21. Spear, *The Educator*, 239-54. All subsequent citations from this text are cited parenthetically.

22. Emma Hardinge, *Modern American Spiritualism: A Twenty Year's Record of the Communion Between Earth and the World of Spirits* (New York: The Author, 1870), 221. As described by A. E. Newton, "Upon the centre of an ordinary circular wood table, some three feet in diameter, were erected two metallic uprights, six or eight inches apart; between these, and reaching from one to the other, near the tops, was suspended on pivots a small steel shaft, which was crossed at its centre by another shaft, about six inches in length, on the extremities of which were suspended two steel balls enclosing magnets. The first named shaft was nicely fitted with sockets at its extremities, so that the balls could revolve with little friction. Beneath these suspended balls, between the uprights, and the centre of the table, was arranged, a very curiously constructed fixture,—a sort of oval platform, formed of a peculiar combination of magnets and metals. Directly above this were suspended a number of zinc and copper plates, alternately arranged, and said to correspond with the *brain* as an electric reservoir. These were supplied with lofty metallic conductors, or attractors, reaching upward to an elevated stratum of atmosphere. In combination with these principal parts were adjusted various metallic bars, plates, wires, magnets, insulating substances, peculiar chemical

was designed to receive, store, and eventually transmit electrical energy and would run on spirit-power, initiating a loop between this world and the afterlife that would never again be closed. The political payoff of the new motor would be to usher in an age of *spirituality*, a social order in which feelings would take precedent over mere reason. As "spirituality increases," wrote Spear, "there will be more reliance on feeling" (127). The epistemological payoff of the new motor would be the illumination of "heretofore unknown mechanical forces" that would in turn serve to unlock the secret emotional capacities of each and every human, providing an equally affective image of themselves. In order to consummate our knowledge of "mechanical forces," humans must comprehend the principles of "circulation" and "perpetual motion." Only then will they understand themselves — the "ultimate of Nature" — and be able to apply this life force to themselves — constructing "mechanisms . . . in harmony with the human body" (256-57).

The new motive power offered Spear an opportunity to feel, firsthand, the laws of circulation and centralization, to transform himself into a proper subject of governance, and in turn to demonstrate to others how they could be transformed. Spear was clear as to what this new sensorium logically entailed. "The Divine Mind works in man by influx," declared the Association, "not only controlling his will, but his very acts. Man is as much a free agent as is Mars, Jupiter, or Saturn, and no more" (514-17). Spear sought to reconcile the difference between the fixity of human being and the circulatory directives of technology. He sought to bring this difference into a perpetual harmony, to make one an extension of the other. This reconciliation was an aesthetic and emotional affair.[23] It was also masochistic — not in the sense of painful submission but in that of an eroticization of

---

compounds, etc., arranged by careful direction in accordance with the relations of positive and negative, or masculine and feminine, as set forth in the foregoing treatises. At certain points around the circumference of the structure, and connected with the centre, small steel balls enclosing magnets were suspended. A metallic connection with the earth, both positive and negative, corresponding with the two lower limbs, right and left, of the body, was also provided. Certain portions of the structure were subjected to very peculiar processes, such as immersion for a time in novel chemical preparations, exposure to heat and electrical action, etc. etc., designed apparently to fit them to perform their respective functions. . . . Besides the elevated conductors connection with the *brain*, already alluded to, and representative of *vital influx* through that organ, provision was made for *inhalation* and *respiration*, — thus recognizing the three essential vital processes. . . . Animated life, be it remembered, has many *forms*, but the ultimate *source* and *laws of motion* are undoubtedly the same in all" (240).

23. Indeed, according to Spear, the veracity of his own "Electrical theory of the universe" was a matter of feeling rather than linguistic proof (iii). "Words are but signs of ideas. They are less than the ideas of which they are types. But behind *idea* lies *feeling*, and yet back of *feeling* lies *inter-consciousness*" (525).

subjection in the service of securing the elusive foundation of self.[24] For to read Spear's words about the new motive power and to appreciate the emotions involved in his activities is *to sense a desire to feel* these metaphysical principles at work, to feel the inherency of self as a matter of circulation.

Spear's longing owed much to the metaphysical pronouncements of Andrew Jackson Davis. Spear first encountered the work of Davis in 1847, when he noted his "new and wonderful book" (*Principles of Nature*) in the pages of the *Prisoners' Friend*. Spear and Davis became friends in 1851, and it was Davis's 1852 vision of a "Spiritual Congress" that catalyzed Spear's own interest in the interplay between spirits, government, and technology. In August 1852, while residing at "High Rock Cottage" in Lynn, Mass., Davis had a vision of a Spiritual Congress thirty miles in the air, a little east of Boston. A "thin mellow atmosphere," wrote Davis, "full of glory and beauty, emanates from and surrounds" an "assemblage of men from the Spirit Land." These spirits were righteous men "skilled in the divine art of self-government and individual culture." They included a veritable who's who of philosophers, statesmen, and doctors from the ancients to the recently deceased. An emissary from this congress, moving in an "immense white cloud" along a "river of electricity" toward Davis, told him that these designated spirits had assembled "for the purpose of weighing kings, emperors, tyrants, teachers, and theologians in the balance of Justice and Truth." Davis's vision was formative for Spear—not only its location and suggestion of a new political blueprint revealed by spirits but also Davis's insistence that such a blueprint would remain "incomprehensible" and "impenetrable" for the time being.[25]

The example of Spear's Sisyphean desire suggests how social norms are both internalized and transformed in the process of encountering them.[26] In and through his feelings Spear learned to inhabit, in comfort *and* anxiety, new iterations of social reality. And these were the feelings that would eventually provide him terms for thinking about such iterations—defining patterns of subjection as well as possibilities of critique.

In order to charge—"impregnate"—the new motor, Spear drew up plans

24. Asad, *Formations of the Secular*, 119–20.

25. Andrew Jackson Davis, *The Present Age and Inner Life* (New York: Partridge & Brittan, 1853), 82–89. See also Davis, *The Principles of Nature, her divine revelations, and a voice to mankind*, edited, with an introduction and biographical sketch of the author, by William Fishbough (New York: S. S. Lyon and Wm. Fishbough, 1847).

26. Raymond Williams, *Marxism and Literature* (New York: Oxford University Press, 1977), 128–35. See also Judith Butler's theory of subjection in *The Psychic Life of Power: Theories in Subjection* (Stanford: Stanford University Press, 1997).

for a ménage-a-trois between human, spirit, and machine—a "severe course of bodily as well as mental and spiritual discipline." In the spring of 1854, Spear first "copulated" with the machine. As one witness later described the scene, Spear "desired to submit himself to an operation" and "was encased . . . in an apparatus . . . composed of a combination of metallic plates, strips, and bands . . . and including, at proper locations, some of the precious metals, jewels, and other minerals." Upon being encased, Spear entered into a trance state for over an hour and entered into relations with the machine. One witness "described 'a stream of light, a sort of *umbilicum*, emanating (from [Spear]) to and enveloping the mechanism.'" Spear was found in a "condition of extreme exhaustion. The witness concluded that 'virtue,' of *some* sort, 'had gone out of him,' by this novel mode of transfer" (245).

Spear's dissemination was then followed by the "labor" of Sarah Newton, then married to A. E. Newton, Spear's close associate and someone who had already exhibited exceptional mediumistic gifts.[27] Newton's "labor" lasted for two hours and was accompanied by the "pulsation," "throbbing," and "visible vibratory motion" of the machine. As one witness declared, "in these agonizing throes the most interior and refined elements of her spiritual being were imparted to, and absorbed by, the appropriate portions of the mechanism." For upon Newton's engagement, "slight pulsatory action became perceptible in . . . the pendent magnetic balls around the circumference of the mechanism. . . . This . . . throbbing, was perceptible first to the touch, but gradually increased until it produced a visible vibratory motion. . . . This motion was quite variable" in Newton's presence and began to lessen once she left the room (247).

The strange and sexually charged actions of Spear and Newton are remarkable only because they actively sought to become the objects of a technological totality, to feel as though they had become perfected, that is, mechanical versions of themselves. For them, the new motive power was an invitation to be haunted through and through by technology—to be systematically treated by "ethereal laws" and "heretofore unknown mechanical forces" that were part and parcel to divinity (147). For once treated as such, Spear and Newton could then recognize themselves as human, feel themselves as divine, and invite others, by way of the new motive power, to do the same. In consummating their theological vision,

27. "Intelligently satisfying herself that the purpose intended involved neither wrong nor impropriety . . . she resolutely decided to comply with their wishes, and put the matter to the test, so far as she might be the instrument of so doing" (246). See also John Murray Spear, "Of the Electric Motor" (June 2, 1860), Box 1, Folder 48, Sheldon Papers, Darlington Memorial Library, University of Pittsburgh.

a radical egalitarianism of minds, bodies, races, and sexes would result. "Persons must be so educated, purified, and spiritualized," wrote Spear, that they "come to that state wherein [they] will feel that the human form is divine, that every organ is holy" (257).

Spear and Newton were certainly not alone in participating in the eroticization (and erotics) of technology. Many other Americans at mid-century were also feeling their way across an affective threshold, into a material and conceptual space bound up with the imagination of technology as a matter of intimacy. And it is this "indeterminate"[28] space, a space in which technology was passionately engaged rather than visibly seen or reasonably understood, that is the distinguishing mark of agency within the secular age—of persons, to be sure, but also the technics and technologies.

To say as much is to admit that technologies are laden with metaphysics of their own. As machines change—becoming better, stronger, faster—so too does the form and content of the first principles emanating, with moral force, from these machines. What demands attention, I have argued, is not so much the force itself but the effects, registered in uneven ways, in the practices and documents of humans. Consequently, I have focused on the ways in which the shimmering sheen of steam-powered machines became aesthetic matters, affecting modes of sense perception, channeling senses in particular directions, recording them, and making some feelings more real, more textured, more reliable than others. Admittedly, this is a perverse exercise, moving from a depth in order to figure out a surface. But it is on the surface that secularism operates, itself a discourse, which is just another way of saying an assemblage of forces that challenges the demarcating tendencies of either/or grammars of agency. Machines inflect aspects of that assemblage, but the assemblage of forces cannot be reduced to those machines. As Deleuze reminds us, social experience cannot be reduced to the technologies that inform that experience. "The machines don't explain anything," he writes. "You have to analyze the collective apparatuses to which the machines are just one component."[29] In other words, machines alone cannot explain how secularism insinuated itself into the very pores of social being, making certain sensibilities feel right and rendering particular feelings nonsensical.

Consequently, Spear's "high and holy feelings" do not provide a defini-

28. In his desire to be subject to technology, Spear considered the notion of selfhood as perpetually happening within what Jeremy Stolow calls the "indeterminate spaces of exchange between humans and their machines" (Jeremy Stolow, "Salvation by Electricity," in *Religion: Beyond a Concept*, ed. Hent de Vries [New York: Fordham University Press, 2008], 686).
29. Giles Deleuze, "Control and Becoming," in *Negotiations: 1972–1990*, trans. Martin Joughin (New York: Columbia University Press, 1995), 175.

tive answer to whether the electric motor assumed a degree of agency in a process whereby Spear assumed his own. They do, however, open a line of questioning that serves to highlight how subjectivity, at least within the conditions of the secular age, has as much to do with passionate responses to those conditions as with beliefs about them. For Spear's emotional affair with technology was in the service of affirming a self open to the radical and creative possibilities of continual diffusion. And it was precisely this "porous world" that the blueprints of the new motive power would usher into being.[30] For even as he entertained the idea of fucking machines, enchanted by their perpetual undulations, throughout Spear imagined himself to be in the missionary position, in charge, and on top. "When a full and thorough knowledge of *man* has been obtained," wrote Spear, "when the laws of motion, as exhibited in man, are discovered,— then mechanisms may be constructed which shall perform the various offices which are exhibited by and through the human structure" (255). For the Association of Benificents had told him, "*Each person is a distinct individual, a sovereign, having a perfect right to do as he or she pleases, in respect to his or her person, his or her property, to follow his or her pursuits, to seek his or her happiness in his or her own individual way*" (404-5).

———

Spear's encounter with the new motor was fraught with tension. It remained a negotiation, an attempt to experience something that did not make any sense at all—the demands of liberation made upon him and in his name by the machines that surrounded him.[31] For at the end of that crisp spring day in 1854, Spear experienced what the Association of Benificents had predicated in their plans for a new era of social relations—the felt exercise of freedom against overwhelming, perhaps even monstrous odds.

30. Spear, "Of the Electric Motor."
31. According to Spear, the primary manifestation of God was ineffable yet nevertheless subject to analysis and veneration. It was, in short, a principle that already inhered in the very fabric of reality: "The First Cause of all Causes is INHERENCY. The Deity of deities cannot pass that line. How that Inherency came to be, can never be comprehended. Every attempt that ever has been or ever will be made to pass that line must end in disappointment. Let this last remark be carefully noted, and constantly remembered" (141). For to inquire into the matter of inherency was to begin to feel the power of divinity. As the Association of Electric-izers made clear, the "idea of Divine Existence is one to be *felt*, rather than *expressed*. It lies within the province of inner consciousness, rather than of verbal description" (147). In short order, Inherency possessed the element of Life, the power of Motion, otherwise known as electricity (159), the power of Attraction, the power of Expansion, and the power of Enlightenment (141-42).

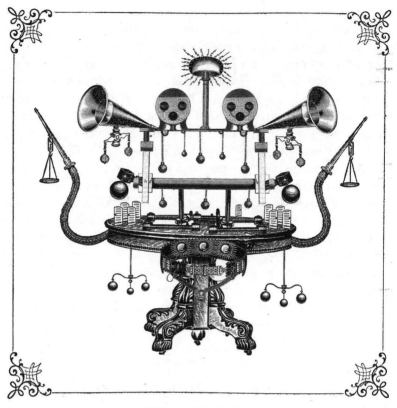

NEW MOTIVE POWER

FIGURE 23 · Libby Modern, *The New Motive Power* (2011). Illustration based on a true story.

Victim of collision on the open sea
nobody ever said that life was free
sink swim go down with the ship
but use your freedom of choice.

DEVO

INDEX

phrenology (*continued*)
with Unitarianism, 12, 23, 30n74, 221;
and revivalism, 161–64; as social physics, 244n12. *See also* Fowler and Wells
(institution); Fowler, Lorenzo; Fowler,
Orson
Pierpont, John, 150
pluralism (concept), 3–4, 6, 12, 15, 21
Poe, Edgar Allen, xxix, 170n134
poesis, 7, 45–46
Polk, James (President), xxii, 214
population (concept), 12, 29, 45, 50, 84n101,
90n117, 113, 178; as leverage for governance, 64, 67, 78, 80n90, 81, 85–88,
89–94, 97–104, 274. *See also* masses;
public opinion
Post, Amy, 222
Post, Isaac, 41n113, 222–23, 223n116
Princeton Theological Seminary, 75, 77,
146n60, 198
Prison Association of New York (PANY), 14,
243–46, 259–60, 267–70, 271, 275
Prisoners' Friend, The (Spear), 259n44,
267n62, 268n63, 268n64, 293, 296
Protestantism, liberal, 122, 127–28,
131–32, 142–50, 161–62, 186. *See also*
Unitarianism
psychometry, 223–25. *See also* Buchanan,
James R.
public opinion, 60–61, 125–26, 140n46, 142,
156–57, 201n9, 254, 260n47. *See also*
masses; population
Puritans, 62n36, 91, 92, 217

racial codification, 15n35, 18n45, 20n49,
68, 84–88, 110n187, 110n190, 116n209,
130n26, 146n62, 148, 157n89, 168n124,
168n125, 216n91, 230n142, 243, 262,
263–65
railroads and railways, 13, 27, 31, 32, 33,
34, 36, 38, 39, 67, 68n52, 107–10, 183,
184, 189, 195, 199, 204, 231–33, 241, 243,
267n62, 279–80, 288
reading, xx, 23, 42–43, 50, 55, 62, 67, 76,
103, 104–13, 202, 205, 219, 221, 262
Reichenbach, Baron, 34
Reid, Thomas, 22, 23, 72, 79, 80, 135,
138n39, 145, 146n60, 155
religion: concept, 1–21 passim, 290n14;
disestablishment of, 15, 20n49, 61, 121;
falsity of, 5, 15n35, 18n45, 36n94, 78n81,

200, 201n39, 217n94, 246; liberation
from, 20; liberation of, 4–20; as mode
of liberation, 4, 6, 150; truth of, 5, 6, 8,
10, 11, 12, 13, 16, 18, 25, 29, 47, 50–51,
53, 66, 70, 75–76, 78, 79, 84–88, 92,
98–99, 107, 113, 121, 134, 150, 151, 167,
178, 205, 216, 245, 283, 285, 291
religious-secular binary, 8n20, 15n35,
18n45, 53, 55, 83, 107, 111, 113, 200,
226–27, 235–38
religious-secular continuum, 7n20, 8,
19n48, 21n5166, 65, 70, 71, 72n60,
76–84, 108–13, 121, 161–65, 234–38, 240,
246–68, 277–78
republicanism, 22, 24–25, 34–35, 38, 41,
46, 59, 86, 108, 161n99, 247, 250–52,
256–57, 266; interplay with Scottish
Common Sense, 22, 24–26, 72–76,
79–80, 99, 114, 145, 155, 240, 246, 284;
and Iroquois, 212; language, 107
resonance, 9, 10, 12, 24–25, 38, 76, 172, 283
revivalism, xxxi, 13, 18n45, 91, 106, 143n52,
161–62, 201–2, 225, 240, 251n27
Roberts, Tyler, 46n121
"Rochester knockings," 39, 177, 202–3,
222, 247
Rochester, New York, 13, 177, 184, 194–96,
201–3, 225–27
Rocket, The (Knight), 107–13
romanticism, xxxii, xxxiii, 40, 57–58, 60,
130n26, 180–81, 209, 216n92, 217. *See
also* Scottish Common Sense philosophy: going to romantic seed
Roof, Wade Clark, 119, 123
Rush, Benjamin, 25, 251–52, 294
Ryan, Susan M., 15n34, 114n201, 188

Sampson, M. B., 166n117, 244n12, 261–64
Saturn, 295
savagery, 10n25, 14, 56–57, 65, 68, 84–88,
110, 148–49, 221n110, 228–34, 283
Schmidt, Leigh Eric, 5n10, 122–24, 174n141
Schoolcraft, Henry, 130n26, 218, 231. *See
also* metaphysics: of Indian-hating
Scott, Walter, 241
Scottish Common Sense philosophy,
22–24, 35, 38, 44, 46, 60, 105–6, 108;
of beavers, 233–34; contested deployments, 132, 134, 144–47; on emotion, 23;
interplay with republican modes of governance, 22, 24–26, 71–76, 79–80, 86,